STUDIEN UND MATERIALIEN ZUR GESCHICHTE DER PHILOSOPHIE

Herausgegeben von Yvon Belaval, Gerhard Funke, Heinz Heimsoeth † und Giorgio Tonelli

Kleine Reihe
Band 1

ANTHONY PREUS

Science and Philosophy
in Aristotle's Biological Works

1975

GEORG OLMS VERLAG HILDESHEIM · NEW YORK

ANTHONY PREUS

SCIENCE AND PHILOSOPHY
IN ARISTOTLE'S
BIOLOGICAL WORKS

1975

GEORG OLMS VERLAG HILDESHEIM · NEW YORK

© Georg Olms, Hildesheim, 1975
Alle Rechte vorbehalten
Printed in Germany
Herstellung: fotokop wilhelm weihert KG, Darmstadt
ISBN 3 487 05832 4

TABLE OF CONTENTS

CHAPTER I   OBSERVATIONS AND THEORIES

A. Introduction

Aristotle's *Parts of Animals (PA)* and *Generation of Animals
(GA)* were written after his philosophical position was already rather well-developed, and after a period of gathering
observations of biological facts.[1] Aristotle's interest in
biology probably influenced the development of his philosophy, and his philosophical concerns no doubt determined
the direction of some of his biological investigations, but
Aristotle's philosophy and his biology do not meet head-on
until the *PA* and *GA*. In these works he is not satisfied with
an arrangement of data, as he had been in the *History of
Animals (HA)*;[2] he looks for an explanation of the facts which
will enable him to integrate his biological investigations
into his philosophy, an explanation which will extend man's
comprehension of the world, and validate the explanatory
concepts and approaches being developed in the works which
we call the *Physics (Phys.)* and *Metaphysics (Met.)*.
When the philosophical concepts and the observational data
meet in *PA* and *GA*, sometimes the philosophical position is
bent to fit the observed facts, and sometimes the observations are adjusted to fit the philosophical position. When
Aristotle's position is faced with a serious difficulty, one
may see more readily the character of the commitments made
to various parts of that position; at the same time, the
nature of his observations appears more clearly when we see
which observations he is willing to disbelieve in the face
of theoretical difficulties. Aristotle does not stick to the
letter of his theory, no matter what; not everything in the
biological books is consistent with the positions in the
Physics and *Metaphysics*; but Aristotle does not give up his
presuppositions without a struggle.
It is hoped that these claims will be substantiated by the

1

present work, and that it will help to illuminate the character of Airstotle's philosophy and science, not only in
broad outline, but also in some details. In this chapter we
will investigate some of the preconditions of the *PA* and *GA*,
both the sources of Aristotle's data, particularly in the
HA, and also the philosophical positions which affect the
PA and *GA*, at least in a general or introductory manner. In
the second chapter, we will explore parts of the *GA* which
are concerned directly with the problem of the generation
of new entities, the problem of 'existential change', a phenomenon which should be eminently explicable according to
Aristotelian principles, if Aristotle is right about the
virtues of his philosophy as against that of Plato, for example.[3] Chapter III takes Aristotle's theory of the 'four
causes' seriously and attempts to find the theory applied,
somehow and somewhere, in the explanations of the development and function of the organic parts of members of the
animal kingdom. The *PA* generally sticks to the functional
account, the form and end, and only to a much lesser degree
discusses the matter; rarely is the moving cause of development of a part described in that book, so we have imported
from the *GA* whatever might assist us in giving a genetic explanation of the individual parts of animals, and of the
variations in the parts of animals. The fourth chapter discusses the concept of necessity, as it appears in the biological books, and the apparent personification of nature,
especially as one may find it in phrases like 'Nature uses..';
our objective is to see how close Aristotle comes to a mechanical notion of necessity, on the one hand, and to a teleology of intention, on the other, for these would be the
limits of his middle path between the materialists and the
mythologers.

2

B. Aristotle's Teleology

Aristotle as scientist and as philosopher of science is most
generally remembered for his explicit defense and enthusi-
astic use of teleological modes of explanation. Since teleological explanations are not very popular today, perhaps it
would be well to say something about Aristotle's version of
teleological explanation. He regarded teleology as an important innovation for science and philosophy, with its
earliest roots in Empedocles and Anaxagoras, and not maturely
stated even in Plato. He did not think that his teleology
was an attenuated survival of primitive animism, as indeed
it was not. He does say, "Just as the mind acts for the sake
of something, so does nature, and this is its end" (*de An.*
II.4, 415b16), but in this comparison, the similarity between mind and nature is in that both mind and nature act
"for" something, and the contrast is in that nature is not
a mind, does not act intentionally. Aristotle believes that
teleological explanations do not imply, or even suggest, intentional actions as causes of the event or fact explained.

A statement in *GA* II.1 may be taken as making explicit
the implicit principle upon which Aristotle's teleology is
based:

> Soul is better than body, and that which has soul
> in it is better than that which has not, because
> of that soul; being is better than non-being, and
> living than non-living (731b28ff, after PECK).

If one favors a deductive model of explanation, this assertion could be taken as a major premiss not only for the
explanation of sexual generation, where it appears, but also
in the greater part of the teleological explanations in the
biological books. This proposition could not be established
by observation or by induction, nor could it be demonstrated
within a science. Very likely, it cannot be demonstrated at
all; rather, such a principle has to be supported by persuasive arguments if it is to be supported at all. Aristotle
proposes at least three such persuasive arguments, or we may

extract at least three from what he says. One sort of argument is that which depends upon the notion of a 'function',
in the biological sense; modern biologists, particularly
organismic biologists, talk of the 'significance' of certain
features of organic wholes. In Aristotle, this argument
starts from the notion of 'health' or 'flourishing'; 'flourishing' may serve as a translation for the word *eudaimonia*
as it appears in the *Nicomachean Ethics*. Another sort of
argument is presented in *Physics* II as a conclusive argument
for the priority of teleological explanations; it may be
called 'the argument from the logical priority of purpose'.
A third sort of argument, familiar to readers of almost any
part of Aristotle's work, is the analogy between art and
nature; although it is even farther from being conclusive
than the other two, it is perhaps the most persuasive, and
the most revealing of the trend of thought which leads to a
general scheme of teleological explanation.

1. Function and health

Aristotle affirms that certain states of being are valuable
relatively to the entity of which they are states. The most
general of the good states which are applicable in biological
explanations is 'being alive' or 'having a soul'. Closely
related is the state called 'health'. We regard health as a
valuable state for ourselves; no one would choose to be un-
healthy unless it were to achieve something which he regarded
as better than simply being healthy. Health is a condition
which is describable in physiological terms; it can be a condition of any living organism, independently of the use which
another organism might make of it. Health is a good for an
organism because it contributes to its life, and is its
living well.

> We say that all excellences depend upon particular
> relations. Thus bodily excellences such as health

4

> and a good state of body we regard as consisting
> in a blending of hot and cold elements within the
> body in due proportion, in relation to one another
> or to the surrounding atmosphere; and in like
> manner we regard beauty, strength, and all the
> other bodily excellences and defects. Each of them
> exists in virtue of a particular relation and puts
> that which possesses it in a good or bad condition
> with regard to its proper affections, whereby
> 'proper' affections I mean those influences that
> from the natural constitution of a thing tend to
> promote or destroy its existence.[4]

It is not only the case that there are irreducible values
for organisms, but also, according to Aristotle, these organisms are understood in terms of these values. Although we
may speak of the physiological balance as a necessary condition for health, that balance (or whatever) does not ex-
haust the meaning of the word 'health' as we use it.

This last point may be made clearer by distinguishing between description and explanation. The same system may be adequately described or mapped in any number of ways, some of
which make no reference whatever to the purpose or point of
the system, but not all of these descriptions would count as
an adequate explanation of the system. If a system or part
of a system has a function, it must be mentioned in the explanation of the system or part.

> There is nothing to prevent the teeth being formed
> and being shed in the way (Democritus) says; but it
> is not on that account that it happens (*GA* V.8,
> 789b6, PECK).

Similarly, organismic biologists argue:

> ... an enormous preponderance of vital processes
> and mechanisms have a whole-maintaining character;
> were this not so the organism could not exist at
> all. But if this is so, then the establishment of
> the significance for the life of the organism is
> a necessary branch of investigation.[5]

Many modern accounts of teleology in explanation do not meet
this kind of point, because they tend to concentrate on end-
directed *behavior*. Teleological explanations of behavior
naturally begin with ascriptions of intentions or choices
or desires to the organism whose behavior is to be explained,

but the approach gets into difficulties very rapidly. At best, intentions are demonstrable only for man; the behavior of lower animals is then either inexplicable or explained *obscurus per obscurius*. Even for man the causal relationship between intentions and action is difficult to trace, or perhaps the attempt to trace such a relationship is wrong from the start. Faced with such problems, forcefully driven home by the critic of teleological explanations, those who remain attached to teleology may forego talk of intentions, but claim that there is something inherently special about systems which overcome obstacles to reach a goal, through 'feedback', for example. The critic of teleology has but to reply that such systems can be completely described without reference to goals, that the feed-back mechanism is, nonetheless, still a mechanism. But this entire line of criticism gets started in the first place because many writers suppose that 'behavior' exhausts the relations to be investigated; the emphasis upon behavior leads the discussion astray, because the bogey of intention, conscious or unconscious, continues to permeate the discussion when the problems are posed in this way.[6]

Functional explanations are concerned with interrelationships between parts, organs, and processes, rather than with any derivation from antecedent conditions. That which is to be explained is the simple fact that this unity *is* a whole, and a whole of a certain type, different from units of other types. The biologist has an interest in discovering why and how this organ is an organ *of a seal*, for example; such a question would not be answered by any ascription of intention to the seal -- "the seals *choose* to have ears like that" would be clearly a joke, and Aristotle does not joke in that way. Nor does Aristotle suppose that features of organisms exist because of *God's* intentions; he avoids that blind alley. Rather, he explains the parts and processes of animals by describing the role which they play in the life of the animal.

6

Although Aristotle asserts that health can be described as a
relationship between the parts of the animal (or whatever),
it is not simply that relationship, but also 'excellence',
(*aretē*, 'virtue' in the ethical books). Many of the parts
of animals, and many of their life-activities, have a function, preserve the life of the individual animals or preserve the species; one important task of the biologist is to
discover which organs and which activities have what 'significance'.

The point which we are ascribing to Aristotle may be compared
to one which many moral philosophers, at least since G.E.
MOORE, make about words like 'health' and 'virtue'; these
words, as they are used in our language (English or Greek)
have an irreducible evaluative element. We find that we must
use these words in order to express our understanding of the
world; without these evaluative words we find that we cannot say what we think. The notion that evaluative terms are
somehow reducible to non-evaluative terms, in science at
least, has been dogma for so long in certain circles, that
the constant effort of moral philosophers to resist reduci-
bility at least for ethics has not been entirely successful.
It is well to realize that Aristotle supposes that evaluative concepts are not derived from non-evaluative concepts,
whether in ethics, or biology, or anywhere else.[7]

2. The Logical Priority of Pointedness

In *Physics* II, Aristotle presents an argument which purports
to demonstrate the irreducibility of purpose or rather point-
edness in explanation. This argument reveals a good deal concerning his philosophy, and could lead us in paths which we
will not explore in the present work; the central idea of
this part of the *Physics* is that processes in which a purpose
or point can intelligently be discerned are intrinsically
more comprehensible, more explicable, than pointless processes.

There are indeed processes which are pointless,[8] but if
those pointless processes are to be understood at all, it
would be in relation to or in comparison with some processes
which are understood teleologically.

Democritus, like some others of Aristotle's predecessors,
had attempted to explain the world without the use of teleological concepts. Aristotle regards this attempt as misguided
because the non-teleologist, whether he says so or not, is
using chance and accident as his ultimate explanatory concepts, and the description of an event as a chance event is
not an explanation. In fact, it seems to Aristotle and ad-
mission that the event is partially or wholly inexplicable.
He contrasts chance and purpose in *Physics* II and tries to
show how purpose is conceptually prior:

> Chance and luck are causes of that which mind or
> nature could cause, when some accidental cause
> brings these about; nothing accidental is prior
> to that which is essential (*kath hauto*); there-
> fore, no accidental cause is prior to an essential
> cause. Conversely, chance and luck are posterior
> to mind and nature.

According to Democritus and others the universe has come to
be what it now is spontaneously or by chance:

> but if chance is the cause of the universe, then
> necessarily mind and nature are a prior cause of
> this Everything, and of many other things (*Phys.*
> II.6, 198a5-13).

This too might be seen as a linguistic argument, but it does
not turn simply upon usage; Aristotle seems to claim that
one does not have the right to assert that an event is accidental if one denies that any event could be pointed.
This is based upon the idea that the concepts of 'accident',
'chance', and 'spontaneity' are defined negatively, that they
mean 'not essential', 'not deliberate', 'not pointed'. 'Accidental' and its relatives are meaningful only if 'essential'
and its relatives are meaningful; both sets of terms are
predicable of events or processes or results, but something
in the class must be essential if anything can be accidental.

8

The priority of the teleological concepts is both logical and metaphysical; nothing can be accidental unless something is essential, and nothing can happen by chance unless something happens for a purpose.

This criticism might look misdirected to the presocratic philosopher, for he contrasts necessity and chance, for everything occurs according to necessity and nothing is really at random.[9] Aristotle contends that the presocratic philosopher cannot *show* that the world is comprehensible by his methods, and could not ever succeed with the presuppositions with which he begins.

> In general, to think that the fact that something has always been or always happened thus is a sufficient principle of explanation is to fail to understand correctly. Democritus reduced the explanation of nature to this, that it happened thus before; he did not think it worthwhile to look for an explanation of what always happens.[10]

If one does not explain why the regularities exist, then these regularities themselves seem to be understood as coincidences or accidents, but of a higher order. Thus despite the contrast which Leucippos made between "necessary" and "random", Aristotle supposes that there is no difference between chance and necessity in the philosophy of the atomists; thus, he describes the position of Democritus at *Phys.* II.8, 198b17ff, using the words 'chance' and 'necessity' indiscriminately.

At 198b33ff (as at *Cael.* III.2, 300a20ff) Aristotle argues against the position that all events are 'coincidental' (*symptomata*).[11]

a) Natural occurrences are those which happen regularly.

b) Coincidental occurrences are those which happen irregularly.

c) Every occurrence is either pointed or coincidental, not both.

d) Therefore, all natural occurrences are pointed. There are natural occurrences, such as the development of the teeth, so there are pointed occurrences. This argument looks valid, and seems rather strong in the context of a criticism of the presocratic position, but it might be misleading to interpret

Aristotle's own theory on the basis of this argument. Premise a) has the virtue of being acceptable to the presocratic, but it is not Aristotle's definition of 'nature', nor does he believe that the classes 'natural occurrences' and 'regular occurrences' are coextensive. The premise is rhetorical. Premise b) seems to be established (again) by an appeal to usage; it would be bad Greek to call all events '*symptomata*'. However, the presocratic philosopher would suppose that this appeal to ordinary language begs the question, since Democritus, at least, supposes ordinary language to be wrong about the true nature of the world (cf. fragment 125, for example); he is recommending a new way of looking at things. That new way of looking at things includes supposing that everything is regular; if you don't see the regularity, then suppose that "hidden harmony is better than apparent harmony" (Heracleitus fragment 54). Nothing is coincidental, or if purpose and coincidence are contrasted, everything is coincidental, because everything happens regularly but nothing for a purpose.

There are several ways in which the presocratic philosopher might attack Aristotle's argument. For example, the disjunction in premise c) may be criticized from three directions, two mistaken, but one very damaging. i) One might point out that some events are both pointed and irregular, for example some cases of deliberate choice. But this does not touch the claim that all regular occurrences are pointed. ii) One might claim that regularities *must* be pointless, but that position assumes a heavy burden of proof; it could not be established empirically, and seems *prima facie* false. It would mean that it would be pointless to do anything regularly, for example, eat. iii) The point which is really at issue is this, are there any pointless regularities? Aristotle's argument may seem to fail here; he does admit the existence of some pointless regularities, although he attempts to assimilate them to pointed processes.[12] For example, the eclipse of the moon seems to be a regular occurrence, but probably has no special point (*Met*. Eta 4, 1044b12).

In order to defend his argument against this criticism,
Aristotle could say that the eclipse is, in a way, a coincidence, a concomitant result of the process of revolution
of the moon and sun, and these (in turn) are pointed processes. But this takes us from biology into the strange world
of Aristotle's astronomy. More relevantly for our present
investigation, we would say that Aristotle must show that
some regularities are pointed, and that he must find grounds
for distinguishing pointed from pointless regularities. But
those grounds are already provided by the 'functional' argument: if health is a good, then a process which results in
health is a pointed process; if this process happens regularly, we understand the process partly on the ground that
it happens regularly, but also and more importantly because
it results in health. So also in the generation of new individuals, the existence of an individual entity is a good
in itself and as the instantiation and continuation of the
species; the process is regular, and happens for this purpose.

3. The Analogy of Art and Nature

Aristotle's use of the analogy of art and nature seems to be
partially a matter of aesthetic appreciation of natural species, rather than an ascription of mind to nature.

> Though there are animals which have no attractive-
> ness for the senses, yet for the eye of science, for
> the student who is naturally of a philosophic spirit
> and can discern the causes of things, Nature which
> fashioned them provides joys which cannot be mea-
> sured (*PA* I.5, 645a8-11, PECK).

When a comparable appreciation occurs in a writer like J.B.S.
HALDANE, no one accuses him of animism or of a teleology of
intention:

> In an evolutionary line... we perceive an artistic
> unity similar to that of a fugue, or the life work

> of a painter... . Possibly such artistic work
> gives us as good insight into the nature of the
> reality around us as any other human activity.[13]

Aristotle, like HALDANE, considers the possible intention-
ality of actions of mind as a point of difference between
mind and nature, rather than as a point of similarity.
In *Physics* II.8, Aristotle presents what he seems to consider a clinching case for teleological explanation:

> Where there is an end, the prior steps are for
> that end (τούτου ἕνεϰα). As in action, so in
> nature; as in nature, so in action, if nothing
> interferes. Action is purposive (ἕνεϰά του).

The point is clarified by examples:

> If a house had been generated naturally, it would
> have been generated as it now is by art; if na-
> tural things were generated not only in nature
> but also by art, they would be generated as they
> are in nature (199a8ff).

(I have taken some liberties with the translation in order
to bring out the form of the argument). The statement "as in
action, so in nature..." asserts that there is indeed an
analogy between art and nature; the example of the house is
meant to show the character of the analogy. If art and nature had the same ends (and they sometimes do), the processes
which would bring about those ends should be identical. If
the process is regarded as pointed when carried out intentionally, Aristotle supposes that the process should equally
be regarded as pointed when carried out naturally.

> If it is both by nature and for an end that the
> swallow makes its nest and the spider its web...
> it is plain that there is this sort of cause in
> those things which are generated and exist in
> nature (199a26).

The swallow builds its nest naturally (not intentionally),
but the process is quite comparable to the building of a
house. We understand the process partially by the similarity
of function in the lives of birds and men of nests and houses.

Nature is defined thus: "Those things are natural which,
by a continuous movement originated from an internal principle, arrive at some end" (199b15). 'Artificial' would be

12

applied to 'those things which, by a movement originated from an *external* source, arrive at some end.'[14] In the biological books, there are a number of similarities between art and nature which are used fairly frequently by Aristotle in order to explain natural phenomena: 1) Both nature and art use or work upon a material, presumably a material appropriate for that which is to be made.[15] 2) Both nature and art tend to use tools or instruments in their work.[16] 3) There are similarities in the relationship of form to matter in the works of art and nature; Aristotle expands upon this theme when he talks of 'ratio' and 'symmetry'.[17] 4) Of course, the analogy of art and nature is used to show the likelihood of final causation in nature on the ground that it is certainly present in art.[18] We will look more closely at many of these passages in the pages which follow, and we will investigate more thoroughly the degree to which Aristotle's Nature is an Artist, in the latter part of Chapter IV; however, it would be well to give an example of the sort of passage which one finds in Aristotle, but taken from the literature of recent work in biology. The concepts and moves which are made here are those which seem essential in biology, and which are certainly central in Aristotle's biology:

> It then became evident that metabolic activity in the skeleton is a vital necessity for at least two reasons. For one thing, such activity allows remodeling of the skeleton to enable it to deal with the developing mechanical stresses on the body. It is as if each bone were an elaborate Gothic structure in which a resident engineer, in response to changes in stresses, continually directs the replacement of supporting arches with new ones providing a slightly different center of thrust. The other vital function of metabolic activity in bone is that, by allowing an exchange of minerals (calcium and phosphate ions) with the blood, it provides a storehouse of these materials to help meet the body's general requirements. And in fact normally there is an overall balance of supply and demand for bone materials.[19]

Aristotle's 'nature' is that 'resident engineer' of RASMUSSEN and PECHET; this is what must be understood in the analogy of art and nature.

C. Aristotle's Explanatory Modes and Concepts

In this section the reader will find a brief resumé of some
elements of Aristotle's philosophical positions as they bear
upon his biology. Anyone who finds it too elementary is invited to proceed to the next section immediately.

1. Function and Genesis

The great majority of Aristotle's accounts of characteristically biological phenomena fall into two general classes which
modern terminology would label "functional analysis and explanation" and "genetic analysis and explanation" (these terms
are borrowed from Morton BECKNER, *The Biological Way of
Thought*, chapters V and VI).

a) Being and Function

Individual entities (*ousiai*) and species of individuals are,
according to Aristotle, ontologically prior to attributes or
relations (see *Cat.* 5, *Met.* Zeta 1, etc.); animals and men
serve as paradigm cases of entities. Thus the question 'what
is it?' is logically prior to other questions. The first sort
of answer to this question may be a statement of species or
genus membership (Socrates is a man, man is an animal), but
a further demand must be satisfied either with a description
of the individual or with a listing of the attributes common
to the species. Certain attributes of species are called
'essential'; these are the differentia in the definitions of
the species and the genera to which it belongs. The selection
of certain attributes as the essential attributes is not
arbitrary; there is a principle of selection which is fairly
clear in the case of living beings. The essential attributes
of a living thing are those which enable it to live (without

14

which it would die) and to reproduce (without which the species would become extinct). Thus Aristotle divides the animal kingdom into those species with red blood (for him, coextensive with the chordata) and those which do not have
red blood (but an analogue of blood); these two large genera
are further divided according to their mode of reproduction.[20]

"A functional analysis attributes to a part or process
a role in the performance of some activity."[21] This charac-
terization includes Aristotle's analysis of the 'being' of
animals, especially as presented in the *PA*. Closer to Aristotle's special sense of 'function' is a sense described by
NAGEL:

> ... the vital functions can be taken to be the
> *defining* attributes of *living* organisms (or pos-
> sibly of some particular type of living organism),
> so that if an organic body lacks one of these at-
> tributes it does not count as a living organism
> (or a living organism of some stated type)
> (*Structure* p. 524, italics by NAGEL).

Classification is not the object of Aristotle's biological
investigation; rather, correct classification explicates the
teleological understanding of the species and genera. It
therefore depends upon the discovery and description of the
'vital functions' as described by NAGEL. This is the sense
in which Aristotle gives functional analyses of living beings
in the biological books.
His word for function is '*ergon*'; '*energeia*', usually translated 'actuality' or 'activity', could be translated as
'functioning'. The word '*dynamis*' is used for a class of
functional concepts.

b) *Genesis* and genetic analysis

A genetic analysis, as the term is used today, shows a being
or state of being to be the outcome of prior changes in one
or more series of moving causes. Each series of moving causes
has a source of movement (Aristotle calls it an *archē*); the

15

generation of the being or state of being analyzed is the last member of the series.[22] For Aristotle, only individual entities (*ousiai*) come-to-be in the unqualified sense; attributes come-to-be in an individual, or rather individuals come to have attributes (*Phys.* I.7, 190a32). Aristotle's *GA* deals primarily with the genesis of individuals; his genetic analyses are almost entirely limited to accounts of ontogeny. He does not concern himself with phylogeny and probably believed that it does not occur.[23]

2. Explanation

An analysis states a fact or set of facts, but an explanation is meant to give an understanding of the relationship between facts. This relationship may be a causal relationship; one fact may be the 'reason for' the existence of another fact. Such a distinction appears in Aristotle as that between 'knowledge of the fact' and 'knowledge of the reasoned fact' (*APo.* I.13, 78a22).[24] According to him, we understand a fact if we can construct a demonstrative syllogism with the fact as the conclusion, and the cause (*aition*) as the middle term (I.24, 85b22). Thus stated, Aristotle's theory resembles the 'deductive' or 'entailment' model of explanation outlined by NAGEL, and by HEMPEL and OPPENHEIM.[25] Although in the logical works Aristotle makes it a requirement for explanation that the explanandum be logically entailed by the explanans, he does not usually cast his explanations in the biological books into anything resembling syllogisms.
Of course the logical requirement would not necessarily specify the type of premises which should appear in the explanans. Although modern writers have, in general, a bias against teleological premises,[26] such premises would seem to Aristotle to fulfill the logical requirement as well as any other.

> It is clear that we must obtain knowledge of the
> primary causes, because it is when we think that

> we understand its primary cause that we claim to
> know each particular thing. Now there are four
> recognized kinds of causes. Of these we hold that
> one is the essence or essential nature of the
> thing (since the 'reason why' of a thing is ulti-
> mately reducible to its formula...)
> (*Met*. Alpha 3, 983a24-28, TREDENNICK).

The phrase 'the reason why of a thing' is, Aristotle notes, radically ambiguous, for one may ask why something simply *is*, or why it is qualified as it is; in either case one may ask for a functional or a genetic answer. Furthermore, one may be demanding an account of any one or more of the four causes. In fact, Aristotle tends to suppose that all of these demands should be satisfied if we are to understand completely ge-nerated entities.

An explanation enables us to know the nature of the thing, and a generated thing's nature must be stated in terms of all four causes. A thing is for us what we can say about it; a thing truly is what can be said truly about it; a thing's na-ture is what it really is. If some statements about the thing tell you why it exists, then those statements tell what it really is. Telling what a thing really is, is explaining the thing.

When explanation is described in this way, we can see that it is possible to get away from the deductive sort of explanation which we may find in the *APo*. Recently, Maurice MANDELBAUM has shown that functional explanation in modern anthropology is neither deductive nor probabilistic in character, but of-ten depends upon the principle that "descriptive analyses constitute explanations". "The various elements in a culture", he says, "were held to be what they actually were because of their interconnections with each other".[27] If we substitute 'organism' for 'culture', this sentence would be a fair de-scription of Aristotle's functionalism, though Professor MAN-DELBAUM claims that biology and anthropology are *not* similar in this respect.

3. *Dynamis* and the causes

We may explicate the notion of 'cause' as it appears in Aristotle by relating it to the various senses of the word '*dynamis*'. The causes are: matter, source of movement, form, and end. The two basic senses of '*dynamis*' from which any others are derived are: a) a source of movement or change; b) a source of a thing's being moved. These are, respectively, the active and passive 'powers' (potencies, potentialities). Fire, for example, has the active power to consume wood; wood has the reciprocal passive power to be consumed by fire (*Met.* Delta 12).

Both senses of '*dynamis*' are intimately related to teleological concepts. The active power is closely identified with the moving cause, and appears in analyses and explanations of the generation of entities. One seeks, in such analyses, the agent which has the power to generate such an entity, and has actualized that power in this case. Thus the sculptor has the power to generate statues, and a male animal the power to generate offspring. The 'power' is understood in terms of its valuable ('significant') results. In the functional analysis or explanation of an entity, or part of an entity, the ascription of active powers (abilities) is essential to the understanding of the entity or part as 'natural'. "Nature is a source or cause of movement and rest in that to which it belongs primarily" (*Phys.* II.1, 192b22). The passive power is closely identified with the material cause, and both the material cause and the passive power are understood in terms of ends. A passive power or material character is such simply because it is or has the potentiality *to be made into* something, or because it can have this form, whether be it a statue or a sphere or a man. In the context of an analysis or explanation of generation, matter and the passive power are potentially what they can become actually. In biological analyses Aristotle investigates matter and the passive power in two ways: a) he sometimes analyses the entity into its con-

18

stituent parts, which may in turn be analysed into their constituent parts, until something is reached which is no longer
analysable. Aristotle's unanalysed elements are earth, air,
fire, and water, or rather the elementary powers, hot, cold,
fluid, and solid/dry;[28] b) he investigates the passive powers
of the parts of the organism as such, e.g. the power of the
sense organs to be acted upon by other organs.

The relationship between *dynamis* and the formal cause (*eidos*)
is complicated by the ambiguity of the word '*eidos*'. On the
one hand, the *eidos* is the form of the individual; as such;
it is the dynamic structure of the individual (*his* powers,
potentialities); on the other hand, the *eidos* is the species
or class of individuals which share (in principle at least)
a similar dynamic structure. The individual entity is this
eidos in 'this' matter, but one cannot, finally, say anything
about the matter as such. What we can say about the individual
is that which is potentially common or general; for example,
we can state the relationships between the various powers or
dispositions of the entity and its parts. Such a statement
is a *logos* which tells the nature (*physis*) and the essence
(τὸ τὶ ἦν εἶναι) of the thing.[29]

The agent which generates an entity must have, at least vir-
tually, the form which is generated, for he cannot generate
the form; he transmits it to the material. In the case of a
natural species, this power to generate new individuals is
part of the definition of the species, a criterion for species
membership. The possession and the transmission of such a
form is an end in itself.

Aristotle emphasizes a special relationship between the notions of power and purpose in the passage where '*dynamis*' is
defined, *Met.* Delta 12:

> In virtue of that principle in virtue of which a
> patient is acted upon we call it 'able' (*dynaton*)
> to be acted upon; and this sometimes if it is acted
> upon in any way, but sometimes not in respect of
> every passion, but only if it is acted upon for
> the better.

> The power of performing well or according to
> choice; for sometimes we say of those who merely
> can walk or speak but not well or not as they
> intend that they cannot (do not have the power
> to) speak or walk.30

This purposive sense of potency often appears in Aristotle's
explanations; he speaks of 'actualizations' or 'realizations'.
When an active power (one able to effect some change for the
better) acts upon a passive power (one able to be changed
for the better) the result is an *energeia*, an activity or
actualizing of potentialites. The result of an *energeia* is an
entelecheia, a state of being in which certain potentialities,
thus understood, have been realized. This state of being, in
turn, will have further active and passive powers for further
actualizations.

Thus, for example, the organic parts of animals have functions
(*erga* or *ergasiai*), and it is just because they do have these
functions that they are understood as parts *of animals*. Aristotle uses these concepts in this way in his explanation of
the most obvious differences between male and female:

> Since they are different in respect of power,
> they are also different is some function (*ergon*);
> for every function (*ergasia*) there must be a tool
> (*organon*), and the tools for the powers are parts
> of the body; therefore ·there must be parts for
> childbirth and copulation (*GA* I.2, 716a23-27).

This argument follows nicely from his general definition of
the soul, as it appears in *de An*. II.1, "the first *entelecheia*
of a natural organic body". This definition in turn is related to the teleological principle stated at *GA* II.1, which
we have already discussed, by the elaboration of the definition at *de An*. II.4: "For living things, to live is to be,
and the soul is the cause and source of living and being;
furthermore, the *entelecheia* is the *logos* of that which is
potentially" (415b12).

Enough, for now, of the form; let us turn to the matter from
which the biological books were made, the data, the observations, and their sources.

D. The *History of Animals* and Aristotle's Sources[31]

Aristotle's sources of biological information were of three
general sorts: 1) written sources, literary, philosophical,
and otherwise; 2) the oral tradition and interviews with
fishermen, farmers and others; 3) his own dissections and
observations. One may wonder which predominate: does Aristotle rely mostly on books, on word of mouth, or on his own
observations? How careful and critical was he in the use of
his sources? How accurate are his observations? But the
question with which we are most concerned is this, to what
extent do theoretical considerations determine the direction
or even content of his observations? Answers to questions
like these have been developed very often on the basis of the
point of view and enthusiasms of the interpreter: G.H. LEWES,
a pioneer in this investigation, was a positivist and scientist; he represents an extreme position, that Aristotle did
not make important discoveries in biology, and was more influenced by theoretical considerations than by his own meager
observations.[32] Most writers about Aristotle love the object
of their research, and find it more congenial to defend him
than to attack him. The result is a tendency to try to show
that Aristotle was similar, in some important respects, to
contemporary scientists; the analyses which result differ to
the extent that the opinions of interpreters concerning the
nature of scientific thought differ. JAEGER has Aristotle
looking rather like the positivist's idea of a biologist;
RANDALL's Aristotle looks like John DEWEY's idea of a biologist; Marjorie GRENE brings Aristotle into line with her own
naturalism; and the Thomists, like Theodore TRACY, make Aristotle seem atemporal, neither contemporary nor ancient.[33]
Several difficulties complicate an assessment of Aristotle's
use of data. For one thing, it is not perfectly clear which
books are authentic, and which passages within authentic
books may have been inserted after Aristotle's death. The
principle which we follow in this section is generous: we

will accept *HA* I-IX, *PA*, *GA*, *IA*, *MA*, *de An.*, and the *Parva Naturalia* except the *peri pneumatos* as genuine. No doubt some inauthentic passages are taken as authentic in the process, but nothing of capital importance hangs on it.[34] Another difficulty is that the general style of the biological books is expository, stating the facts as Aristotle understands them without reference to the source of the information. Even when he does indicate that his information has come from someone else, the source is usually anonymous; he says, "some say", "it is said", or the like.[35] Sometimes the same fact is attributed in this vague way in one place, and to a particular source in another. For example, in the *HA* he says that "some suppose that fish conceive by swallowing milt", but in the *GA* he blames Herodotus the "mythologos" for this absurd notion.[36] This happens with oral material too, perhaps even more often; "some" describe the mode of copulation, peculiar to the octopus, involving hecatolization of one of the tentacles; in another place it appears that the acute observers are certain fishermen (*HA* V.6, 541b8; 12, 544a12). This, incidentally, is one of the true stories which Aristotle heard but rejected on the ground that it was too strange to be believed.[37] Unless we can trace a story to a particular writer, it is difficult or impossible to guess its source, or even to guess whether Aristotle is taking the story from a written source or an oral source. Thus one cannot support any very definite statements about the relative proportions of his uses of oral and written sources; the relative infrequency of any attribution at all prevents the substantiation of any very precise claims concerning the proportion of the material which he checked himself and of that which he incorporated without checking. For example, Aristotle describes a method of making sea water into fresh water by percolating it through a thin wax vessel, and even recommends the experiment.[38] AELIAN[39] reports that this idea comes from Democritus; D'ARCY THOMPSON (as he says in a note to the passage in *HA*) tried the experiment and it doesn't work. Unless there is something more

22

to the method that Aristotle does not report (I doubt it),
then he did not try it himself, but accepted it on the authority of someone else, probably Democritus. In fact, if
the experiment were to work it would corroborate the physics
of Democritus, not that of Aristotle, in that the wax would
be filtering out the larger, rougher, salt atoms, and letting
the smaller, smoother, water atoms through.

1. Written sources

Aristotle does name some of his literary sources, and there
are some surprises in these citations: Plato is never named
in the *HA*, *PA*, or *GA* (but he is cited in the *de An.* and
Parva Naturalia), nor is Hippocrates. Various poets are cited,
especially Homer, and such obscure individuals as Syennesis,
the doctor from Cyprus (*HA* III.2, 511b24), and Herodorus of
Heraclea, father of Bryson the Sophist, and author of the
History of Heracles.[40] Because we have the text of Herodotus,
we are able to trace a good many places where Aristotle relies upon him,[41] but he is named only once in *HA*, as the
source of the story that the semen of Ethiopians is black.[42]
Aristotle rejects that story, as he does one which can also
be traced to Herodotus III.103, that the camel has four knees
(*HA* II.1, 499a20). But Aristotle accepts the description which
Herodotus gives of the crocodile, especially that it moves its
upper jaw rather than its lower jaw.[43] He also accepts the
(true) story of horned serpents in Egypt,[44] of the smallness
of animals in Egypt,[45] of the varieties of the Egyptian ibis,[46]
and the description of the hippopotamus.[47] One might detect a
note of skepticism in Aristotle's report of the stories,
traced to Herodotus, of birds with no feet,[48] of bearded
priestesses in Caria,[49] of the fabulous cinnamon bird, who
makes his nest of cinnamon sticks, gathered one knows not
where,[50] that the lioness discharges its uterus on giving
birth,[51] and of the oxen which graze backwards, because if

they grazed forward their horns would stick in the ground.[52]

If we had a text of Ktesias, another tireless traveler, we probably could find many indirect references to his work too, for there are several direct references. Ktesias "assures us that there is a wild beast in India called the 'martichoras' which has a triple row of teeth in both upper and lower jaws...," describing the tiger in exaggerated and fanciful terms (*HA* II.3, 501a25); Ktesias tells us that the semen of the elephant becomes as hard as amber (there is no truth in the story, says Aristotle).[53] Ktesias says that there is neither wild nor tame pig in India, "but he is not trustworthy", says Aristotle (*HA* VIII.28, 606a8). Nevertheless, Aristotle seems to have trusted Ktesias about the Indian rhinoceras (*PA* II.2, 663a15) and seems to have been in agreement with him concerning the method used by Thracians for hunting birds with the aid of falcons.[54]

The references to various poets, especially to Homer, are rather more frequent than one would expect in a book devoted to biological facts. It may be that this has something to do with one of Aristotle's earliest writings, if we can trust the reported title, "ὑπὲρ τῶν μυθολογουμένων ζῴων",[55] which means not simply "On Mythological Animals", but more generally, "On Animals Mentioned in Stories". Herodotus is called a *mythologos* (*GA* III.5, 756b7), and one of his stories is called a *mythos*.[56] "Myths" are told about the deer, that they are very long-lived, but the evidence points to the contrary (*HA* VI.29, 578b22); according to the "myth" the crane carries a stone for ballast, but this is untrue (VIII.12, 597b1); it is a "myth" that the 'lazy-bird' heron was generated from slaves (IX.18, 617a5); there is a "myth" about the punishment of the eagle (IX.32, 609a18). One "myth" of special interest, in that Aristotle's account is more detailed, is the one about the she-wolf who brings forth her young only on twelve particular days of the year.

> The reason that they give is that when they brought Leto in twelve days from the Hyperborean land to

24

the island of Delos, she took the form of a she-
wolf to escape the anger of Hera (VI.35, 580a15ff).
Aristotle goes on to say that he does not know whether the
story about the she-wolf is true or not, that he is just
giving it as it is told.[57]

Some of Aristotle's references to Homer show signs of having
been guided by an examination of secondary sources on the
poet, as well as his own considerable familiarity with the
text.[58] For example, he says, "Some think that Homer did well
to represent Odysseus' dog as dying in his twentieth year;"[59]
"some say that Homer does well to depict... ."[60] He even
cites a verse of Homer and follows without credit the interpretation and commentary given this verse by Herodotus.[61]
Aristotle mentions Homer's name several times in connection
with odd bits of animal lore: the size of the self-castrated
boars,[62] the various names of a particular bird,[63] the fear
which lions have for fire,[64] where to hit a horse in order to
kill him,[65] the mention of a species of eagle.[66] He also
quotes with approbation one of Homer's fine clinical desciptions
of a killing blow with a spear,[67] along with a bit of
linguistic analysis: if a severed head were to talk, it would
be the head that spoke, not the man whose head it had been.

Several other poets are cited: the poems ascribed the
Orpheus are mentioned for their comparison of the embryonic
formation of the animal with the weaving of a net;[69] MUSAEUS
is cited for the number of young of the eagle ("lays three,
hatches two, raises one" *HA* VI.6, 563a18); four lines of
Simonides are quoted concerning the Halcyon (V. 8, 542b6);
an allusion to Stesichorus continues the discussion of this
bird (542b25); a passage in Epicharmus is taken as an example
of a series of moving causes.[70] In a pair of disputed passages,
Hesiod, it may be, is cited concerning the siege of Ninevah
(*HA* VIII.19, 601b22) and Aeschylus concerning the changing
appearance of the hoopoe (IX.49b, 633a18).
The influence of medical writers and philosophers is, for
the most part, not explicit in the *HA*, at least not as ex-

plicit as it becomes in the *PA* and *GA*; in fact, apart from
III.2-3, where Diogenes of Apollonia, Syennesis of Cyprus,
and Polybus the son-in-law of Hippocrates, are quoted at some
length, there are but three explicit references to philosophical and medical writers in the *HA*. Alcmaeon of Croton is
cited twice, once to criticize his claim that goats can
breathe through their ears (I.11, 492a13), and once in approbation of his comparison of the growth of the hair on the
pubes to the sprouting of flowers in springtime (VII.1, 581a
15). Although Aristotle seems to have been taken in by the
'wax bottle in the sea' experiment (note 38 above), he cites
Democritus by name only once (IX.39, 623a30) to attack the
(essentially correct) theory of the extrusion of spider web
filament, an attack all the stranger in that Democritus'
theory is really more consonant with the theory of 'residues'
developed in the *PA* than is the theory of spider webs defended by Aristotle in the *HA*. CHERNISS (*Presocratic* 333-4)
suggests that Aristotle was misled by his theory here, but
he does not actually show how. I think it more likely that
he was misled by somebody's theory, but that his theory was
not yet developed.

In a unique section in the biological books, Aristotle quotes
extended passages of several writers, and then discusses them.[71]
Syennesis, Diogenes, and Polybus had treated the subject of
the blood vessels 'very unsatisfactorily' because of the manner in which they dissected; he quotes their descriptions,
describes his own method of preparing animals for dissection,
and describes the observations made as a result. In this case,
at least, he is working within the medical tradition, on a
medical problem which he regards as central to his interests
in philosophical biology.

Given the systematic approach shown in this passage, it is
all the more surprising that he never cites medical writers
elsewhere in the *HA* except with a vague "some say". However,
we may discern extensive influence of several works which
survive in the Hippocratic corpus, and there is probably also

26

influence of medical works now lost. One of the more obvious
cases is his agreement with the Hippocratic texts in the error that the brain is located solely in the front part of the
head.[72] The account of menstruation and pregnancy in the *HA*
is also similar in many details to the position stated in several Hippocratic works.[73]

In the *PA* and *GA* Aristotle's citations are mostly of philosophical writers. General references to his predecessors
abound in *PA* I.1, which is a kind of protreptic to biology,
and in much of *GA*. He speaks of "the ancients who first philo-
sophized about nature",[74] "some of the ancient *physiologoi*",[75]
"some of the physiologoi" (*GA* IV.3, 769a7), or simply of "the
physiologoi" (*PA* I.2, 641a7); he writes of the "*physikoi*" in
the same manner (*GA* II.5, 741b10); the terms seem inter-
changeable, for he writes of "Anaxagoras and some of the
other *physikoi*", and "Anaxagoras and others of the *physiologoi*".[76]

The Hippocratic writers would count as *physiologoi*;[77] A.L.
PECK has found many passages which rely upon or are closely
related to passages in many of the Hippocratic books,[78] but
Aristotle refers to these books only in indirect ways, e.g.:
"the ancients thought that the semen was a *syntēgma*..." (*GA*
I.18, 724b35); "those who say that children suckle in the
womb..." (*GA* II.7, 746a19); and the like. He uses with easy
confidence information gained from the medical tradition and
perhaps from personal contact with medical men (his father
had been a doctor), as when he says that 'the old doctors'
reduced dislocated fingers with an instrument which works in
a manner similar to the suckers in the tentacles of the octopus.[79] He is aware of a medical use for the sea urchin (*HA*
IV.5, 530b10), a method for recognizing tapeworm (*HA* V.19,
550b13), the practice of midwives with umbilici (*HA* VII.10,
587a22);he is familiar with the pharmacology and the contents
of the pharmacy,[80] and with the practice of the *pharmacides*,
sellers of various remedies. But the *pharmacides* are closer
to witches than to medical doctors.[81]

27

Heracleitus is cited explicitly only once in the biological books,[82] and that is for a story likely to be apocryphal, about how he invited his guests into the kitchen, saying, "there are gods also here".[83] But his influence, even if indirect, pervades the *PA*, for the theory of the soul which is used in this book emphasizes the similarity, but not identity, of the vital heat with fire; Aristotle also uses the notion of a balance of opposites throughout his work. Although both these ideas are common in presocratic philosophers, one thinks of Heracleitus especially in connection with them.

Another sort of theory of opposites, that of the Pythagoreans, is cited without naming its author.[84] Alcmaeon of Croton, close to the Pythagoreans, and named in the *HA*, is attacked in the *GA* for his theory that the yolk of the egg is the germ and the white the food; Aristotle's theory is that the white is the germ and the yolk the food.[85] Parmenides is mentioned not for his striking metaphysical theses, which are discussed in some detail in the *Physics*, but for his belief that women are hotter than men, on the ground of their menstrual flow (*PA* II.2, 648a25). Socrates is mentioned[86] for his advances in philosophical method, "but the study of Nature was given up in his time". A certain Leophanes is noted for his supposed experiment of tying up the testicles individually in order to see whether males come from the right and females from the left;[87] the method would be of considerable value if it were to work.
Diogenes of Apollonia is not named in the biological works (he is named in the psychological books[88]), but his influence is most important on the development of Aristotle's theory of *pneuma*, for it is he who compares semen to foam most explicitly, and explains the derivation of the name of Aphrodite on this basis.[89] Plato is not named either, but one may compare several of the theories attacked with those which Plato defends; for example, the theory of classification criticized in *PA* I.2 resembles that developed in the *Sophist* and *Politicus*. Of course, Aristotle may here be attacking

28

someone like Speusippos, rather than Plato, for taking the
theory of collection and division too seriously.[90] But the
Timaeus, one of Aristotle's favorite targets in any case,
comes in for its share of fairly direct criticism in the biological books:[91] for example, Aristotle attacks the theory
of the marrow which one finds in the *Timaeus*,[92] the account
of the purpose of the lung,[93] of the purpose of the gall
bladder,[94] and, at some length, the theory of vision shared
by the *Timaeus* and Empedocles.[95]
Aristotle's major opponents in the *PA* and *GA*, as often in
other works, are Empedocles, Anaxagoras, and Democritus, yet
one may say that he is guided by the advances made by these
philosophers as often as he finds that he must disagree with
them; it is only his habit of naming his predecessors most
often when they are the object of attack that leads us to
suppose them less influential than they must have been upon
his development. Indeed, he gives Empedocles special credit
for hitting the truth, even if a bit grudgingly:

> In some places even Empedocles, being led and
> guided by truth herself, stumbles upon this, and
> is forced to assert that it is the *logos* which
> is a thing's essence or nature. For instance,
> when he is explaining what bone is, he says not
> that it is any one of the elements, or any two,
> or three, or even all of them, but that it is
> "the *logos* of the mixture" of the elements. And
> it is clear that he would explain in the same
> way what flesh and each of such parts is.[96]

Empedocles is also cited for his brilliant analogy, "The great
trees lay eggs; the olives first...",[97] and for his claim that
men are hotter than women (rather than colder, as Parmenides
claimed) on the grounds that women have the menstrual flow
(*PA* II.2, 648a30); this is Aristotle's own opinion, although
he does not say so in this place (cf. *GA* I.19, 726b31ff).

Aristotle's major criticism of both Empedocles and Democritus is that they rely upon the notion of chance in explanation; for example, he objects to Empedocles' claim that
the backbone is segmented because it was accidentally broken
"in the process of formation".[98] But there are also many cri-

ticisms of details of their theories. In the *GA*, Empedocles'
theories concerning animal generation are discussed at some
length;[99] this discussion is, in fact, one of the major
sources of information concerning this aspect of Empedocles'
thought. Aristotle's major objection in *GA* I.18 is that Empedocles supposes parts of the animal to be able to live separately, which is absurd even in the generative fluids. This
criticism is taken up again in IV.1, where the issue is the
development of males and females; apparently Empedocles
thought that if the embryo got a male organ, it would turn
out male. Aristotle retorts that sexual differentiation is
not simply a matter of having a male organ or not. Empedocles
also thought that a difference in temperature in various parts
of the womb made some difference in the sex of the offspring;
Aristotle is more tempted by this theory, but has observational evidence that disconfirms it.

Empedocles had a theory about why mules are infertile; Aristotle discusses this theory at some length without, however,
making very clear what the theory was, although it might not
have been too clear in the poem either (*GA* II.8, 747a25ff).
Aristotle criticizes Empedocles for comparing milk to 'pus',
which would imply that it was an unnatural formation (*GA* IV.8,
777a5); he attacks aspects of Empedocles' theory of vision.[100]
Probably Empedocles is discussed anonymously in a number of
passages, but we cannot discern his influence exactly because
we do not have his entire work. We may discern that Aristotle
has him in mind when he alleges that sharks are ovoviviparous
because they are cold, not because they are hot, as "some
people" say; this should include Empedocles, because he did
indeed believe that water animals are hotter than land animals.[101] Despite these disagreements, we may recognize that
Aristotle respected Empedocles, and that he was influenced by
him in more ways than one usually notes.

Democritus too must have influenced Aristotle extensively.
We have already noted one or two places in the *HA* where we
may trace an idea to *Democritus*; in the *PA* and *GA* the ci-

tations are many, for entire chapters in these books have
been written expressly to refute or to amend the theories of
Democritus, or of Democritus and Empedocles taken together.
Aristotle takes exception especially to the philosophical position which Democritus defended:

> If each animal and each of its parts is what it
> is in virtue of its shape and its color, what
> Democritus says will be correct, since that was
> apparently his view, if one understands him aright
> when he says that it is evident to everyone what
> "man" is like touching his shape, for it is by
> his shape and color that a man may be told.[102]

To this position Aristotle opposes his functionalism, no
doubt justly. But Aristotle does recognize that Democritus
had some comprehension of a solution to the philosophical
problem, for he says that Democritus was the first to touch
on the essence and the entity:

> he did so, not because he thought that it was
> necessary for the study of nature, but because
> he was carried away by the subject in hand and
> could not avoid it.[103]

Possibly Aristotle has in mind the theory which he discusses
in *Met.* Alpha (I.4, 985b10ff), that formal relations can be
reduced to three, 'rhythm', 'intercontact', and 'turning'.

The theory of the soul which Democritus shared with
Leucippos (*de An.* I.2, 404a1) holds that the soul is iden-
tial with spherical atoms, which make us move, perceive (i.e.
'touch'), and even think and dream. Since life is the renewal
of these spherical atoms, Democritus seems to say that all
animals breathe, and renew their soul and mind through this
means.[104]

As in *Phys.* II, so in *GA*, Aristotle attacks Democritus on the
subject of necessity and chance. The idea that something is
necessary because "this is how it has always happened" (*GA*
II.6, 742b18) is criticized on the ground that it would de-
stroy the possibility of mathematics, an unusual argument in
a biological context. Aristotle seems to recognize that the
definition of 'necessity' as 'that which always happens' has
some (misleading) plausibility in a biological context, but

none at all in a mathematical context. The final passage in the *GA* (V.8, 788b10ff) is devoted to a refutation of Democritus' position on biological, rather than mathematical, grounds. Democritus, says Aristotle, has attempted to explain the appearance of teeth in the development of the growing animal, but his attempt fails partially through defective observation, and partially (but this might be the same point) through omission of the purpose of teeth.[105]

Aristotle supposes that Democritus' neglect of the functional or teleological aspects of biological phenomena led him into a variety of observational, or scientific, errors. For example, the notion that 'man is just what we see' led him to regard too highly the external parts of the animal, and too lightly the internal organs. Democritus seems to have thought that the internal organs of animals which do not have red blood were quite like the internal organs of those that do, but that we cannot see them because the animals themselves are too tiny (*PA* III.4, 665a30). Democritus seems even to have thought that the external parts of animals were formed first in the process of development, and then the internal (*GA* II.4, 740a10ff). Aristotle spends some effort attacking this position on the ground that it makes the mother and her womb seem rather too much like the sculptor, that the process seems not natural but artificial. There are also, says Aristotle, observational reasons for rejecting the hypothesis that Democritus provides.

Aristotle criticizes Democritus together with Empedocles on the subject of the generation of mules (*GA* II.8, 747a25), on the generation of the differences between males and females (IV.1, 764a5), on the explanation of monstrosities (IV.4, 769b31), and on the theory which we call 'pangenesis'.[106] Aristotle says that Democritus' explanation of the generation of sexual differences is better than that given by Empedocles because "he is trying to find out what is the difference inherent in the process, and endeavoring to state it, though whether he is right or not is another matter" (IV.1, 764a20).

32

In the *PA* and *GA*, Aristotle, unlike Plato (who never mentions
Democritus by name) takes the atomists as worthy opponents,
and gives credit to Democritus for some correct positions;
he also works at destroying the philosophical basis of atomism, and sometimes criticizes Democritus for poor observation.

Anaxagoras is not mentioned in the *HA*, but his views are discussed in the other biological books. Most notably, his theory
that man is the most intelligent animal because he has hands
is the occasion of an important little essay (*PA* IV.10, 687
a7-b25) in which Aristotle argues that man has hands because
he is the most intelligent animal. The disagreement between
Anaxagoras and Aristotle on this point is one which still appears among scientists, for it depends upon a distinction
between two ways of understanding organic functions. Anaxagoras seems to have quite a lot to say on biological and
medical questions: "those around Anaxagoras" argued that the
gall-bladder is the cause of acute diseases, but this is incorrect, says Aristotle, and if one were to dissect those who
suffer from these diseases one would find that they have no
gall-bladder at all (*PA* IV.2, 677a6ff). The theory of sexual
generation which Anaxagoras proposed is attacked along with
those of Empedocles and Democritus (*GA* IV.1, 763b30, 765a5),
although Aristotle does give him credit for thinking up a
plausible if incorrect solution for many of the problems with
his theory of 'homoiomeries' (*GA* I.18, 723a5, see chapter II
below). Given the attention which Anaxagoras must have paid
to the problems of generation, it is surprising to find that
he is among those who believed that some birds copulate mouth-
to-mouth and that the weasel brings forth its young from its
mouth (*GA* III.6, 756b13ff). Incidentally, Anaxagoras is criticized together with Diogenes for his opinion that all animals breathe, including fish and shellfish; this comment
might bring Anaxagoras closer to the 'pneumatic' tradition
than is ordinarily supposed.[107]

Aristotle surely was influenced by, and took information from,

33

many writers whom he does not mention by name. In his lifetime, the Academy was populated by many clever thinkers on a
variety of subjects. If Xenocrates, Speusippos, Eudoxos, or
the others, had anything to say on biological questions,
Aristotle would have been aware of it. After his departure
from the Academy, Aristotle spent about two years on the island of Lesbos, probably investigating marine life part of
the time (he was also on his honeymoon, it seems); Erastos
and Coriscos were with him part of this time, and Theophrastos
joined them.[108] We know Theophrastos as much interested in
biological problems, and generally concerned with scientific
questions. It is not necessary to accept the extreme position
expounded by Josef ZÜRCHER, that much of the Aristotelian
corpus was really composed by Theophrastos, to assert that
this younger friend must have influenced the development of
the *HA* as well as that of the other biological works.[109]
One might also mention another, even younger (probably) biological writer who could have influenced Aristotle: Diocles
of Carystos. According to JAEGER, Diocles was indeed a student of Aristotle at the Lyceum.[110] If he did influence Aristotle, it might have been in regard to the changing attitude
toward *pneuma*.

Aristotle probalby used other written sources of information,
but the evidence is rather indirect.[111] My own guess (and it
is no more than a guess) is that among the books which Aristotle had available to him as he wrote his biological treatises were: one or more guides to soothsaying, at least one
bee-keeper's guide, other traveler's reports besides Herodotus and Ktesias, possibly a treatise on veterinary medicine,[112]
possibly a written source on the habits of fish, and possibly
others.

One may be led to suppose a written source concerning soothsaying, partially because the references to *terata*, unnatural
or portentous events, are rather unevenly distributed through
the biological books. In *HA*, VI has several references to such
things as "monstrous" eggs (VI.2, 559b20), "monstrous" copu-

34

lation of oxen (21, 575b13), and the search of the *pharma-kides* for "hippomanes" (18, 572a22; 22, 577a13). Again, in IX, there are many examples given of friendships and enmities among animals, probably appropriate to a catalogue of such relationships compiled for the sake of the *manteis*, or sooth-sayers.[113] In the same book we are told that people say that the left (or right) horn of the stag is never found because the animal hides it because of a "medicinal" property (5, 611a29); that a stag was found with ivy growing over its horns;[114] that the afterbirth of the deer has medicinal pro-perties (611b26); that a man in Byzantion got a big reputation by foretelling the weather by looking at the habits of hedge-hogs (6, 612b8), and so on. In *GA* IV, there is a long group of explanations of *terata* which must depend upon a fairly ex-tensive collection of descriptions of these phenomena (some described are rather rare). Elsewhere, he mentions the use of internal organs for soothsaying, and seems to have de-rived some of his information about unusual formations from soothsayers, possibly by word of mouth or (more likely) from a written guide.[115] He also mentions the belief in prognostic-ation by dreams (*HA* IV.10, 537b17), a subject which he treats in a small essay, *Div. Somn.* In the *Meteorologica* he writes of οἱ τερατολογοῦντες (II.7, 368a25), which could imply more than one written source on the subject of *terata*.

Although a "Compleat Mantis" might account for all these kinds of information, the relationships between different varieties of soothsaying are complicated enough that one may suppose a plurality of sources. Dream interpretation (*oneiro-critica*) was to have its own literature; Artemidorus, in the second century A.D., wrote a rather extensive treatise on the subject, using literature which might have origins before Aristotle's time. Very different, and also very ancient, is soothsaying on the basis of the inspection of the internal organs of sacrified animals, *hieroscopia*. Another school specializing in the observation of the behavior of animals, especially of birds, and of peculiar meteorological phenomena,

35

was known as 'augury' in Rome. A special branch of mantic lore
surrounded the birth of human infants and of domestic animals.
Finally, ancient pharmacology tended to make little distinction between magic and medicine, despite the usually confident
naturalism of the Hippocratic writers.

Aristotle, in contrast to Plato,[116] uses this information with
considerable confidence in the accuracy of the observations,
and little confidence in the explanations devised by the mantic band to account for the peculiarities which have been observed.[117]

2. The oral tradition

It is obvious to anyone who reads the text that Aristotle
talked to many people from many vocations in the attempt to
acquire information concerning the animal kingdom, as indeed
he gained information from them concerning other subjects as
well. He gives credit in the biological books to fishermen,
spongedivers, hunters, eelkeepers, farmers, shepherds, cattlemen, pig breeders, horsetrainers, beekeepers, bird fanciers,
and he probably talked with an elephant keeper and a camel
driver too, to cite exotica.

The fishermen gave him more and better information concerning
animals than anyone else. Aristotle mentions the "more ex-
perienced" fishermen[118] who have seen examples of odd-look-
ing fish in the sea; the methods of fishermen demonstrate the
existence of the senses of smell, taste, hearing, and vision,
in many species of sea-creatures.[119] The fishermen had observed hectocotylization in octopi,[120] and had noticed that
the octopus devours members of its own species.[121] They were
well informed about the habits and character of the purple
murex (*HA* V.15, 547a25), about the parasites of the pinna
(547b30), and of course about the havoc wreaked by the starfish on beds of shellfish (548a9). Fishermen are credited
with something resembling an experiment, for they nicked the

36

tails of dolphins, then let them go, in order to establish
how long members of that species might live (VI.12, 566b24).
Aristotle frequently gives credit to fishermen as the source
of his information about marine life, and they are probably
the source of much information which is not specifically
credited. But Aristotle does not simply repeat their stories;
he has checked their stories by observation, or so at least
he pretends. For example, he says that fish copulate, although
the fishermen do not think so; fishermen do not notice it because fish do not take much time over it, and "of course no
fisherman ever watches this sort of thing for the sake of
pure knowledge". Fishermen, it seems, think that fertilization
occurs through the fish swallowing the milt. [123]
Spongedivers have reported concerning the fish which they see
(*HA* IX.37, 620b34), and eelkeepers are well-informed about
the character (if not the origin!) of the fish which they
sell (VIII.2, 592a2). These eelmen are associated in the passage with the river Strymon, which flows through Amphipolis,
not far from Stageira, Aristotle's home.
Hunters are closely associated, in Aristotle's way of thinking,
with fishermen, particularly when they use decoys of 'bait',
as the partridge hunters are said to do. [124] Possibly Aristotle
followed Xenophon's *Kynegetikos* [125] or a similar book, for example for the story about the use of human excrement to catch
panthers (*HA* IX.5, 612a10) or about the ways to hunt deer
(VI.29, 579a6); he seems pretty clearly to have talked per-
sonally with the hunter who said that out of eleven hyenas he
had caught, only one was female (VI.32, 579b28).
Aristotle does not rely much on the authority of farmers
(*geōrgoi*), no doubt because their experience is largely limited to botany; one botanical fact, at least, is noted (and
it is important to him): that farmers tie wild figs to fig
trees to make them fertile (*HA* V.32, 557b30, and THOMPSON
ad loc.), Farmers do report on the character and habits of
cicades (V.30, 556b15), complain of the rapidity of a plague
of mice (VI.37, 580b17), and use the appearance of flies from

piles of manure to judge that the manure is sufficiently rotted to use for fertilizer (*HA* V.19, 552a20); Aristotle agrees with the farmers that the flies have been generated spontaneously.

Aristotle distinguishes those concerned with the breeding and training of animals from farmers. He has great confidence in the information which he acquires from animal-keepers, as much as in the fishermen.[126] Aristotle reports that shepherds (*nomeis*) know how much cheese to expect from the milk of sheep and goats (*HA* III.20, 522a29), and are full of information concerning the reproduction of their charges (*HA* VI.19, 574a11). Aristotle believes them when they say that it makes a difference which way the animals are facing when they copulate (*GA* IV.2, 767a8). The shepherd (*poimēn*) knows the character of his sheep (*HA* IX.3, 610b27ff), watches for signs portending the birth of lambs (VI.18, 573a2), and has been known to catch the 'hybris' bird and eagle in mortal combat (IX.12, 615b15).

Cattlemen (*boukoloi*) report the character of cattle (IX.4, 611a8; VI.18, 572a33), and tell how they tame castrated bulls (VI.21, 575b1). Horsebreeders say how they allow intervals between breeding times (VI.23, 577b14), and must be the source of much of the information about the breeding of mules. Those who occupy themselves with the raising of pigs seem to have been consulted about their methods.[127]

Aristotle's description of the habits and structure of the elephant are presented in considerable detail, and from the point of view of an elephant trainer. The source of this information may be indicated by the statement that the elephant can eat nine Macedonian medimni (VIII.9, 596a3), which may mean that he was acquainted with these animals during a stay in Macedonia, perhaps during the period in which he was the young Alexander's tutor; in the context, Aristotle goes on to talk about camels. Perhaps Philip had built up a small menagerie of animals reputed to have military significance. There is an old story that Alexander sent an elephant to

38

Aristotle from his military campaigns;[128] chronologically
this is impossible, because Aristotle's familiarity with elephants must date from an earlier period than the last two or
three years of his life. But there may be this much in the
story, that Aristotle found out about elephants, and about
camels too for that matter, in the company of the adolescent
Alexander.

Beekeepers must have been interviewed at some length, for
Aristotle twice in *HA* discusses several different theories
about bees. Noting that various theories are held concerning
the way in which bees generate (V.21, 553a16), he discusses
at least four such theories under the rubric "some say...
others say...". An essentially correct theory[129] is rejected
on the ground that observation does not support it; his own
incorrect but oddly ingenious theory is defended in *GA* III.
10, 759a8ff. In *HA* IX.40, 623b29ff, several different sources
have obviously been consulted; probably there was at least
one written source and several oral sources. We may note also
that he has talked with birdfanciers as well, for they have
told him of their habit of putting a second cock to the hen
in order to improve the breed, a practice which Aristotle
tries to explain (*HA* VI.9, 564b2; *GA* I.21, 730a12).

We have noted (n. 33) that Aristotle often says simply "some
say..." or the like, and this may indicate that his sources
include not only "experts" but also a more or less undiffer-
entiated oral tradition. He wavers between a skeptical attitude and some degree of gullibility, toward this tradition.[130]
One of the more striking instances of his credulity is his
apparent acceptance of the notion that there exist "fire-
animals".

> In Cyprus, in places where copper-ore is smelted,
> ... an animal is engendered in the fire, somewhat
> larger than a bluebottle fly, furnished with wings
> which can hop or crawl through the fire. And ...
> these animals perish when you keep (them) away
> from the fire ... . The salamander is a case in
> point, to show us that animals do actually exist
> that fire cannot destroy; for this creature, so

the story goes, not only walks through the
fire but puts it out in doing so.[131]

In later books he is more skeptical on this point; even in
the *Meteor.*, which should be from about the same period as
the *HA*, he writes: "animals exist only on land and water,
which are the matter from which their bodies are compounded,
but not in air or fire."[132] In the *GA*, again, he writes,

> Fire does not generate any animal, and we find
> no animal taking shape either in fluid or solid
> substance while they are under the influence of
> fire; whereas the heat of the sun does effect
> generation... . (II.3, 737a1, PECK).

The tradition was strong, however, for he says later in *GA*,

> As for the fourth tribe, we must not look for it
> in these regions, although there wants to be a
> kind corresponding to the position of fire in
> the series, since fire is reckoned as the fourth
> of the corporeal substances. ... No, this fourth
> tribe must be looked for on the moon, since the
> moon, as it appears, has a share in the fourth
> degree of remove (III.11, 761b16ff, PECK).

Also, in *Resp.* 13, 477a28, he speaks of a higher proportion
of earth in plants, water in water animals, of air or fire
in land and air animals; this is tied to the principle of
natural directions. The myth has been rationalized.[133]
Another story accepted by Aristotle in *HA* (VI.2, 560b13) is
that the hen-partridge can conceive by standing to windward
and within scent of the male; again the mistake is corrected
in the *GA*, where the scent of the male is said rather to
stimulate the production of infertile eggs (III.1, 751a15).

3. Aristotle's own observations

Although Aristotle relied upon many written and oral reports,
he also observed many phenomena himself, and sometimes went
out of his way to observe phenomena which he thought might
interest him. It would be difficult to ascertain just what
percentage of his statements he checked with his own eyes;
the correctness of the statement is not a guarantee that he

checked it, for sometimes he judges against the correct reports which he has received (the information about the hectocotylization and cannibalism in octopi is rejected, it seems,
on the basis of his own incorrect observation). Nor is the
falsity of a statement a guarantee that he did not check it,
for many of his false positions are supported by (casual)
observation and (primitive or sloppy) dissection. All the
same, it is obvious to readers of the biological works that
Aristotle did check many of his statements, and did it correctly, especially when it was possible to check them by
simple observation. He often recommends such observation: the
beneficial effects of the sun on vegetation "can be seen in
any garden" (*HA* VIII.13, 598a4); the industriousness of the
ant is recommended for the consideration of the reader (*HA*
IX.38, 622b23), though not with the moral fervor of *Proverbs*
6:6. He has carefully observed the development of fertilized
eggs, by opening them at different times in the gestation
period, and he recommends methods for repeating his results
(*HA* VI.3, 561a4ff). In the *PA*, he says, "To study nature one
must look at the majority of cases, for the natural is either
in all or in most" (*PA* III.2, 663b28). He seems to have acted
upon this principle of investigation as faithfully as anyone
in ancient Greece, and his recommending it to his followers
surely had something to do with the great collections of data
which typified the Alexandrian school (see EDELSTEIN, *Ancient
Medicine*, pp. 429-39).

Aristotle's dissections are of special interest. It is esti-
mated by LONES that Aristotle dissected some fifty species
of animal, from bees to elephants, including aborted human
embryos but not cadavers, and no vivisection of mammals.[134]
Drawings of these dissections were preserved in a lost work,
to which he often refers, the *Anatomy*.[135] He often recommends
dissections to the student of biology, with directions for
the mode of operation.[136] For example, he says that one should
understand that the bloodvessels of the lungs are full of
blood in the living animal, but this blood runs out of the

lungs when the animal is killed if the dissector is not careful (*HA* I.17, 496b5). He means, of course, that the blood
vessels of the lung are infused with blood, not that the
lungs contain blood as a sac. When he describes the course
of the bloodvessels, he criticizes the methods of his predecessors and suggests,

> If anyone be keenly interested in the matter, his
> best plan will be to allow his animals to starve to
> emaciation, then to strangle them on a sudden, and
> thereupon to prosecute his investigations.[137]

Aristotle's account of the generation of sharks is developed
on the basis of considerable dissection and careful observation (*HA* VI.10-11); he says, for example, that the sperm-
ducts in sharks are quite indistinct at any other time than
at breeding time, if one is not accustomed (συνήθος) to looking for them (VI.11, 566a8). In the *PA* and *GA*, he sometimes
says that the mistakes of his predecessors could have been
avoided by a bit of dissection and observation.[138] No doubt
we might make the same objection to a number of Aristotle's
claims, but we must recognize that he was on a promising
track, and that he did not single-handedly set back empirical
science for hundreds of years, as some people say.
Although it is possible to make much of Aristotle's errors,
errors inherited from others and errors of his own making,
one may find that the overwhelming majority of his observation
-reports are, as such, accurate; the famous inaccuracies are
usually a matter of the interpretation of the phenomena, and
especially the manner of explaining the phenomena, as will
be seen in following chapters. Often he failed to see what
was right there in front of him, sometimes he accepted un-
critically false reports, sometimes his eye was prejudiced
by *a priori* reasonings, but Aristotle and his ancient suc-
cessors had less taste for the fabulous and more for expe-
rienced reality than most other ancient philosophers, and
even more than many modern philosophers.

42

E. On the Chronology of the Biological Books

The basic dates for Aristotle's life are as follows:
384/3: born, probably in Stageira.
367/6: Aristotle arrives at the Academy as student.
348/7: Aristotle leaves Athens, Plato dies.
345/4: Aristotle at Mytilene in Lesbos.
343/2: At Pella, as Alexander's tutor.
340/39: Alexander regent; Aristotle probably to Stageira.
335/4: Aristotle returns to Athens, teaches at the Lyceum.
323/2: Alexander dies, Aristotle retires to Stageira, and
dies.

Much effort has been spent in attempts to develop a consistent and reasonable chronology of Aristotle's works which
could fit into this life history. The task is made difficult,
if not impossible, by the character of the works, for they
are notebooks, repositories of arguments and observations
dating from very different periods of the author's life. They
are more or less organized into coherent wholes, but they are
not polished or 'finished' in the sense in which a Platonic
dialogue is finished.[139] If the 'date' of the treatise is to
be taken as the time in which it received its present organization and the last additions of material, then one may assert
that the majority of the major works of Aristotle which we
have in their entirety date from the last, or Lyceen, period
of his life, since the works are, at least superficially, in-
terdependent, each one showing relationships to several others
in an overlapping fashion. If, however, the 'date' of the
treatise is taken to be the time in which most of the material was first thought out and written down, then one may
well find great variations in the relative ages, in this sense,
of individual works (or even of parts of works), since many
works were likely to have been much advanced when Aristotle
was still a member of the Academy.[140] Other works seem to have
been developed during the period of travels, after leaving
the Academy;[141] still other works may have been begun only

43

when the Lyceum had already been founded.[142]

In regard to the biological books in particular, Aristotle
seems to have had a life-long interest in biological problems
as D'ARCY THOMPSON noted and Thomas CASE argued.[143] Werner
JAEGER, however, in the course of his famous attempt to order
the books of the *Metaphysics*, argued *en passant* that all of
the biological books were written during the latest period,
as the consequence of a turning away from the Platonic metaphysics toward a more scientific orientation.[144] JAEGER's argument has been criticized in this particular by quite a few
scholars, and the point seems sufficiently established today
that some have been able to make a continuing interest in
biology pivotal in their general interpretation of Aristotle's
philosophy.[145]

F. NUYENS attempted another general chronology of Aristotle's
works, claiming that he had found evidence of three stages in
the development of the theory of the soul: first a Platonic
soul-body dualism, then a closer relationship, an 'instrumentism', in which the soul makes special and particular use
of the body and its organs, and finally 'hylomorphism', in
which the soul is simply the dynamic form of the body, which
is the matter.[146] This theory has been soundly criticized by
Irving BLOCK and W.F.R. HARDIE, among others.[147] Although
LE BLOND follows NUYENS for several pages (17ff), he gladly
gives plenty of evidence for 'instrumentism' in *de An.* (27ff)
and hylomorphism in *PA*, which goes counter to NUYENS' position.
In this section LE BLOND follows Alexander Aphrodisiensis,
and this is a virtue of this part of his book, though out of
accord with his apparent earlier acceptance of NUYENS' dating
system. A little later (p. 40) Le BLOND compares the evidence
for monism and dualism of mind and body in Aristotle thus:

> Ce serait une erreur, croyons-nous, de vouloir à
> tout prix présenter cette diversité d'attitudes
> comme une succession; nous croyons au contraire
> que les deux attitudes coexistent, comme tant
> d'autres prétendues incompatibilités, dans la
> recherche aristotelicienne.

44

As BLOCK and HARDIE show, this sensible position effectively
reduces the central arguments of NUYENS to little or nothing.

The difficulty inherent in the method of both JAEGER and
NUYENS is that they suppose that Aristotle went through dramatic changes in fundamental philosophical positions, and
that the various works of Aristotle might be put into a relative chronological ordering in terms of these dramatic
changes. This methodological assumption appears to be in for
trouble, for we have reason to suppose that the works of
Aristotle included in the Corpus never left his possession
until his death, and thus that points of view which he had
quite given up ought to be rather difficult to find in these
works. It is very generally supposed that Aristotle had to
be a follower of Plato during the Academic years, but although there has been quite a lot of investigation of works
supposed to have been written in these years, there is little
agreement about the respects in which Aristotle was a Platonist in that time and not later.
We can, in any case, lay down a rather dependable ordering of
the biological books, as the major works are systematically
related. 1) The *History of Animals* is systematically first
(the other works explicitly depend upon it); the bulk of the
information seems to hive been gathered during the period of
travels, soon after the death of Plato. This has been argued
by H.D.P. LEE, by Pierre LOUIS in the Intro. to the *HA*, by
Le BLOND and others, and DÜRING agrees. 2) The *Progression
of Animals* (*IA*) is close to the *PA* in viewpoint and method;
it might be a little earlier than the *PA* since it refers to
HA but not to *PA*, while *PA* refers both to *HA* (constantly) and
to *IA* (e.g. IV.11, 690b16; 692a17; 13, 696a12). 3) Of the
Parva Naturalia, *Respiration* is often mentioned in the *PA*,
and some of the others are sometimes mentioned. These references cannot always be matched with passages in the works as
we have them; it is possible that some of the essays in *Parva
Nat.* were first written at about the same time as *PA*, as topics not quite fitting the plan of *PA*, but related in that

45

they stem from the same sorts of evidence. 4) The *Parts of Animals* was obviously written in two pieces, II-IV, and I. DÜRING puts I in the Lyceum period, which is possible but not necessary (it would fit equally well or better in the middle period). Book I might be two pieces, one the protreptic, and the other the essay on classification; as it stands it looks later, rather than earlier, than II-IV, since II has a separate introduction. 5) The *Generation of Animals* seems to have gone through at least one revision; an early version may date from the period of travels, but the more philosophical aspects seem to depend upon the development of problems which do not appear to have disturbed Aristotle during the years of the earlier biological works. 6) The *Motion of Animals* (*MA*), as JAEGER argued but NUYENS denied, should be a late work, later than even the *GA*, since it uses the notion of *pneuma* confidently in explaining animal behavior, while *GA* II is almost apologetic about the concept.

The difficulties increase when one attempts to match the series of biological books with the composition of the *de Anima*, *Physics*, *Generation and Corruption* (*GC*), and various parts of the *Metaphysics*. NUYENS wanted to put the *de Anima* very late, perhaps even after the present *GA*; however, there seem to be several references in the present *GA* to the present

This is not a conclusive argument, but makes NUYENS' argument less probable.[148] The relationship between the *PA* and *de An.* cannot easily be determined since possible references from one to the other are not sufficiently clear, but I would guess that the present *de An.*, and the psychological parts of the *Parva Naturalia* at least were written between the *PA* and the present version of the *GA*.

At least some parts of the *Physics*, and the *GC*, seem earlier than the present *de An.*; *Physics* VIII is roughly similar in doctrine to the *MA*; *Physics* II seems strongly influenced by biological interests, and has a number of similarities with *PA* I (I would question DÜRING's early dating of *Phys.* I-VII). *PA* II and *GA* IV seem to depend upon parts of *GC* (see LE BLOND

46

p. 19).

Many similarities may be found between individual passages
of various biological books and individual passages of the
Metaphysics, but the problem of dating various parts of the
Metaphysics is even more difficult than the other problems
which we have mentioned. Here, in particular, the skeptical
reader might suppose that such similarities show only that
Aristotle was in the same frame of mind, or considering similar problems, when writing similar passages; this might be
possible for him at quite widely separated periods.

Such problems have led some students of Aristotle to consider
the development of stylistic methods for the chronological
analysis of his works; such methods have met with considerable success when applied to Plato and some other authors.
Unfortunately, but not very surprisingly, the results for
Aristotle seen thus far have been inconclusive.

Many writers have turned to the reconstruction of Aristotle's
earlier works;[149] we need not involve ourselves in the disagreements concerning the contents of these works to note
that Aristotle was concerning himself with philosophical problems of life, of being and becoming, of the explanation of
the world, in his earliest years. These philosophical concerns, at least, are prior to the actual production of the
biological books, and must have guided the investigations
which Aristotle carried out. Philosophical positions similar
to those found in the *Physics* and *Metaphysics* were being developed when Aristotle was working on the biology; the two
parts of his work were not compartmentalized, but rather,
the philosophical interests helped to guide the direction of
biological investigation, and the biological investigations
gave insights into the metaphysical problems. More than that
we cannot say without a much more detailed examination of
many sorts of evidence, and this is not our object here. We
will, however, point out similarities between particular passages as cases of parallels are important to our argument.

47

CHAPTER II   SCIENCE AND PHILOSOPHY IN ARISTOTLE'S
             GENERATION OF ANIMALS

Introduction

In the *Generation of Animals*, Aristotle tries to solve a
group of problems which are central for biology and for Aristotle's philosophical system. The biologist supposes that he
has made some progress toward the understanding of life if he
has understood how a new life begins; Aristotle shares this
concern with origins, and the explanation of animal generation
also has metaphysical importance for him. Individual animals
are among his paradigm cases of "entities" (*ousiai*); if his
metaphysical system (which depends so much upon the concept
of an entity) is to be validated, then the generation of an
entity must be explicable within that system. He sketches
the sort of explanation which he supposes must be given, in
the *Metaphysics*:

> When one inquires into the cause of something,
> one should, since "causes" are spoken of in se-
> veral senses, state all the possible causes.
> E.g., what is the material cause of man? Shall
> we say "the menstrual fluid"? What is the moving
> cause? Shall we say "the seed"? The formal cause?
> His essence. The final cause? His end. But per-
> haps the latter two are the same.[1]

Here the explanation of generation seems to be proposed as
a model of explanation; Aristotle shows no fear of the difficulties of his problem. Sketched briefly, the problem is
of the change from non-being to being. Since Parmenides,
philosophers had had to deal with the problem of change: how
is change thinkable? How can a changing world be understood?
Roughly speaking, Parmenides had argued that non-being is
unthinkable, that all change involves non-being, and therefore that change is unthinkable. Philosophers before Plato
had tried to get round this argument by trying to find a way
to deny that change involves non-being (perhaps the atomists

48

were an exception). Plato did grapple with the problem in his
later dialogues, but Aristotle is clearly dissatisfied with
the solution proposed by Plato in the *Timaeus* (*Generation and
Corruption* II.1ff). Aristotle's theoretical solution may be
found in *Physics* V-VIII; it depends upon the persistent application of the distinction between potentiality and actuality to each variety of change which may be distinguished,
as this distinction was made central in the definition of
'change' given in *Phys*. III.1: "the actualization of that
which is potentially, as such". This general definition works
out fairly well in the case of change in any of the categories where the "is" of the definition is predicative, that
is, except the first category. Change in the first category
(entity) must, however, involve a radical difference in the
definition itself, because in this case the "is" is *existential*.

Plato, particularly in the *Timaeus*, resolved the problem
of change by making it disappear. In Plato's analysis, there
is no special problem about substantial or existential change,
because the form, or *eidos*, is the truly existing thing, and
the form is changeless and eternal. The phenomenal world, by
contrast, is analyzed into attributes, fleetingly found together. The phenomenal attributes have a kind of dependent
being, a being in relation to the eternal *eidos*, which alone
deserves to be called an *ousia* (entity, real being). This solution seemed to Aristotle no solution at all, since one of
the most obvious truths about the phenomenal world was that
it was composed of *things*, of men and animals, and other individual objects. Aristotle's objection to Plato's metaphysical analysis is that it makes the ordinary entities of the
world disappear by turning them into a conglomeration of
predicates, and gives the predicates or attributes an existence which they cannot support by turning them into eternal
entities (see *Metaphysics* Zeta, 13-14).
Aristotle's solution to the problem of existential change is,
none the less, based upon much of the Platonic analysis. For
Plato, phenomenal attributes have their reality in relation

49

to the *eidos*; for Aristotle, phenomenal entities have their
reality as examples of the *eidos*, which he understands as an
everlasting object existing in and through the individuals.
Although for Plato the *eidos* alone is an *ousia*, for Aristotle
both the individual and the species (*eidos*) may be called
ousia. For both philosophers, everything which is not an
ousia has its being in and through some relationship to an
ousia.

A potentiality (*dynamis*) is such in relation to the *ousia*
which it can become (passive *dynamis*) or can bring about in
something else (active *dynamis*). Potentialities answer the
Eleatic problem of non-being to Aristotle's satisfaction, because that which is potentially an X is not an X, but it is
not nothing either. Potentiality gives Aristotle a way to
save both *ex nihilo nihil fit* and substantial (existential)
change. There need be no absolute non-being (no void of the
atomists); everything which can be made into something is
matter for such a generation; it is potentially, but not actually, the result of such a generation.

An active power belongs to something which already has the
eidos (form, species) actually, but which is potentially the
generating cause of a different individual with the same
eidos. While the source of movement is actually a member of
the species, it is not (even potentially) another member of
the same species; rather, it has the potentiality of causing
such an individual. In this way it too generates from a kind
of relative non-being.

So much may be taken as an all too brief summary of the teaching of the *Physics* and *Metaphysics* with regard to the problem
at hand. In the *Generation of Animals*, Aristotle turns to the
problem of showing that his metaphysical analysis does indeed
account for the phenomena of generation. The application of
the metaphysical concepts to the phenomena results in a number of problems in explanation for Aristotle. In this chapter I shall try to describe some of these problems, how they
arise, and how Aristotle tries to solve them. In *GA* I, Aris-

totle uses his concepts of matter and form to provide a
starting point, at least, for the explanation of generation.
The rigorous distinction between matter and form assists in
the refutation of some earlier theories of generation, but
it also causes difficulties for Aristotle's own account. In
Part A we examine the manner in which the problem concerning
matter and form arises in *GA* I, and how an attempt is made
to resolve the difficulty.

As a result of the investigations recounted in *GA* I, Aristotle
is sure that the male provides the moving cause of generation;
that which provides the moving cause also provides the form.
In nearly all species, the male contributes to generation by
means of semen; in order to fit the theory to the phenomena,
Aristotle must show how semen transfers movement from the male
parent to the material for generation, and how semen transfers
the form (*eidos*) and the soul from male parent to offspring.
In *GA* II.1-3, Aristotle attempts a solution of the problem
of the transfer of soul; he juxtaposes explanatory analogies
with a subtle development of the implications of the distinction between potentiality and actuality, and he introduces (to
the surprise of readers of the *de Anima*) a special material
basis of the soul, which is said to carry the soul from male
parent to offspring. In Part B Aristotle's explanation of
generation as it appears in II.1-3 is critically examined,
and some related problems which arise in the interpretation
of these chapters are commented upon-among them, the problem
of the origin of mind.

Aristotle's explanation of animal generation often utilizes
the ramifications of the concept of *energeia* (activity, actuality). This part of his explanation has the closest relationship with the theoretical philosophical positions expressed in *Physics*, *Metaphysics* and *de Anima*, and is most typical of the more theoretical sections of the remainder of
the *GA*. Part C discusses the explanation of generation which
appears in II.4, and which relies heavily upon the concept of
energeia rather than upon the concept of *pneuma*, the supposed

51

physical basis of soul. Also discussed are the ways in which
the concepts of matter, movement, form, and end are related
to *energeia* in the context of the explanation of generation.
Finally, we show how the developed concept of *energeia* is
used in the solution of the problem, especially difficult for
Aristotle, of the resemblance and lack of resemblance between
parent and offspring.

A. Male and Female, Form and Matter: *GA* I

The major problem in explanation which Aristotle faces in
I -- and it plagues him for the rest of the work -- arises
from an initially too rigid application of the distinction
between form and the active power, and matter and the passive
power, to the natures of male and female.[2] Matter and movement are strictly segregated to female and male respectively,
the female bringing about no change, and the male providing
no material, for that which is produced.
In I.17-23, Aristotle defends this thesis through the examination of a series of "problems" which his own theory proposes to solve more adequately than any other. The resolution
of these puzzles leads to an exposition of individual elements
of the Aristotelian solution to the general problem of generation.

1. The refutation of "pangenesis" and preformationism: the
   male principle as "organizer" (I.17, 721b6, - 18, 724a13)

The theory which may be called "pangenesis" held that the
spermatic materials were drawn from the entire body of one or
both parents, and that the fact that these materials were so
drawn should explain the resemblance of offspring to parents.[3]

52

The tactic which Aristotle uses to refute this theory is typical, and our understanding of the refutation will help in
the understanding of the theory which he develops for himself. He argues that even if parts from every region of the
parents' bodies were to mix together, one would still have
no reason to expect an organized whole, an organism, to result.

> If something were to come from a written word,
> the whole word, then it would have to come from
> each of the syllables, from each of the letters,
> and from the synthesis (combination). If flesh
> and bones are constructed from fire and so on,
> then the spermatic secretions would come from
> the elements only; how could they come from the
> synthesis? But without the synthesis there is no
> similarity. And if something makes the synthesis
> later, then *this* is responsible for the similarity,
> and not the fact that the spermatic secretions
> come from the whole.[4]

The arrangement of parts is not a material thing, but it is
the principle of resemblance. Thus the pangenesis theory does
not solve the problem which it is meant to solve. This refutation uses the principle upon which Aristotle bases his more
general criticisms of reductionist theories of various sorts:
they generally reduce any organizing principle out of their
analysis. Aristotle's theory is precisely that theory which
makes the organizing principle central, for his *eidos*, as the
active power, functions as a kind of "organizer", in something
akin to the modern sense of the word.[5]

The theory thus refuted supposes the individual parts to be
scattered in the spermatic secretion, but another popular
theory, like that which has been called "preformationism" in
modern times, held that all these parts were connected, in
which case it should be "a small animal".[6] The trouble with
this theory is that it cannot explain how a female animal could
be generated, how a male parent could implant a seed with female parts rather than with male parts.

The theory of Empedocles represents a compromise position
between the Hippocratic pangenesis theory and the preformationist theory, in that according to Empedocles, each parent

53

is supposed to provide half of the offspring.[7] Aristotle's objections to the most obvious interpretation of this theory are perfectly straightforward: a) the parts could not remain healthy and alive if separated; b) it is not reasonable that two halves of animals should grow together to form one animal; c) the parts would have to be separated several ways, not just in half (they would have to be separated into up and down, right and left, front and back).

In contrast to all these theories, Aristotle argues that one ought to look for some *one* material which can carry the active principle for making all the others; one should look for a spermatic material which is not *from* all the parts of the body, but *for* the whole body. Thus the correct explanation must, in Aristotle's view, have an irreducibly teleological character.

2. The nature of the spermatic secretions, *sperma*

Having disposed, to his satisfaction, of some of the more popular theories of sexual generation, Aristotle must proceed to show how his *a priori* description of the character of male and female fits with the observed phenomena concerning the contributions to generation of the two sexes (he has described many of these phenomena in I.3-16). His general name for semen and menstrual fluid is *sperma*; he proposes a definition of this word for examination: "*Sperma* wants to be this sort of nature: the first 'from what' in the generation of natural constructions."[8] Characteristically, Aristotle lists a number of senses of the word "from" with an eye to showing which are applicable in this case.[9] As we should expect, the two senses which he chooses are "from matter" and "from something in that it is the source of movement."

The source of matter and movement for the independent living body is, to a great extent, its food; it is reasonable to suppose that there should be some close relationship between

54

both sorts of *sperma* and food. Aristotle finds this relationship by arguing that both the menstrual fluid and the semen
are residues[10] of blood, which is the final food of the body.
Thus in a sketchy way (the full discussion is reserved for
Book IV) the problem of family resemblance which had given
rise to the pangenesis theories and their variations may be
solved, for it is reasonable that "there is a resemblance
between (the blood) which is distributed to the various parts
of the body and that which is left over" (I.19, 726b14).
Given Aristotle's notion that the "menstrual fluid" is the
female *sperma* of the mammalia, the most obvious resemblance
between blood and *sperma* is found in the female. The mense is
obviously bloody in character; the problem which faces Aristotle is to show that it is in fact the material for generation.[11] His argument in support of his notion that the menstrual fluid is spermatic in character is, in part, observational. He argues (727b) that females with no menstrual
flow do not conceive, nor usually when the menstrual flow is
in progress, but after the flow is over.[12] Since the menstrual
(or estrous -- he does not distinguish) flow is the only observable function which varies concomitantly with conception,
it must have some causative connection with conception; this
material seems the only possible candidate for the female
contribution to generation in the mammalia.
From a philosophical point of view, Aristotle is happy to
fit the explanation of the behavior of the menstrual flow into his doctrine of the "mean", of neither too much nor too
little. But the argument at 726b30ff leads more directly to
the philosophical problems developed in the rest of *GA* I. He
says that the female is weaker, and therefore likely to produce that which has less form; that which has less form is
matter; therefore the female is likely to produce the matter
for generation. Consequently, the menstrual fluid should be
that spermatic contribution which serves as matter for generation. He could have phrased the argument thus: the female
is weaker, and therefore less active; that which is acted

upon is matter; therefore the female is likely to produce
the matter for generation. The continuing question with which
he must deal is this: to what extent does the female provide
something which has, after all, some form, and is to some
extent active. The possible answers to this question might
be anything from an assertion that the female contribution is
almost completely passive and formless, to the claim that the
female contribution needs only the smallest additional activity and form to develop into a new individual. But I would
suggest that Aristotle did not understand the problem in this
way when he wrote *GA* I; if he had, his argument would have
developed more clearly along these lines. Indeed, different
sorts of evidence lead him toward both extremes; the philosophical argument seems to lead him toward an assertion of
extreme passivity of the female *sperma*, while observations
of resemblance of children to their mothers, and of parthenogenesis in fish, for example, lead him toward a claim of almost equal formal activity in the female *sperma*.

3. How mense serves as matter for generation

Given the assumption that the male provides the form and the
female the matter (cf. 729a10-12), how can generation proceed?
Aristotle actually gives several separate accounts of generation, each more sophisticated than the last, each from the
point of view of a particular problem in his account. At
I.20, 729a10ff, he gives a provisional account into which
mense as spermatic can fit. He supposes that he understands
the role of mense through this analogy: "In the coagulation
of milk, the milk is the body, but the fig juice or rennet
is that which has the constructing principle. The semen of
the male acts in the same way" (729a12-14). Both milk and
mense are "residues" of blood; both rennet and semen contain
vital heat -- these are points made clear elsewhere.[13] This
analogy gives him a further occasion for the development of

56

the consequences of his definitions of male and female in a
"general rational account":

> There must be that which generates and the "from
> what"; this is true even if they are the same in-
> dividual. They at least differ in form (*eidos*)
> and in that the definition (*logos*)of each of them
> is different; in those which have the powers se-
> parated, the bodies and the nature of the active
> *x*   and of the passive are also different. Now if "male"
> means "mover" and "doer", and "female" (*qua* female)
> means "passive", the female would not contribute
> semen to that of the male, but matter. This is what
> is seen to occur, for the nature of the menstrual
> *y*   fluid is in the class of proximate matter.[14]

The force of the original definitions is increased by tying
them in to the notions of *eidos* and *logos*, and the notion of
power (*dynamis*). Male and female each has, per se, its own
form and definition, and its own power. This statement seems,
in its context, reasonable enough, but the net result is the
driving of a further wedge between the characteristics which
one may expect to find in actual individuals of each sex.

4. How the male contributes to generation; the carpenter
   analogy

No ancient Greek author seems to have doubted that in most
species the male contributes to generation by means of semen.
Aristotle need not argue that this, rather than something
else, is the male contribution. He has, however, more difficulty describing *how* semen contributes to generation, once he
has rejected the ancient version of preformationism as a possibility. His position is already clear, in one respect: the
male provides the form, the dynamic structure.
Even though preformationism has been rejected, two ways of
sharing in generation seem possible for semen, from Aristotle's
viewpoint: (a) Semen might mix with the menstrual fluid and
remain present in the embryo as a part of the generated body;
(b) Semen might not be present in the embryo as a determinate

part, but only as a power or movement. The strict interpretation of the original definitions of 'male' and 'female' lead him to reject the first alternative and to accept the second. This choice results in a number of difficulties, particularly those with which he deals in *GA* II.3; we must examine the argument which he offers in support of his choice.

a
b
c

> To those who examine the problem in general it does not appear that one thing is generated from the passive and the active with the agent immanent in that which is generated, nor in general from the moved and the mover in this way. The female, *qua* female, is passive, and the male, *qua* male, is active and the source of movement. If the extremes are taken, on the one hand the active and mover, on the other passive and moved, that one thing which is generated is not "from" them except in the sense that the bed is "from" the carpenter and the wood, or the ball "from" the wax and the form (*eidos*). It is clear then that it is not necessary for anything to be emitted by the male, nor, if something is emitted, does this mean that that which is generated is from this as immanent in it, but as from the mover and from the form, as one who is cured by the medical art.[15]

At *a* Aristotle gives what amounts to a deductive demonstration of his point, based on the original definitions. While the argument may be taken as disclaiming a position like that of certain modern vitalists,[16] the question at issue is rather this, whether the semen makes a material contribution to the offspring. Matter is by definition that which is acted on, not that which acts; anything that had both powers would change itself, but the female does not generate without the male.[17] Thus the definitions lead us to the conclusion that the powers are separate not only logically, but also in fact.

The analogy of fig juice or rennet, as used to illustrate the role of mense in generation, was admirably suited to show the way in which a natural material serves for change, but it was not a close analogy for *pointed* change, for fig juice or rennet and milk result in cheese, but semen and mense may generate a living being.

The analogies used to illustrate the role of semen are not

deficient in this respect, for they are frankly teleological
in character. This is not an unreasonable difference between
the two sets of analogies, for although matter is to be understood teleologically too, the end is more truly present in
that which has the form and source of movement. The source of
movement and end are most clearly related through the notion
of form, for a movement is a pointed movement in virtue of
its form, the structure of the movement itself (which may be
per se valuable), and the normal results of that movement in
a material, if they are valued results.
The use of these analogies at *b* and *c* in the passage quoted
above leads us to a further understanding of the thought process which led to the rejection of the theory that semen par-
ticipates materially in the generated embryo; they are examples
of the general tendency to draw analogies between the workings
of art and the workings of nature. These analogies lead Aristotle to suppose that the fact that the artist does not become
a material part of his product shows somehow that the natural
generator does not become a material part of his product either.
The analogy of the carpenter is explicitly used in this way;
he makes the bed, but neither he nor a part of him becomes
or becomes a part of the matter of the bed.[18] The analogy of
the wax emphasizes the distinction between the form and matter of the particular thing. If it is true to say that the
male provides the form, someone might say that he is providing
a "part" of the generated thing. Aristotle simply reminds us
of the distinctions made elsewhere (*de Anima* II.1, 412b7-9;
Physics VII.3, 245b11, *et al.*), that the form and matter of
the individual are one, and not "parts" of the thing. It is
odd to find the form of the wax ball classed with active principles in this place; all I can do to reduce the sense of
strangeness which I feel with that notion is to point out
that in the case of the male principle, at any rate, the form
is thought to be provided as a movement.
The analogy of the medical art brings the analogical account
closer to the circumstances of the natural event to be ex-

plained. We are reminded of the passages in the *Metaphysics*
and *Physics* in which the medical art is taken as paradigmatic
in the understanding of nature, and of many passages in the
biological books in which a medical predicate is attached to
"nature".[19] Aristotle's trust in the general analogy between
natural and artificial generation is one of the causes of his
only slightly modified confidence that the matter for a particular generation is totally passive in respect of that generation, and that the source of change provides only form
and movement, and no material contribution.
I believe that this trust is greater than is strictly demanded
by the metaphysical presuppositions which govern his explanatory scheme. In *Physics* II.1, 192b24, the doctor who cures
himself is said to do so "accidentally". This is taken to be
a general truth about the relation of efficient and formal
causes on the one hand, and matter on the other, in all the
arts. Yet the products of nature are taken to be analogous
to the doctor who cures himself, except that in nature this
process is essential, not accidental (192b14). If these distinctions are taken into account in relation to the use of
the analogy of the medical art at *GA* I.21, 729b, one notes
that not only semen but also mense is a natural product; mense
exists *physei*, and should therefore have a source of movement
within itself. Thus Aristotle has a possible alternative position regarding the activity and passivity of these contributions to generation: the mense may have *some* source of movement, some form, some power, even active, but it may lack
something which the male can provide. Under this interpretation, parthenogenetic production of things different in kind
becomes comprehensible : if parthenogenetic reproducers did
have that which a male could provide, they could produce things
like in kind to themselves.
Something like this alternative solution does begin to appear
in the later books, not only in the case of the generation of
bees, but also in the various discussions of the generation
of infertile eggs,[20] and most of all, in the discussion of

60

the resemblance of offspring to parents, in Book IV.
However, in *GA* I, Aristotle remains committed to the radical
separation of matter and maker; this commitment may be seen
in his attempt to find (at 729b22ff) empirical evidence in
support of this separation. Most important to his case, if
accurate, is his alleged observation that some insects copulate without transfer of semen from male to female.[21] In I.22,
739b27-32, Aristotle fits this case into the analogy of art
and nature with evident satisfaction:

> It is as if someone were to bring the matter to
> the craftsman. Because of the weakness of this sort
> of male, "the nature" is not such as to act through
> something else; the movements seem scarcely strong
> enough with nature sitting right there. Here nature
> seems to resemble modellers in clay, not builders,
> for she does not fashion that which is constructed
> by means of something else, but does it with her
> own parts.[22]

In further support of his case, he cites the production of
infertile eggs by birds prior to copulation. The implication
drawn is that the material is all there; only the cause of
growth and development must be missing. He goes on to cite
the practice of chicken breeders of putting a second cock to
the hen in hope of improving the breed, believing that the
brood would resemble the second cock.[23] Aristotle seems to
think that the second cock adds to the vital force of the
offspring, and gives it some of its valued characteristics.
As a final bit of evidence, Aristotle calls attention to the
mode of fertilization in oviparous fish, in which the male
sprinkles milt over the eggs; those which the milt touches
are fertile, while the others are not, "as though the male
contributes not to the quantity but to the quality" (730a22).

Aristotle is now ready to account for semen, which could
readily have been thought to become some part of the generated offspring, in terms of his carpenter analogy. In the
case of the carpenter, the form is present in his soul, and
is

> generated in the matter by means of the movement,
> and his soul and knowledge move his hands or some

> other part in a particular movement, different
> for different products ... his hands moving the
> tools and the tools the matter (I.22, 730b13-19).

Aristotle here regards carpentry as strictly analogous to the
male role in sexual generation in that semen is viewed *pre-*
cisely as a tool, for the tool does not become a material
part of the production (not in carpentry at any rate), but
serves to transmit the formative movements from the maker to
the made. The distinction which Aristotle finds here between
semen and the tools of carpentry is this: the semen is a tool
which "has the movements in activity", while the tools of the
arts have their movements "somehow". Semen has an actual "disposition"[24] to act in a certain way; tools of the arts have
certain potentialities, powers, but they are not in themselves
sources of movement; semen is a source of movement.

5. The accomplishment of *GA* I

Aristotle set out, in the first book of the *GA*, to describe
many of the phenomena related to generation, particularly
phenomena related to sex differentiation (we have not discussed this aspect of the book), to refute some of those who
had proposed explanations differing from his own, and to understand the phenomena of sexual generation in terms of his
own philosophical system.
The major distinction which Aristotle uses in the explanation
of sexual generation in Book I is the distinction between matter and form. I have argued that he gets himself into difficulties through his rigorous application of this distinction
to the distinction between male and female; he seems to have
been led to this rigorousness as much by the explanatory models, the carpenter and the doctor, as by demands of his philosophical system.
The application of the distinction between matter and form
and the analogies of art and nature as presented in Book I

62

are understood by Aristotle as substantially correct, since
he continues to use them through the *GA*, but they leave problems in explanation which force him to more drastic measures
in *GA* II. There is a certain plausibility in the view that
the menstrual fluid serves as the material for generation,
for the body is fed by blood once it is born; it should have
been made of blood, or something very like blood, in the first
instance. But the notion that the semen does not become any
part of the generated embryo would seem implausible to many
members of Aristotle's audience. Thus the climax of the first
book is the explication of this relatively unpopular thesis.

Aristotle's account of the soul in the *de Anima* had identified the soul, or all the soul but the mind, with the dynamic structure of the body; as a first approximation, it
seems to him appropriate to argue that the male has as its
function the installation of the soul in the body. In defending this doctrine it is constantly necessary for him to argue
against those positions which identify the soul (*psyche*) with
some material. As far as it goes, the analogy of craftsman
and procreator seems appropriate as a defense of his position.
Aristotle knows very well, however, that his materialist opponents can persuasively argue that the relevant difference
between craftsman and procreator is just that the procreator
passes on the soul, and the craftsman does not. Aristotle
must, therefore, defend the validity of the analogy. In order
to do so he will have to explain just how semen functions as
a tool for transferring the soul from procreator to offspring.
This is the major problem of the first part of *GA* II.

B. THE PROBLEM OF THE TRANSFER OF SOUL (*GA* II.1-3).

In II.1-3, Aristotle takes up the account of generation from
the direction of a teleological analysis. In *GA* I, a teleological theory of generation operated implicitly rather than
explicitly; his commitment to a teleological explanation may
be seen in the use of the analogy of the craftsman, as well
as in his constant reliance upon the idea of form, but he does
not clearly say that these concepts directly involve finalistic concepts, in his system of explanation. In the second
book of *GA*, by contrast, he begins with an account of the
teleological principles which must operate in an adequate explanation of animal generation, and then works back to the
problem of the role of semen in sexual generation. When the
problem has been presented, he proceeds to examine the "nature" of semen, and finally to give an account of its role
in generation which he hopes will be acceptable.

1. The purpose of sexual generation (II.1, 731b18-732a25).

The question "why is there sexual generation?" may be analyzed into (a) "why is there animal generation?" and (b) "why
are there sexes?" The answer to the first question is easy
enough. Animals (or plants) cannot last forever as individuals,
due to the imperfections in their matter, their potentiality
for non-existence. However, everything that exists aims at
continued existence. This is possible for a species of animals or plants, through reproduction. Thus the purpose of
reproduction is the continued existence of the species.
The normally observed mode of reproduction in animals is
sexual, so the distinction between sexes exists for the sake
of reproduction. Aristotle's *a priori* explanation is this:

> As the proximate moving cause is better and more
> divine in nature, in that the *logos* and the *eidos*
> are present in it, than the matter, so it is better
> that the superior be separate from the inferior.

64

> That is why the male and female are separate in
> as many species as possible and to the greatest
> degree possible; for the male is better and more
> divine in that it is the source of movement in
> generated things; the female is the matter.[25]

Aristotle argues in much the same fashion in *de Anima* II.4,
415a26ff, in his explication of the nutritive and generative
function of the soul; in *Generation and Corruption* II.10
there is also a general relation established between the stars
which are everlasting as individuals, and the continuation
of species on earth.[26]

Several commentators have argued that the *GA* gives a large
place to "material necessity" in explanation, instead of and
in opposition to teleological explanation.[27] The present passage, particularly given its placement in the book, should
discourage the view that Aristotle has softened his position
on teleology in nature. We note that he closely relates the
moving and final causes in this passage. Indeed, he regards
the "participation" of the source of movement in the end as
a sufficient reason for the distinction between the sexes and
the purported superiority of male animals over female animals.

This tack of the argument is by no means accidental, for
Aristotle is aiming at a final defense of the notion that the
male provides the soul and the female the matter. If the
notions of "male", "moving cause", and "better" can be closely
related in the minds of his audience, he is that much closer
to convincing them of the truth of his position. The arrangement of the exposition may owe something to his view of rhetoric (*Rhetoric* I.1, 1355b27; *Topics* I.2, 101a30-34), for he
seems to begin his argument in *GA* II with something which his
audience will be ready to accept: that the male is superior
to the female. He can then proceed to argue that it is better
to provide the form than to provide the matter. From these
premises it "follows", by a kind of rhetorical move, that
the male provides the form rather than the matter.

2. The statement of the problem of semen (733b23ff)

"It is necessary for that which is generated to be generated *from* something and *by* something, and to become something."[28] The "from what" may be treated summarily; it is the matter, whether mense or egg, or the material derived through the umbilicus, or the later milk, and other food. The new individual, the new entity, is a "this something" of the same species as its parents (as in *Met*. Zeta, 7-9, and Theta 8). The problem at hand is the "by what", the moving cause of generation.

Aristotle develops and tries to resolve (733b23-735a29) a dilemma in regard to the relationship between semen and the source of movement in generation. The source of movement for generation, the "by what" of generation, should either be in the semen, or outside the semen; it should be either in the embryo, or outside the embryo. However, whether we say that it is 'within' or 'without' either semen or embryo, we are involved in a multitude of difficulties.

It seems unreasonable to suppose, Aristotle claims, that something external makes each of the parts of the embryo; it would be especially unreasonable in the case of the internal organs, because nothing can be changed except by something which is in contact with it.[29] So on this showing the construction of the internal organs requires the presence in the fetus or embryo of something which, either as a part of it or not as a part of it, constructs at least these organs. But it could not be separate from or different from the fetus itself: if there were such a thing, it must either remain in the fetus or disappear. If it were to remain, it would be distinguishable, a detectable entity within but not a part of the living body, but no such entity is discoverable.[30] Furthermore, it is "absurd" to suppose that it fashions either all or some of the parts and then disappears. If it fashions only some of the parts, then something else fashions the rest; suppose that something else to be the heart -- does the heart disappear when

it has fashioned the rest of the parts? Aristotle does not
consider here the possibility that it fashions   the parts,
then disappears; apparently that hypothesis would be open to
the same criticism as the hypothesis that it persists, for an
organizer of that kind would be apparent, at least in semi-
developed individuals. Furthermore, whatever fashions all
the parts ought to be the same as that which maintains them.
Thus whatever it is that fashions the animal persists, and
since no separate entity can be distinguished, we must suppose that it is part of the whole, and present in the semen
from the outset, if the semen is that which has the source
of movement and development.

One might, alternatively, argue that there is some part of
the body of the fetus which is present in the semen, and that
this "part" constructs and is the source of movement for the
rest of the body of the fetus. This suggestion would indeed
make the source of movement "internal" at every stage, but
Aristotle argues that this hypothesis has as many difficulties
as the other; the agent must be either internal or external,
but it cannot, it seems be either. The dilemma is drawn out
with a series of arguments. Aristotle argues first that the
principle of change cannot be internal in the manner proposed
on the following grounds: either this supposed part forms all
the other parts simultaneously, or it forms them successively.
By observation we know that the parts are not formed simul-
tanously, because the heart appears before other parts which
are ultimately larger than it will be. So the parts are formed
successively: but is this succession causal, or merely temporal? If the succession is merely temporal, then we must still
seek the cause of the generation and the cause of the succession; but if the succession is causal (if the hypothetical
'part' makes the heart, and the heart makes the liver, for example)[31] then because that which is potentially (*dynamei*) is
generated by that which is in catuality (*entelecheia*), and because that which generates must have the same form as that which
is generated, the heart would have the form and shape of the

liver. Such an account, he says, would be an absurd fabrication.

In fact, Aristotle argues, no part of the plant or animal which is to be generated can be contained in the semen or see, whether that part is supposed to make anything or not, and the semen or seed cannot become a part of the generated individual. Nothing can be maker of itself *simpliciter*; thus the agent which makes the individual cannot be a part of the individual; if, as we have been supposing, the semen is (or contains) the agent which makes the individual, then it cannot be a part of the individual. The male parent makes the semen, the semen makes the parts; the semen transfers the form from the male parent to the offspring, but the form is not a *part* of the thing. We may see from this argument that Aristotle's theory resembles that which has been called "epigenesis" in more recent periods, but Aristotle's theory is an epigenetic theory which is still struggling with the central problems.

The most immediate problem is the dilemma, that the agent which brings about development must either be external or internal, but it seems (according to the arguments adduced) that it can be neither. It cannot be external, because then it could not bring about internal changes; it cannot be internal, because the agent cannot be a part of that which is generated. In general, dilemmas are resolved by making distinctions; Aristotle points the direction toward the required distinction by asking, "In what sense is it not possible for something to be generated by something external? In one sense it is impossible, in one not" (734b5-7). It is not possible for something to be generated by something external in the sense that it is "separated and not touching", since if it does not touch it cannot have a causal effect. But "external" is a word subject to some interpretation. There might be something which sets up a movement in a second thing, which in turn effects the movement or change in question. This interpretation, too, seems to bring about the same dilemma, for each mover in the series of movers must be either internal or external to the next member of the series.

68

One might also ask, with more effect perhaps, 'In what sense
is it possible for something to be generated by something
internal, and in what sense not?' It is the answer to this
question which resolves the dilemma, as we can see in advance,
for the form can be 'within' and yet not 'part of' the individual. But the attempts at resolution show that a juggling
of the concepts cannot, by itself, resolve the problem of
the generation of new individuals; we must show how the form,
which is at first 'outside' the individual which is to become,
gets 'inside' that individual. It is not enough to say that
the semen begins as internal in the male parent (and outside
the matter for the embryo), thus acquiring its form from the
male parent; then that it ends as internal in the matter for
the embryo (and outside the male parent), and thus transfers
its form to the matter, with an embryo resulting. Among other
difficulties, this solution does not explain how the semen
has the form.

3. Toward solution: two analogues and potentiality/actuality
   (734b5ff)

In order to distinguish the senses of *internal* and *external*,
as applied to moving causes, Aristotle uses an illustrative
analogue, that of the self-moving puppets. He also discusses
the principle behind the use of this analogue, the distinction
between potentiality and actuality: "The parts of these
automata have somehow the potentiality in them while at rest;
when something external sets the first part moving, the next
becomes actually."[32] According to Aristotle, if something is
to be a source of movement, it must have an active power
(potentiality) for that sort of movement or change. An agent
may initiate a series of movements by exercising only the
active power, and the matter for a change may have only the
appropriate passive power, but anything which is to serve as
an intermediary between agent and matter must be both passive

and active -- passive in relation to the agent, and active in
relation to the matter, or in relation to the next member of
the series. Such an intermediary is known as a "moved mover".
This characteristic of a moved mover may be understood as the
same power; for example. the potentiality of some materials
for being heated is at the same time the potentiality for
transferring that heat to something else. It is in this way
that the puppets are understood as passive in relation to the
puppet-master, and active in relation to the movement which
they initiate. Semen, it is suggested, is similar to the puppets in respect of this kind of potentiality; semen is understood as a moved mover.

One may be uneasy with this analogy, however, for semen is not
a mechanical device, but a natural product. Pushing the analogy of the puppet might even reintroduce a preformationist
theory in a new and peculiar form. In order to still this un-
easiness, I suppose, and in order to relate the present account to that given in *GA* I, Aristotle introduces another
analogue. He claims that the power of semen which we are discussing is within the semen in the way in which"housebuilding
is in the house" (734b17). Housebuilding is in the house, we
may suppose, by virtue of the activity (artistic and intentional) of the builder. Semen is not as mechanical as a puppet,
but it is not as human as a builder; the puppet and its parts
are moved movers, as semen is a moved mover; but housebuilding
is a kind of unmoved mover, for in the case of housebuilding,
the origin of movement is internal, the builder works inside
the house in virtue of an unchanging art, which guides all of
the movements without being acted upon in return. Aristotle
no doubt means to suggest that the truth lies somewhere between, but one wonders just how to find that middle ground.

  The conclusion of the present set of arguments is, as a result, more negative than positive: "It is clear now that there
is something present which makes the embryo, but it is not an
individual itself, nor is it the first completed part of the
embryo."[33] Semen is "something" but it is not an individual,

not an *ousia*. That which builds is, strictly speaking, a
movement (*kinesis*), or, in the language of the *Parts of Animals* (I.1, 641b32), a *genesis* or "becoming": "Seed (*sperma*)
is a *genesis*, but the end is an entity (*ousia*)." PECK translates *genesis* in this place as "formative process"; a "becoming" or formative process is not thought of as an entity.
Aristotle, by referring to the *art* of housebuilding at 734b,
rather than to the builder himself, wishes to abstract or
separate the movements from the individual who effects them.
Even the puppet is an individual of a sort, but evidently
semen is not. It has a form, but only "as a power" and not as
"something perfected".
It should be pointed out that this argument has consequences
for Aristotle's metaphysical position: it develops that semen
has both a matter (which we discuss below) and a form, that
of the male parent, which it transfers to the matter provided
by the female parent; but although it has both matter and
form, it is not itself an entity. In general, if anything is
a compound of matter and form, it is either an entity or a
part of an entity. Perhaps Aristotle sidesteps the metaphysical issue by claiming that the semen is 'simply' a part of
the male parent, but it is a very odd sort of part which
functions only when separated from the entity of which it is
a part. In other cases, when a part of a living entity is
separated, it is no longer an organic part of that entity.

4. Semen and the distinction between *energeia* and *entelecheia*
   (734b21ff)

   Whatever is generated naturally or artificially
   is generated by something which is "in activity"
   (*energeia*) from something which is such "potentially"
   (*dynamei*). Semen is such, and has such a movement
   and principle, that when the movement stops each of
   the parts is generated and is ensouled (734b21-25).

This is an approach to the positive solution of the problem

of the activity of semen. The key word in the understanding
of the middle ground which Aristotle attempts to take is
energeia, which I here translate "activity", but this word
is often translated "actuality". In the passage which follows,
and in general, the movement in the semen is described as an
energeia rather than as an *entelecheia*. The latter word often
conveys a sense of perfectedness, and might be reserved for
the parent and the offspring, while the semen should be or
have an *energeia* (734a30, b35, 735a19).

There is a fairly precise distinction between *energeia* and
entelecheia in the case of the productions of a craft; Aristotle calls attention (734b28ff) to the way in which the analogy between art and nature explicates the concept of an
energeia. Heat and cold do not make the *logos* of their product either in art or in nature; whether in art or in nature,
it is the "logical movement" which makes the entity. Thus the
movement of the tools has the *logos*, or form, of the art, and
this is the *energeia* of the art; semen has the *logos* of the
species, and this movement is the *energeia* of this nature.

Aristotle recognizes that using the analogy between art
and nature in this way makes his problem arise again, in yet
another way: "for art is the source and form of that which is
generated, but 'in another'; but the movement of nature is
'in itself', 'from another' nature which has the form actually"
(735a2-5). The translation preserves the opacity of the original in respect of the term "in itself"; one immediately
supposes that the "itself" referred to in this case must be
the semen, but that is not said. In the context, Aristotle
must show that the movements proper to the *eidos* are in the
semen, but if the semen has these movements, one might suppose that it is a member of the species, for it is matter
which has, somehow, the form of this sort of nature.

5. Does semen have soul? (735a5-26)

The question, "Does semen have soul?" takes us to the heart
of the problem. In one way, the answer must be affirmative,
for semen effects natural production, and only that which
has a soul can effect natural production. In another way,
the answer must be negative, for semen is not an individual
entity. Aristotle discusses this question *twice* in *GA* II.
Chapter I ends with the assertion that the explanation of
generation has been given, leaving only the physical analysis
of semen to be taken up in Chapter 2; in Chapter 3, however,
the question of the relationship between semen and soul is
again raised, this time at greater length and in greater
depth.

These passages answer this question in different ways; the
first depends upon a philosophical analysis and the use of
analogies, while the second succeeds the physical investigation
of semen. The philosophical argument proceeds thus:

> The same argument holds for semen as for the other
> parts of the body: a) there is no soul elsewhere
> than in that of which it is the soul; b) a part
> which does not share in the soul is a part only
> *x* "homonymously", like a dead man's eye. It is there-
> *i* fore clear that semen has a soul and is a potential
> soul. The same thing can be potentially in varying
> degrees, as the sleeping geometer is farther than
> *ii* the waking geometer, and he is farther than the
> working geometer. Now no part is the cause of
> generation; the cause is rather the first external
> mover. For nothing generates itself, but when it
> has been generated, it grows by itself.[34]

It is for this reason that the principle of growth, that which
has the nutritive and generative power, is generated first.
Aristotle goes on:

> To be generative of another like itself, this is
> the function of every animal and plant perfect in
> *x* nature ... Though it was generated by something
> bearing the same name (a *synonymon*) as a man
> generates a man, it grows by itself; thus there
> is something which makes it grow.[35]

Thus the heart or its analogue is generated first.

In an important respect, the problem of semen and soul is

evaded in this passage. Aristotle brings himself to say that
semen is an organic part of the male parent, and all organic
parts share in soul (735a8), namely, the soul of the individual living being of which they are parts. But this is not
enough, as can be seen from the ambiguity at *i* in our translation (καὶ ἔχει καὶ ἔστι [ψυχὴ] δυνάμει). On the one hand,
the word *dynamis* has the effect of taking away something: not
actually, but potentially, semen has and is soul. On the other
hand, one is tempted to read the phrase as if it were written
"καὶ ἔχει καὶ ἔστι ἡ τῆς ψυχῆς δύναμις" - both has and is the
power of the soul.

The first interpretation is reinforced by reference to degrees
of potentiality. At *de Anima* II.5, the same doctrine is applied at length to the account of perception and knowledge.
At 417b16, Aristotle speaks of degrees of the potentiality
of knowledge, claiming that learning is a change in habits
and nature: "The first change in the faculty of perception
is generated by the male parent; but when generation is effected the individual already has knowledge, in the sense of
perception." The passage in *GA* II has the effect of inserting
the activity of semen into this process. It would seem that
semen has the potentiality of perception, but even farther
from actuality than the potentiality which the embryo has.

Semen must, however, have *actually* the power of generation, and if it has that power, then it "has and is" soul.
We wonder again just what a *dynamis* might be. If a *dynamis*
may be ontologically independent, as hot, cold, fluid, and
solid seem to be, then perhaps a power of soul may exist
without its being the soul of an individual. Aristotle seems
to suppose that the soul is a power, or a closely interrelated
group of powers, which may be the soul of an individual, to be
sure, but which may also be transferred by means of semen
without being the soul of anything at the moment.

Given the statements which Aristotle has made up to this
point in the *GA*, we may suppose that the powers of soul present in the semen are there as heat and as movements. The male

parent imparts movements and vital heat to the semen, and the
semen in turn is said to impart the movements and heat to the
menstrual fluid. It therefore seems that semen "transfers"
the powers by preserving the form of the movements by which
it was itself moved and by imparting them to the menstrual
fluid which it finds in the female.

Aristotle uses the ambiguity inherent in the word *dynamis* in
his account of semen and soul in II.1. Semen is, in respect
of its *dynamis*, soul. But the actuality of a soul is its exercise, its activity. Semen does not have the activity of the
sensitive soul; thus it is not an animal. It does have the
generative faculty of soul, to the extent that its activity
is precisely a generation.[36] It generates an animal, which
has the faculties of perception and movement. These faculties
are thought of as the same power in parent and offspring;
this power must be in the semen too, but "potentially". Thus
we get the "potential presence of a power" all packed into
the word *dynamis* at 735a9.[37]

Supposing that we were to accept this theoretical account of
the character of semen, there would still remain a specter of
the continuing problem which Aristotle faces in his account
of generation. This specter is suggested by the pair of terms
"homonymous" and "synonymous" at 735a8 and 735a21, marked "*x*"
in the passages quoted above. On the one hand, semen would be
only "homonymously" a part if it had no soul; it would be like
a dead man's eye. On the other, generation is effected by the
"synonymous", as man generates man. Semen is not even homonymously a man, although it is part of a man; it cannot, it
seems, be said without qualification that semen generates.[38]

For the time being, it seems that the dilemma posed at
734a (p. 67 above) has been theoretically solved. Generation,
it would appear, is effected both by something external and
something internal. The male parent is external, but he is
the source of the power of soul which is in the semen; the
semen ensouls the menstrual fluid largely by fabricating the
embryonic heart, which in turn "makes" the rest of the animal.

6. Semen as phenomenon (II.2, 735a30-736a24)

In order to show how semen can be the sort of material to be
able to carry, to transfer, such a complicated set of movements and powers, Aristotle provides an observational description of semen and attempts to explain its non-generative
behavior. This explanation turns upon the hypothesis that semen is a foam of water and *pneuma*; in support of this notion
he calls upon Hesiod's derivation of the name Aphrodite from
aphros, or foam.
Aristotle is gradually working in his (new) theory of *pneuma*
as the special physical basis of the soul. For the most part,
pneuma had no more special connotation of soul in the Greek
of his day than does "breath" in English, and Aristotle does
not show his hand in this chapter, for he says simply that
pneuma is "hot air" (736a2). There is little indication of
the role that *pneuma* will play in the next chapter, where it
is even true that the physical characteristics of semen are
again investigated (736a30ff).

7. The extended analysis of semen and soul (II.3, 736a24-
    737a34)

A seemingly innocent question, "What becomes of the physical
part of the semen when it has done its work?" (the problem
was already noted at 734a8), introduces one of the most important chapters in the *GA*. This question arises from Aristotle's position that the male provides the form and the
female the matter; semen should provide none of the matter
for the embryo (fetation), but it does provide the soul. If
it provides none of the matter, what happens to its physical
nature? Before answering this question, Aristotle proceeds
to an analysis of the way in which semen has the powers of
the soul, including the power of reason (*nous*). This analysis
involves a radical development of the theory of *pneuma*, which

is seen in this chapter as a terrestrial analogue of *aither*, the matter of the heavenly bodies.

Rather than following Aristotle's argument step by step (MORAUX does this in his *"nous thyrathen"*[39]) we shall investigate certain key topics: a) what happens to semen? (II. 3, 737a8-18); b) *energeia* in II.3; c) *"nous thyrathen"*; d) *pneuma* and the bodily powers of the soul (736b22ff); e) *pneuma* and *aither* (736b30-737a8).

a) What happens to semen?

"It dissolves and evaporates, having a fluid and watery nature" (737a12). The foam "breaks down" (διαλύεται) and "turns into *pneuma*" (πνευματοῦται). That is, the water evaporates; the *pneuma* in the semen is already *pneuma*. It is for this reason that "we should not look for semen leaving the female, nor as a part of the fetations". i) If it all becomes gaseous, even if it were to escape we could not see it. ii) Semen acts on mense as fig juice acts on milk, and we do not look for the fig juice either, "for this also changes (μεταβάλλει) and is not part of the systematized mass" (a15).

Both the fig juice and semen work on their material in virtue of their vital heat,[40] but this is not the whole story in the case of semen. There is a sense in which *pneuma* does not become "part" of the fetation, but there is a sense in which it does too. *Pneuma* does not become a part of the developing organism in any of the Aristotelian senses of the word *morion*, for it is neither a *homoiomeros* nor an *anomoiomeros* which can be distinguished by anatomical investigation. On the whole, in anatomical investigation Aristotle does not find *pneuma* in any special location or reservoir, although he surely thinks that there is more *pneuma* in some parts than in others. But *pneuma* does become a part of the developing organism in this sense; the *pneuma* is there, in the organism. It is *everywhere* in the organism, and is indistinguishable from the compounds

into which it enters. The *pneuma* which the semen has become
cannot be found in the organism because it cannot be distinguished from the organism. It has entered into the compounds
which are the *homoiomere*, giving them their form, maintaining
their form, and giving form to the *anomoiomere* and their activities.

Even if we could, in some way, distinguish the *pneuma* from
the other elements of the body, we would still not be certain
to have found the *pneuma* from the father distinguished as a
separate nature. i) The female contribution also contains
some *pneuma*, even if insufficient for generation by itself;
ii) once the male *pneuma* has been introduced, and the individual begins to develop, there is a constant production of
pneuma which cannot be distinguished from the *pneuma* which
was in the semen or mense. All of the *pneuma* is now the *pneuma*
of this individual; it is "with" his "nature", *symphyton*, as
the *Movement of Animals* puts it.

b) *Energeia* in II.3

"Fetations" and "seed" (*sperma*) have at least the nutritive
and generative function of the soul, as was shown in II.1.
As the fetations of animals develop, the sensitive soul appears, for it is the defining characteristic of animals.
"'Animal' and 'man', or 'animal' and 'horse', are not generated simultaneously, for the end is generated last, and the
particular is the end of the generation of the individual"
(736b2ff). This statement comes near to an assertion of a
phenomenon made abundantly clear in modern embryology, that
the fetuses of different species of animals are very similar
at the beginning of their development. Aristotle had sufficient acquaintance with various embryoes to make the assertion on this ground; he makes a similar assertion, on the
basis of observations of various sorts of failure of offspring
to resemble their parents, in *GA* IV.3, 768b10ff, and 769b9ff.

78

In II.3, however, it is more nearly a question of the se-
quence of development of various functions of the soul; the
nutritive and generative functions of the soul are present
from the beginning, the sensory and motor functions develop
during the embryological process. But Aristotle's goal is to
discover when and how the mind comes to be in the individual
man, for 'mind' is the defining characteristic of the human
species.

In order to get at the problem of the development of the sensitive and motive faculty, and of the development of the mind,
Aristotle works out some of the consequences of his theory of
potentiality and actuality:

> It is clear that not yet separated (x) spermata
> and fetations have nutritive soul potentially, but
> they do not have it in actuality (*energeia*) before
> (as separated fetations) they draw in food and
> exercise the function of this sort of soul; for
> all such fetations seem at first to live the life
> of a plant.[41]

Some interpretation is required. (i) The sense of the word
dynamis is unclear. Are both active and passive, or only active powers considered? If both, then the semen must have an
active power and the menstrual fluid a passive power. The
fetation has both, but especially the active. (ii) Saying
that something has something potentially is not simply a
tricky way of saying that it does not have it. If something
has an active power, it is something in virtue of that fact.
The soul is a *dynamis*, or set of powers. This is the point
of the analogy of the sleeping geometer: he is a geometer,
although he is not actually doing geometry. The faculties of
the soul do not simply appear and disappear as the organism
acts or desists. (Aristotle thus seems to think that the
nutritive and generative faculty is in the spermata and fetations, although not yet functioning.) (iii) There is a direct
correlation between this passage and the definition of the
soul in the *de Anima*: "The soul is the first *entelecheia* of
a natural body having the power of life; such will be whatever is organic" (II.1, 412a27). This passage reads, δυνάμει

ζωὴν ἔχοντος, and the *GA* passage reads, ψυχὴν ... δυνάμει ...
ἔχοντα. Just as we read the *de Anima* passage as affirming the
life of that which has soul, so we should read the *GA* passage
as affirming the existence of soul (even if not yet in *energeia*) in seed and fetations. (iv) It has been suggested[42]
that Aristotle here tries to resolve a conflict between Diogenes of Apollonia and Empedocles: Empedocles had argued that
embryos are alive; Diogenes thought that they did not have
life because they did not breathe. At this point Aristotle
tries to provide a theoretical basis for the solution of the
puzzle, operating in conjunction with his new version of the
theory of *pneuma* as the physiological part of the solution.
This theoretical solution must provide for some sort of life,
and therefore some sort of soul, in seed and fetations, but
Aristotle cannot make the observational errors of Empedocles
and Democritus which give spurious independence to seed and
fetations. (v) The distinction between *dynamis* and *energeia*
drawn here may then be the distinction between having (but
not exercising) and exercising a power.
Two interrelated problems arise from this interpretation: (i)
Can it ever be proper, within or without Aristotle's system,
to say that something has a power which it cannot exercise
now? (ii) Is it not self-contradictory to say that something
has a soul (defined as first *entelecheia*) but does not have
it in *energeia*? That is, are not *entelecheia* and *energeia* so
closely related that the ascription of one necessarily involves the ascription of the other, or else that an *energeia*
is a necessary precondition for the existence of the correlative *entelecheia*?
(i) There is no question that Aristotle envisages powers which
are present but need further preconditions for their actualization. The sleeping geometer, and the puppet before being
wound up, are cases of entities with potentialites which need
prior conditions for their actualizations. In general, given
the analysis in terms of potentiality and actuality, one may
grant "submerged" potentialities. Matter, for example, has

levels of potentialities of the passive sort. As elements,
matter has limited immediate potentialities, but immense secondary potentialities; as matter is presented in more and
more organized forms, new potentialities come to the surface
and become immediately possible. There is no reason I can
think of for the same not to be true of active potentialities;
they too may be submerged only to appear as their activity
works itself out in the presented material.

(ii) The supposed contradiction between the presence of an
entelecheia and absence of an *energeia* may be resolved by the
specification of the precise *entelecheia* and *energeia* involved in the discussion. In the *de Anima* passage, the *entelecheia* is the presence of a power which is present by virtue
of the presence of an organ. In the *GA* passage, the *energeia*
is the activity of an organ. Semen *is* an organ.

As for the higher powers, the sentient and rational, Aristotle
gives a complicated "rational argument" which purports to ex-
haust the possible locations and sources of the various powers
of soul, in the process of generation:[43]

   I. Possible powers in matter provided by female
      (mense or egg).
     A. None in matter, but all generated in it.
     B. All in matter beforehand.
     C. Some in matter, some not.
  II. If A or C is true, then either
     D. Not by semen (what, is not clear) or
     E. By semen.
 III. If generated by semen, when did they come to the
     semen? (It is suggested that they may come from
     "outside", though where outside is not specified;
     we may suppose that the heavenly bodies have some-
     thing to do with it).
     F. All the powers generated by the male come "from
     outside";
     G. None of them do;
     H. Some do, some do not.

The combinations are these:

B. If all the powers are in the matter, then they are not generated in it, so none of the other possibilities would apply. Aristotle has, of course, argued against this position before, and will do so again at 736b22.

FGH apply only to E.

A, D: "No powers of the soul in matter, all generated in it but not by semen." This may be the proper understanding of spontaneous generation where the matter is slime or the like; the generation is said to be effected by the sun or by warm weather.

C, D: "Some powers in the matter, others generated by a non-spermatic agency." This would, I suppose, be the interpretation of parthenogenesis, for the female *spermata* (e.g. eggs) even if not fertilized, seem to have some share in life; again heavenly bodies or the weather effects the rest.

AE: No powers of soul in matter, all generated by the male:

AEF: all the powers generated in the male from without;

AEG: all the powers generated in the male, not from without;

AEH: all the powers generated by the male, in whom some are from without, some not. But all the AE possibilities seem unlikely, since Aristotle posits the presence of nutritive and generative soul in the female matter.

CE: some power of soul pre-exists in the mense or eggs; the other powers generated by semen. So if nutritive and generative soul is mainly in the matter,

CEF: sensitive and rational soul may be generated by semen in which they were generated from without;

CEG: same, but not from without;

CEH: nutritive in the matter, sensitive and rational generated by semen, in which sensitive is generated not from without and rational generated from without.

[PECK thinks that only CEH is operative, but a combination of CD and CE is also possible, since they are not mutually exclusive.]

82

The upshot of the argument seems to be that some of the nutritive and generative power is provided even within the female matter, although some must be provided by the male, in
species which generate sexually. Aristotle seems still committed to the view that the male provides the power of the
sensitive and motive soul. Unfertilized female *spermata*
(menstrual fluid or eggs) develop to a point, then stop short
of the development of animal organs which would be sensitive
or locomotive; the male must provide something which is
"higher". The simplest account which one may dig out of
(Aristotle's text is that the male semen adds the faculty of
sensation and movement to the faculty of nutrition and generation already more or less present in the female spermatic
contribution.)

c) "*Nous thyrathen*"

Aristotle's "most vexed" problem concerns the rational power
of the soul, mind (*nous*). It may be that this problem moti-
vates the exhaustive account of the possibilities of the
sources of the faculties, for at 736b5-8 Aristotle has said
that his biggest problem is "how and when and whence" mind
arises in those that have it.[44] This problem arises largely
because there is serious question whether mind has any share
in physical nature, that is, in matter. Aristotle says in the
de Anima that "it is unreasonable to suppose that (mind) is
mixed with the body".[45] This theme is developed in *de Anima*
III.4-6; there, mind is opposed to matter in a particularly
striking way: not only is mind "separate" and "unmixed", but
it is also *apathes*, which means "un-acted-upon" (being acted
upon is the essential characteristic of matter), perfectly
active, for its being is activity, and it is immortal. We are
reminded of this passage at least twice in *GA* II.3 (736b28,
737a8). These passages lead us to suppose that *nous* cannot be
(as *aisthesis*, on the contrary, can[46]) the name of movements

in matter, at any rate not bodily matter (*somatike hyle*). If
this is so, then there has been *no* progress toward solving
the problem of the origin of mind in the rational being. Although Aristotle uses language[47] which seems to indicate that
mind has a locality in semen or fetus, this seems inconsis-
tent with its nonbodily character, for only bodily things can
have a place (*Physics* IV.1-5; *Generation and Corruption* I.5).
If Aristotle were committed to a placeless mind, then his
problem would be partly insoluble; one might ask when and
how it comes to be for the individual rational animal, but
one could not reasonably ask whence, nor could one respond
"from outside" (*thyrathen*).

The difficulty may be reduced by the careful handling of the
senses of the word *choriston*, which may mean either "separate"
or "separable", and either of those in any of three ways:
a) in place, b) in *logos*, c) by intellection (*Metaphysics*
Iota [X] 1052b17). It seems unlikely that Aristotle means
to tell us that mind is "separable in place" (a). The notion
of "separable by intellection" seems in the *Metaphysics* to
apply to mathematical objects, which are not (according to
Aristotle) separate in reality, but treated as separate for
intellectual convenience; this seems unlikely to be applied
to mind except in a truistic way. Joseph OWENS claims that
Metaphysics Eta seems to argue that there are individual separate forms; although Aristotle does not actually say this,
he does seem to suggest that the mind is such an eternal separate form.[48]

MORAUX, in his "*nous thyrathen*", attempts to play down the
reference to "mind coming from without" at 736b28. The theory
of an adventitious mind is fraught with difficulties, some
of which I have hinted at. Yet any interpretation which makes
this passage disappear must contend with the Greek commentators, who took this passage as an indication of Aristotle's
own position, and even more with the puzzle of Theophrastus:
"*Nous*: how and when it is from outside, and is, as it were,
adventitious as well as connate."[49] Put in this way, there

84

seems to be a self-contradiction: how can mind be both "adventitious", "from without", and "connate"? In spite of the difficulties in MORAUX's position, I agree with him that Aristotle does not confidently assert that mind is immaterially adventitious. In spite of all, Aristotle seems to believe, and tries, on the whole, to convince us, that there is no essential difference between the inheritance of mind and the inheritance of the other powers of the soul. This interpretation is, I believe, supported by a casual comment a little later in the chapter:

> The body of the semen, in and with which some of the psychic principle goes away, some being separable from the body, in those in which there is something divine wrapped up (such is the so-called *nous*), some being inseparable.[50]

Here, in the space of a half-sentence or less, Aristotle says that *nous* "goes away" (from the father) in and with the semen (or body of the semen, which is the same thing); that it is separable (*choriston*) from body. Not only is it separable, but something divine is "wrapped up in" those individuals which have it. I suppose that here, as in other passages which speak of *nous*, Aristotle is purposely ambiguous. Certain epistemological considerations lead him to separate or dematerialize the mind, but biological and physiological considerations lead him to avoid dematerializing the mind too much. Perhaps we do not find (try as we might) a solution to the mind-body problem in Aristotle because he intentionally does not give a solution.

In fact, there is a way in which the problem of *nous* is external to the problem of the *GA*. If *nous* is immortal, then it is not subject to substantial change; if it is not subject to substantial change, then its generation need not be explained, for it is not generated. It simply manifests itself in the appropriate vehicle.

d) *Pneuma* and the bodily powers of the soul (II.3, 736b22ff)

It is not the presence of mind in "some animals" that requires the elaboration of the theory of *pneuma*, but the generations of the *bodily* powers of the soul in matter. "Those principles whose *energeia* is bodily cannot be present without body"; for example, "walking without feet" (736b22). This seems quite clearly to be an Aristotelian (hylomorphist) position, but it seems equally a difficult problem for the explanation of the subrational powers, as SOLMSEN points out.[51] In one respect, Aristotle has already solved part of the problem which this doctrine poses, with his elaboration of the theory of *dynamis* and the analogy of the sleeping geometer; he has already explained how the power of walking, at several removes, may be present in that which causes the power of walking, in that which becomes the organ for walking. But this power must be in the semen (it is active, and the active powers must be from the male). What is there about semen which has this potential power? After all, "semen is (only) a residue of changing food".[52] Yet semen does have in it *pneuma*; this material must have some special characteristics which allow it to have the powers without being the entity.

e) *Pneuma* and *aither* (736b30-737a8)

> Now it seems that the power of all soul shares in a body different from and more divine than the so-called elements; as souls differ in value, so the relative nature also differs. In every *sperma* there is present that which makes all *spermata* fertile, the so-called "hot". But this is not fire nor any such power, but the *pneuma* wrapped up in the *spermata* and in the "foamy", and the nature in the *pneuma*, which is the analogue of the element of the stars. Thus fire does not generate any animal constructed in either fluid or solid under the influence of fire; but the heat of the sun and the

86

> heat of animals do generate, not only through
> the *spermata*, but also any other residue of
> their nature likewise has the principle of
> life.

In the preceding chapter Aristotle has simply said that
was "hot air"; now, without giving up that view, he wants to
relate *pneuma* to the divine *aither*.

MORAUX[53] argues that it would be a misunderstanding to identify *pneuma* and *aither*, and in the strongest sense of the
word "identify", his position is surely correct. However,
MORAUX does not provide a clear discussion of the relationship which Aristotle does find between *pneuma* and *aither*. One
of the most important clues in the present passage is this:
"As souls differ in value, so the relative nature also differs" (b32). This statement suggests a proportion or *analo-
gia*; the suggestion is confirmed when *pneuma* is called the
analogon of *aither*. Expressed as an "analogy", Aristotle's
statement is this: Value of soul A : value of soul B :: value
of nature A : value of nature B. If value (*timiotes*) is ex-
pressible as a quantity, or is quasi-quantifiable, then if
the souls differ in value, then the relative *physis* (nature)
of the souls differ in value.

One cannot, or ought not, push the analogy too far: although
the *physis* of animal souls differs, it is all *pneuma*. But how
closely are *pneuma* and the element of the stars to be related?
PECK[54] discusses the problem, noting this passage:

> Air, water, and many solids (are transparent); but
> neither air nor water is transparent *qua* water or
> air, but because the same nature is present in both
> these as also in the eternal bodies above. Light is
> the activity (*energeia*) of this transparent *qua*
> transparent (*de Anima* II.7, 418b6-10, after HETT).

the same *physis* as is found in heavenly bodies is here supposed to be present in a number of terrestrial materials; the
sole *physis* of the stars is *aither*. Therefore, there is a
sense in which there is *aither* in some terrestrial objects.

In harmony with these passages is *GA* III.11, 762a19-27,
where Aristotle argues in the course of his explanation of

spontaneous generation as follows:

> Animals and plants are formed in the earth and in
> water because in earth water is present, and in
> water *pneuma* is present, and in all *pneuma* soul-
> heat is present, so that in a way all things are
> full of soul; that is why they quickly take shape
> once it has been enclosed. Now it is enclosed as
> the liquids containing corporeal matter become
> heated, and there is formed as it were a frothy
> bubble. The object which thus takes shape may
> be more or less valuable in kind, and the dif-
> ferences depend upon the envelope which encloses
> the soul principle; the causes which determine
> this are the situations where the process takes
> place and the physical substance which is en-
> closed.[55]

a) It may be that both *aither* and *pneuma* are present in water,
being different natures, but I doubt that Aristotle makes
this distinction. That which is, by inference, called *aither*
in the *de Anima* is, I feel, called *pneuma* in this passage.
b) The scale of value is again referred to, but with an addition. In the earlier passage (736b32) the value depends
directly, it seems, on the relative *physis*, the quality of
the *pneuma* "which is enclosed" (762a27); now the "place" is
said to make a difference.[56]
We may phrase the theory in modern biological terms. Aristotle
seems to suppose that *pneuma* functions as an *organizer*, and
that the surrounding material is that which is organized.[57]
This understanding of his account seems confirmed by this
passage:"The portion of the soul-principle which is enclosed
or separated off in the *pneuma* makes and puts movement into
the fetation" (762b16-18). Thus it seems that generation and
the character of the result of generation depends upon at
least two factors: the character of the *pneuma* which is either
already in, or introduced into, the material for generation;
the character of the material which is to be organized by
the *pneuma*. A third factor must be mentioned, regarded as
essential at least in plant generation and in a large range
of animal generation, including all "spontaneous" generation:
the environmental temperature, that is, the activity of the

heavenly bodies upon the *pneuma* and the material.
The mention of this third factor re-emphasizes the importance
of *heat* in this analysis; Aristotle finds a qualitative as
well as a quantitative difference in various lots of heat.
The sun and other heavenly bodies participate in generation
because their heat is in fact soul-heat,[58] and not radically
different in kind, although radically different in value,
from the soul-heat of temporal souls. The heavenly bodies
thus participate in generation by providing one source of
movement and organization for that which is organized. But
that which provides the source of movement and generation
must, according to the principles already elucidated, have
the form. The sun *et al.* are not actually members of animal
species; how then do they have the form? Aristotle seems committed to the sort of distinction made clear later, between
formal and eminent reality. The souls of the heavenly bodies
must contain all these species eminently, for they do not
contain them formally, in the Cartesian senses of these words.

8. The accomplishment of II.1-3

The problem which Aristotle set out to resolve in these chapters was primarily that of the mode of operation of semen in
generation. In Book I, semen was supposed to provide the form
and source of movement to the female spermatic contribution.
How it could do this seemed difficult to explain, and we may
be excused if we are still puzzled by the end of II.3. Aristotle sought a material which could serve as a tool when no
longer in contact with the male parent, and a material which
could at the same time be understood under some teleological
rubric. The *pneuma*, as the special vehicle of vital heat,
seems to serve the purpose of the explanation. In the first
place, Aristotle has essentially three analogies which con-
verge to an understanding of what "must" be the manner of
operation of the semen. These analogies are those of fig juice

(or rennet), which comes close in that natural materials are involved in the change; of the puppets, which is as good as Aristotle can do at finding an analogy of a tool acting at a distance; and of the working of a craft, which illustrates the manner in which form and movement are given to matter without becoming a part of the matter. Secondly, *pneuma* is brought more or less forcibly into line with these analogies. There is no special problem in bringing *pneuma* into line with the fig juice analogy, because he believes that fig juice coagulates milk by virtue of its *pneuma*, or the vital heat which the *pneuma* carries; it is not, in this respect, an analogy but an identity. But the puppet analogy seems forced, for the complicated movements of the puppet, and more, are demanded by the results. But those complicated movements are the result of the already quasi-organic structure of the pupet. Semen, and more especially the *pneuma* in the semen, cannot be understood to have an organic structure in this sense; however it may be that *pneuma* preserves the dynamic structure (*eidos*) of the male, Aristotle does not really tell us at all. The analogy of housebuilding or doctoring tells us what *must* occur, without really telling us how, and it leads Aristotle to suppose that no material of the semen becomes material of the fetation.

Since the inspection of semen, and the analogies which occur to Aristotle, seem to be insufficient to carry the day, Aristotle puts a considerable weight on the fateful theory that *pneuma* is a special material quite unlike anything else one might find in the world, but rather strikingly like the material which one might find out of this world. There is something of the myth-maker about Aristotle here; he seems to bring the gods, or at least the divine, down to earth in order to explain that which he finds otherwise inexplicable. His hylomorphic theory of the soul is up against the wall in the explanation of generation, and he knows it, so he decides to support the notion of a particularly formal material. That it is a rarefied material, his audience would readily accept;

90

that it is to be found everywhere, or nearly so, would also be accepted. But that *pneuma* may be a kind of divine *spiritus* would not be too readily accepted, at least not, or especially not, by those who had taken the rest of his physical philosophy seriously.

Aristotle knows that he must explain the generation of animals in order to make good his claim to have developed the only philosophy able to account for all kinds of change, while remaining rational and preserving the phenomena. Yet in order to make good his claim he must resort to a quite unverifiable theory. One gets the impression that Aristotle ultimately tries to trick us into thinking that he *has* solved the problem, for he could as well have admitted his inability to explain the manner in which semen does its work, even while maintaining that his general philosophical principles (for example, the four causes) do in fact work out in animal generation as in all other sorts of change.

Yet this criticism may be somewhat harsh. If Aristotle is to gain an understanding of this phenomenon, it must be a theoretical understanding. For only now, with enormous progress in techniques of investigation, are the empirical data accessible. Aristotle knew that there must be something in spermatic secretions which provides the form for development, something which would perform the functions which we assign to sperm and egg cells, or more precisely to DNA and related factors. He was mistaken in supposing that his functional equivalent of our DNA was to be found only, or pre-eminently, in the male semen, but he knew that something had to carry the dynamic structure from parent to child. His version of the theory was a considerable advance on the theories of his predecessors. No appreciable further advance was made until the discovery of spermatozoa (1679), and even this discovery was accompanied by a step backward to preformationism. Not until the nineteenth century did epigenesis, the theory suggested by Aristotle, win general scientific approval.

C. *Genesis* and *Energeia*

Aristotle uses analogies, the ramifications of the concepts
of potentiality and actuality, and the notion of *pneuma*, to
explain animal generation in *GA* II.1-3. We tend to suppose
that *pneuma* is the central concept in those chapters, partly
because it appears so surprisingly. The concept of *energeia*
is, however, still important in II.1-3, as we have shown above. Elsewhere in the *GA* the central explanatory concepts are
energeia and the related four causes, and *dynamis*. This is important to note, for it is the use of these concepts which
most closely relate the *GA* to theoretical works such as *Physics, Metaphysics*, and *de Anima*.
We begin this part with a discussion of an especially important passage, *GA* II.4, 740b13-741a3, which gives an account
of generation relying upon the nuances in the sense of *energeia*
and upon the analogy of art and nature, rather than upon the
concept of *pneuma*. The particular emphasis here is the relationship between activity and the matter of which it is the
activity. A finer appreciation of the character of the concept of *energeia* may be gained by an investigation of some
of the concepts related to it; we will summarize some of our
findings concerning Aristotle's concept of matter and his
concept of a source of movement. We may then show how *energeia*,
form and end, develop out of the idea of a dynamic moving matter.
Of the appearances of the notion of *energeia* in the *GA* which
we will note in this part, one of the most important is its
use in the explanation of resemblance and lack of resemblance
of offspring to parents, in Book IV. It is an especially difficult problem for Aristotle, as shall be shown; it is a phase
in his explanation of generation which requires a further development of the concept of *energeia*. Some general remarks
concerning the character of the teleology of the *GA* conclude
this chapter.

1. Summary of the explanation of animal generation
   (II.4, 740b13ff)

> (1) The differentiation of the parts is ge-
> nerated...[59] because the residue of the fe-
> male is potentially such as the animal is
> in nature, and the parts are in it poten-
> tially, but not actually (in *energeia*), for
> this reason (cause) each of the parts is
> generated; and because the active and the
> passive, when they touch, in the way in which
> the one is active and the other passive (by
> "way" I mean how, where, and when) immediate-
> ly the one acts and the other is acted upon.
> The female provides the matter and the male
> the source of movement.
>
> (2) (a) Just as that which is generated by
> art is generated by means of tools, it would
> be truer to say by the movement of tools,
> and this is the activity (*energeia*) of art,
> "art" being "the shape of that which is ge-
> nerated in another", so also the power of
> the nutritive soul, (b) as it even later ef-
> fects growth in animals and plants, using as
> tools hot and cold (for its movement is in
> these, and each thing is generated according
> to a certain *logos*), so also from the beginning
> it constructs that which is generated naturally;
> (c) for as it is the same matter by which it
> grows and from which it is constructed at the
> beginning, so also the making power is the
> same;[60] now if this is the nutritive soul,
> then it is also the generator; and this is
> the nature of each thing, present in all plants
> and animals.
>
> (3) But the other parts of the soul are present
> in some living things, and not present in
> others.

The passage is structured thus: (1) A general account of generation, including both reproduction and embryological development, is proposed in terms familiar in Aristotle. (2)
Two analogies and one other argument develop the account; analogy (a) extends over analogy (b), and argument (c) supports
analogy (b) without being a part of analogy (a). (3) Conclud-
ing remarks tie the passage together.

(1) Aristotle begin with the matter provided by the female, explaining its role by reference to the distinction between *dynamis*, in the sense of potential, and *energeia*, in the sense of actual. *Physis* and *energeia* seem to be identified. Having distinguished matter and end, Aristotle proceeds to the source of movement, which he presents in terms of the distinction between active and passive powers.[61] (The process of generation depends upon the contact of the (right) active and passive powers.)

(2) The role of analogy (a) may be stated thus: art : movement of tools (*energeia* of art) : product of art :: nature : movement of hot and cold in the semen and in the body = power of the nutritive/generative soul (apparently, = *energeia* of nature) : natural product. 'Art' is defined as 'the shape or form of that which is generated in another'; the correlative definition of 'nature' would be 'the shape or form of that which is generated in itself'. This definition of 'nature' works well in the account of the later development, as in the first part of analogy (b) and at (3), but it is puzzling when it is applied to the first movement of generation. What, after all, is the "itself" that the shape of nature is "in" at the moment of conception? Aristotle seems to be continually uneasy that his account of the first movement of generation is *too* like his account of the productions of art, and he seems relieved once the nutritive soul is installed in the heart. This is, I suppose, the motivation of analogy (b) and argument (c); he must make it perfectly clear to himself and to his auditors that it *must* be the same power, movement, and activity in both cases, that the nutritive and generative power of the soul has a continued existence between parent and offspring, although one cannot say clearly *whose* soul it is during this period.

The problem is not solvable by empirical investigation. One has to have available a criterion for what will count as "a soul" in order to discover it (or not) in the phenomena. By implication, but not straightforwardly, this passage says

that the power of the nutritive soul is the *energeia* of nature; this would provide an appropriate criterion.)
From analogy (b) it is clear that the semen generates by
virtue of the nutritive soul; if it is to provide the sentient soul, as Aristotle surely believes, it must do so by
means of the nutritive and generative soul.(One may put it
this way: the nutritive and generative soul of animals is
able to generate sentient beings. The parts or functions or
powers of the soul are not very strictly delimited from each
other.)
The form of argument (c) is: if matter 1 is the same in character as matter 2, then mover 1 is the same in character as
mover 2; if mover 2 is nutritive soul, then mover 1 is nutritive soul; but matter 1 *is* the same in character as matter
2 (cf. 740b3). Thus it is the same power which makes the
heart (or its analogue) as constructs the rest of the body
once the heart (or analogue) is established.

2. Matter in generation

Given the role of the notion of "matter" in this account, and
its similar role in the other related accounts of generation,
it will be worthwhile to examine Aristotle's concept of matter more generally than we have done thus far.
Aristotle's matter is not the atoms of the atomist, nor the
matter of anyone who finds material reduction to be an adequate explanation of physical phenomena. Nor are Aristotle's
four 'elements' even roughly comparable to the modern 100-odd
elements.(Aristotle's matters form hierarchies; each material
has more form than the material from which it is made, but
has less form than whatever it can be made into, whatever it
is matter *for*.) In the biological books, the highest level in
the hierarchy is occupied by animals and man; these are the
entities for which all the other components of the world exist. The lowest level in the hierarchy (cf. *PA* II.1, 747b13)

is occupied by the simple powers, hot and cold, fluid and solid. These powers are qualitative, and their presence or absence is discovered more or less empirically.[62] They are also "causative" for as active and passive they enter into changes and constructions. The most truly active power (the hot), as active, seems to have a share in finality, for it is (at least insofar as it does something good) a cause for the noble and good. It should be pointed out that the (essentially scholastic) distinction between *materia prima* and *materia secunda* does not appear in the biological books at all. Aristotle seems to play with the notion of an absolutely final, or primary, material in some places in the *Metaphysics*, notably at Theta 7, 1049a25ff, but in the biological books the elementary powers seem sufficiently basic. Since Aristotle's system is perfectly opposed to any materialistic reduction, the most important material for any explanation is not the ultimate material, but the proximate material; in scholastic terms, the only matter which appears in the biological books, and with good reason, is the so-called *materia secunda*.

The hierarchy of materials is, simultaneously, a hierarchy of forms; even the elementary powers are found in the world only in materials which are already somewhat organized. Most of the time, in the biological books, Aristotle is interested in the materials which one finds in living bodies, the materials which compose living bodies. These are, in the first instance, the *homoiomere*, the parts of the body of which the (gross) constituents are identical, or bear the same name. This does not mean that *homoiomere* are unanalyzable; they are, after all, compounds of the elements or powers. Blood, for example, is described by Aristotle as a rather complicated *homoiomeros*.[63] These *homoiomere* either compose the *anomoiomere* (arms, legs, head, etc.), or are food for the parts (e.g. blood), or are "residues".

Menstrual fluid, semen, and milk are residues and *homoiomere*. They are the result of concoction, and semen is more concocted

96

than menstrual fluid. Concoction changes a material more or less radically;[64] in these cases the concoction is toward greater perfection, toward more closely resembling in heat and movement the character of the heat and movement of the parent animal. Through the concoction, *pneuma* is either generated or gains the character of the animal in which it finds itself. I hesitate to say that it becomes organized, for it has no organs, but one might say that it becomes more sophisticated, or at any rate it becomes more useful for generating new individuals of the same species.

Of the generative materials, the male semen, Aristotle repeats again and again, provides the source of movement (only). We have found reason to suppose that the semen becomes some of the *pneuma* of the new individual, but Aristotle does not see this as providing material for generation. Two sorts of consideration may lead to this position. The first is that semen is said to have little or no *earthy* material in its make-up.[65] The second sort of consideration is presented in *Generation and Corruption*:

> When a whole changes, nothing perceptible persisting as its substrate, e.g., blood from the whole semen or air from water or water from a lot of air, this is already a genesis of the one, a destruction of the other; especially if the change occurs between perceptible and imperceptible (either to touch or to all the senses), as when water is generated from or is destroyed into air; for air is more or less imperceptible (*Generation and Corruption* I.4, 319b15ff, my translation).

In this passage, semen is said to be literally destroyed in the generation of blood, and there is no perceptible substrate or material which persists through the change. It is interesting and important to note that the process is immediately compared to the change between water and air, which, I have already argued on the basis of *GA* II.3 itself, is the essential answer to the problem of the disappearance of the semen. In Aristotle's view, if there is a change in the matter, then matter is not contributed, since it is not the same matter.

According to Aristotle's generally stated position, only

the menstrual fluid is the matter from which the new individual is generated;)the female provides all the matter for the
initial fetation, and for the first period of growth and development.)In comparison with the male, what the female lacks
in concoction of its material is made up for in readiness for
construction, like the materials of the artist or builder.
The female contribution may be passive, but it is conditionally necessary. It is worked up to the point that it is *almost*
a new individual, lacking only something of a push, some formation by the power of soul. It is proximate matter.
This is even more clear in the case of the oviparous or larva-
producing animals; indeed, in the latter instance, there seems
to be relatively little need for a male animal at all, for
they sometimes produce parthenogenetically (as the bees do -
GA III.10, 759a8ff), or are even produced out of the lively
earth or sea by the power of the heavenly bodies (*GA* III.11,
cf. II.6, 743a35).

3. The source of movement

The proximate source of movement in generation is normally
the male semen; this is in turn derived from the male parent.
The sun, and to a lesser extent the other heavenly bodies,
seem to have a role in imparting movement and form to the
proper matter for generation. The male parent got his proper
movements from the semen of his father, and so on, more or
less indefinitely. One might mention that these proper movements are preserved in the individual by his eating his proper
foods, which contain a measure of the natural heat by which
they grew; this heat, in the *pneuma* apparently, takes on the
proper degree and form so as to become co-natural with the
individual. The sun and moon also have a role in the well-
being of the individual.[66]

4. *Energeia*, and movement, form, and end

An examination of the occurrences of the word *energeia* will
help us see how movement, form, and end are closely interrelated, yet distinguished in the *GA*. According to BONITZ and
to my own examination of the text, there are just two occurrences in Book I, but several in II and III. The first appearance contrasts *dynamis* and *energeia* in the familiar po-
tentiality:actuality way: what each part of the developed
animal is in *energeia*, the *sperma* is in *dynamis* (I.19, 726b
17). Such passages by themselves (they are frequent enough in
II) might suggest that the *energeia* or *entelecheia*[67] exerts
some occult finalistic causation on the development from seed-
The second occurrence (I.22, 730b21) should show otherwise.
Here nature in generation is compared to the carpenter; as
the carpenter uses his tools, so nature uses semen "as a tool
which has the movement in *energeia*". The implication here is
that the natural tool has a movement of itself which counts
as an *activity*, and indeed the *right* activity. The tools of
the carpenter have only potential movement in and of themselves.
The first appearance of the word *energeia* in II is at 1, 734
b13; here it is used in connection with the analogy of the
puppet, which somehow has a *dynamis* when at rest, and an
energeia when set in motion. We infer that semen has both the
dynamis and the *energeia*. Aristotle goes on to assert that a
source of movement must be something which "is actually something (x)",[68] and that it acts upon something which is potentially (*dynamei*) x. It was at this point that the problem
about semen and the *energeia* arose, for as activity, semen
must have the *energeia*, but as actuality there is some doubt,
since this seems to imply the possession of the *eidos* actually.
One wants to say (735a5) that only parent and child have the
eidos in the full "actuality" sense of the word *energeia*. The
difficulty, seen from the direction of the use of the word
energeia, may be expressed as a tension between the rather

simple sense, "activity", and the metaphysically portentous
sense of "reality".

This, or something like this, must be the reason why the un-
exercised movements of the semen are no longer called unqua-
lifiedly *energeiai* in II.3; these movements are now called
powers (*dynameis*), in the active rather than in the passive
sense of that word. The powers in the semen are those which
do something, bring something about, not the capacity of being
acted upon; these potentialities become *energeiai* only when
they are actually working on the matter, and during the development of the individual (736b10). The line between an
active power and an activity is a very narrow one, to be sure,
but the theory behind the present passage seems to be as follows: everything in the physical world must exist as a *dynamis*
before it can exist as an *energeia* (736b16); if it is only a
dynamis, and not an *energeia*, then it cannot be a source of
movement without a prior *energeia*. Mind seems to escape this
problem (736b29), because its *energeia* seems independent of
physical activities. Semen and fetations, then, are said to
have the soul as a power (*dynamis*) but not as an *energeia*
(737a18). Aristotle has not satisfied himself concerning the
relationship of semen and *energeia*.

The problem is not as difficult in the case of the female contribution to generation (737a24). It is easy enough to fall
back on the passive sense of *dynamis*, and to say that the
matter has all the parts potentially, but none in *energeia*

In II.4 Aristotle traces some of the implications of his
course of reasoning. The heart, he believes, is the first part
to have the *energeia*, to be actually (740a4), to exist; this
is a reasonable assumption when the problem of development
is seen from the material constituent, the menstrual fluid.[69]
He still has the problem of semen. Recalling the analogy of
the semen and the tools of art (740b26), he says that the
movement of the tools of art is an *energeia*. But while this
implies that the movements of the tools of nature are *energeiai* too, he forebears and says simply that the movements in

100

the semen are "the power (*dynamis*) of the nutritive soul".
He goes on to say (II.5, 741a12) that they are the cause of
the sensitive soul in the developing animal. Sitting directly
on the fence, he says that nothing can be the part of an animal unless there is in it the sensitive soul, "either *energeia*
or in *dynamis*, either qualified or unqualified." To say that
the sensitive soul is present 'somehow or other' is precisely
not to tell how it is present, but only to insist that it
must be, despite all the problems.

By II.6 Aristotle has gone back to the language of Book I.
Describing the solidification of bones and sinews by the
agency of heat, he argues that there must be the right material and the right mover:

> for that which is potentially will not be (brought
> into being) by a mover which does not have the
> *energeia*, nor will that which has the *energeia*
> make it from just anything; just so the carpenter
> cannot make a chest out of anything but wood, and
> without him there will be no chest from the wood.
> The heat is present in the spermatic residue, and
> has the right amount and character of movement
> and *energeia* as is proportionate to each of the
> parts (743a23-29, after PECK).

This seems to be the original position. Semen, or the heat in
the semen, has the "movement and *energeia*" without worry about
its status as an entity. It is considered as an organ of the
father, but it is a very special organ, which has all the
powers but can actually exercise just one power: the power to
pass the other powers along to the proper material.

5. The explanation of resemblance between parents and offspring (*GA* IV)

The term *energeia* appears again in the explanation of resemblance and lack of resemblance of offspring to parents.[70]
Aristotle begins Book IV with an explanation of the generation
of offspring of different sexes. Treated briefly at the beginning of II, Aristotle's explanation is presented in the context

of a discussion of earlier writers on the subject.[71] (He begins his positive account with a reprise of the definitions
of male and female, this time emphasizing the difference in
ability to concoct seminal residue. The male can concoct semen, but the female gets only as far as menstrual fluid. The
semen in turn concocts the menstrual fluid, and always "tries"
to make it into a male; sometimes however, it fails, due to
the recalcitrance of the material.[72] The next best thing is
the sexual opposite, a female.)

The same general principles are applied to the degrees of
lack of resemblance of offspring to parents (767a35ff). Some
offspring resemble their grandparents, or more remote ancestors; some do not have the form (*idea*) of a man, but of a
monster (*teras*, 767b6). This is a kind of scale of deviation
of nature; although females are a conditionally necessary deviation, they are also naturally necessary for the species
(767b9). Monsters, however, are necessitated by the character
of the material, for they do not, in themselves, serve a purpose.

The movement or power in the semen constructs the menstrual
fluid according to the *logos* which it has; this *logos* depends
not only on the immediate parent but also on the ancestors,
the species, and the genus. All of these "are at work in the
act of generation",[73] but the individual parent most of all,
"for this is the *ousia*" (767b34). That which is generated has
a character like the movements in the semen, but it too is an
individual, a *tode ti*, "and this too is the *ousia*".

Here, at 768a12ff, the distinction between *energeia* and *dynamis* is recalled in order to explain two different kinds of
departure from similarity to the male parent. As I understand
the passage, Aristotle supposes that resemblance to the female parent (or ancestors on the female side) is due to "departing from type and changing over" (PECK's translation of
ἐξίστασθαι καὶ μεταβάλλειν) to the opposite. Resemblance to
ancestors rather than to immediate parents is due to "relaps-
ing" (*lyesthai*). "Some of the movements are present (*x*) in

102

energeia, some in *dynamis*; in *energeia*, those of the generator and of the universals (e.g. 'man' and 'animal'), in *dynamis* those of the female and of the ancestors" (IV.3, 768a
12).

Two questions arise for us: a) Where are the "movements present in *energeia* and *dynamis*?" b) What are the senses of the
words *energeia* and *dynamis* in this passage? PECK gives his
answer to the first question by inserting the words "in the
semen" at 768a12, in the place marked x in the passage quoted,
and he inserts the words "the seminal substance" at 768b4 and
7 in his translation.[74] The second sort of insertion is nearer
the truth than the first. Aristotle cannot possibly be taken
to be saying that the semen is in *energeia* generative of an
individual like the father and in *dynamis* generative of an
individual like the mother, particularly if one takes into
account the individual peculiarities of the mother, which do
not belong to another individual, even potentially. What the
father can have, potentially as opposed to actually, are the
faculties of the female, or (in general) characteristic variations of the species which he does not actually show. If
one were to put the idea into Mendelian terms, one might say
that Aristotle claimed that female characteristics were re-
cessive. However, Aristotle's system is quite different from
the Mendelian genetics. He distinguishes between 'rational'
(*meta logou*) and 'non-rational' powers; according to *Met.*
Theta 2, 1046a36-b28, a rational power or *dynamis* can have
either of two opposite effects. He gives as examples the powers of the arts, especially of the art of medicine (1046b8).
But Aristotle argues constantly in *GA* that the power of generation is a 'rational' power, analogous with the powers of
the arts. Just as the doctor, having the power to heal, passes
over to the opposite and kills when he is defeated by the recalcitrance of the material, so semen, having the power to
generate a male, when it is defeated by the recalcitrance of
the material, passes over to the opposite and generates a female. Or, perhaps, "dark eyes" pass over to "light eyes". This

103

is what Aristotle means by going over to the opposite.
Aristotle makes clear that the movements (whether *energeia*
or *dynamis*) are also present in the female contribution to
generation,[75] so that seminal substance more closely desig-
nates the location of the movements; I should prefer the plu-
ral (seminal substances), as though Aristotle understood,
but did not write, σπέρμασι after ἔνεισι at the places noted
above (see note 74). It is of course equally true that *all*
of these movements are especially "present in" the first process of systematization of the original fetations.
Energeia and *dynamis* seem to be understood in both the ways
which we have distinguished, in this part of Book IV. Particular movements seem to be both *energeia* and *dynamis* in That
the *energeia* has the *dynamis* of bringing about its opposite
(that is, femaleness), and in that an *energeia* has or is the
dynamis for bringing about the generation of the developing
individual.
A further nuance in the distinction between *energeia* and *dy-*
namis may be found in its use in explaining resemblance to
more remote ancestors. Aristotle seems to understand that
movements proper to the immediate parents are all, in some
sense, present in *energeia* in the spermatic materials, while
the movements proper to the ancestors as individuals are present as *dynameis* but not as *energeiai*. Somehow the various
senses of *dynamis* are combined here again, thus: they are
back-up powers, which come into action (*energeia*) when the
primary (parent) powers fail to do the job. They are potentially generative, as the second and third lines of soldiers
are potential first-line soldiers. These lines, or powers,
come into action, says Aristotle, "because the active is also
acted upon by the passive, as the cutter is blunted by the
cut, and the heater is cooled by the heated".[76]
Thus *GA* IV.3 illustrates, in the stress of a difficult explanation, how Aristotle sees the interaction of mover and
moved, how both mover and moved have their formal character
(but more so the mover), and how mover, form, and end in the
sense of activity for an end are intertwined in a genetic
explanation.

Conclusions: Teleology in Aristotle's Explanation of
            Generation

There is little indication that the teleology of the *GA* has
anything to do with the notion of a consciousness of purpose.
At most there are hints that minds, and the intelligent stars,
are the best things that exist; self-consciousness belongs to
them, to be sure, but it is not by virtue of that self-consciousness that the process of generation may be understood
teleologically. Semen acts purposively,but not consciously.

   Aristotle does not make much use of the notion of "obstacle avoidance" in his explication of the finality of generation. He does say that "everything strives to share in
the eternal and divine insofar as it is able",[77] but he does
not attempt to show that this might be accomplished in a variety of ways. There is an element, in the account of the resemblance of offspring to parents, of the notion of reserve
troops to combat the recalcitrant matter; in more general
terms, the existence of many. *kinds* of natural beings is also
a sort of cosmic obstacle avoidance. Being *is* as much as possible.
Professor CHERNISS criticizes Aristotle's teleological account
of generation thus:

> ...the fortuitous birth of monsters is "contrary
> to nature" not in the sense that it does not pro-
> ceed from natural causes, but only because the
> form fails to master the matter completely; the
> whole doctrine rests upon a circular argument,
> for when the variations are frequent they can no
> longer be called monsters.[78]

The argument is circular, however, only if regularity is the
only argument for teleology, or if nature has only one sense,
the regular. However, nature does have several senses (*Met.*
Delta 4, *Phys.* II.1), and regularity is only one, not the
most important, argument for teleology.
Specifically, in the case of generation the steady repetition
of generation of new individuals of a species is *not* what
shows it to be a teleological process, but rather the way in

which the end, being, is achieved.) To be sure, Aristotle believes that monsters do not reproduce themselves, but if they
did, the result would be something inferior to the species
which originated it.

The end in generation is rather understood as "perpetual being", a cyclical return of genesis and decay for individuals,
but the permanent existence of the kind, the preservation of
the *eidos*. This is the end of the development of the individual and its parts. Since this perpetuity of the species has
a cyclical character, there is indeed a repetition of processes. It is for this reason that the repetition of processes may be taken as *prima facie* evidence of the purposiveness
of the process, but it is only *prima facie* evidence; one must
ask further, "Does it serve the end of more being, more soul,
and so on?" Aristotle believes that the species which do exist
do serve being in this way.

If we ask how final causation operates in the individual case,
we are led inevitably to see the close relationship between
the notions of form and end in Aristotle's account. Teleological explanations of a non-Aristotelian sort are sometimes
offered in the case of generation and development: some have
supposed that there is a special "thing" in developing embryos which "guides" its development; others have supposed
that the final state of the mature individual exerts an influence upon the development, from the future.[79] Both sorts
of statement might find some support in Aristotle's text; the
first might find it in his theory of *pneuma*; the second might
find it in his often repeated assertion that the developed
individual is the end or *telos*.)

We must be careful, however, with the idea of causation. If
Aristotle gives the "end", it is in answer to the particular
question, "What is this for?" or "in order for what?" The end
does not, per se, exert a movement on the material, surely
not backward in time. *Pneuma*, on the other hand, is able to
structure the material because it already has, Aristotle supposes, the dynamic structure of the individual, although it

does not have the (earthy) material.

(The soul, the *ousia* in the sense of form of the individual living being, reproduces itself for its *own* sake.) This is because the soul is somehow both individual (and mortal) and universal (and immortal) at least in that it continues itself through *spermata* to offspring, perpetually. This is its nature, form, and end.)

CHAPTER III   UNDERSTANDING THE ORGANIC PARTS

Introduction

As the *Generation of Animals* is an attempt to resolve a central philosophical problem, that of existential change, so
too throughout the biological books Aristotle defends his
teleological mode of explanation of the world by explicating
what is, for him, the paradigm case of something which demands such an explanation: the functional dynamic system of
the organic parts of animals. For Aristotle, an organ or
tool is understood in terms of its functions; we have now to
see the manner in which this general principle or point of
view is applied in specific cases.
The observational data which Aristotle uses in the cases
which we will discuss are such that they are nearly all open
to immediate inspection, simple dissection, or a relatively
uncomplicated investigation. Aristotle usually differs from
the ordinary observer only in that he has a particular viewpoint, an interpretation which fits into a philosophical
system.
We will discuss two related groups of cases in this chapter.
The first group concerns the inter-relationship of development and function in the understanding of parts of animals.
Paying special attention to the structure and physiology of
the 'blooded' (chordate and vertebrate) animals, Aristotle
gives accounts (usually separate) of the development of individual parts, and of their functions. The developmental
account is usually to be found in the *GA*, especially in the
later chapters of II, while the functional account is usually
to be found in the *PA*, and is more hylomorphic in character
than the pneumatic theory of *GA* II.3 would allow.
The second group of problems arises from the comparison of
different species of animals with each other. Any observer
should be struck by the diversity of the forms of animal

108

life; Aristotle, a man with some taste for the unusual, found
much worthy of explanatory comment. Within the diversity, he
finds many unexpected similarities; Aristotle's accounts of
the variations among species are characterized by the sorts
of similarities and differences which he chooses to discuss.
He lavishes more care than usual on his account of the variations in the organs of perception in various species; for
this reason, and for the related reason that such a study
might help in an understanding of Aristotle's theory of perception, I have chosen to investigate these explanations, in
order to find the relationship between theory and observation
in these cases.

The principles of explanation

> At the beginning of the inquiry we must postulate
> the principles we are accustomed constantly to
> use for our scientific investigation of nature
> (*IA* 2, 704b11, FARQUHARSON).

The laudable practice which Aristotle here recommends is followed to some considerable degree in the biological books,
although in the passage in the *IA* he mentions only his teleological principle. Usually he mentions several or all of
the four causes; sometimes he mentions other explanatory principles in addition. *PA* I is a particularly extensive discussion of his methods of explanation; Aristotle here explores
in detail the problems of classification, relates the formal
and final causes to each other and to the concept of necessity, and connects the genetic account of the parts to these
concepts. He compares his own notion of matter with that of
the Ionian philosophers, as he interprets them, and he contrasts his general approach to explanation with the approach
of Democritus. At the end of *PA* I.1 he fits the notions of
physis and *psychē* into the structure of the 'causes', and
contrasts two concepts of necessity, both of which are said
to operate in his explanations. At the beginning of book II

he again summarizes his explanatory concepts, adding his
distinction of potentiality and actuality.[1] In the *GA*, there
is a brief summary of the four causes at the beginning of
book I, and a defense of teleology at the beginning of book
II; he again summarizes his principles at the beginning of
book V. The first chapter of *de An.* indicates the scope of
that work, and the first chapter of *Sens.* forms a transition
from the *de An.* to the *Parva Nat.* by distinguishing the sorts
of explanatory principles to be used.

None of Aristotle's accounts of his explanatory principles
is exhaustive, however. In Chapter I, we presented an analy-
tical exposition of the most important explanatory principles
particularly of the teleological principles as they are presented in the *Physics*. We tried to show how the four causes
are inter-related, and ultimately dependent upon the notion
of a final cause; we explained the concept of *dynamis* in
terms of the four causes. It might be possible to relate all
of Aristotle's explanatory concepts to the four causes (he
seems to suppose this to be possible), but some of them do
not fit easily. Most notable of these relatively independent concepts are those which may be ranged under the head-
ing of 'polarity and analogy'.[2] For example, Aristotle sometimes uses the idea of bilateral symmetry, an idea which is
more formal than final; it is expressed (e.g. at *IA* 5, 706
b 10) in terms of the supposed superiority of right to left,
front to back, and up to down, a notion which is teleological, to be sure, but not so obviously functional as Aristotle's usual explanation of the final cause. Another sort
of explanation which stands somewhat outside the analysis in
terms of the four causes is that which depends upon analogies
drawn not only on functional grounds between the parts of
different species, or between various biological facts and
the productions of art. The analogy between art and nature
especially transcends the analysis of the causes, for it
is thought to provide one of the major grounds for the teleological understanding of nature. Another form of analogy,

the continuous, appears in the idea of a scale of nature,
from lifeless things, to the highest animate beings. Although
this notion of an ordering of nature is made teleological in
Metaphysics Lambda, for example, it is not so much teleological as 'polar'. Perhaps the origin of these polar and analogical modes of explanation is mathematical, or perhaps it
is mythical and religious; at any rate, a reliance upon polar and analogical arguments is presupposed by Aristotle,
and is not explicitly supported within his explanatory system.

One sort of explanation which Aristotle does not ever give
is a mathematical analysis and explanation; he does not give
equations, he does not give numerical values. He does speak
of proportion and symmetry, but unlike the modern investi-
gator, he does not feel called upon to put numbers into his
proportions. Aristotle does not attempt to calculate quantities, to measure temperatures, volumes, weights, and so on,
even though he sometimes gives a sketch into which such
quantities could be fitted.

It is often said that Aristotle's biological investigations
suffered from the lack of a thermometer and a microscope. This
is probably true of the microscope, which he would no doubt
have used if he had had one. But I doubt that he would have
been much interested in using a thermometer had he had one;
he does not seem to have bothered to use the measuring techniques which were at his disposal, linear measures and weight
measures. Aristotle envisioned the marriage of geometry and
biology, but did not perform the ceremony; he does not seem
even to have envisioned the marriage of arithmetic and biology.

A. DEVELOPMENT AND FUNCTION OF THE PARTS

Aristotle's general account of the parts which may be found
generally in the chordata or 'blooded' animals, or in some
large group of species in this phylum, may be pieced together
from the various biological books. We can, following the
distinction made by Morton BECKNER, find both a genetic account, tracing the development of a particular part or group
of parts, and a functional account, describing the value of
the part in the life of the animal.

The genetic account of the parts given in *GA*, mostly in II.
4-6, overlaps with the explanation of conception, and actually plays a part in that explanation. We might distinguish,
somewhat artificially, between the two explanations on the
ground that at some moment the source of movement for development is *in* the developing organism rather than contin-
guous with the material for the organism. Until the moment
of conception, the source of movement must be regarded as
'external' to the organism which is explained in terms of
that source of movement, because until that moment, that organism does not exist as an individual; after the moment of
conception, the source of movement is within the organism,
continuing as its source of movement. A distinction may also be found in the precise character ascribed to the final
cause: in sexual generation, Aristotle proceeds directly to
the ultimate end, the preservation of the species; in the
account of development, the achievement of each stage is in
itself an end, and the most ultimate end which operates in
the explanation is the achievement of the adult form.

Form again plays a dual role: the achievement of the adult
form is the end of development, and yet the soul, the entity
of the individual in the sense of form, brings about the
development through its nutritive and generative function.
No matter how 'mechanical' a particular analysis may seem,
an explanation is always sought for the fact that a particular movement brings about a particular -- and correct --

change; this explanation can only be in terms of the 'form' of that movement.

The account of the material cause is comparatively devoid of complications. In conception the material was the menstrual fluid; the growing animal is nourished by food from outside. A small problem arises in the account of the transition from conception to development.[4] In the case of the viviparous animals, the first external nourishment comes through the umbilicus, but the first organization is of the heart, and not of the food for the development of the umbilicus. But there is blood in the heart to begin with, and it did not come through the not yet formed umbilicus; blood is nourishment. The solution is stated thus: "As in the seeds of plants there is some such stuff which appears at first to be milky, so in the material of the animal the residue from the first organization (*systasis*) is food (II.4, 740b6)." This food is the material for the growth of the umbilicus (II.7, 745b 26) and perhaps starts the development of some other internal organs. It is significant that Aristotle says that the first food is 'milky', for it is thus thought of as analogous to the milk which feeds the vivipara (mammalia) after birth. Of course the food must be that which is appropriate to the species, and so on.[5]

1. The beginning of embryological development: *pneuma* and the heart

For Aristotle, the heart is the *archē* of the living animal in several senses of the word '*archē*':

1) The heart is the 'beginning' of the body, for it is the first part formed.[6]

2) The heart is the 'origin':
   a) of the blood vessels,[7]
   b) of the entire body, in that it is essential in the process of nutrition. The digestive tract carries out

the process of concoction only to a degree; its product is carried to the heart, where it is turned into
blood, the final food, and moved out to the rest of
the body, where it becomes the parts and feeds them.[8]

3) **The heart is the 'sovereign' of the body,**[9] and this in
several ways:
a) it is the seat of the senses,[10]
b) it is the origin of movement.[11]

Because it is the 'origin' and 'sovereign' it is called the
seat of the nutritive and sensitive soul.[12]

Aristotle argues that it is both evident to observation, and
necessary, that the heart is formed first. The observation
is not quite correct, but is easy enough to make: the backbone and nervous system begin to develop before the heart,
but they are transparent at this stage, and the heart is a
very obvious red spot. The necessity to which Aristotle ap-
peals is a functional necessity, and it is illustrated by a
forceful analogy:

> Once the fetation which has been formed is se-
> parate and distinct from both the parents, it
> must manage for itself, just like a son who has
> set up a house of his own independently of his
> father. That is why it must have an *archē*, from
> which the subsequent ordering of the animal's
> body is derived.[13]

It seems clear from this passage that the heart must be
formed first because it, in turn, forms the other parts, and
is, in general, the *archē* of the individual living body.
PECK, however, suggests a somewhat different account; he
finds that "the heart must be formed first, *because it is
the seat* of the *symphyton pneuma*" (*GA* app. B 11, his italics).
He admits that the italicized words

> do not actually occur in the passage DGA 742-743,
> but they are to be supplied from the doctrine of
> other passages here examined, and we must realize
> that they represent the chief consideration, though
> unexpressed, in Aristotle's mind as he writes the
> present passage (*ibid.*).

PECK supposes that *pneuma* is that for the sake of which the
heart exists, but this is mistaken. Aristotle clearly starts

114

with the belief that the heart is all-important in the living body, then must explain *how* the heart carries out its functions, and how these functions are transferred from parent to offspring. *Pneuma* appears in the *GA* as part of the solution to these problems in explanation; indeed, in *GA* II.6 he is still at some pains to distinguish between the 'breath' sense of *pneuma* and the 'connate' sense (741b37ff). These confusions could not exist if PECK's interpretation were correct.

There is an old puzzle in the interpretation of the role of *pneuma* in Aristotle's solution of the problem of the embryonic heart: is the *pneuma* which differentiates the parts the same *pneuma* which came from the male parent, in the semen, and formed the original systasis?[14] PECK seems to think that the *pneuma* in the two cases *is* the same, for he says (*GA* app. B) that it is "there from the start".[15] Elsewhere[16] he writes: "As the heart concocts, by means of heat, the nourishment into blood...the heart *pneumatizes* the blood; this is what its pulsation indicates: it is a phenomenon similar to that of boiling water in a vessel, when we see bubbles rising up in the liquid: the heart charges the blood with *pneuma*...This *pneuma*, of course, is not the breath which is breathed in from outside, but is *connate* (*symphyton*), there from the start." The strongest version of this position would face great difficulties: *pneuma* would have to be present in man or semen in a certain quantity; if all the *pneuma* present in man is inborn, then that quantity of *pneuma* must have been present in the semen which generated him. But the father could have given only a portion of his *pneuma* to this semen, so the child would have only a small percentage of the *pneuma* of the father, and could pass on to his child only a small percentage of that. Such a view would reintroduce the infinite regress of the preformationists in a particularly virulent form.[17]

A different interpretation of the character and origin of *pneuma* may resolve our puzzle. The starting point for the

investigation must be this statement: "*Pneuma* is present
necessarily, because fluid and hot are present, the one active, the other passive."[18] Aristotle must, in *GA*, propose
either a) that heat and *pneuma* in the heart, originating
from semen, separate further *pneuma* from the fluid nourishment, or b) that the heat and *pneuma* in the heart, originating from the semen, change the fluid nourishment into
further *pneuma*. The first interpretation (a) is supported
by Aristotle's assertion that *pneuma* is present in all water;[19] spontaneous generation occurs when it is enclosed and
heated. Enclosure and heating occur in the heart; would not
the *pneuma* then be separated and become life-giving?

The second interpretation (b) is correct, however. The passage which demonstrates this point comes from *On Respiration:*

> The characteristic beating of the heart... is like
> boiling; for boiling occurs when fluid is pneuma-
> tized by heat. ... In the heart pulsation occurs
> due to the expansion by heat of the liquid food-
> product which continually enters it... there is a
> continuous influx of this fluid, of which the blood
> is constituted... . Pulsation is the pneumatization
> of the heated fluid (*Resp.* 20, 479b27-480a16, HETT's
> translation with some changes).

PECK indeed calls attention to this passage, and to the analogy with boiling, but his account of 'pneumatization' sounds
more like the charging of soda water with carbon dioxide. This
cannot be a correct account of Aristotle's position. But is
boiling a separation of elements or a transformation of elements in Aristotle's chemistry? "Water is the *hyle* of air,
and air the *energeia* of water" (*Phys.* IV.5, 213a2). "Fire,
air, water, and earth are generated from each other, and
each is present in each of these potentially."[20] We remember
that *pneuma* was called 'not air' (*thermos aēr*, *GA* II.2, 736a1);
the 'powers' associated with air are heat and fluidity. We
may suppose that *pneuma* is superheated air, and that the
added heat is the vital heat, or body heat, at first of the
father.

This interpretation of *pneuma* makes comprehensible Aristotle's

116

acceptance of two senses of the word 'pneuma' in one argument, breath and vital spirit.[21] Not only the pneuma in the blood but also the breath can be called superheated air; exhaled breath has a higher temperature than the surrounding atmosphere, and the added heat is in fact 'vital' heat.

Aristotle's notion of the generation of the heart and of the pneuma in the heart seems to run something like this: the pneuma in the foamy semen does its work by means of the vital heat and movement imparted to the pneuma by the nature of the father; the movement and heat are transferred to the material present to the pneuma. This material is a fluid; whether or not it contains air or pneuma already, some of it may be turned into pneuma by the introduced heat; the movement is also transferred. I cannot demonstrate that pneumatization is a change rather than a separation of elements, but this is possible for Aristotle's theory, for pneumatization is compared to boiling. If boiling were simply a separation of elements one could not boil away all the water in a pot. Once all the pneuma or air was gone, continued application of heat would have no effect. Perhaps when Aristotle says that pneuma is present in water (GA III.11, 762a 20) he means nothing more or less than 'potentially' present as the Meteorology and Physics suggest. Aristotle goes on to say (762a24) that as liquids are heated "there is formed a frothy bubble;" the froth should be pneuma which was not present in a gaseous form until the liquid was heated.

According to my interpretation, one could call the pneuma in the heart 'symphyton' if one were very careful about the sense of the word 'symphyton' applied in this case.[22] One might emphasize the 'connate' character of the pneuma, in that it is 'with the nature', but it would be incorrect to emphasize the sense of 'symphyton' which could be translated 'with or in the birth'. At any rate, Aristotle envisages the fluid portions turning into, or becoming, gaseous in character, at least some of them; in Mete. IV.3, the process of concoction is described as one which tends

to solidify the earthy materials as the liquid becomes gas.
It would be reasonable to expect that this separation would
occur in a sphere, around the center of heat, around the developing *pneuma* and blood, and this more solid sphere would
be the first formation of the walls of the primitive heart.

2. Matter and Movement in Embryological Development

> As the parts of the animal to be formed are present
> potentially in the matter, once the source of move-
> ment has been generated one thing follows another
> without interruption, just as in the marvelous
> automatic puppets. And the meaning of the state-
> ment, made by some of the physiologers, about like
> "making its way to like", must be taken to be not
> that the parts of the body move in the sense of
> changing their position, but that while remaining
> in the same position they undergo alteration as
> regards softness, hardness, color, and the other
> differences which belong to the uniform parts; they
> become actually what previously they had been po-
> tentially (*GA* II.5, 741b8-15, after PECK).

The analogy between the changes which occur during conception and embryological development and the changes which
occur in mechanical automata was introduced at II.1, 734b10
(see chapter II.B.3, above), and these automata occur again
in the explanation of animal movement at *MA* 7, 701b1-32
(see III.A.3.c.i., below). It is introduced here to emphasize the continuity of the process of development, once it
begins. One may be tempted to find in it the germ of the
idea of mechanical necessity, but Aristotle distinguishes
immediately the kinds of changes which occur in each case.
The automata, he suggests, change in position only, while
the changes which occur in embryological development are not
primarily changes in location, but qualitative changes. This
is sufficient to distinguish the embryological process from
a mechanical process in the primary sense, and constitutes
the difference in this analogy.
Aristotle does not only wish to distinguish spacial and

118

qualitative processes, he wants to emphasize the teleological aspect of biological change as well. For Aristotle, the automata have a kind of built-in purposive character; their parts have, by design, the potentiality of moving in certain ways, which are actualized when the mechanism is set in motion. Rather than taking the automatic process of the mechanism as a model for the explanation of biological processes, he calls attention to the fact that the mechanism has a builder, and argues that 'nature' similarly *uses* heat and cold as tools in making the organism grow.[23] Heat and cold, in turn, "have the power necessarily to make one thing into this and another into that" (II.6, 743a37). As in my translation of this phrase, so in the Greek, there is an ambiguity: the powers are 'necessary', their activity is 'necessary'. This necessity is a hypothetical or conditional necessity, for heat and cold are understood as necessary for their products, rather than the products being necessitated by the nature of heat and cold, independently of any goal or purpose.

The heat introduced by the seminal residue is proportionate (*symmetros*) to the tasks which it must perform (743 a28). Again, matter and movement are directly related to teleological concepts, since proportionality of power to task is precisely a teleological notion. The analysis becomes still more teleological with the use in explication of the distinction between power and activity.

> That which potentially is cannot be brought into being by a motive agent which does not have the actuality, nor will that which has the actuality make it out of any casual material. No more could a carpenter produce a chest out of anything but wood, and equally without the carpenter no chest will be produced out of the wood (743a22ff).

Not only is the motive agent required to 'have the end', to have whatever the product will become, but also the matter must be 'for' the end -- that is what makes it matter for this particular production.

So the heart, from the beginning, must have the proper *energeia* (actuality, activity). This *energeia* is a *kinesis*,

an active *dynamis*, which may be said to be the nature of
the father, and of the semen, and of the heart, and of the
offspring. The 'nature' is, as an activity, continuous from
parent to offspring. As one finds it in the heart, at the
beginning of embryological development, it is nothing other
than the soul. A part of the body is a part only by presence
of soul (II.5, 741a10), and the heart is the 'ruling' part
from having the activity of all soul. The generative function
is most obviously in operation at every stage; apparently
Aristotle believes that the sensitive faculty develops out
of the generative faculty, but that that development requires the influence of the male (cf. II.3, 736a24ff, and
ch. II.B.5.above).

3. Examples of the explanations of the parts

a) The brain (a 'uniform' part): development and function

The *GA* says only this about the development of the brain:

> On account of the heat of the heart, and to provide
> a corrective to it, the cold causes the brain to
> set, where the blood-vessels terminate above. That
> is why the regions around the head begin to be
> formed immediately after the heart, and bigger than
> the other parts, the brain being large and fluid
> from the outset (II.6, 743b27-32, PECK).

The blood, or product of blood, which becomes the brain, is
thought to be cooled by the surrounding environment, but to
become somewhat harder under the influence of heat (744a13).
Aristotle thinks that the brain is fluid and cold in nature,
and that it becomes smaller and harder as it develops and
ages. In *PA* II.7, 652b22, 653a21, he says that the brain is
a "compound of water and earth". The evidence for this assertion is a kind of analogical experiment: he thinks that
the brain becomes solid and hard under the influence of heat
(for example, when it is cooked), because

120

the earthy substance is left behind after the
water has evaporated owing to the heat. It is just
what happens when pulse (beans, etc.) and other
vegetables are boiled (653a22, after PECK).

The way the heat gets to the head, according to Aristotle,
is this:

there is a great deal of heat and blood in the
region around the heart and lung... . This explains why man is the only animal that stands
upright. As the *physis* of the hot prevails in
the body it induces growth, beginning from the
center along its own line of travel. It is
against great heat that a large supply of fluid
and cold is provided (*PA* II.7, 653a29ff, after
PECK).

Heat and hot substances rise; the hotter they are, the more
they rise. But this thrust must come to an end, and come to
an end by being cooled (even though it has lifted man's body
to an erect position along the way). This might help to explain the fluidity of the brain, for fluid has more natural
heat than solid, and more likely to rise, but it does not
explain the 'fact' that the brain is cold. Indeed, one might
suppose that it would be hot, like the attic of a well-heated
building. Aristotle recognizes this problem in a passage explaining why there is almost no flesh on the head:

If the part surrounding the brain were fleshy,
the effect of the brain would be the very reverse of that for which it is intended: it would
be unable to cool the rest of the body because
it would be too hot itself.[24]

Thus the head is like an attic which is not too well insulated; the blood may be cooled there. A genetic account of
the brain may be constructed from Aristotle's statements
about it (collected above), but the most important material
datum is that it is cold, and this, he says, may be determined by touch (*HA* I.16, 495a5; *PA* II.7, 652a34).

Thus the function of the brain is the cooling of the blood,
and consequently the general preservation of proportion of
heat in the organism. Animals must have heat in them

and everything needs a counterbalance, so that
it may achieve moderation and the mean; for it
is the mean, and not either of the extremes

apart, which has the entity and the *logos*. For
this reason nature has contrived the brain to
counterbalance the region of the heart and the
heat in it.[25]

One might ask, might not the animal have just the right
amount of heat provided by nature, so that no counterbalance
be needed? Two sorts of answers might be suggested within
Aristotle's system: i) the temperature of the environment
varies, and means of both cooling and heating are needed to
counteract the extremes;[26] ii) heat is introduced into the
system from the ingested food, and this must be balanced,
smoothed out.

Just as important for the understanding of Aristotle's account would be the philosophical aspect of his answer: only
those entities which achieve a mean through the balance of
opposites have a *logos* in the primary sense, a ratio of polar
opposites.[27]

For Aristotle, all existing things, and especially all living things, exist as balances between hot and cold, fluid
and solid, and perhaps between other less primitive oppo-
sitions as well. Man achieves this balance between the widest
extremes, for the heat in the heart is greatest in man (*GA*
II.6, 744a30) and thus the brain of man is largest and most
fluid; it makes "the heat and boiling in the heart well-
blended (*eukraton*)" (*PA* II.7, 652b26).

The brain has some subsidiary functions, and is a more or
less accidental agent of some other physiological phenomena.
Hair on the head is generated by the fluidity of the brain
and the sutures of the skull, through which the fluidity presumably is supposed to seep and then to solidify; the function
of hair is the protection of the brain from excesses of cold
and heat.[28] Some of the senses are placed in the head partly
because the brain makes it a congenial location considering
their nature and function,[29] although the brain itself, according to Aristotle, plays no part in sensation. Vision is
placed in the head because the brain is fluid and cold, and
the *physis* (material nature) of the organ of vision is water;

122

also, it is necessary that the most precise sense be where
the blood is purest, for the movement of the heat in the heart
cuts the sensitive function.[30] Indeed, in their embryological
development the eyes are

> produced by the purest part of the liquid around
> the brain being secreted off through those passages
> which are to be observed leading from the eyes to
> the membrane around the brain.[31]

Hearing too, although its material medium is air, benefits by
being placed in the head, "for the so-called empty part is
full of air..., a passage runds from the ears to the area behind the brain."[32] Aristotle, like some Hippocratic writers,
thought that the brain occupied only the front part of the
head; he seems to have thought that the empty back part of the
head acted as a resonating chamber for sounds. The sense of
smell is in the head because of the brain too; Aristotle says
in *Sens.* that this sense is "proper to the region of the brain,
for the matter of what is cold is potentially hot."[33] In this
place he argues that the object of smell is a certain 'smoky
vapor', which might be thought to introduce some heat into the
region, actualizing the potentially hot, and occasioning the
sensation of odors. By contrast, the fact that the organ of
taste is in the head has nothing to do with the brain, according to Aristotle; the mouth, and the tongue, are in the head
for the sake of mobility.[34]

An untoward result of the nature of the brain is the symptom
of runny noses (*rheumata*):

> The occur when the parts around the brain are colder
> than the rightly proportioned blend (*symmetros krasis*).
> As the nourishment exhales upwards through the blood
> vessels, the residue from it becomes cooled due to the
> power (*dynamis*) of this place, and produces fluxes of
> serum and phlegm.[35]

He goes on to compare this process to that which causes the
fall of rain:

> Damp vapor exhales up from the earth and is carried
> into the upper regions by the heat; and when it reaches
> the cold air up aloft, it condenses back again into wa-
> ter owing to the cold, and pours down towards the earth.

Here again, the functional characteristic of the brain is its coldness; here the brain is said to get colder than it really should, causing *rheumata*. This is not the only place where Aristotle compares physiological processes with meteorological phenomena. then adds that menstruation seems to follow the same cycle, and for the same reasons. A good deal is made of these periods, and other related periods, in *GA* IV.10, 777b 17ff, and *GA* V.3, 784a12, although not as much mysticism enters the discussion as in Plato's *Timaeus*, for example at 41D. The brain also plays a part in causing sleep:

> It cools the onflow of blood which comes from the food... and weighs down the part where it is (that is why when a person is sleepy his head is weighed down), and causes the hot substance to escape below together with the blood...[36]

Without commenting on the oddity of the physics implied in this passage (Aristotle's peculiar physics is fairly well known), we can add that these peripheral results of the nature of the brain may be considered as part of its function to the extent that they are 'for the better'; sleep is clearly 'for the better', for it is a resting of sensation, and evidently Aristotle believes that it plays a part in good digestion. Runny noses might do some good, but whether they do or not belongs to the study of diseases (*PA* II.7, 653a9).

Aristotle's concept of the brain is very different from ours, and thus can be instructive. He supposes that the brain is a 'uniform' part, which means approximately that it does not divide into further organic parts, that it is simply tissue. If we were to use this criterion, we would tend to think of the brain as the most complex part of the body, rather than as a simple part, for it is comprised of a very large number of constituent organic parts. Starting from the supposition that the brain is not complex, Aristotle cannot reach a concept of the brain as the organ of the complex functions which we ascribe to it.

The modern reader of Aristotle may well be surprised that he makes the heart the center of perception and movement, espe-

cially if he considers the fact that Plato in the *Timaeus*
(44d, 69e, 90a) had already said that the brain was the seat
of reason, and that the Hippocratic medical writers had tended to think of the brain as the seat of senstation (*Morb. Sacr.*,
Coac. XXVIII [Littré V.697]). But Plato had also argued that
many of the functions of the soul were to be located in the
heart (and some in the stomach). Aristotle begins by supposing the soul to be more unified than Plato had thought, and
if it is unified, it should have one principle origin or
archē. Plato had made the brain the seat of reason, but Aristotle supposes that the active reason, at least, does not
need a physical basis at all (*de An*. III.4-6), so the brain
need not serve this function. Several bits of evidence point
to the heart as the seat of the soul: philosophically, it
seems more satisfying that the psychical center be at the
topical center (and the brain is at an extremity); also, the
beating of the heart must indicate something important. If
it is not understood that the heart serves as a pump, then
one might associate this movement with the animal functions
of the body, in a more general way. The brain, on the other
hand, does not seem to be active in any way. Finally, the
heart seems to appear first in embryological development; the
fact that the brain is a close and dramatic second does not
impress Aristotle sufficiently with the possibility that it
might serve more than a cooling function.
He comes to the conclusion that the brain cools the blood
more or less *faute de mieux*; he cannot accept the evidence
which had been introduced to give it a more nearly correct
function, and so he proceeds on the phenomena as he has observed them. The brain seems 'cool', and yet well-supplied
with blood, which is normally 'hot'. Given that combination
of facts, and the supposed simplicity of the organ, the
brain seems capable only of serving a colling function. This
is not to say that it is not important, for Aristotle is in-
tensely aware of the importance of the maintenance of a
proper bodily temperature, even if his reasons for this

125

awareness may seem to us rather primitive.

b) The viscera: uniform/non-uniform

The viscera (*splagchna*) include heart, kidneys, liver, spleen,
and lungs, and the digestive tract. They are 'uniform' in the
sense that they can be divided into pieces which still have
the same name, but are non-uniform 'in respect of shape and
form' (*PA* II.1, 647a33). Taking this as a point about language, he means that *a* heart or *a* kidney is, when divided,
'heart' or 'kidney', but is no longer *a* heart or kidney.
Morphologically, he means that these parts are, each of them,
constructed of the same tissue throughout, but they are not,
for all that, amorphous, for their structure has a functional
role, just as their tissue has.
The viscera are similar to each other in these respects,
Aristotle explains, because they are all generated in the
same way and of the same material:

> the nature of them all is blood, because they are
> situated on the channels of the blood vessels and
> on the points of ramification. All these viscera
> except the heart may be compared to the mud which
> a running stream deposits; they are as it were
> deposits left by the current of blood in the blood
> vessels (*PA* II.1, 647b1-4, after PECK).

> The viscera... have been generated necessarily at
> the inner ends of the blood vessels, because
> moisture necessarily must make its way out, and
> this moisture is bloody; as it is set and soli-
> dified the body of the viscera is generated from
> it. Therefore they are bloody, and they all have
> the same nature of body, though it is different
> from that of the other parts.[37]

Aristotle thus claims that the 'matter' of viscera is blood;
the moving cause is vaguely introduced through two images
which differ in accordance with their assumptions concerning
the positions of the organs. It may be that Aristotle believed that both processes operate in the generation of the
viscera. On the one hand, the 'mud bank' analogy is supported

126

by the assertion that the blood vessels traverse all the
viscera except the heart (*HA* III.3, 513a22); on the other,
extrusion is the normal mode of generating parts (see note
24 above). In any case, Aristotle's genetic account of these
parts is sketchy at best.

It is of special interest, however, that he closely relates
the two senses of the word 'nature' (*physis*) in both passages.
In the first passage, all the viscera are said to resemble
the heart in being uniform materially but non-uniform in
form because they have the same nature of material as the
heart. Thus it seems that the form of the product depends
upon the nature of the material, which is all the more remarkable when one considers the fact that Aristotle believes
the blood to be the material for the entire body, and to
carry the form of the entire animal.

From the point of view of a teleological explanation, there
are more problems raised by a rather insistent application
of the principle of bilateral symmetry of these internal organs (*PA* III.7, 669b13-670a8; LEWES, pp. 310ff). The lungs
and kidneys are obviously double, just as the brain and sense
organs are double; the problems arise with the heart, and
with the liver and spleen.

He insists that the heart in larger animals has *three* chambers
(e.g., at *PA* III.4, 666b22). Many people (e.g., TRACY, pp.
188-9) take this as a more or less obstinate application of
the doctrine of the mean in the face of observations to the
contrary, but this is a mistake, or partly a mistake. He has
a rather strong *a priori* reason to find an even number of
chambers in the heart: bilateral symmetry; and this could
easily override the considerations which he uses to support
his ultimate position. However, as T.H. HUXLEY showed almost
one hundred years ago,[38] the manner in which Aristotle dissected was likely to lead to the mistaking of the right
auricle as a part of the vena cava. Once this observation was
made, the theoretical considerations noted by TRACY (p. 188,
with note 48) and many others were thought to override the

principle of bilateral symmetry. Observation overrides theory here, and the *a priori* considerations are brought into explicate the observations.

In the case of the liver and spleen, the principle of bilateral symmetry is almost solely responsible for the existence of the spleen in some species, it seems:

> In those animals which necessarily have a spleen it seems to be a sort of bastard liver; in those which have it but not necessarily (they have a rather small one as if by way of a token, σημείου χάριν) the liver is patently double, and the larger part of it tends to lie towards the right... Because the liver is placed rather to the right the nature of the spleen has been generated, so that in a way it is necessary, but not very (ἀναγκαῖον μὲν πῶς, μὴ λίαν δ'εἶναι), for all animals (*PA* III.7, 669b27ff).

So Aristotle interprets the liver and spleen as two sides of the same organ, in spite of the fact that their functions vary, on the ground of bilateral symmetry.

In connection with this passage, I would like to comment on the notion of a 'token', and on the peculiar phrase 'necessary but not very'. The word 'σημεῖον', like the words in English which translate it, 'sign' and 'token', is a noun which needs some completing description, in English a phrase, in Greek a word or two in the genetive case. Aristotle usually provides such a descriptive phrase: physical characteristics are taken to be σημεῖα of psychological characteristics in analysis of physiognomy (*HA* I.9, 491b15ff); mist is a 'sign' of fine weather in meteorology (*Mete*. I.9, 346b34), and so on. It is an easy step to the frequent usage of σημεῖον in the sense of 'evidence',[39] but the evidence is always evidence *of* something. Of what is the 'very small' spleen a sign or evidence? The locution is repeated at *PA* III.7, 670b12, where the sorts of animals which have this token spleen are mentioned; at IV.10, 689b5, it is said that nearly all quadrupeds have a tail, but in some it is not large, it is there (according to BÜSSEMAKER's reading) 'σημεῖου ἕνεκα' (cf. *HA* II.10, 502b34). A comparable use of the word may be

found at *HA* IX.5, 611a31, where the small bumps of horns of
the yearling stag are called σημεῖα. In this case one may
guess that they are signs of the great antlers to come, but
the tiny spleen and small tail are not quite analogous, for
they do not portend a later development.

The modern biologist would be likely to regard such parts as
are present but apparently not functioning as signs of the
evolutionary ancestry of the species; in man, the appendix
and the pineal gland have sometimes been described as 'vestigial' in this way.[40] But this cannot be Aristotle's idea,
for he does not believe that there has been a descent of
the species in this sense.

Although there is no clear statement by Aristotle to this
effect, we may speculate that he regarded σημεῖα as signs
of the membership of this species in a larger genus in which
these parts do, as a rule, have a function. That larger genus
would be that of 'blooded animals', perhaps, which could be
said to produce this organ or that 'necessarily', as the
normal outcome of the process of generation shared by the
entire genus, or in the sense that having this organ is included in the definition of the genus.[41]

The second aspect of the passage *PA* III.7, 669b27ff, which
may be remarked, is the statement that the spleen is 'necessary but not very' (ἀναγκαῖον μὲν πῶς, μὴ λίαν δ'εἶναι,
670a2). Our analysis of the expression 'σημείου χάριν' suggests that the necessity is formal, that the animal must
have a spleen because the principle of bilateral symmetry
and the *logos* of the entity demand it, in spite of the fact
that the organ does not have a function in this species. If
the organ were functional in this species, then it would be
conditionally necessary in the ordinary way.

A difficulty for this interpretation of the spleen as formally necessary may be posed by the statement, "The spleen is
present in those which have it κατὰ συμβεβηκὸς ἐξ ἀνάκης",
(670a30) which suggests that the necessity is one which
arises within or as a result of the process of generation.

PECK, for example, translates the phrase which we quote in Greek as follows, "*of necessity* in the sense of being an incidental concomitant", which does convey the usual notion of 'συμβεβηκός', "coming together", as an 'accident' in the Aristotelian sense. In the context, the spleen is compared to the heart, liver, and lungs (where present); these organs are conditionally necessary in the strong sense, for without them the animal could not live. The spleen, where it functions, assists in digestion by drawing off 'residual humors' from the stomach. Apparently the worst that could happen without a functioning spleen would be a poor digestion. There are reasons for the existence of the spleen, conditional reasons, but the conditional necessity is not strong (it is not a '*conditio sine quā non*'); if the spleen is necessary, it is necessary 'for the better'. Although the spleen is normally generated to serve a function, sometimes there is no discoverable function; in this case, it is generated as a part of a normal generative process common to the genus to which the species belongs. In this way the necessity is both formal and accidental, but not very necessary. If this account seems somewhat cryptic, the reader may be assured that the concept of necessity will be examined in greater detail in chapter IV.B, below.

We may rapidly summarize the normal functions of the viscera generally. We have already noted Aristotle's ideas about the functions of the heart; the lungs, he supposes, have the function of cooling the body with the external breath, in species which need such cooling (*PA* III.6, 668b33ff; *Respiration*). To be sure, he does say that the lung serves "the *archē* in the heart" (*PA* III.3, 665a17), which might be identified with the *pneuma* in the heart; by a bit of scholarly legerdemain one might make Aristotle say, however obscurely, that the lungs help the external *pneuma* become internal *pneuma*, and thus to make him approach the modern concept of respiration. This would, however, be untrue to the evidence, for he argues in the *Respiration* against

130

theories which approach more closely to the modern point of
view, the theories of Anaxagoras and Diogenes of Apollonia.
Aristotle remarks that there is no name given to the group
of animals which have lungs, but that there ought to be,
"for the fact that they have a lung belongs to their *ousia*"
(*PA* III.6, 669b10). It is one of the defining characteristics
of such a group; it belongs to their *eidos*, or rather, such
animals form an *eidos* because of this characteristic. One
might note that Aristotle avoids inventing a name for this
class of animals, in spite of the fact that he thinks that
there should be one.

All the viscera below the diaphragm have one odd function in
common, Aristotle believes:

> They are, as it were, anchor-lines thrown out to
> the body through the extended parts..., like rivets
> they fasten the great blood vessel and the aorta to
> the sides of the body (*PA* III.7, 670a11ff).

The reference to 'anchor-lines' may remind us of the Orphic
notion that the body is generated in the manner of the plaiting of a net (*GA* II.1, 734a19), or even more definitely of
plaiting or twining of the aorta and 'great blood vessel'
which binds the front and back of the body together (*PA* III.
5, 668b20).[42] Besides holding the insides together, the
liver and spleen are involved in the concoction of food
(670a21), and the kidneys "assist with the residue which is
excreted into the bladder" (III.9, 672a1ff).

The digestive tract is explained with the use of a functional
analogy:

> The natural heat comes into play in the upper and
> lower gut, which effect the concoction of the food
> by its aid... . There must be passages through
> which, as from a manger, the body as a whole may
> receive its food from the stomach and from the
> system of the intestines... . Practically all ani-
> mals, and unmistakeably those which move about,
> have a stomach or bag -- an earth inside them, as
> it were -- in order to get the food out of this.[43]

Aristotle does not further enlarge on his explanation of the
digestive tract, although he does often describe the anatomy,
or the process of digestion.[44] He seems to suppose that the

two analogies in this passage are so powerful, so convincing that nothing else need be said. The analogy of the manger is introduced to make a point relating to function and structure: if the stomach is the source of the food for the body, there has to be some way to get the food out, just as there are slits in the sides of the manger. He looks for 'passages' and finds them, it seems, in the blood vessels which rather copiously come to the wall of the stomach, as they do (to more effect) in the walls of the small intestine. With the analogy of stomach and earth, Aristotle's scientific imagination has touched just the most enlightening point, for this is the basis of our kinship with all natural beings, including plants, that we take nourishment 'as from the earth'. He uses the same central notion in a number of related analogies. For example, the system of blood vessels is compared with an irrigation system. In *PA* III.5, 668a14, 'nature' is understood as a gardener or farmer who traces out the irrigation channels in the body; flesh is generated by the smallest vessels being clogged with the solid portions of the blood. In fat animals, the blood vessels get especially clogged, "like water-channels choked with slush" (*HA* III. 4, 515a22). We have already noted the formation of viscera as 'deposits like those of mud which a stream deposits' (*PA* II.1, 647b3ff) and the description of multiple fetuses as lined up to their individual umbilici as to runnels in a garden (*GA* II.7, 746a16).

Plato had already compared the digestive functions of the soul with the life of plants, to the point of describing the blood vessels as an irrigation system (*Timaeus* 77C); he had also compared the stomach to a manger (*Tim.* 70D). But although Aristotle uses these analogies, and develops them, he avoids, for the most part, the wilder sorts of speculation found in this part of the *Timaeus*; he does not compare the appetitive part of the soul to an untamed beast, likely to cause tumult and clamor (70E), nor does he describe the liver as shiny,

132

that the influence proceeding from the reason should
make impressions of its thoughts upon the liver,
which would receive them like a mirror and give back
visible images (71B).

Aristotle, well aware of the passage and probably borrowing
from it, not only avoids its excesses, but also avoids the
ridicule which he could so easily have exercised.

c) The non-uniform (*anomoiomerē*) parts

The non-uniform parts are those which, when divided, no longer
have the same name; they are organic parts which are composed
of more than one kind of tissue. Of such parts, we will discuss in some detail the account of the organs of locomotion,
and we will briefly discuss the general account of the organs
of perception, leading toward an account of the variations in
the organs of perception from one species to another.

i) The organs of locomotion

The organs of local movement are excellent examples of true
non-uniform parts, since they are non-uniform both in matter
and in structure. In the 'blooded' animals they are composed
of bones and marrow, sinew and flesh, blood vessels and blood,
skin and nails, hair or feathers or the like. Structurally,
a part of a leg is no longer 'leg'; organs of local movement
are essentially articulated, and without such articulation
would no longer be genuine organs (*MA* 1, 698a15-b7). As the
structure is complicated, so too would be an account of the
generation of such organs, were Aristotle to provide an exhaustive account. One would have to start with an account of
the generation of the *homoiomerē* which compose the part, then
give an account of the generation of the arrangement of those
parts. We have mentioned aspects of the account of the generation of flesh and blood; we have not, however, sufficiently
noted the most important function which Aristotle assigns to
flesh: "'animal' exists in virtue of the sensory part, and
flesh and its analogue are sensory" (*PA* II.5, 651b4). Since

133

'sensory' (*aisthētikon*) is part of the definition of 'animal', and touch is the most primitive, most basic sense, flesh or its analogue is formally necessary for the existence of an animal. This argument is worked in the other direction too: Aristotle finds that sponges appear to be fleshy, so he argues that they have the sense of touch, and thus are animals (*HA* I.1, 487b10). Flesh, as the organ of touch, is so important that Aristotle even asserts that all the other parts exist for the sake of flesh.[45] But Aristotle does not recognize the importance of flesh, as muscle, for locomotion. The movement of the limbs he ascribes to the 'sinews', which might include the harder and stronger muscles, but not the soft 'fleshy' parts.

The embryological development of the sinews and bones is discussed in *GA* II:

> The sinews and bones are formed by the agency of
> the internal heat; hence bones (like earthenware)
> cannot be dissolved by fire; they have been baked
> as it were in an oven by the heat present at their
> formation (II.6, 743a17-21, PECK).

The contrast in the generation of flesh and bones is rather neat. Both are formed from the same material, approximately, but the moving cause is different: flesh is formed by the agency of the external cold, while bone is formed by agency of the internal heat. This contrast is meant to account for their resultant differences in character, so far as matter and movement are concerned. The argument in the case of bones and sinews is supported by a telling analogy between bones and earthenware. Aristotle appears to claim that the flesh and other surrounding parts form a kind of insulated oven, the vital heat baking the ceramic bones. Thus, since flesh is formed by cold, it may be dissolved by fire, but since bone is formed by heat, it cannot be dissolved by heat.[46]

There is a difference in the materials as well as in the agency between flesh and bone, noted both in *GA*[47] and in *de An.*: "The mixture of the elements which go to make the flesh has not the same ratio as that which makes the bone" (I.4,

134

408a15, HETT). Wholes, such as bones, "do not consist of the
elements arranged at random, but in a certain ratio (*logos*)
and with some principle of composition" (I.5, 410a2, HETT).
Aristotle goes on to quote Empedocles on the matter (see Ch.
I.D.1, above).

The account of marrow presents a problem of theoretical interest in regard to Aristotle's concept of necessity. He
gives a reasonably clear genetic account of the marrow: the
part of the blood which, in the embryo, goes to make bone
does not all actually become bone. Some is shut up inside
the bones and is gradually concocted by the heat: it is the
fatty part of the blood which is separated off, and becomes
some form of fat, depending on the species of animal. No particular function is assigned to the non-spinal marrow, except
perhaps the further feeding of the growth of the bones (*PA*
II.6, 652a11). The spinal marrow, however, is said to have
two quite different functions: a) it holds the vertebrae together, while allowing flexibility of the spine; b) its heat
helps counterbalance the coldness of the brain. In accounting
for the possibility of performing these functions, Aristotle
runs into an unusual contradiction in his account of the nature of spinal marrow.

> a) The spinal marrow cannot possibly be of a (fatty
> or suety) nature because it has to be continuous
> and to pass without a break right through the whole
> spine which is divided into separated vertebrae; if
> it were fatty or suety it could not hold together
> as well as it does, but it would be either brittle
> or fluid (*PA* II.6, 651b33ff, PECK).

> b) The marrow is hot in nature, as is shown by the
> fact that it is greasy and fat. That is the real
> reason why the spinal marrow is continuous with
> the brain. Nature is always contriving to set next
> to anything that is excessive a reinforcement of
> the opposite nature (II.7, 652a27ff, after PECK).

No minor textual 'corrections' could resolve the opposition
between these passages. In the first, the marrow of the spine
is not fatty, in the second it is. Both contentions are
argued through several lines of text. If passage a) had stood
alone in the text one might have supposed that Aristotle

135

regarded purpose as over-riding material factors; the function might be said to 'make' the material change its nature. If passage b) had stood alone, one might argue that it is evidence for the close working together of matter and end. Given both passages, the evidence is rather for a confusion on Aristotle's part. It is not just a question of his contradicting himself on the nature of marrow. He seems even to think of the relationship between matter and end in both the ways stated. This raises a serious problem in the interpretation of Aristotle's analysis according to the 'causes', and the problem is raised by his own lack of precision in the use of that analysis.

There are no particular problems which I intend to discuss now concerning the other uniform parts which constitute the organs of local movement. Aristotle lists nails, hooves, talons, and the like, as well as skin and hair and their analogues, as uniform parts which make up these organs. We may note again that the *neuroi* ('sinews') perform the functions which we ascribe to muscles and sinews together. He notes that they hold the bones together, and that they are abundant in the shoulders, arms, hams, and heart.[48]

Aristotle's genetic account of the organs of movement as articulated wholes is especially interesting. He has two approaches to this account in the *PA* (the question is not discussed in *GA*). Both of the *PA* passages are more directly concerned with the explanation of variations between species; among chordates some of the most striking variations are in these organs, wings, arms, legs, feet, hands, fins, tails, and so on.

In *PA* IV.10, 686a24-688a11, Aristotle compares the stature and natural position of man with those of other animals, particularly other chordates. The theme of this singular essay on the unity and diversity of animal forms, and on the scale of nature, is that all animals apart from adult man are 'dwarf-like' in comparison to man. Aristotle finds that children are 'dwarf-like' for a while, *HA* VIII.1, 588b1. In

136

regard to the organs of local movement, this dwarf-likeness
of inferior species has the following effect:

> When the bodily part and its weight become ex-
> cessive, the body must lurch forward to the ground;
> for safety's sake, nature has provided forefeet in-
> stead of arms and hands (686a32-35).

> If the heat which raises the organism wanes and the
> earthy matter waxes, then the animals' bodies wane,
> and they will be many-footed (686b29-30).

Rather than evolution, Aristotle thinks in terms of devolution;
the best possible thing to be, for an animal, is a man; to be
anything else is to be something inferior, something less
good. The same assumption seems to be the driving force behind certain post-Lamarkian evolutionary theories too, but
they suppose that the best comes last, while Aristotle thinks
that the best comes first. How could that which is better
come from that which is less good? As DESCARTES says in *Me-
ditation* III, "It is manifest by the natural light that there
must be at least as much reality in the efficient and total
cause as in its effect". This principle was tacitly presupposed by both Plato and Aristotle, and became explicit later
in Plotinus and medieval philosophers.

Aristotle does not emphasize the 'chain of being' aspect of
this passage; he does not explain the existence of inferior
species on the basis of a need for a variety of species to
make up a world. To be sure, in the *Politics* he says, "As
nature makes nothing purposeless or in vain, all animals
must have been made by nature for the sake of men" (I.8,
1256b20, BARKER), to the considerable dismay of some contemporary ecologists, I might add. But in the passage in *PA*
Aristotle is chiefly interested in explaining the differences
between species, rather than in explaining the existence of
different species.

In inferior species, Aristotle seems to suppose, the material
available permits the actualization of only a limited proportion of man's characteristics, and nature does the best
possible with the material available. Since hands would be

an inferior arrangement for animals which must use their forefeet for support, the forefeet are thus adjusted to the mode of life made necessary by the failure of the natural heat and the relative predominance of earthy material. At any rate, that is what he says here.

The relationship between the mode of life and the resultant form is clarified in a later passage, *PA* IV.12, 692b3-695b1. Aristotle here discusses variations within the genus of birds, particularly variations in legs, claws, talons, and beaks. The various formations in various species are, he says,

> the necessary result of the process of their de-
> velopment. There is earthy substance in the bird's
> body which courses along and issues out and turns
> into parts that are useful for weapons of offense.
> When it courses upwards it produces a good hard
> beak, or a large one; if it courses downwards it
> produces spurs on the legs or makes the claws on
> the feet large and strong. But it does not pro-
> duce spurs and large claws simultaneously, for
> this residual substance would be weakened if it
> were scattered about. Again, sometimes this sub-
> stance makes the legs long; and in some birds, in-
> stead of that, it fills in the spaces between the
> toes. Thus it is of necessity that water-birds are
> web-footed... . But they also conduce to a good
> end and are meant to assist the birds in their daily
> life (694a22-b8, after PECK).

"Courses along" and "issues out" hardly adds up to a genetic account, but these words are at least an indication that Aristotle supposes that he really ought to try to give such an account. In fact, he puts rather a lot of weight on them, for they are the major ground for saying that 'water-birds are necessarily web-footed'. Of course that phrase by itself might mean several different things: a) it might mean that 'web-footed' is part of the definition of 'water-bird', so that a non-web-footed bird wouldn't count as a water-bird, even if one found it swimming somehow; b) it might mean that webbed feet are necessary to the survival of swimming water-birds, which might be true; c) it might mean that internal processes associated with the nutritive-generative soul bring about the development of webbed feet as a consequence

138

of their growth. It is plain from the passage that Aristotle
means the last, and then that he adds a weak sense of conditional necessity rather than the strong sense (b). To say
the least, he has not demonstrated the point that webbed
feet are a necessary consequence of the development of water-
birds, but he must suppose that this is in principle demonstrable.

Aristotle says a great deal about the functioning of the organs of local movement.[49] The *MA* is particularly rich in its
suggestions concerning the relationships of various parts of
Aristotle's philosophy; it has been mentioned rather frequently in regard to the psychological problems discussed
therein, for it is a contribution to the philosophy of action,
as it is called today.[50] Although I intend to discuss this
treatise more fully elsewhere, I will briefly comment here
on the physiological aspects of Aristotle's explanation of
animal movement in the *MA*.

The *MA* uses several analogies, the four causes, and the distinction between *dynamis* and *energeia*, in its account of the
physiology of animal movement. Aristotle insists first upon
the mechanical requirement of the proper leverage conditions.
There must, he says, be an external point which remains relatively unmoved; mice on loose soil and people on sand make
headway with difficulty; a boatman who pushes on something
external to the boat moves the boat easily, but can never
move it if he pushes on something within the boat itself. He
adds an analogy between man and the universe, which only
raises problems in the present context, without explaining
anything.

In order to give a picture of the way in which the leverage
may operate internally Aristotle uses the analogy of the
'marvelous automatic puppets' already familiar from the *GA*.[51]
The question is, how can a small alteration result in a large
change of movement?

> Animals move themselves and the automatic puppets
> move themselves, after a small movement is generated;

> the strings are released and they strike one an-
> other; and the toy wagon, when the one riding on
> it moves it in a straight line, moves itself in
> a circle because it has unequal wheels... . Animals
> have similar organs, the nature of sinews and bones.
> The latter correspond to the wooden pieces and the
> iron, the sinews are like strings which cause the
> movement when loosened and released. [52]

In the puppets, a small movement generates a bigger movement, because there is 'stored energy', as we would put it, and the small movement releases the energy. But Aristotle also thinks of it in terms of leverage, as can be seen by his reference in the context to the activity of the rudder of a boat (7, 701b27; see n. 42 above). As in the *GA*, the answer involves a 'dynamic' analysis, an analysis which makes much use of the notions of active and passive powers both in the analogue, the puppets, and in that which is to be explained. The parts of the body which are involved in local movement change easily from fluid to solid and the reverse under the influence of heat and cold; a small variation in the heart, and each part acts upon the next, effecting both alteration and local movement.

> Since the passive and active have the sort of
> nature which we have often said, whenever it hap-
> pens that one is active and the other passive,
> and neither fails to fulfill its definition, im-
> mediately the one acts and the other is acted
> upon. [53]

As in the *GA pneuma* is the essential factor; here it is its potentiality for expansion and contraction which makes it suitable for effecting movement.

The generation of animal movements proceeds, according to the *MA*, in the following steps:

1) A perception, imagination, or thought, of a real or apparent good or evil, occurs. Perception is already a physiological alteration, and "imagination and thought have the power of their objects" (7, 701b20). Pleasant and painful objects cause heat and cold in the heart or elsewhere in the body (7, 701b28; 8, 702a2ff).

2) Heat and cold are also spacial alterations, in that heat

140

expands and cold contracts; *pneuma* is especially sensitive
to the influence of heat and cold. This is especially true
in the heart, the *archē* of perception, imagination, thought,
and movement (8, 702a22; 9, 703a3).

3) *Pneuma* causes the sinews to contract or expand, rotating
the limbs and the parts of the limbs about the joints.

4) Local movement of the animal results, and the (apparent)
good is grasped for, or the (apparent) evil is avoided.

The teleological aspect of Aristotle's account of movement
has ofent been emphasized, but usually in relation to the
Nicomachean Ethics, where it is most obviously human intentional action which is at issue. The *MA* makes it quite clear
that even where intention does not come into play, the real
or apparent good is still a kind of unmoving mover. The object of desire is the source of movement in this sense; however, there is the source of movement within the animal itself, for the first movement is a movement in the animal.

One may ask why the animal moves in this way, rather
than pursuing evil and eschewing the good. The first part of
the answer must be that that is how it is constructed; the
second part of the answer must be that it is constructed thus
because it is better thus. This evaluation seems to Aristotle
to be irreducible, and any attempt to eliminate this evaluation seems misguided and wrong.

> The animal must be understood to be constructed
> like a well-governed city, for when order is once
> established in the city, there is no need for a
> separate monarch which has to be present for each
> activity; each individual does his own work as
> ordered, and one activity follows another from
> custom (*ethos*). In animals this comes about by
> nature; each of their parts is naturally so con-
> structed as to do its own work, so that it is not
> necessary for the soul to be in each part, but as
> it is in some origin (*archē*) of the body, the
> other parts live by natural attachment to this
> and do their work naturally (703a29-b2).

This analogy, quite comparable to the analogy of soul and
state in Plato's *Republic*, and reminiscent of the political
analogy of the universe in *Met*. Lambda 10,[54] powerfully

brings to our attention the attempt which Aristotle makes
to unify his view of nature by means of organic concepts. It
may be that the image of the state which is here proposed
developed in earlier philosophers from an attempt to understand the state from a biological point of view (cf. GUTHRIE,
In the Beginning pp. 102ff). Aristotle is ready to accept
the implications of this organic view of the state without
searching too much for its origin; the analogy returns to
its source, perhaps, as Aristotle applies the organic picture
of the state to the psychophysiology of the animal in local
movement. He is aware of a distinction between state and animal in this analogy: the individuals who compose the state
act, for the most part, from *ethos* (custom, habit), while the
parts of animals act, for the most part, from nature. This
would be particularly true of those parts which seem to act
more or less independently of volition.[55] These parts are the
heart and the sexual organs (cf. *Timaeus* 91b); they acted
non-rationally, but not dysteleologically of course.
Our investigation of the locomotive organs has led us somewhat away from the strictly biological mode of explanation,
and into the philosophy of action. I have made this excursion
a brief one, but it should be sufficient to show where Aristotle marks the border between natural philosophy and moral
philosophy. Although a teleological explanation may be given
in either natural philosophy or moral philosophy, Aristotle
does move from functional activity in the one area to intentional activity in the other. The practical syllogism
appears in the *MA*, as it does in the *EN*, and it does not
make much sense to suppose that spiders and sparrows (*Phys.*
II.8) make up practical syllogisms in order to arrive at
their action. At the same time, the distinctions made between voluntary, involuntary, and non-voluntary action in *EN*
seem to ride on the existence of a theory of non-intentional
animal movement. Aristotle assumes the possibility of a man
acting in the way that spiders do, when they build a nest,
from '*ethos*' or (we would tend to say) from instinct; if men,

142

as well as animals, act in accordance with their natures,
then one has to have a theory of moral responsibility which
takes this fact into account. But now we are wandering into
the heart of moral philosophy.

ii) The organs of perception, especially the eyes

The organs of perception are non-uniform parts too, at least
most of them are. Aristotle's explanation of these organs will
be treated in a rather summary fashion here, for this section
is intended mostly as an introduction to the discussion of
the variations in these parts in the following section.

Perception (*aisthēsis*) may be investigated in two quite
different ways. One may carry out a 'psychological' or essentially introspective investigation of the phenomena of
awareness; Aristotle does psychology in this sense in several
works, especially in the *de Anima* and in the *de Sensu*, and
touches on this aspect of perception only in passing in the
zoological books.[56] One may also study the physiology of the
perceptual process in various species of animals, and the
relationship of this physiology to behavior. Investigations
of this kind have again come into favor; contemporary psychologists may be both surprised and pleased to learn that,
despite his teleological bent, Aristotle carried out essentially behavioral investigations of a number of species. To
be sure, he is not experimental in the modern sense, but many
contemporary psychologists would say that he was pursuing
the right direction of research.
The generation of the various sense organs is discussed
briefly. The organ of touch, Aristotle supposes, is flesh or
its analogue:

> As food oozes through the bloodvessels and passages
> in each part, like water in unbaked earthenware,
> flesh or its analogue is formed; it is the cold
> which sets flesh, and that is why fire dissolves
> it.[57]

We have already mentioned this passage, and discussed the
generative theory involved, at the beginning of the previous

section (III.A.3.c.i). We may add that taste is closely related to touch, partially because its organ is fleshy in
character; possibly Aristotle supposes that the generation
of the tongue proceeds in the same way, since its material
is similar.[58] The analogy of 'oozing' is not particularly
helpful; Aristotle is obviously at a loss to know quite what
to say on the matter.

He does not give a special account of the generation of
noses or ears because they do not have any special 'body' of
their own; these organs are simply

> passages connecting with the outer air, full of
> connate *pneuma*, terminating at the blood vessels
> around the brain leading from the heart (*GA* II.6,
> 744a2-5).

He does say some rather odd things about the sense of smell
in *Sens*. 5, 444a8ff. For one thing, he distinguishes between
'functional' smells, smells having to do with the preservation of the organism, which all animals share, or most of
them anyway, and smells which are pleasant for their own
sake, smelled only by man or chiefly so. He claims that this
second sort of odor has the function of preserving man's
health; although the passage is by no means clear, it seems
to say that smelling pleasant odors operates against runny
noses. For another thing, the sense of smell is closely related to the brain in this passage, which runs counter to
the theory that the heart is the center of perception, not
the brain. Finally, he does not mention *pneuma* in this passage.

In the *de Anima*, at II.8, 420a13, the ears, at least, are
said to be full of 'συμφύη ἄηρα'. This is clear reference
to the middle ear, and seems to indicate that Aristotle knew
of the eardrum but not of the Eustachian tube. 'Συμφύη ἄηρα'
means 'connate air', which is just about what '*symphyton
pneuma*' means; however, there is an important difference
which must be noted. Aristotle in *GA* II.3, not many pages
before he says that there is *symphyton pneuma* in the ear and
nose, has made *pneuma* central in his account of generation,

144

and made it close to identical with a physical basis of soul.
In the *de Anima*, Aristotle defends hylomorphism and does not
mention *pneuma*; ἀηρα at 420a13 is rather neutral by comparison.
According to the theory propounded by F. NUYENS, this difference might be understood as evidence for the idea that Aristotle had given up the theory of *pneuma* between the time that
he wrote *GA* II and *de An*. II; according to the theory which
makes the *GA* later than *de An*., once *pneuma* was introduced
as an explanatory concept, Aristotle finds himself applying
it even in cases which had already an acceptable alternative,
as in the case of the contents of the ear. *Pneuma* becomes the
special body of hearing, instead of plain air.

Vision is discussed in the *de Anima* without any discussion
of the organ of vision, the eye; in *Sens*. Aristotle is careful to refute various theories of vision, but he says little
more about the eye than that its 'medium' or special body is
'water' (2, 438b8). *Insomn*. 2 has a number of rather peculiar
things to say about vision, which I have discussed in *Phronesis*
13, 1968. But the most complete account of the eyes is to be
found in the *GA*, for Aristotle gives a brief genetic account
in book II, and an explanation of the variations in eyes, as
well as of the existence of eyes in animals, in book V.

Because the eyes have a 'special body' (*soma idion*), a
problem is developed concerning their generation, for they
appear to be large at the beginning of their development,
then appear to shrink slightly as the embryo develops. The
body of the eyes

> is fluid and cold, and unlike the other parts,
> which are present in their places first potentially,
> then actually, this one is not there at the start,
> but is produced by the secretion of the purest
> part of the liquid around the brain through those
> passages which are to be observed leading from
> the eyes to the membrane around the brain.[59]

Since the 'special body' of the eyes is generated from that
of the brain (Aristotle saw but did not understand the op-
tic nerves), the process of generation of the eyes is similar
to that of the brain. This explanation is not determined by

functional considerations, not very much so at least, but
rather guided by the desire to account for the similarity in
the developmental process between brain and eyes, and by a
supposed observation that the brain and eyes are similar in
being fluid and cold materially. It would not be stretching
matters at all to say that Aristotle emphasizes this relationship in order to support the refutation of the emanation
theory of vision; various predecessors (Plato, Empedocles in
particular) had argued that something goes out from the eye
in the process of vision, and this theory was attacked particularly in *Sens*. If the body of the eyes is fluid and cold,
then it should not be the case that 'fire' or anything resembling fire be emitted by the eyes; this seems to be the
motivation of this passage in *GA* II.6, or to be one of the
possible motivations.

Later, in *GA* V.1, Aristotle uses his explanation of the process of development of the eyes as an illustration of the
senses of necessity which will appear in his account.

> X will *of necessity* possess an eye ('a' because
> that characteristic is included in the essence
> of the animal as posited), and it will -- also
> *of necessity* -- possess a particular sort of
> eye, but the latter is a different mode of ne-
> cessity from the former, and is 'b' derived from
> the fact that it is naturally constituted to act
> and to be acted upon in this or that way (778b
> 16ff, PECK).

The text of the key phrases is:

'a': τοιόνδε γὰρ ζῶον ὑπόκειται ὄν

'b': τοιονδὶ ἢ τοιονδὶ ποιεῖν πέφυκε καὶ πάσχειν.

PECK's translation of the first phrase is somewhat interpretative for a literal rendering of it might be, 'for it is
posited that it is such an animal'. This means that one of
the senses in which an animal must have an eye is this, that
it is a member of a species which has eyes; if it didn't have
any eyes, it wouldn't count as a member of that species at
all. Of course this is what PECK means by saying that it is
'included in the essence', but Aristotle makes quite clear
that it is a matter of *definition*, that in one sense of

146

'necessary' an animal has an eye because it belongs to an
'eyed' group. PECK, in his notes to the passage, indicates
that he supposes that sense 'a' is indicative of the Final
Cause, but as I indicate, this is not as simple as it might
at first appear.

PECK also indicates in his notes that he supposes that the
second phrase, 'b', describes "the necessity implied by the
Motive and Material Causes", which puts the emphasis upon a
contrast between the senses of necessity only, and that would
be a mistaken emphasis. There is also a contrast between (a)
having an eye at all, and (b) having an eye of a certain
sort. Having an eye at all depends upon the definition of the
species, but having an eye of a certain sort might not; there
can be variations in the characteristics of eyes even among
members of the same species. It is characteristics of this
kind which concern Aristotle in *GA* V, and motivate the contrast in the passage quoted.

This contrast demands a contrast in the kinds of explanation
required, and thus a contrast in the 'senses' of necessity.
But the sort which is meant to be explicated by phrase 'b'
remains puzzling. Immediately before the passage quoted he
has said that the explanation of these variations are to
sought "in the movement and generation, that they get their
differences in the *systasis*;" phrase 'b', however, does not
quite have this sense, as is obvious even in PECK's translation. Phrase 'b' talks of the eye's 'natural constitution'
(*pephyke*), which could involve an idea of having grown to
be that way, but there is no mention of just what it is that
might have happened in the process of generation which makes
the differences. Rather, "to act and be acted upon thus and
so" looks rather more like a reliance upon the idea of fit-
ness of organ to function. It may be that this second sort of
necessity is even more nearly teleological than the first; we
will argue this point more fully in the next Part and in
Chapter IV.[60]

Summary of Part A

We have examined the relationship between the genetic and
functional accounts of the parts of animals as Aristotle presents them in the *PA* and *GA*. The genetic account begins with
the embryonic heart; we have seen how the theory of *pneuma*
works together with Aristotle's more typical concepts in this
account. Examining examples of Aristotle's explanations of
various parts, we have seen how Aristotle sometimes gives
both a genetic and a functional account, and yet puts greater
emphasis on the functional or organic analysis.
The greater emphasis upon the functional analysis may have
several causes. The actual physiology of growth and development is very difficult to observe in detail, and any reasonable precise account requires very sophisticated methods, and
some theoretical developments which were far from achievement in Aristotle's day. He lacked, and we cannot blame him
for this, the concept of a biological cell, yet growth is to
be understood largely in terms of cell division. Once the
notion of a cell has been developed, one can give an organismic account on the microscopic level, and such an account may
in turn assist one's genetic analysis.[61] Aristotle has the
possibility only of observing parts and their relationships
with the naked eye; he asserts organic relationships with
the theory of *pneuma* on the microscopic level, or of non-
observed parts, but such assertions were and could only be
guesswork, and could not be tested with his techniques.

Aristotle's accounts of the parts of animals are most
plausible when they concern the organic inter-relationships
of the major organs of the body. One may see his biological
investigations as an attempt to test and support his philosophical theories; the investigations which we have discussed
in this Part support the theory of the soul as organismic,
'hylomorphic', as asserted in the *de Anima*. This is perhaps
despite the development of the theory of *pneuma* in the *GA*;
the functional account found in *PA* is most consistent with

148

the *de Anima* version of the nature of the soul, even if Fr.
NUYENS was dubious of this fact. We might find that the account of the brain is the least successful part of his story
about the parts of animals, but a further investigation of
the *de Motu Animalium* and *de Incessu Animalium* might well
show that Aristotle's theory has considerable interest and
value to modern philosophers and perhaps even to scientists.

B. VARIATIONS AMONG RELATED PARTS IN DIFFERENT SPECIES

In this part we will examine some of Aristotle's explanations
of observed phenomena which have been used to support, in more
recent times, evolutionary theory. Species of animals differ
in a variety of ways, and not all of the differences can be
explained easily by reference to function (survival value);
evolutionary theory depends upon a concept of genetic inheritance to explain non-functional aspects of animals, but
Aristotle does not leave himself much room for this sort of
explanation, or indeed some of the other sorts which modern
biologists apply. As a result, he struggles to use his teleological concepts even where they would seem difficult to
apply; we can better understand his theory when we see it
faced with difficulties of this kind.
We will look in particular at Aristotle's explanations of the
variations in three sense organs, the eyes, the ears, and the
tongue.[62] These explanations use most of the explanatory
principles and modes which appear in the biological books,
and several instances are especially detailed, as though
Aristotle paid particularly great attention to these problems.
He shows considerable interest in problems of perception in
many of his treatises; much of *de An.* II, all of *Sens.*, and
many other passages are concerned with the nature of perception. Aristotle thinks that he can arrive at a more

satisfactory understanding by comparing the modes of perception in various species (*Sens*. 1, 438b8ff), a program that he does not really carry out except for some few comments, as at *de An*. II.9, 421b13ff.

1. Variations in eyes

Aristotle tells us what he is looking for at the very beginning of his account of the variations in eyes, limiting the possible range of solutions to his problem. Having discussed the variations in blood, he says,

> Similarly, one may assume that the other uniform and non-uniform parts present variations; some of these variations will be related to the activities and the *ousia* of each animal, others to the 'better or worse'. For example, some animals have hard eyes, others fluid eyes; some have eyelids, others do not, but in both cases it is for the greater accuracy of vision.[63]

We will discuss what he says about these variations in the order in which he mentions them here.

Hard eyes, which are less discriminating than fluid eyes,[64] are typical of bloodless animals, particularly of the crustacea and insects which may live out of water.[65] He does not seem to have determined the relative capacities of hard and fluid eyes by experiment; he probably decided that hard eyes were inferior because the animal was generally inferior in capacity. At any rate, the crustacea and insects 'have their skeletons on the outside', so that they do not have the soft skin necessary for a movable eyelid.[66] They do need protection however, so their eyes are constructed as if they saw through attached eyelids. This is a disadvantage, but unavoidable considering the material available. Hard eyes are 'movable' normally, which Aristotle regards as a compensation.[67]

In his discussions of hard eyes, Aristotle contrasts the exigencies of the material with the functions of good vision and

protection of the eyes; he does not bring into the explanation
any account of the moving cause. He clearly expects to find
teleological explanations of the variations among eyes, as
elsewhere. Those variations which depend upon activities
(*erga*) should be those which are consequent upon special adaptation; although all eyes have the function of sight, nevertheless they vary according to the sort of objects which
they must see (prey or attacker), or according to additional
functions which they may have for a particular species, as a
modern biologist might find certain characteristics of eyes
to be secondary sexual characteristics in some species. Incidentally, the attraction of the opposite sex is one function
which Aristotle emphasizes less than modern naturalists do.

The variations which depend upon 'entity' (*ousia*) are
those which are related to the general character of the species, for example the 'hard eyes' of the crustacea, which
accord with the hard exterior generally of this class. He
adds the words 'better or worse' for a somewhat complicated
reason: if he explains a part in terms of a function or 'activity', it is by saying that such and such a part or variation in a part is *better* for the species; if he can show
this, he is satisfied that he has explained the part. However, there remain related parts in other species which do
not perform the function as well, which are 'worse' in this
respect. How can he explain them? By arguing that this part,
though inferior to that in some other species, is nevertheless the best that *this* species can do, given the general
character of animals of this species. That general characteristic is supposed to have some over riding value, finally
related to the place of this species in the scale of nature.
Thus the hard and mobile eye belongs to the 'nature' of a
large genus of animals, and to their *ousia*, despite the intrinsic inferiority of this adaptive solution.
In animals with blood, except fish, protection for the eyes
is provided by eyelids. A peculiarity of many birds and of
the oviparous quadrupeds (lizards and such) is that they use

the *lower* lid rather than the upper, which is the normal
mode for viviparous animals, and for some birds. This peculiarity is explained, in the case of the heavy-bodied birds,
thus: "since they do not fly much, the growth for the wings
is turned to the thickness of the skin."[68] In the case of
the oviparous quadrupeds, their scaly skin is particularly
hard in the region of the head. For both groups, the terrestrial life and the need for protection of the body explains
the need for such hard skin; in the case of the birds, the
material is the same as in the species which use the upper
lid, but the apportionment is different. In both groups, the
use of the lower lid is a concomitant result of a conditionally necessary adaptation to a particular mode of life.
Within the group of oviparous quadrupeds, the chamaleon is
apparently described in *HA* as permanently open-eyed, like a
fish or hard- and mobile-eyed bloodless animal. In the chamaleon a membrane covers all but the center of the eye (this
approaches the adaptation which fish have), and something
like the bloodless animals

> it keeps twisting its eyes around and shifting
> its line of vision in every direction, and thus
> contrives to get a sight of any object that it
> wants to see (II.11, 503a31, THOMPSON).

Although he seems to have dissected the eye of the chamaleon,
Aristotle does not try to explain this oddity.
Blinking is regarded as a problem for the heavy birds. They
need to have the ability to blink in order to protect themselves against dust, and because they need to see farther
than the oviparous quadrupeds; however, the lower lid is too
slow. They therefore have a membrane, which we call the nictitating membrane, which proceeds from the corner of the
eye nearest the nostril "because the front is more of an
archē" (*PA* II.13, 657b16ff); LLOYD, in *Polarity* pp. 52ff,
adequately discusses this sort of explanation; he makes clear
that Aristotle means approximately that the front is a better
starting point for movement. There are no very good reasons
given for this assumption; Aristotle seems to think that it

152

is obvious.

Fish do not have eyelids at all, for there are fewer dangers
in the water, and "nature does nothing in vain".[69] The eyes
of fish are particularly fluid, thinks Aristotle, for it is
more difficult to see through water, and fish need to see
through it to some distance; the more fluid the eye, the
more easily it sees at a distance, according to his theory
of vision.

In *GA* V several other variations in eyes are discussed. This
book sets out to examine the necessary concomitants of the
generative process, but the stated theme in no way prevents
Aristotle from providing functional explanations of the phenomena mentioned. His account of the color of eyes is an especially interesting example. He finds that in most species
all members of the species have the same typical color of
eyes, while in man there is a range of possible shades, and
furthermore the color often changes between birth and a more
developed state. These two peculiarities of the human species
must, he thinks, be due to the same cause (*aitia*): the fact
that in other species there is just one natural eye-color,
while in human beings there is more than one natural eye
color.[70] Horses, he says, are like man in this respect; one
wonders whether all Greek cats had the same color of eyes,
or whether Aristotle had seen the blue eyes of puppies of
a brown-eyed race of dogs.

Development, Aristotle believed, is a process of differentiation. As the living organism develops it becomes more in-
dividuated, develops more peculiarities, becoming simultaneously more like its parents, less like the offspring of other
species (see *GA* IV.3, and chapters II.C and III.A above).
The young of other species do not become further differentiated in respect of eye color, so there is no reason for them
to change from one to the other; in the absence of any 'cause'
they will not.

Young human beings have *blue* or light colored, eyes, rather
than some other color, because "the parts of the young are

153

weaker, and blueness is a form of weakness" (779b12). The
young are, of course, weak in many ways. To put it in the
Aristotelian way, they are material for a better development,
and the material is weaker than the final product, for that
which is added is increased power derived from the sources
of movement and growth. It remains to show why *blue* is a
form of weakness.

> Some eyes contain too much fluid, some too little,
> to suit the right movement, others contain just
> the right amount; and so those eyes which contain
> a large amount are dark, because large volumes of
> fluid are not transparent; those which contain a
> small amount are blue. (Sea water is a parallel
> instance; transparent sea water appears blue, the
> less transparent pallid, and water so deep that
> its depth is undetermined is dark or dark blue).
> Eyes intermediate between these two extremes differ
> merely by 'the more and the less' (*GA* V.1, 779b
> 26-34, PECK).

The general idea behind this passage is that the color of
the eyes depends upon the material, rather than upon function.
There are some oddities in this explanation, or perhaps one
should say that Aristotle is careless here. 1) Aristotle
fails to distinguish between iris and pupil; it is the iris
and not the pupil which varies in color. Elsewhere[71] he calls
the pupil 'the black' or '*korē*' (girl), and recognizes that
vision proceeds through it. He may have included both pupil
and iris under the term '*korē*', but his explanation of color
variation would then be difficult to apply to the entire
korē. 2) One is led to suppose that the only way an eye could
be different in color is to be different in size, in order
to have more fluid in it, as the sea is darker where it is
deeper; however, the color of eyes obviously does *not* vary
directly according to size. One might add that the other part
of the analogy is somewhat faulty too, for even the sea does
not vary in color directly with depth. For the sea to be very
blue, it must be quite pure, have a light colored bed (white
sand for example) and be from about one to ten meters deep;
it is darkest when it is both deep and pure. Any impurities
change the color of water radically, even in rather small

154

quantities. Air bubbles, for example, make water greenish
and opaque. The sea can be very green due to minute plant
life; it can also be red or any of several other colors due
to this and similar causes. There seems to be careless observation on both sides of the analogy which Aristotle draws;
this is especially odd here, since Aristotle had direct acquaintance with human eyes and the sea.

Aristotle argued in *de An.* II.12, 424a17ff, that perception
is a mean, that we perceive in virtue of a ratio between extremes in the organ. This should help to explain the idea behind the first sentence in the passage quoted; he also thinks
that the extremes are closely related to certain diseases or
functional difficulties. Blue eyes do not see as well in daylight, but better at night, because, having less fluid, "they
are unduly set in movement by the light and by visible objects" (780a1). Dark eyes see better in the day but less well
at night, "for the light is weak during the night, and besides fluid is generally not easily set in movement at night"
(780a8). The diseases which attack eyes of each extreme color
vary too; cataract arises more often in blue eyes, because it
is a sort of dryness of the eyes; night-blindness arises in
darker eyes, for it is a superabundance of fluid (780a20). As
we might suspect, those eyes are best which hit the mean between extremes.

PECK is troubled about the comments about 'nightblindness' or
'*nyktalops*'. Aristotle says in the context that this disease
particularly affects the young because their brain is more
fluid; PECK is worried about the fact that Aristotle says that
the eyes of the young are blue, and that nightblindness affects dark-eyed people and especially the young. This apparent
contradiction is only apparent, however, for Aristotle does
not mean that this disease affects those so young that their
eyes are still blue but about to change; rather, it affects
those young people whose eyes have developed to the point of
extreme dark color, extreme fluidity; in the one case he refers to new-born infants, in the other to older children and

155

adolescents, who have much fluid (according to him). This is
borne out by the Hippocratic *Epidemics* VI.7 (pp. 332-335
LITTRE), where it is said that '*nyktalōpes*' effects those
with large eyes, those who are children, and those with dark
eyes with small pupils. "Most of them also had straight black
hair." Women were not affected as much, probably because they
did not go out as much, according to the author. This ought
to hold for infants as well.

Aristotle comments on some other factors in good vision in
the same passage. The skin on the pupil (*korē*) must be thin,
white, and even, so that it may be transparent (780a26ff).
Old people do not have good vision because the skin of the
eyes, like the rest of their skin, becomes thick and wrinkled.
PLATT is puzzled, in his note to this passage, by the word
'white' as it appears here: "By 'white' Aristotle sometimes
means transparent, but what he means here is very obscure."
This obscurity is diminished by the comparison of the eye to
a skin lantern: "Lanterns cannot give any light if they are
made of black skin" (780a35). The contrast is that of ordinary skin-colors; you can make a skin-lantern out ot the
white skin of a lamb, perhaps, but not out of the black skin
of a goat. Even an Ethiopian must have white skin on the pupils of his eyes if he is to have good vision. White skin,
in this sense, is in fact transparent, rather than opaquely
white as paper.

Aristotle points out in the context two ways in which vision
may be good or bad: a) the ability to see at a distance;
b) the ability to discriminate differences. Different species
and individuals may be superior in one respect, deficient in
the other. The discriminative ability depends upon having
"a pure fluid in the eyes and a pure covering around it"
(780b27).

> Just as quite small stains are plain and distinct
> on a pure clean shirt, so quite small movements
> are plain and distinct in a pure, clean sight, and
> they give rise to sense-perception (780b31).

If one compares this statement with what was said earlier

about blue eyes, one is led to suspect the possibility of a somewhat different theory concerning the cause of light and dark eyes. Blue eyes might be 'purer' than darker eyes; this would also explain their ability to distinguish small differences, and to see in the dark, while dark eyes, less 'pure', would have the advantage of filtering out, so to speak, the stronger rays of daylight. Aristotle seems to have missed out on a better guess from his data.

The ability to see well at a distance is explained here by reference to the position of the eyes and the surrounding structure. It helps to have a "considerable projection over the eyes" (780b23), or to have "sunken eyes placed in a hollowed recess" (781a1). It does not matter whether vision 'issues forth' from the eyes, or is derived from a movement from the seen object; the important thing is not to have the rays scattered. A tube all the way from the eyes to the object would be best of all, but otherwise a tube as long as possible.[72] The optics and physics of this theory are rather primitive, of course, but there could be some observational data to support it. Before the invention of the telescope observers of the stars seem to have used tubes as an aid to observation. If nothing else, such a tube would help the observer keep his attention on the same visual object, and it might help reduce interference from peripheral light. Aristotle does not refer to such a device in this passage however; rather, he uses an analogy with smell and hearing: the long nose of the Laconian hound improves his ability to perceive odors at a distance (V.2, 781b10), and there are quadrupeds with ears designed for long-distance hearing, though none are named here (781b13). The elephant has the longest nose of all, of course, but Aristotle does not mention a talent at scenting odors from a distance in his discussion of this magnificent organ. Also, when he discusses eyebrows in *PA* he says that their function is protection 'like the eaves of a house'; he does not mention their benefits for the ability to see at a distance (*PA* II.15, 658b14ff). At *GA* V.1,

157

781b10, it is the ears which are like the cornice of a house. In *HA* I.10, 492a7ff, he does say that receding eyes are most acute, but a sign of bad disposition. He doesn't give any examples; probably he had some human individuals in mind, as Theophrastus had in the *Characters*. Good vision at a distance is cited as a characteristic of certain species: the crook-taloned birds,[73] fish,[74] and perhaps by implication all or many carnivores, especially hunting carnivores. The river crocodile, for example, is said (*HA* II.10, 503a9) to have 'especially acute' vision out of the water. He doesn't say whether this is acuteness in discrimination or good vision at a distance, and perhaps didn't have the distinction in mind as he wrote that passage.

Man, by contrast, is said to have very great powers of discrimination, but in proportion to his size very poor vision at a distance (*GA* V.2, 781b20). In none of these individual cases do we find any statement to the effect that the presence or absence of the ability to see well at a distance depends upon the structure around the eyes. Possibly Aristotle came to this conclusion relatively late in his biological investigations, on the basis of an analogy, and without thinking about it very much. He certainly doesn't explain his position on this question very well.

It might be well to summarize the principles which are used to explain the variations in eyes. 'Hard' eyes were said to be due to the sort of *material* available, but the mobility of hard eyes was explained by an appeal to *function*. Closure with the lower lid was explained as functionally necessary, and the best that could be done with the material. A genetic account seems behind the idea that the material available is turned to heavy skin in heavy birds; the presence of the nictitating membrane is explained mostly by appeal to function, the point of origin to the peculiar principle that the front is 'more of an *archē*'. The operative phrase in the explanation of the absence of eyelids in fish is "nature does nothing in vain", while fluidity of the eyes of fish is explained functionally.

The change of eye color in man depends mostly on the material and developmental process characteristic of the species; functional considerations are quite secondary here. The available matter is responsible, he believes, for the blueness of the eyes of infants, while good and bad vision (elsewhere explained on functional grounds) is in *GA* V explained on the material of the eye itself, and the material structure of the surrounding parts.

Thus Aristotle sometimes emphasizes material factors, sometimes functional factors, in his explanations of variations in eyes; many of his explanations of variations involve both sorts of considerations, especially if we bring separated passages on the same topic together. Material factors are understood either as a limitation (hard eyes, lower lid closure), or as an opportunity (fluidity of man's eyes). When Aristotle offers a functional account, this does not preclude a genetic account; he may very well give one at another point.

2. Variations in ears, and a 'deformed dualizer', the seal

Most of Aristotle's comments about the variations in ears are to be found in one relatively short passage in *PA*,[75] which again illustrates the explanatory use of the concepts of function and matter.

> The quadrupeds have their ears 'detached', and
> (apparently) higher than the eyes... . As they
> are usually on all fours when they move, it is
> useful (*chresima*) to have their ears up in the
> air and movable -- this allows them to turn them
> in every direction to catch sounds better.[76]

He is thinking of donkeys and horses, in particular, in which the turning of the ears is more noticeable. The moveable ears, for quadrupeds, are thought of as adaptive in much the same way as the moveable eyes of the crustacea, which we discussed in the preceding section.

Also related to matters discussed in the preceding section
is the explanation of the lack of ears in birds:

> The birds have the passages only because of the
> hardness of their skin and because they do not
> have hair, but feathers; thus they do not have
> the sort of matter from which ears could be formed.
> The same is true of the oviparous quadrupeds with
> horny scales; the same *logos* fits them too.[77]

Since the 'nature' of external ears is similar to that of
eyelids, the entity (*ousía*) of the animal is the explanation
of a condition which one would tend to think of as 'worse'.

The explanation of the absence of external ears in seals,
however, introduces a principle which we have not yet examined
in any detail.

> The seal, a viviparous animal, does not have ears,
> but only auditory passages, because it is a de-
> formed (πεπηρωμένον) quadruped (*PA* II.12, 657a23).

Aristotle recognizes that one would think it odd to say that
the absence of earlobes in certain seals is a 'deformity',
and he is quite aware that this 'lack' has an adaptive value
in an aquatic animal, as he says in the *GA*:

> Nature has worked out reasonably (εὐλόγως) in the
> case of the seal, for although he is a viviparous
> quadruped, he does not have ears, but passages
> only. The reason is that his life is in the water,
> but the ear is a part added on to the passages in
> order to save the movement of the air coming from
> a distance. This is not useful for the seal, but
> would work out rather the opposite, for ears would
> take in a quantity of water (*GA* V.1, 781b22-28).

The apparent disagreement between these two passages is due
to the fact that the seal is one of those animals which,
Aristotle says, 'dualizes'.[78] The seal, he says, dualizes
between 'land animal' and 'water animal',[79] to use the most
general terms; it is true that the seal is amphibious, but
Aristotle means more than that. To dualize is to belong to
two different groups of animals at the same time, and one
group may be regarded as 'higher', the other as 'lower', in
the scale of nature. To be a land animal is better than to
be a water animal; land animals (mammals) have earlobes;
therefore to have earlobes is, in this respect, better than

not having them, and the seal is deformed without them. But
it is better for water animals *not* to have earlobes, for
functional reasons, so the seal 'reasonably' does not have
them.

Aristotle says rather similar things, in more detail, about
the feet of the seal; although he often says that it is a
quadruped,[80] he adds that the hind feet of the seal are similar to the tail of a fish.[81] Although the shape of the limbs
clearly aids in swimming, nevertheless they are 'deformed'.[82]
This means not only that the legs of a seal are defective for
the purpose of walking on land (which they are), but also
that inasmuch as they depart from the normal form of the limbs
of land animals, their owners are somehow defective as members
of the natural order.

It might be interesting to narrow down the classes to which
the seal is thought to belong. According to the manuscripts,
there are two passages in which Aristotle says that the seal
is a cetacean, a member of the same class as the whale and
dolphin: *HA* I.11, 492a26, and III.20, 521b24. THOMPSON, in
the Oxford translation, does not like this, but there seems
to be no alternative, at least in the former passage. Although
PECK has an amendment here, his text gives this sense, which
he has in his translation; Louis preserves the standard manuscript reading, but slides around the problem in his translation ("... du phoque, du dauphin, et des autres animaux
conformés comme les cétacés..."). The manuscript reading
gives "... the seal, the dolphin, and whatever other animals
are cetacean in this respect".

In the second passage, 521b24, THOMPSON, PECK, and LOUIS follow KARSCH's emendation of 'φώκαινα' (porpoise) for 'φώκη'
(seal). Aristotle here lists animals with mammae, which he
says are identical with those animals which have hair, and
says that cetaceans belong to this class. The main reason, it
seems to me, for emending the passage is the conviction that
the seal is not a cetacean; but Aristotle may well, in these
passages, be thinking of the seal as a cetacean in spite of

the fact that the animal does, in its way, have legs. The
manner of life, the general form, and the lack of external
ears (492a26) are similar in both groups, seals and cetaceans.
But seals and cetaceans dualize between land and water animals. It seems then that seals are considered to be at least
in some measure members of the class of cetaceans.
One may note, finally, that at *HA* V.12, Aristotle seems to
compare the female organ of the seal with that of the ray,
a selacian. This may be considered an indication of the general dualizing with water animals.
A modern taxonomist might take facts like these as evidence
of convergent adaptation, if not of genetic inheritance;
there does not seem to be much inclination to say that some
species really belong to two different genera simultaneously,
even if they are 'intermediate' or structurally similar.
Aristotle's biology has been understood as an attempt at
taxonomy, but it is not; although there is some support for
a fixity of natural kinds, he does not suppose that natural
kinds are separated into perfectly distinct groups. Some
variations, the lack of ears in certain seals for example,
are explained as instances of the fuzziness of distinctions
between natural species.

3. Variations in tongues; tongues and stings in insects

a) Tongues for speech
.

Aristotle often mentions the special adaptation of the tongue
for speech.[83] According to him, not only man, but also other
animals use their tongues for communication. For example, at
the end of *de An.* (in its present condition) he says that the
animal has:

> taste for sweet and bitter, in order that it might
> perceive this in food, desire, and move; hearing
> that something may make significant sounds (σημαίνει)
> to it, and a tongue that it may make significant

sounds to another (III.13, 435b23-26, after HETT).
He adds that all of these senses, and sight, "are not for the
sake of existence but for the better (οὐ τοῦ ἕνεκα ἀλλὰ τοῦ
ἐῦ, b21). This is in contrast with the sense of touch, without which "it is impossible for an animal to exist" (b16).
In other words, the senses are regarded as conditionally necessary, but not in the strongest sense. He probably supposes
that the function of communication also is 'for the better'
and that its presence in animals which have it is explained
on that ground.
The human tongue, he says,

> is the freest, broadest, and softest, so that it
> is useful for both kinds of function: a) for the
> perception of taste (man has the most delicate
> perception among animals, and has a soft tongue;
> it is also sensitive to touch, for taste is a
> form of touch); b) it is useful for the articu-
> lation of sounds, and for speech, because it is
> soft and broad.[84]

Thus Aristotle supposes that man must have the most delicate
sense of taste because he has the most delicate sense of
touch.[85] In *PA* II.16, 660a9-13, the explanatory order is different:

> It was necessary from the start that the lips and
> tongue function well for the use of articulated
> speech, and that they have this sort of nature;
> therefore they are fleshy. But the flesh of man
> is the softest; this is because his sense of touch
> is more perceptive than that of the other animals.

Here the function of articulated speech is made the teleologically prior reason for the fleshiness of the tongue, whereas in the other passage, the nature of the tongue is presented
as an opportunity for speech. Perhaps there is not that much
difference in the point of view. The more serious problem is
this, why is it that man has the most delicate sense of
touch? We might speculate that the sensitivity of his flesh
is due to his perfection *qua* animal, for the sense of touch
is the essential characteristic of animal; man, as perfect
animal, should have the essential characteristic in the highest degree. Thus the material would be perfect for taste, and

163

articulation.

It is also important that the tongue be soft and broad, and
'detached' or free if an animal is to use it for communication.
Aristotle does suppose that it is relatively free in most of
the vivipara. The functional reason, in land animals generally, for this mobility of the tongue is the movement of food
in the mouth:

> the epiglottis and the movement of the tongue are
> well contrived so that when the food is being chewed
> in the mouth and passing over the epiglottis the
> tongue rarely falls beneath the teeth, and hardly
> ever anything gets into the windpipe (*PA* III.3,
> 664b33-36).

Elephants, it seems, have a very small tongue, which hinders
their ability to articulate sounds (*HA* II.6, 502a3); dolphins
make various sounds, but their tongue is 'not detached', nor
do they have lips, so they cannot articulate. The small tongue
of the elephant might be due, according to Aristotle's principles, to borrowing for the length of the nose, but he does
not say so. He definitely missed a great opportunity in failing to notice the high degree of articulation in the sounds
made by dolphins. In this case, his dissections seemed to
rule out the possibility of articulated significant sounds
(*HA* IV.9, 536a1), in spite of the fact that he had heard the
'squeaks' and 'groans' of the dolphin out of water.

b) Various tongues of the vivipara

Aristotle says that the tongue is 'practically the same in
all land animals' (*PA* II.17, 660a15); he notes some variations even so. For example, the colors of tongues differ in
these animals according to the color of the skin; "One ought
to understand the tongue as one of the external parts, like
a hand or foot, disregarding that it is covered in the mouth"
(*GA* V.6, 786a26). This is the source of certain variations in
hair color (*HA* III.17, 508b17); in fact, the shepherds think

164

that the color of the ram's tongue determines the color of
the lamb which he sires (*HA* VI.19, 574a5). The externality
of the tongue agrees with his position that the tongue is
essentially flesh. The tongue in dark-skinned animals tends
to be dark, in light-skinned, light; in animals with varie-
gated or '*poikila*' coloring, the tongue tends to be *poikila*
too. It should be noted that hands and feet tend in man to
have anomalies of coloring which could be called *poikila* too,
in that dark-skinned men have the palms of the hands and
soles of the feet lighter in color. I don't know whether the
reference to hands and feet at 786a26 is motivated by this
fact or not.

One might say that the small tongue of the elephant and the
attached tongue of the dolphin, noted above, would be exceptions to the great similarity of tongues in land animals
asserted at 660a15; he also says that seals have forked
tongues (*HA* II.17, 508a27; *PA* IV.11, 691a8). However, none
of these animals are strictly land animals (*peza*); the elephant has his 'life' in the water, and the seal even more
so; the dolphin is completely a water animal, in the sense
that it is *enhydra*. Thus the statement that all the 'land
animals' have similar tongues remains consistent.

He does not explain why seals have forked tongues; this comes
as an afterthought to the description of the forked tongue
in serpents. In *PA* IV.11 he says of both seals and serpents
that the forked tongue explains the 'gourmandise' of both
species. Elsewhere[86] he says of serpents only that they get
a 'double pleasure out of their tastes'. We may also note
that the forked tongue emphasizes bilateral symmetry; Aristotle does not suggest that the seal dualizes with reptiles.[87]

c) The tongue in birds

Aristotle thinks that the birds are a good example of animals
which articulate sounds with the tongue:

> All birds use the tongue for communication with
> one another, but some more than others, so much
> so that it seems in some cases information is
> exchanged (*PA* II.17, 660a35-b2).

In fact, the small polyphonic birds do not use their tongues
to articulate voice. Aristotle does not actually say that
their tongues are the sort for speech, but he does not make
an attempt to discover how they make the large variety of
sounds. He does say that the clearest articulators are those
that have the broadest tongues; or, as at *HA* IV.9, 536a21,
those that have broad or light tongues. The crook-taloned
birds have broad tongues (660a34), and some other birds have
particularly long tongues (*PA* IV.12, 692b6; *HA* II.12, 504a
35). The wryneck (504a13ff) has a tongue so long that he can
extend it four finger-breadths, as a serpent can; as for his
voice, he only chirps (*trizei*). The "glottis" (perhaps a
landrail) also has an especially long tongue, as his name
indicates (*HA* VIII.12, 597b20). Aristotle notes that the
hoopoe and the nightingale do not have their tongues pointed,
and they are both fairly good articulators (*HA* IX.15, 616b8);
the woodpecker has a broad flat tongue (IX.9, 614b2), but
Aristotle does not comment on his speaking abilities.
All of this is description, rather than explanation; his
notion that the tongue should be broad and flat seems to be
derived from the form of the tongue in man, rather than observations concerning the articulated sounds made by birds
in relation to their mouth-structure.

d) The tongue in land ovipara, frogs, and crocodiles

All the oviparous quadrupeds have a tongue, for the same
reason that the vivipara have one, with the exception of the
crocodile (to whom we will soon return) (*PA* IV.11, 690b20).
In many cases this tongue is fastened down and hard in conformity with the general hardness of the flesh and skin of
these animals (*PA* II.17, 660b3); snakes and lizards, however,

tend to have an exceptionally long and fine tongue, often forked. Aristotle describes this tongue several times[89] and says that it is due to the 'gourmandise' of their nature (II.17, 660b9). Such a tongue is useless for speech, but excellent for sensing tastes. It seems odd that Aristotle does not attempt to explain how these forked-tongue ovipara, belonging to a class which normally has a hard tongue, solidly fastened down, in accordance with their flesh and skin, can have such an agile tongue, contrary to expectation.

The tongue of the frog is most peculiar, observes Aristotle:

> it is attached in front like that of a fish, where
> in other animals it is detached, and the part near
> the larynx is detached and folded, which permits
> him to make his special sound (*HA* IV.9, 536a8-11).

Aristotle properly recognizes that this croaking is the call of males to females at mating time, like that observed among domestic animals. He does not, however, notice that the frog also catches insects with his tongue, although that would be just the sort of thing that would interest him. He doesn't remark this characteristic of the chamaleon either, in his description of that animal.[90]

Aristotle's account of the crocodile's tongue has several peculiarities; one peculiarity is that he discusses this matter twice in *PA*. The passages to be investigated include *HA* II. 10, 503a1; *PA* II.17, 660b11ff; and *PA* IV.11, 690b20ff. In the *HA*, the Egyptian crocodile is said, somewhat ambiguously, to be an exception to the general rule that oviparous quadrupeds have a tongue:

> he is more similar to certain fish: for in general
> fish have a prickly and non-detached tongue, and
> some of them have a smooth unarticulated surface
> unless the mouth is pulled well open (503a1ff).

We will return a bit later to the tongue in fish; let us turn now to the *PA*:

> all the blooded animals have an organ for taste,
> including those which most people would say had
> not, e.g. certain of the fishes, which have a paltry
> sort of tongue, very like what the river crocodile
> has. Most of these creatures look as if they had no

> tongue, and there is a good reason for this.
> 1) All the animals of this sort have spiny mouths;
> 2) the time which water animals have for perceiving
> tastes is short; hence, since the use of this sense
> is short, so is the articulation of its organ (660
> b11, PECK with minor alterations).

The other passage in *PA* does not quite say the same thing:

> he would not be thought to have one, but only the
> place. The reason is that in a way he is simul-
> taneously a land animal and a water animal; be-
> cause he is a land animal he has the place for a
> tongue, because he is a water animal he is tongue-
> less (690b20ff).

Aristotle goes on to refer to the earlier passage, and closely paraphrases the reason given there for the almost invi-
sible taste organ in fish. He indicates that fish and crocodiles gain more pleasure through swallowing their food than
through the taste.

We have here an interesting example of the extent to which
two kinds of *a priori* principles influence Aristotle's thought:
i) he is led by general opinion to say that the crocodile has
no tongue; but ii) he is led by his doctrine of natural kinds
to affirm, and to look for, an 'organ for sensing tastes',
in all animals, but especially in those with blood, and real
flesh. The general opinion is, of course, that of Herodotus
(II.68-70), although Aristotle has gone beyond Herodotus on
some points of information (see MANQUAT, pp. 38-39). Aristotle accurately describes the shortness and the fastened-
down character of the crocodile's tongue, and accurately
describes the tongue in fish; but the story was that the
crocodile has no tongue, so Aristotle must find a way around
that notion. In 660b, where PECK translates, "a paltry sort
of tongue", the text actually reads "in a way something
sticky"; the word 'tongue' (*glōtta*) does not appear at that
point.[91] It seems that the word '*glōtta*' implies not only an
organ for sensing tastes, but such an organ which protrudes
a little; Aristotle uses roundabout expressions such as
'something sticky' or better, 'sensorium of taste'.

The remainder of the account reveals some typical character-

istics of Aristotle's explanations. The crocodile is a dualizer, and this helps to explain the deformity of the tongue;
the material character of the crocodile's mouth also helps
to prevent the development of a normal tongue. The converse
of the functional principle appears; instead of, 'for every
function, an organ if possible', we have, 'for no function,
no organ'. This principle is usually stated as the maxim,
'Nature does nothing in vain'; as it appears at 691b4, the
formula is, "Nature does nothing superfluous (*periergon*)".

But a more peculiar reason, inherited from Herodotus,
is also given for the 'deformity' of the crocodile's tongue,
the crocodile's jaws are on upside-down.

> Something which contributes to the deformity of
> this part (a) is the immobility of the lower jaw.
> The tongue is naturally conjoined with (*symphyes*)
> the lower jaw, but in the crocodile they are in a
> way upside-down; in other animals it is the upper
> jaw which is immobile. He does not have the tongue
> on the upper jaw, because it would get in the way
> of the entry of the food, but on the lower, (b)
> because the upper is as it were substituted (for
> the lower). Besides, this happens to the crocodile
> because he is a land animal living the life of a
> fish, so that for this reason too he necessarily
> has this part not distinctly articulated (II.17,
> 660b26ff).

PECK inserts the word 'tongue' at (a), although it does not
appear until the places where I have it in my translation.
In the first appearance, the statement is a general rule
about tongues; in the second, it is negative. The crocodile
does *not* have a tongue on the upper jaw (which is somehow
the lower in the wrong place) because it would get in the
way of the food if it were really a tongue, and thus 'hanging
down'. By inference, he might be said to have his tongue on
the lower jaw, but in order to understand the explanatory
phrase which follows (b), we must assume some such phrase as
'and so the crocodile has something which is hardly a tongue
at all' (because the upper, etc.).
At 691b5ff, Aristotle explains why the crocodile moves the
upper jaw instead of the lower: the feet of the crocodile

are too small to hold anything, so "nature has given him" a
mouth which not only bites and cuts the food, but also holds
it. The upper jaw can give more of a blow in biting, and
thus it is more useful to the crocodile this way. This much
of the explanation seems reasonable, given the false assumption that the upper jaw and not the lower is hinged.
The argument at 660b26 is less reasonable. The sense seems
to be this: the tongue is naturally attached to the lower
jaw, and not attached naturally to the upper jaw; the crocodile has his jaws upside down, so to speak; he cannot have
his tongue in the upper jaw (which is similar in its mobility
to the lower jaw to which tongues are naturally attached)
because then if it were really a tongue, it would hang down
in the way of the food; he cannot have it in the lower jaw,
because that is, in a way, an upper jaw; therefore the crocodile does not have a tongue worthy of the name.
"Naturally attached" translates "*symphyes*". This word has
two general senses: one is directly related to the verb φύω,
to grow, the other more closely related to the concept of
physis in its various ramifications. '*Symphyes*' should mean
either a) 'grown together, attached', or b) 'co-natural'.
Aristotle, at 660b28, seems to imply a bit of both senses,
and PECK translates accordingly, and I follow him. LOUIS and
OGLE translate 'adherent', without the sense 'co-natural',
but this does not reveal the remark as part of an argument.
The considerations which would lead Aristotle to make the remark should be something like this: in all, or nearly all,
species other than the crocodile, the tongue is in the lower
jaw, for functional reasons (it would hang down if it were in
the upper jaw), and also perhaps because the lower jaw is the
mobile jaw, so as the location of mobility, it is a proper
location for a mobile tongue. This is, then, a characteristic
of blooded animals, at least, that if there is a tongue, it
is in the lower jaw. But the crocodile cannot have it there
because his lower jaw is really an upper jaw in respect of
its immobility, and so on.

170

If my account is correct, then one may accuse Aristotle of making 'nature' to be rather inflexible in dealing with odd contingencies, but it would be nearer the truth to say that Aristotle is out to explore the extent of nature's flexibility as against inflexibility, and to explain why nature is flexible in some cases, and not in others.

e) The tongue in fish

The normal arrangement in fish is to have a 'tongue' like that of the crocodile (*HA* II.10, 503a2), hardly a tongue at all, but in this case there is a functional reason, in that the fish has little time to linger over the taste of his food (*PA* IV.11, 690b24). Aristotle adds (*HA* IV.8, 533a26; *PA* II.17, 660b34) that fresh water fish, especially carp, often have a very fleshy roof of the mouth, so much so that some observers think that it is a tongue. He does not say that the roof of the mouth serves as the sensorium of taste, but rather suggests that the 'tongue' in these fish is like that in others. Actually, the ciprinoi do taste with this organ,[92] but Aristotle was not prepared to locate a sensorium of taste in the roof of the mouth.

Certain fish, he remarks, have teeth on their tongues and on the roof of the mouth (cf. *HA* II.13, 505a30). He gives an explanation of this fact in *PA*:

> Being in the water, it is necessary to take in water with the food, and quickly to get it out again. They cannot waste time chewing, for the water would run down into the stomach. Because of this they all have sharp teeth for cutting up only, many of them and all over, so that instead of chewing they tear up their food into many little pieces with the quantity of teeth (III.1, 662a8ff).

In this case, the manner of life sets requirements which a variation solves; this is called adaptation nowadays, or conditional necessity by Aristotle.

f) 'Tongues' and related organs in bloodless animals

Aristotle seems to have believed that the sense of taste,
after the sense of touch, was the most widespread of the
senses in the animal kingdom. No doubt the ground of this
belief was in part the notion that taste is most closely related to touch, and in some sense developed out of that sense;
he probably also believed that the sense of taste was the
next most necessary functional sense for the preservation of
the individual, for one must discriminate between objects
offered as food (*de An.* III.12, 434b18-24).
He finds a 'fleshy analogue of the tongue' in the crustacea,
particularly in lobsters and crabs (*PA* IV.5, 678b10); he
finds a 'fleshy body' in sea urchins, which they have 'instead of a tongue' (*HA* IV.5, 530b25); he finds a 'so-called'
tongue in the testacea, with which they taste food;[93] the
cephalopods 'do not have a tongue, but a fleshy part instead'
(*HA* IV.1, 524b5); the analogous part in insects he tends to
call a tongue, without qualification, following general usage,
and says that it too is used to taste food (*PA* IV.5, 678b8;
6, 683a2).
In many insects and in some testacea (e.g. sea-snail, pur-
pura, whelk) there are various sorts of additional utilization
of the tongue. This 'additional utilization' we call 'katachresis', from the verb *katachrētai* which sometimes appears in
passages describing such utilizations. In the case of these
'tongues', these additional uses fall into two categories:
a) drawing liquid food into the mouth with the elongated
organ; b) serving instead of a posterior sting. A passage in
HA describes this organ:

> In some insects there is something like a tongue
> (which all the testacea have), with which they both
> taste and draw food into themselves. This is soft
> in some, but in others it has great strength, as
> in the purpurae. Both the horsefly and the gadfly
> have strong ones, as do pretty nearly all the others
> in this class; for in non-rearstinged insects this
> is present as a weapon. But those that have this do

not have teeth, except for a few, since flies
touch with this and suck blood, and mosquitoes
sting with this (*HA* IV.7, 532a5-14).[94]

Three passages in *PA* also describe and discuss this tongue-
like part:

> 1) Some of the insects have a tongue-like organ
> inside the mouth (e.g. the ants), as do many of
> the testacea. Others have it outside, like a
> sting, but spongy in nature and hollow, so as to
> taste and to draw in food with it simultaneously.
> This is clear in flies, bees, and all such, and
> also in some testacea.[95] In the purpurae this
> part has so much power that it can even pierce
> the shell of univalves, including those of the
> stromboids which are used as bait for them.[96]
> Also, some of the gadflies and cattleflies can
> pierce human skin with it, and some can even
> pierce the skin of other animals. Now in these
> animals such a tongue is naturally comparable to
> the nose of the elephant, for they have a tongue
> instead of a sting, as he has the nose for help
> (II.17, 661a16-29).[97]

> 2) The parts for nutrition are not the same in
> all insects, indeed they differ greatly. In some
> the so-called sting is inside the mouth, and is
> in a way a combination of tongue and lips having
> the power of both; in those not having the sting
> in front this sort of sense organ is within the
> teeth. ... The class of cicadas has the most pe-
> culiar nature of the insects, for it has mouth
> and tongue grown together (*sympephykôs*) into the
> same part, and through it takes in food from
> fluids as through a root. All the insects take
> in little food, not so much because of their
> smallness as from coldness (for heat needs food
> and quickly concocts it, but cold is unfed), most
> of all the class of cicadas; for the fluidity
> deposited by the *pneuma* (wind?) is enough for the
> body (IV.5, 682a9-27).[98]

> 3) Some insects also have a sting for protection
> against attackers. In some it is in front and in
> others in back; in those which have it in front
> it is on (a) the tongue, in those which have it
> in back it is on (a) the tail. Just as in the
> elephant the organ of smell is generated in such
> a way as to be useful both for defence and for
> getting food, so in some of the insects that which
> is placed on (a) the tongue is generated (so as
> to be useful for defence and for getting food),
> for they perceive the food with this, and pick it
> up and draw it to the mouth... .

173

> It is better, when possible, that the same organ
> not be put to unlike uses, that the defensive
> organ be as sharp as possible, and the tongue-
> like organ be spongy and able to draw up food.
> When it is possible to use two parts for two
> functions and they do not get in each other's
> way, nature does not usually make, like a copper-
> smith for cheapness, a spit-and-lampstand. But
> when it is not possib̲le, nature makes extra use
> of something (*katachrētai*) for two functions
> (*PA* IV.6, 682b33-683a26).

First we will identify the insects of which Aristotle writes
in these passages, then we will proceed to more theoretical
issues. The identifications are complicated by the fact that
Aristotle uses several ways of classifiying insects, and
several identifications of individual species are disputed,
though they might give us a better idea of which classes he
means.[99] In *HA* I.5, 490a13ff, he divides 'bloodless fliers'
into: I. sheathed winged (cockchafer *et al.*), which have no
sting; II. four winged, which are largish and tend to have
a sting at the rear; III. two winged, which are smallish, and
tend to have a sting at the front. At IV.7, 531b22ff, from
which our first passage is taken, he complains that *entoma*
are not properly classified, and proceeds to show how many
complexities there are by including centipedes and millipedes,
scorpions and chelifer cancroides, and spiders of all sorts,
among the *entoma*. He might as well have included crabs, lobsters and prawns for good measure, and classified all the
arthropods at one time. At any rate, his objective here is
the description of some of the variations in the external
organs, and in some internal organs; he describes the tongue,
sting, wings and legs, in a rather cursory fashion.
Later, in V.19, 550b21ff, he sets out to describe the various
modes of generation which appear among insects; according to
his usual principles, a description of these phenomena should
result in a satisfactory classification, and so it would ,but
he has not enough of the truth about the phenomena in question
to achieve his goal.[100] For example, he has an entire class
of insects which are normally produced by spontaneous generation.

174

This section does not help us with our present problem.

In VIII.11, 596b10ff, Aristotle examines the feeding
habits of various species of insects, and divides them into
'those with teeth' (mandibles, for the most part), which are
omnivorous, and 'those with tongues' which feed on liquids.
He means, of course, the external sting-like tongue of the
passages in question. Of those which have this tongue, some
take any liquid, and thus are in a way omnivorous (the common
fly is an example); some prefer blood (gadfly, cattlefly);
others live from the juice of plants and fruits. The bee is
the fussiest eater of all, sucking only the sweetest flowers
and pure cool spring water.
In *PA* II.17, from which the first of the passages from this
book was taken, Aristotle is concerned with comparing tongues
in various species, so he manages to find one in every species of insect, and elsewhere; he even finds one in species
with 'teeth', in ants, for example. The classification implied by this passage looks like this:

    i) Internal tongue-like organ;

   ii) External tongue-like organ;

       a) Spongy and soft tongue (bees, some flies);

       b) Hard and strong tongue (gadflies, cattle-
         flies, as well as the testacea).

In the second passage quoted from *PA*, IV.5, 682a9, Aristotle
discusses the internal organs of various animals in parallel
with *HA* IV.7, but he here includes the 'so-called sting' as
an internal organ. This 'so-called sting' is probably the
same as the 'so-called tongue' of *PA* II.17. The negative
description 'not having the sting in front' seems to mean
'having the sting in back'; this is true of bees and the like,
which also have a soft 'tongue' and mandibles ('teeth').
Ordinary flies (diptera) do not have mandibles; Aristotle
must be including them in the class of those which 'have the
sting in front', although not all of them have a stronger
tongue-sting than the soft tongue of the bee.
In *PA* IV.6, from which the last passage comes, Aristotle

gives an account of the external parts of *entoma* which is
clearly meant to improve upon *HA* IV.7. Thus, he divides
entoma with numerous feet from those with few (six: 683b2)
feet, and tries to explain the general distinction between
four wings, two wings, and sheathed wings. He also gives some
reasons for insection (682b21ff). It is at this point that
our last passage appears; the omitted lines, a4-20, say that
ants and bees have no sting in front, but teeth, which they
use for picking up and conveying food to the mouth. This appears to contradict the earlier assertion (661a20, passage
1) that bees have a tongue 'like a sting'. But in bees the
tongue does not perform the function of a sting, although it
looks like the tongue of flies, and some flies do use the
tongue as a sting. The carriers of the rear sting include
those which have it internally (bees and wasps) and those
which have it externally (scorpions, which are not insects
of course). No diptera have a rear sting, apparently because
it would be too heavy for them. The section concludes with
an account of the legs of various insects. Throughout all of
this there is hardly any notice of lepidoptera, although some
of them have remarkable tongues; Aristotle clearly hadn't
noticed that organ.[101]
It is interesting to note that Aristotle expects to find a
sensorium of taste in all insects, but that he hesitates to
say that all insects have tongues. He prefers to limit the
word 'tongue' to an organ which protrudes, even if that organ
is just as surely a weapon of defense. In *HA* VIII.11, 596a11ff,
he even distinguishes between insects with 'teeth' and insects with 'tongues'.
One of the most remarkable insects in regard to its tongue
is surely the cicada; Aristotle's accounts of this insect
are not, I fear, consistent with each other, and this is particularly true concerning the implications about the function
of this organ. Most blatantly, there is a disagreement between *PA* and *Resp.* about the 'temperature' of the cicada. In
PA IV.5 it is asserted that the cicada is cold, and for that

reason needs little food; the fluidity deposited by the *pneuma* (but see below) is enough. In *Resp* 9, 475a19, however, Aristotle says that the cicada is 'warmer' and sings by virtue of its *emphyton pneuma* ('inborn' pneuma); this *pneuma* also seems (475a3) to have the function of cooling the insects, analogously with the external breath in breathing animals.

At *HA* IV.7, 532b10ff, Aristotle says that the cicada feeds on dew (*drosos*) and nothing else, and that it does not produce residue; at V.30, 556a14ff, there is a much longer description, in which he says that the cicada feeds on dew, and does produce a residue. That the cicada produces a liquid residue is obvious to anyone who has tried to catch a cicada, for as you reach out your hand it flies away voiding its residue. As for the food of the cicada, A.N. BRANGHAM (see note 98) says that the cicada is not very fussy about the liquid it sucks, but generally goes after the sap of the trees in which it perches and sings. If the phrase 'fluidity deposited by the *pneuma*' in *PA* IV.5, 682a27, means 'dew', one may wonder why he didn't say 'dew'. LOUIS is sufficiently bemused by this puzzle that he writes 'σώματος' for 'πνεύματος', implying that the cicada does not eat anything at all, but is nourished by its own body. If one takes that as a possible position, one might also leave 'πνεύματος' at *PA* IV.5, but interpret it by means of *Resp.* 9 by saying that the cicada lives on its internal *pneuma*. I suspect, however, that the corruption in the text at IV.5, 682a27, is not that which LOUIS guesses; 'πνεύματος' could easily have been 'φυτεύματος', 'of a plant'. This would be more accurate than 'dew', which is in turn more accurate than saying that the cicada does not eat anything at all. The objection to this suggestion is that Aristotle goes on to describe an insect which lives for only one day as similar to the cicada in its feeding habits; an ephemeral insect could very well be understood as not eating anything at all.

The length of life of the cicada is also at issue, and this descrepancy is directly related to that concerning the food

of the cicada, and to a discrepancy concerning the temperature
of the cicada. Aristotle nearly everywhere says that the cicada is relatively short-lived, but in *Resp*. he says that it
is long-lived, being especially warm. One might force on the
Resp. the idea that the length of life here, and here alone,
includes the larval stage, which is indeed long (several
years in Mediterranean contries, 14 to 17 years in North
America); the other passages would then be understood to refer to the adult stage, which runs from sometime in June to
August or perhaps early September. But *Resp*. seems clearly to
be talking about the adult stage, not the larval stage; in
HA Aristotle shows that he already knows about the stages of
metamorphosis. I find that the *HA* and *PA* passages are closer
to the truth about the 'temperature' of the cicada, as well
as to the truth about the length of life. The cicada has
little means of regulating its internal heat, and for this
reason avoids deep shade (see 556a) and prefers olive trees
(601a7). It needs an external temperature of about 20° C to
sing, and much below that it hardly functions at all. The
cicada has a dry, almost papery, look, and that would indicate 'coldness' to Aristotle, since that which is essentially
hot has some fattiness. I suspect that there has been some
tampering with the text of *Resp*. 9, 475a1ff; otherwise, Aristotle should have written this passage before he became well
acquainted with cicadas. But the *HA* already has a better account of cicadas than *Resp*. 9, so *Resp*. 9 should have been
written before *HA*; I do not find this alternative attractive,
particularly in view of the reference to '*emphyton pneuma*'.
There are further difficulties with the passage in *Resp*. 9
which I have not mentioned here; perhaps I shall do so elsewhere.

After all of this, we must note that the cicada seems peculiar
but not unique in that its tongue does not serve as a sting,
nor does it have a rear sting, and thus is not armed with a
weapon at all. This tongue is, however, explained by an analogy; it is, as it were, a 'root' through which it takes its

178

food. Of course such an analogy reminds us of passages like
PA IV.4, 678a10ff, in which the stomach is compared to the
ground, and the pores of the mesentery to roots, but we may
also remember the continuity of the lower animals with the
plant kingdom, and the fact that mouths and roots do share
the function of bringing food to the organism, and the cicada like the plant subsists on liquid food alone. The
function is similar, and the form is unexpectedly similar
(see IV.10, 686b34, and *IA* 4, 705a30ff).

A second analogy used in the passages quoted depends upon
a comparison of the tongue-like sting with the nose of the
elephant. The similarity is striking, of course; in English,
all of the organs named share the common title 'proboscis'.
But Aristotle does not have a common name for these organs;
he is pointing out, in the first place, the functional similarity: both the trunk and the sting-tongue are sensory,
both organs are means of gathering food. Furthermore, both
organs perform several functions for their owners. In fact,
the trunk and the 'so-called sting' are both used by Aristotle as paradigm cases of 'katachresis', a notion which we
will discuss at length in the next chapter.

The third analogy which appears may be taken as an apology
for this superabundant utility of a single organ; Aristotle
argues that nature does not usually try to get by as cheaply,
for nature usually does honest work, like a true craftsman,
making specialized tools for specialized purposes, rather
than combining functions of radically different kinds in the
same organ. But the tongue of the insects and testacea which
is used for piercing, tasting, sucking up food, and as a de-
fensive weapon, like the trunk of the elephant, is demanded
by the peculiar way of life of these creatures and by the
limitations imposed by the material and the structure of the
body of the animals.

Summary of Part B: Aristotle's account of variations in the
parts of animals

One of the major causes for variations in a related or similar
part in different species, according to Aristotle, is the quality of the material available for the part in various species. The thick skin of heavy birds, scaliness of reptiles
and fish, the poor imitation of flesh in non-blooded animals,
all seem to Aristotle to limit the possible development of
eyelids, ear lobes, and nostrils. On the other hand, the fine
quality of flesh and other 'uniform parts' in man makes possible organs of vision, taste, and touch which have great sensitivity. The quality of the material sometimes proves a hin-
drance which must be overcome in the way best possible in the
circumstances, and sometimes proves an opportunity which makes
possible a suitable organ for the animal with the other necessary characteristics for the use of an unusually sensitive
faculty of some kind.
To some extent, the environment of the species is understood
as a cause of variations in the parts, but for Aristotle environment is not the kind of cause which it is for modern evolutionary biologists. For the modern biologist[102] environment
is a cause of change in a species; the species is understood
as a changing hereditary line, adapting (or failing to adapt)
through various mechanisms to the challenges and opportunities
of changing environments. Aristotle has foreclosed for himself
the possibility of an evolutionary explanation of variations,
yet he seems to write of variations in a way which is not incompatible with an evolutionary theory. He must suppose that
the environments are relatively stable, and that the relationship between environment and species, so easily observed (in
rough outline), must also remain stable. The character of the
eyes of fish or of birds, and of the 'tongues' of fish, crocodiles, or insects, may be understood as a permanent characteristic necessitated by the permanent relationship between permanent environment and permanent species. If the world does

not change, the species need not change either.[103] So for
Aristotle the environment is a kind of formal-final cause of
the species; the natural environment of the species may well
be part of, or stated in, the definition of the species.
This is true even of the great divisions inherited from Plato:
land animals, water animals, and fliers. But Aristotle goes
farther than that, he points out the minutiae like the fond-
ness of bees for spring water, and the habitat of the cicada
among the branches of the olive tree.

If one has both an evolutionary theory, and a wealth of observational data, one can find explanatory force from the
theory for those data. Darwin's finches, spread into a new
environment, developed new forms to occupy ecological niches;
this is easy to say if you have the theory, and the finches.
The theory itself was more acceptable in the nineteenth century, an age in which man believed that he could better his
life, better his political system, and improve the species
itself. Aristotle did not have some of the more esoteric observational data, and he did not have theoretical use for an
evolutionary theory of biological species.

In fact, Aristotle takes some rather devious roads around data
which might have led him to accept some sort of evolutionary
theory. One such road is the theory of 'dualizing'; the seal
was an example, and the crocodile another. The dualizing species are taken by Aristotle to preserve a certain continuity
in nature, but Aristotle is not so concerned to preserve that
continuity as he is to explain variations which do not fit
with his other explanatory ideas: seals, bats, ostriches, and
apes are animals which do not fit very well into an explanatory
scheme which begins with the assumption of a stable world. Rather than give up the stable world, Aristotle makes use of the
notion of a natural continuum, a notion which finds more support in Plato's metaphysical scheme than it does in Aristotle's.

We have had occasion to comment briefly on some of the
nuances in the concept of necessity as it appears in Aristotle's explanations, especially in *PA*. Sometimes necessity seems

independent from, or other than, functional teleology; often, this possibly non-teleological necessity seems to derive from the character of matter and its movements; sometimes it seems to derive from structural demands which are not directly subservient to functional demands. A non-teleological necessity was a part of the explanatory schemes of several of Aristotle's predecessors, yet Aristotle himself, as we have argued in Chapter I, attempts to show in the *Physics* and elsewhere that necessity of that kind cannot explain natural change. We will try to show, in the next chapter, that Aristotle does *not* revert to the position rejected in the *Physics*, when he attempts to explain biological phenomena.

We have also had occasion to comment briefly upon appearances of the notion of a transcendent Nature. The idea of a Nature which is superior to individuals and to individual species, was not a typical feature of philosophies before Aristotle, since for most of them, the word *physis* was applied more nearly to the material of things, rather than to their form. However, the notion of a Logos, developed by Heraclitus, Parmenides, and Empedocles,[104] was used by Plato in the *Timaeus* as a principle of a transcendent teleology. Aristotle's 'logos' is tied more nearly to the notion of the species, as we shall see in the next chapter. His 'physis', however, might be taken as closely related to the Logos of the *Timaeus* especially in such slogans as 'Nature does nothing in vain', and in the general use of statements of the sort, 'Nature uses...'. We will try to show that such expressions are understood within Aristotle's system as statements of an essentially functional teleology, rather than as assertions of the existence and activities of a being which transcends species of living entities.

CHAPTER IV   NECESSITY AND PURPOSE IN THE EXPLANATION
              OF NATURE

Introduction

In this chapter we explore two main philosophical issues
which are involved in many of Aristotle's accounts of biological phenomena. Aristotle's teleology may be seen as an attempt to take a middle path between two extreme positions
held by some of his predecessors. The one extreme, as he understood it, was the position that denies the validity of a
teleological understanding, and asserts the validity of an
explanatory scheme which we might today call 'mechanistic'.
Democritus, as Aristotle understood him, is an example of one
who held such a position. The other extreme might be called
the 'theological' or 'animistic' position, which holds that
there are divine beings or cosmic souls which purposefully
cause many of the events in the world.[1] Aristotle does not
attack this system directly, but he does avoid the more anthropomorphic version of theism, and he also avoids animism.
He especially avoids any suggestion of the existence of souls
separate from organic bodies; the only exception would be the
prime mover, but that is not a soul, it is pure thought.
Aristotle does *not* believe that there is a separate entity
or soul which may be called Nature, and which (consciously)
brings about the purposive relationships in the world.
Plato had tried to steer a middle course between the position
which we think of as mechanistic, and the primitive animistic
religion; in the *Timaeus*, however, his 'necessity' turns out
to be too like that of Democritus, and his 'reason' (*logos*)
is embodied in a deity who seems as much a superhuman person
as the deities of the poets. Although Plato's *Timaeus* has
many virtues, not all recognized by Aristotle, from Aristotle's point of view it gives too much to both extreme positions,
and thus admits an unnecessary dualism.To obtain an understanding

of living beings as distinguished from non-living, one must understand them as *organic*; in order to understand anything one must avoid basing one's understanding on something which is itself incomprehensible. The cosmology of the *Timaeus* relies heavily on a random shaking of the continuum, or receptacle, in order to account for the variegations of the world (52d-e), and upon the direct activity of God for the establishment of order (53b). These principles seem incomprehensible to the Aristotelian; one ought not search for comprehension in that which cannot be understood. Aristotle does not deny the existence of something like Plato's receptacle (he supposes that the idea of the receptacle is included within his own concept of matter), and he surely does not deny the existence of God, but he does proceed, in the biological books at least, as though an appeal to these ultimate principles, if such they be, could not further our understanding of the species of animals with whom we share the world.

In this chapter we will examine Aristotle's explanations in order to discover just how close he does come to each of the extreme positions. Some have supposed that he does embrace a mechanistic explanation in the biological books and elsewhere; we will see that he does not, for the very concepts in which a mechanistic position would have to be expressed have been turned by Aristotle into essentially teleological concepts. At the other extreme, some of Aristotle's statements about nature, especially those which depend upon and derive from an analogy of art and nature, might be interpreted as making Nature a transcendent agency.

We will see that Aristotle's nature is *not* transcendent, but immanent as the species or soul of individuals. Our special attention will be turned to those passages in which it is said that 'nature uses' something for some purpose; these passages are also interesting because they show the development of the idea of '*katachresis*' as an explanatory concept.

A. ARISTOTLE'S NATURAL NECESSITY[2]

1. The Theoretical Problem

In several passages in the biological works, Aristotle contrasts that which happens 'for a purpose' (οὗ ἕνεκα) with that which happens 'necessarily'. In most such passages, that which happens 'necessarily' is ascribed to the character of the material;[3] we will call the necessity which appears in these passages 'material' necessity, provisionally. In a few passages, the necessity contrasted with purpose seems to derive from the structure of the animal, rather than from its material character; we will call this sort of necessity 'formal'.[4]

Passages which involve 'material' necessity have proven difficult to interpret; the senses of 'necessity' which Aristotle distinguishes in the *Metaphysics* and elsewhere do not seem to fit easily into a contrast of purpose and necessity of the kind found in the biological books. Aristotle distinguishes explicitly three general senses of the word 'necessary' which might apply to natural beings: these may be called 'simple' (ἁπλῶς), 'conditional' or 'hypothetical' (ἐξ ὑποθέσεως), and 'forced' (βίαιον).[5] Various commentators have identified material necessity with each of these senses; others have supposed that Aristotle introduces a fourth sense of necessity in the biological books (and possibly elsewhere), a kind of 'mechanical' necessity. It is my opinion that 'material' necessity is a form of conditional necessity;[6] I will try to show here that it is not any of the other sorts of necessity which have been suggested, and some of the consequences of the position which I share with BALME and WEISS.

Here are some examples of the sort of comment which I find mistaken.

> D'une manière générale, Aristote assigne à la
> nécessité (*anagkè*), c'est-à-dire à des causes
> mécaniques, tout résultat obtenu sans avoir été
> poursuivi comme une fin (S. MANSION).[7]

> ... en général dans l'histoire naturelle --, la
> nécessité dont il s'agit, nécessité opposée à la
> finalité, est la nécessité mécanique, matériel.e,
> conditions que la matière impose à l'intention de
> la nature (LE BLOND).[8]

> At the same time many natural phenomena are due
> to simple or absolute necessity. They flow in-
> evitably from the nature of the matter. Sometimes
> this absolute necessity subserves ends... . But
> apart from the cases in which mechanism and te-
> leology conspire together, there are cases in
> which mechanism alone is at work (W.D. ROSS).[9]

Although he does not accept an identification of material
and mechanical necessity, Auguste MANSION has argued for the
position that there is a "nécessité brute de la matière"[10]
which "s'oppose formellement à la finalité ou, du moins, ne
s'y subordonne pas" (p. 309). He argues that since Aristotle
has an idea of "causes aveugles" which are not spontaneous,
but are involved in all change, then "on conclura que dans
le système d'Aristote le monde de la nature tout entier est
soumis à un déterminisme rigoureux..." (p. 326). Similarly,
Henri CARTERON says that a "déterminisme physico-chimique"[11]
is at work in the biological realm, according to Aristotle,
but CARTERON explicitly denies that this determinism is a
form of mechanism (pp. 178-183). W.D. ROSS has an interpretation which approaches, but is not the same as, that of the
French writers, for he identifies simple necessity, mechanical
necessity, and material necessity.[12]

Most recently, W. CHARLTON[13] has distinguished conditional
necessity from what he calls "unconditional" necessity:
"Sometimes a phenomenon can be explained as the direct outcome of unconditional necessity, and in that case it is
ascribable simply to matter." He makes clear that he means to
ascribe some sort of mechanical theory to Aristotle when he
says,

> In general, changes which Aristotle attributes to
> an external source are changes explained in accord-
> ance with the laws of physics or mechanics, and,
> since these are laws governing or describing in
> general terms the behavior of the elements, this
> is as much as to say that they are changes due to

186

nature in the sense of matter (pp.115-116).

This statement should seem odd to the reader, for "laws of physics and mechanics" had not been formulated in Aristotle's day, nor does he formulate such laws. CHARLTON tries to foist them onto Aristotle by a comparison of "simple" necessity with the modern concept of physical regularity; this commits CHARLTON to an identification of "unconditional" necessity, 'material' necessity, 'mechanical' necessity perhaps, and 'simple' necessity.

I will argue that 'material' necessity is *not* identical with 'simple' necessity, that it is not necessity in the sense of 'force', and finally that Aristotle does not have a concept which may appropriately be called 'mechanical' necessity, in the modern sense of that word.

At the end of *Met*. Delta 5, Aristotle contrasts those things whose necessity comes from something else and those whose necessity is in themselves. If something has its necessity in itself, this is simple necessity, and that which is simply necessary is eternal and immovable (unchangeable): "nothing compulsory (βίαιον) or against their nature (παρὰ φύσιν) attaches to them" (1015b15). The clear sense of the passage is that eternal and unchangeable beings are the ultimate sources of the necessity in that which owes its necessity to something else. The prime mover is said to be simply necessary (*Met*. Lambda 7, 1072b11); the everlasting heavenly bodies are said to be simply necessary at the beginning of *PA* and elsewhere,[14] and are said to be the source of necessity in temporal entities in *GA* II.1 and IV, and *MA*. Aristotle does not say, but everywhere denies, that matter is 'eternal and unchangeable',[15] and he never says that either matter or anything made of terrestrial matter is simply (ἁπλῶς) necessary.

Those who say that the necessity found in matter is, according to Aristotle, simple necessity, have no textual support for their position. To be sure, *Phys*. II.9 has been used as if it were such a support, but Helene WEISS has shown that

Aristotle there interprets

> das Grundsein der Hyle selbst als eine ἀνάγκη
> ἐξ ὑποθέσεως. Die Hyle ist danach für das Wer-
> dende zwar notwendig, das Sein der Hyle ist ἐξ
> ἀνάγκης. Aber dieses "aus Notwendigkeit" ist
> nicht ἁπλῶς, sondern bloss ἐξ ὑποθέσεως.[16]

If she is right, then the 'material' necessity of *PA* and *GA*
should be conditional necessity.

In *GC* II.11, Aristotle poses a problem: 'In continuous processes is there any case in which a future being is necessary?'
We should expect from *Int*. 9, 19a8,[17] that there are some
cases in which a future being is *not* necessary, for example,
tomorrow's sea-fight; the question here posed is, are there
any cases which are not like the sea-fight? Aristotle argues
that only cyclical processes can be 'simply' necessary processes, for to the degree that a series or process is linear,
it is contingent. To be simply necessary, the process must be
continuously actual, never potential (cf. *Met*. 1015b9), since
that which potentially is, also potentially is-not (337b7,33).
Furthermore, an explicable process must have an *archē*, but
the *archē* of a linear process exhibits potentiality of non-
being in that it has not caused the process at one time, and
then caused it at another; such an *archē* might fail to continue the process at any time. Cyclical processes *are* continuously actual, and are understood as having a permanent
archē.

Simple necessity is to be found in the sub-lunar world to the
extent to which cyclical processes are to be found there. In
animal generation, for example (*GA* II.1), the production of
successive generations of a species *per se* is thought to be
cyclical, but the process is linear for each individual member of the species.[18] Linear processes are subject to chance
or accident, and thus cannot be predicted; this is another
way of stating the difference between cyclical and linear
processes. The relationship between cyclical and linear processes in animal generation is well stated in *GA* IV.10. Nature, says Aristotle, tends to measure the lifespans of

188

perishable things by the cyclical periods of the heavenly
bodies,

> but cannot do so exactly because of the inde-
> terminateness of the matter and because a plu-
> rality of principles is generated, which prin-
> ciples often impede natural generations and
> destructions and are causes of those things
> which occur contrary to nature (778a5-9).

A similar position is expressed in *Met*. Epsilon 2. 'Beings'
are classified as a) the necessary, not forced, which cannot
be otherwise and are always the same; b) those which are such
'for the most part'; c) the accidental. The cause of the accidental is 'that which is for the most part', and of such
beings, especially matter: "Matter, which admits of being
otherwise, is the cause of the accidental contrary to that
which happens for the most part" (1027a14). Indeterminateness
and variability, the characteristics of matter which make
dysteleological results possible, are precisely those characteristics which cannot belong to anything which is 'simply'
necessary.

There might be some plausibility in an argument purporting
that the necessity of matter is simple because matter itself
goes through a cyclical process, but this would be a misunderstanding of Aristotle's notion of a cyclical process. That
which is permanent in the cyclical process is form; it is the
continued existence of the form, not the repeated accidental
effects of the matter, which is simply necessary.

The position of Auguste MANSION seems to be that the "brute"
necessity of matter is to be understood as a kind of 'forced'
(βίαιον) necessity;[19] he seems to base this position on *APo*.
II.11, 94b36-95a3.[20] Aristotle does distinguish here between
that which nature does ἕνεκά του and that which is done 'from
necessity', but he goes on to distinguish carefully between
two kinds of necessity, that which is natural and 'in accordance with impulse', and that which is unnatural and forced.
This distinction, repeated elsewhere, should discourage those
who would make the 'forced' into a form of natural necessity;

in fact, the passages in which purpose and necessity are contrasted make clear that the necessity is natural, nevertheless, and κατὰ ὁρμήν. CHARLTON uses this same passage, but argues that "unconditional" necessity is that which is "in accordance with impulse". MANSION too might mean that "brute" necessity is κατὰ ὁρμήν, and would then agree with CHARLTON. This is a quite different sort of mistake; Aristotle clearly identifies the natural necessity which is 'in accordance with impulse' with conditional necessity at *PA* I.1, 642a3ff, and elsewhere, but both CHARLTON and MANSION contrast "unconditional" or "brute" necessity with conditional necessity. This interpretation is, incidentally, committed to the position that Aristotle does not mention any form of conditional necessity at *APo.* II.11, and this is definitely implausible, although not impossible.

Those commentators who identify material necessity with mechanical necessity are the most clearly mistaken, but they are also the most difficult to refute, because they do not define 'mechanical necessity', nor is it easy to find a definition which one can confidently ascribe to these commentators. The 'necessity' of Plato's *Timaeus*, or the 'necessity' of Democritus, must most closely approach a notion of mechanical necessity before Aristotle, but F.M. CORNFORD[21] argues that Plato's 'necessity' was not mechanical necessity in the modern or Cartesian sense, and that the necessity of the early atomists was not understood as a complete determinism. CORNFORD's grounds are rather convincing; the *anagkē* of the *Timaeus* is characterized by a completely *disorderly* motion. There are no inherent regularities in Plato's receptacle; rather, it is the influence of *logos* which imposes order on *anagkē*. GUTHRIE, writing on Democritus,[22] does not hesitate to use the word 'mechanical' in describing that philosopher's theory of necessity; however, GUTHRIE defends the equivalence which Aristotle states between necessity and chance in his refutation of Democritus in *Phys.* II (see Chapter I.B, above), on the ground that Democritus held that most

events are brought about by so many different antecedent
events that no man could possibly predict what will be. If
we accept CHARLTON's notion that a mechanical theory relies
upon success in prediction as substantiation of its validity,
then the atomistic theory, as GUTHRIE describes it, would
not be mechanical at all, because it denies the possibility
of prediction. But there is another reason why the atomistic
theory could not be mechanical: a mechanical theory depends
upon an assertion of an analogy between machines and nature,
an analogy which the atomists did not make, and could hardly
have made, given the simplicity, the lack of complexity, of
machines which existed in the fifth century B.C. It is furthermore clear that machines are understood first teleologically, as implements for some end. Perhaps one could argue
that mechanistic theories should be committed to some form
of teleology as an intrinsic part of their system. This is
not, however, the way in which these theories are characterized by the commentators, so we are at a loss to determine
just what it is that is being ascribed to Aristotle in these
passages.
However the concept of necessity in Democritus or Plato may
be characterized, Aristotle argues against that of Democritus,
at least, quite explicitly in *Phys*. II. It would take far
more argumentation and documentation than S. MANSION, Le BLOND,
W.D. ROSS, or CHARLTON, provides, to establish the position
that Aristotle rejects the concept of necessity proposed by
his predecessors, in the *Physics*, and then uses the same or
a closely similar concept in the biological works. Anyone who
claims that Aristotle uses a concept of mechanical necessity
in the biological works seems to be committed to the position
that Aristotle's predecessors proposed such a concept, and
that he both rejected and accepted it. We know, that Aristotle
did not accept determinism, from *Int*. 9; it should also be
clear that he did not accept mechanical determinism.

2. Conditional Necessity and *PA* I.1

Conditional (ἐξ ὑποθέσεως) necessity is so named because it
is stated in a conditional sentence, 'if p then necessarily
q', rather than in a simple sentence, 'necessarily p'. The
relationship between 'p' and 'q' is thought of as some sort
of causal relationship. In a typical modern theory, the sen-
tences 'p' and 'q' might describe classes of events, and one
class of events is claimed to be the efficient cause of another sort of event. For example, 'if the temperature drops
below 0° C, water (necessarily) freezes'. For Aristotle, by
contrast, the relationship is usually one which we would call
a 'means to end' relationship, a 'necessary condition for'
relationship: 'if x is to be, then y must be'. Aristotle's
own examples both illustrate and reveal some nuances within
his usage of the notion of conditional necessity. In *Met.*
Delta 5, we find two sorts of conditional necessity named:
a) 'that without which a thing cannot live', b) 'that without which good cannot be or come to be'. The first sort is
well illustrated by the functions of nutrition and generation:

> The capacity to absorb food may exist apart from
> all other powers, but the others cannot exist apart
> from this in mortal beings. This is evident in the
> case of plants; for they have no other capacity of
> the soul.[23]

The second sort of conditional necessity is illustrated by
the higher functions of the soul, which are 'for the better',
and thus teleologically prior; the materials and processes
which make these functions possible are conditionally necessary 'for the better'. In *GA* II.6, 742a20ff, the heart, head,
and eyes are said to develop early in the embryological process because they are part of the purpose of the animal, and
are therefore prior in entity (*ousía*). The distinction between two sorts of conditional necessity is also illustrated
by the physiology of the higher animals, according to Aristotle. The diaphragm has the function of protecting the sensory faculty in the heart from the heat and exhalations from

192

food which is being digested, and is, furthermore, designed "to separate the more noble from the less noble, the upper from the lower, in as many species as possible, for the upper is the purpose and better, and the lower is for the sake of it and necessary, as receiving the food" (PA III.10, 672 b21). Here, as often, the first of the two subsenses of conditional necessity is marked by the word 'necessary', in contrast to 'purpose'.

Aristotle discusses the sort of necessity applicable in biology in PA I.1. At 639b21ff, he has distinguished between the final cause (οὐ ἕνεκα) and the source of change (ἀρχὴ τῆς κινήσεως), arguing that the final cause is of highest importance for the understanding of practical processes, such as medicine or building, but the hou heneka and the kalon is even more evident in the works of nature than in art. He goes on to say that necessity "is not present in all the natural things in the same way", although nearly all of his predecessors had tried to use this concept in their explanations. "Simple necessity", he says,

> is present in everlasting things, and conditional
> necessity in those which are generated (in nature)
> as in the productions of art, e.g. a house and
> anything else of that sort. If a house or some
> other end is to exist, it is necessary that such
> and such matter be present; and it is necessary
> that first this be generated and moved, then that,
> and in the same way continually until the end, for
> the sake of which each thing is generated and
> exists. Similarly in things generated in nature
> (639b24-34).

Thus far this passage describes succinctly conditional necessity, and says that it is present in both nature and art. He continues:

> But the manner of demonstration and necessity is
> different in the natural and theoretical sciences.
> (This is discussed elsewhere) (640a1).

On the strength of this sentence DÜRING (see n. 12 above) contrasts the senses or modes of necessity operative in nature and art, but this cannot be quite right, since Aristotle stated that the necessity in both nature and art is conditional necessity. PECK, on the other hand, takes the contrast to be between natural science and theoretical science, in spite of the fact that he notes that *physikē* is theoretical according to *Met*. Epsilon 1, 1025b, just one of several passages presenting this point of view. PECK claims, in his note to 640a, that Aristotle is thinking of *physikē* as productive, because he is thinking of *physis* as a craftsman; this interpretation does not account for the strong contrast implied by ἀλλά at 640a1. LE BLOND similarly takes the contrast to be between physics and mathematics, of which the first uses final causes, and the second does not -- but again, he is mistaken for the same sorts of reasons which apply to the positions of DÜRING and PECK.

As I understand the passage, Aristotle says that the necessity present in art and in nature is conditional, but the direction of the arguments in which this concept of necessity appears varies between art, which is practical, and the science of nature, which is theoretical. Thus we must translate the passage which follows, at 640a3, a passage made more difficult by a surfeit of pronouns of indefinite or indeterminate reference:

> For the starting point in the < theoretical sciences, including natural science > is that which is, but in the < practical > that which will be; for < we may argue that > 'since health or (the) man is so and so, necessarily X is or is to be generated', but not 'since X is or has been generated, Y necessarily is or will be'.
> (< > mark my insertions)

This passage is confusing because Aristotle simultaneously compares and contrasts art and nature, and also because the aorist infinitive γενέσθαι has an indefinite time. I suppose that he means to say that in the case of the man we start from what is, and argue that X (blood, flesh, or the copulation of his parents) must exist or have happened; in the case of health we can argue theoretically, i.e., 'since there is health, X must exist (good blend or whatever) or have

194

happened   (drinking of medicine perhaps), or we can argue
practically, 'if there is to be health, there must be good
blend, or a taking of medicine for the ailment'. But we cannot argue that since there is a copulation, there necessarily
will be a man, or since he takes medicine, he will necessarily be healthy. Conditional necessity, whether natural or
practical, is non-convertible, as he implies a few lines
later, referring to 'another work' which may well be *GC* II.11,
as PECK suggests in a note. In *GC* II.11, as well as in *PA*
I.1, Aristotle adds that reasonings concerning conditional
necessity cannot be carried to infinity.

Although Aristotle says that the necessity which applies in
natural science is conditional, nevertheless he often contrasts 'purpose' and 'necessity', and this is the source of
the difficulty in interpretation which we stated in the previous section. To be sure, in many passages (we will note
some of them below) the contrast is in fact between two sorts
of conditional necessity as defined in *Met.* Delta 5, between
that which is regarded as something of an end in itself, and
that which is necessary for the preservation of an organism.
In much the same way, Aristotle often contrasts the function
of the organ and its conditionally necessary purpose of development; this process he calls 'necessary generation'. So
in *PA* I.1, 640a10, he proceeds to a critique of Empedocles
and Democritus for the attempt to explain biological occurrences with a necessity that resembles all too closely chance
or accident. Rather, he says, the mode of explanation should
be according to one of the modes of conditional necessity:

> The best one could say would be 'since this is
> what it is to be for man, therefore he has what
> he does; for he could not exist without these
> parts'. But if one cannot say that, then the
> next best would be 'quite impossible otherwise'
> or 'well thus'. This follows: since it is as it
> is, thus and so a generation must necessarily
> occur; therefore this part is generated first,
> then that (640a33-b3).[24]

The distinction made here does not seem exactly like that
made in *Met.* Delta 5; here, the distinction is between a 'best'

and a 'second best' mode of statement; both modes seem to include the strong form of conditional necessity: 'he could not
exist without these parts', 'quite impossible otherwise'. The
best mode of statement seems to be to state how the part (or
whatever) belongs to the entity of the species, how it belongs to the logos in the sense of form. The second best mode
seems to be in the form of a general negative proposition like
'there cannot be an X without a Y', or else a proposition like
'X is better off with a Y'.[25]
The best way, giving an account of the essence of the species,
would include stating that which is necessary for simple survival, and that which is necessary for the 'better' life of
the individuals of the species. According to this way of investigation, those qualities which, although rarely found in
actuality, belong to the 'formal intelligible perfection' of
the species. The *eidos* seems to have the kind of being which
the everlasting entities have; it is a kind of everlasting
entity. Conditional and simple necessity coincide in this cyclical generation; in individual members, the functions of nutrition and generation come near to being simply necessary
by this path (see n. 23 above). The higher functions, however, have a teleological priority which is based not upon the
necessity of the continuation of the species, but upon the necessity of the realization of the perfection of the species
(as odd as that may sound). Aristotle often says that the
'point' (*hou heneka*) is prior in entity, while those things
which exist for the sake of the point or end are prior in the
order of becoming; the latter includes the generative functions
and parts which perform them (see *GA* II.6, 742a20ff). 'Prior
in entity' does not simply mean 'prior in the individual', but
also more truly 'prior in essence', essentially prior. In
the individual, he says at 742b12, the parts which will perform the higher functions develop first (heart, head, eyes).
There is a kind of unity between the 'end' or more perfect
functions, and that which is for the sake of the end, in that
the heart or its analogue is the controlling center for all

196

these functions.[26]

At *PA* I.1, 640b5, Aristotle turns his attack upon the idea
of many presocratic philosophers that the matter of the universe has, of itself, a 'necessary nature' (b9). From Aristotle's viewpoint, the error of these presocratics was in
supposing that a discovery of this nature of matter would
immediately convey an understanding of the world. Even if
one had both an understanding of matter as such, and a knowledge of the moving cause of the universe, one would still
not know the form, one would still not know the end. But
matter does not have a 'necessary nature' in itself, nor is
it enough to tell what something is made of, to explain it.
This attack, although directed most definitely at Democritus,
could also be aimed by Aristotelians at many physicists of
the modern era. Many of the commentators on Aristotle seem
to have been so thoroughly indoctrinated into the idea that
matter really does have a necessary nature that they cannot
accept Aristotle's theory as his unless they find him asserting that matter has a 'necessary nature'. However, twentieth
century physics has tended to give up this concept in the
face of W. HEISENBERG's principle of indeterminism, and many
contemporary biologists, like J. MONOD, find 'chance' relationships most typical of the materials on the atomic level.

      Aristotle finds that the necessity of matter and move-
ment described by Democritus would, at best, be the same as
'the forced' (*biaion*), which is contrary to nature.[27] It
seems to him a gross mistake to explain natural beings by
appeal to that which is contrary to nature, so he turns his
attention to the form and purpose of the parts of animals,
and to the soul, which is the essence, mover, and end of the
animal.

At 641b he turns again to the discussion of necessity, contrasting chance and conditional necessity. It is particularly
evident in biological science, he argues, that 'chance' does
not explain what occurs, "for no chance creature is generated
from a particular seed, but this (species) from this (seed),

nor does a chance seed come from a chance body" (641b27). He
therefore enlarges on the theme of the relationship between
sperma and that which generates it, on the one hand, and that
which is generated, on the other. As we know (Chapter II),
the *sperma* is understood as an organ, an instrument, of the
parent, for generating offspring; it is also understood as a
necessary condition for the existence of the offspring.
So, Aristotle continues, "There are then these two causes,
the purpose (*hou heneka*) and necessity; for many things are
generated because it is necessary" (642a2). The necessity, he
says, is *conditional*, and neither of the sorts of necessity
described 'in the philosophical treatises'. OGLE and PECK,
in their notes to this passage, agree that these sorts of
necessity must be the simple (ἁπλῶς) and the forced (βίαιον).
Conditional necessity is essential for an understanding of
"things which are generated" (642a7). For example, an axe
must be hard in order to split wood; to be hard it must be
made of bronze or iron; so the body and its parts, having
each its purpose, must be made of such and such materials.
These then are the two sorts of "causes" which must be described in the explanation of living things. One of them is
evidently the form, the essence, the *physis* of the species,
which Empedocles and Democritus had barely stumbled upon;
in the time of Socrates the *method* was developed, but was
not applied to Nature.[28] The *other* cause must be conditional
necessity, the description of that which is *for* the form,
essence, *physis*. Thus we may gain an understanding of the
difficult passage which appears at 642a31, a passage which
in context is meant to illustrate how purpose and conditional
necessity operate together in the explanation of nature:

> ... respiration exists for the sake of X, but it
> is generated by means of Y and Z necessarily. Ne-
> cessity sometimes means that if that particular
> purpose (end) is to be, it is necessary to have
> these;[29] but sometimes it means that things are
> thus and have naturally come to be so;[30] for it
> is necessary that heat go out and go in again as
> it offers resistance, and the air flow in; this
> is already necessary. But when the internal heat

meets the resistance in the cold there is en-
trance and exit of the external air.[31]

If one takes the last few lines out of context, one might
suppose that Aristotle is talking about 'mechanical' necessity
or some sense of necessity opposed to a teleological explanation, but within the context it is clear that he considers
the process as conditionally necessary *for respiration*, just
as respiration has the function of cooling the body. In many
passages we must understand the contrast between purpose and
necessity as a contrast between a function and a process which
makes the function possible, i.e., between something which is
part of the end, and which is a means toward the end (see
note 3, above); this is one of them.

In this section, I have tried to clarify the fact that Aristotle is talking about conditional necessity and its modes
in *PA* I.1; he does not say that the kind of necessity which
operates in the biological realm is simple necessity, he
does not say that it is the 'forced', nor does he say that
it is a sort of necessity which is neither simple, conditional,
or forced. His language is not always as clear as we might
like to have found it, but its very obscurity in the crucial
passages should warn us not to take it as saying something
which is in contradiction to his very plain language in other
passages.

The frequent contrast between the conditionally necessary
material (organ, part) and the process which brings it into
existence may be illustrated by what he says about the mesentery at *PA* IV. 4, 687a4:

> We shall find that the mesentery has a necessary
> generation, as do the other parts; but the reason
> for which it is present in blooded animals is clear
> to those who consider it.

More amusing, perhaps, is the explanation of the hairiness
of man's head:

> Man has the hairiest head of all the animals. This
> is a) due to *necessity*, because the brain is fluid,
> and the skull has many sutures; and a large out-
> growth necessarily occurs where there is a large

199

amount of fluid and hot substance. But also
b) it is *on purpose* to give protection; that
is, the hair affords shelter both from excessive
cold and excessive heat. The human brain is the
biggest and most fluid of all brains; therefore
it needs the greatest amount of protection (*PA*
II.14, 658b3-9, PECK; see also passages noted
n. 3 above).

3. 'Accidentally necessary' and monsters

The phrases συμβαίνει ἐξ ἀνάγκης and κατὰ συμβεβηκὸς ἀναγκαῖον
appear several times in the biological books, especially in
the explanation of the generation of monsters. 'Accidentally
necessary' may be considered a rather odd phrase; it may be
thought to conflict with *Met.* Delta 30 and *APo.* I.6, 74b12,
where necessity and accident are contrasted (τὰ δὲ συμβεβηκότα
οὐκ ἀναγκαῖα, 74b12). One could lessen the paradoxical look
of the phrase 'συμβαίνει ἐξ ἀνάγκης' by translating it more
neutrally 'it happens necessarily', but the other phrase cannot be treated in that way.

In several passages, the necessity of that which συμβαίνει
ἐξ ἀνάγκης is clearly conditional necessity, the sort found
in a conditionally necessary generation.[32] Sometimes, however,
the phenomena which result from this necessity have no particular function. Much of *GA* V is devoted to a discussion of
that which "happens necessarily" in this way; a distinction
is made near the beginning between two modes of necessity:

> Animal X has an eye necessarily, for it is under-
> stood to be that sort of animal, but it has this
> sort of eye necessarily too, not by the same sort
> of necessity, but another kind, because it is
> naturally constructed (πέφυκε) to act or be acted
> upon thus or so (1, 778b16-19).

The first sense could be called 'essential' necessity, and
is another version of the first sort of conditional necessity
(part of the end). The second sense is obviously related to
the sort of conditional necessity which operates in the
"necessary generation" of functional parts. The difference

200

here is that that which is generated necessarily does *not* have a function, for it is the color of eyes and hair, the changes in the color of hair and in voice, and the like, which he discusses in this book. At *GA* V.8, 789b20, he says that he has dealt with the various παθήματα of the body, as many as 'happen to be generated' (γύνεσθαι συμβαύνει) *not* for the sake of something, but "from necessity and through the moving cause".

In the *PA*, the spleen, and the residues in the intestines and bladder, are said to be κατὰ συμβεβηκὸς ἐξ ἀνάγκης, accidentally necessary (II.7, 670a30). Bile is "not for the sake of something, but is an offscouring" (IV.2, 677a29). Aristotle here remarks that 'many' residues are similar in that they συμβαύνει ἐξ ἀνάγκης. BALME (*Classical Quarterly* 1939, p.135) remarks that the idea seems to be that these materials have no special function as parts of the body; this does not prevent them from being the result of a conditionally necessary process. That is to say, it is conditionally necessary for the body that the bile and the other residues be produced (for the general good of the body), but these residues are not in themselves valuable. This is not a particularly difficult problem for a teleological explanation of the animal economy, and the notion of 'accidentally, but conditionally, necessary' seems to apply rather well, once one gets used to the idea.

The most striking, and possibly the most difficult, case of 'accidental necessity' is in Aristotle's account of the generation of monsters (τέρατα). "Monsters are not necessary according to the final cause or end, but they are κατὰ συμβεβηκὸς ἀναγκαῖον"(*GA* IV.3, 767b14).[33] "The monster is contrary to nature, not all nature, but the general rule; for as for the eternal and necessary nothing is generated contrary to nature, but things *are* generated contrary to nature in the sense of the general rule, for these *can* be otherwise" (770b10). One should note immediately that Aristotle does not say that monsters are generated because of simple necessity;

he says that the generation of monsters is not contrary to
simple necessity. In *Met.* Epsilon 2, Aristotle says that that
which is 'for the most part' is the cause of the accidental;
here this doctrine is exemplified, for the cause of monsters
may be found to be something which is 'for the most part'
(ὡς ἐπι το πολύ, 1026b30). But monsters are said to be 'accidentally necessary', not just accidental, and Aristotle
adds that, "even in these cases it happens contrary to this
particular order, but never by chance, so that it seems to
be less a monster because even that which is contrary to nature is, in a way, nature, when nature in the sense of form
has not conquered nature in the sense of matter" (770b13-17,
after PECK). Aristotle seems to be struggling, in this passage, with the question of the degree to which one could reasonably say that monsters are the result of *force*, of the
sort of necessity called *biaion*, contrary to nature. The problem which he faces in this analysis is that the definition
of βιαία ἀνάγκη necessarily involves the idea that the source
of movement or change is external, rather than internal (cf.
EN III.1, 1110a1-b17).[34] Of course, there might be some cases
in which this would be the case, for example if the female parent were diseased (we would explain deformities caused by ru-
bella in this way); the Hippocratic Περὶ Γονῆς 9-12 gives examples of deformities caused from without. But in some cases
we cannot find an external cause which has 'forced' the monstrosity to occur; how may we find an internal cause of that
which is defective?
Aristotle is not satisfied with the explanation of monsters
commonly offered in antiquity, that they are provided by the
gods for the utility of man's divination of the future and his
guidance for the present, but he does want an explanation.
There is no easy way, however, to appeal to general principles.
Although we may say that he regards monsters as failures in the
process of generation, due to the resistance or variability
of the matter, which brings about the failure of the movement
to generate as it would if the material were all that it
'ought' to be, we actually find several lines of argument in

his explanation.

One sort of monster is explained by the same general principles which explain family resemblance: 'departing from type
and changing over' result from the failure of the movement
from the male to gain the mastery of the material in the female.[35] Another sort of monster, that with redundant parts,
or the 'Siamese twin' phenomenon, had been discussed by Democritus. That philosopher had put the blame for this sort of
monster on the mixing of semens from different copulations.
Aristotle's response is typical of his thinking:

> If one had to find the cause in the male semen,
> one would have to say something like that; but
> in general one ought rather suppose that the cause
> is in the material and in the process of develop-
> ment of the fetations (770a5ff).

He therefore gives examples to show, first, that animal species in which this sort of monstrosity occurs are prolific.
If the animal is normally prolific, the female produces plenty
of material, and the male semen is also plentiful; too much
material may be 'set' by the semen, or the movement may be
divided, 'like the eddies in rivers' (772b14-22). The pro-
lificness itself, however, is explained by an appeal to conditional necessity, for example in the case of fish: "Nature
makes up for the destruction of the fetations by the quantity"
(GA III.4, 755a32). Furthermore, the 'way is prepared' for
monsters which lack certain parts by the fact that prolific
animals normally generate ofsspring which are incomplete at
birth, so a further incompleteness is to be expected as a
'symptom' of the nature of such animals (IV.4, 770b3-7).[36]

One may also relate the 'necessity' of the generation
of monsters to Aristotle's account of 'dualizing' animals.
'Dualizing' animals are often said to be deformed (ἀνάπηρα)
in comparison with the higher of the two species to which the
animal is said to belong. "The reasons for the cause of monsters and of deformed (τῶν ἀναπήρων) animals are close and
in a way similar; for the monster is a sort of deformity
(ἀναπήρια)" (GA IV.4, 769b28-31). If a monster were to breed

true, Aristotle would have to say that it was no longer unnatural in the sense of *eidos*; it would be a definite species,
like a seal or bat. Dualizing will be discussed in section 6;
the matter is worth noting at this point because of the difficulty in discerning what sort of internal principle it may
be which results in something which is somehow inferior, yet
natural.

Monsters are regarded as failures of the conditionally necessary matter and movements to reach their normal end. How
could failures of that which is conditionally necessary be
themselves conditionally necessary? Although that seems a
strange notion, I suggest that Aristotle understands mortal
beings as necessarily made of matter which admits of being
otherwise; if there are to be such mortal beings, the potentiality for non-being must (conditionally) be actualized from
time to time. This I take to be the character of 'accident',
and it is for this reason that Aristotle uses the phrase
κατὰ συμβεβηκὸς ἀναγκαῖον in reference to monsters (767b14)
as in reference to the useless residues generated by the body
(*PA* III.7, 670a30). He is quick to point out that monsters
and useless residues are natural, so the necessity cannot be
'forced', for that is contrary to nature. The useless residues are conditionally necessary because, if matter is vari-
able and indefinite, some of the material ingested by the
organism will not be usable, and thus must be excreted if the
organism is to survive and function well. The case of monsters is similar; the material provided by the female is vari-
able, and lacks the 'definition', the *logos* which the male
provides. Some of the material cannot be formed into normal
progeny, but it does go through some process of development
initiated by the male parent. Since the material is inferior,
the result is a monster (an inferior being); but if there is
to be a process of sexual generation, matter must be used,
some of which will be inferior. Thus there must, in the normal course of events, be a production of monsters from time
to time.

204

4. Aristotle's supposed mechanism: a conclusion

Those passages in the biological books which have been used
to support an interpretation of Aristotle's 'necessity' which
brings it closer to the mechanistic conception popular in
Europe at some times since the Renaissance, at least, do not
fact support this interpretation at all. We have seen that
Aristotle's discussion of necessity in the *Met.* and *Phys.*
make unlikely an identification of the necessity which we
called 'material' with either simple necessity, forced necessity, or some form of mechanical necessity. Aristotle envisages simple necessity as belonging to everlasting cyclical
processes, and forced necessity to processes with an external
source of movement and a direction of change contrary to nature; the necessity which remains in the biological realm,
in most natural processes, is conditional necessity. This is
stated rather clearly in *PA* I.1; those who grasp at obscure
passages in this chapter to twist them into conformity with
modern mechanism are misguided. Although the motive may be
one of friendly assistance to Aristotle, in the midst of attacks from those who identify 'scientific' with 'mechanistic',
nevertheless such charity harms rather than helps Aristotle's
case for a modern philosophical reader.
The central point, which (if properly understodd) should make
Aristotle's conditional necessity tolerably clear, is that
matter itself is, for him, conditionally necessary. Aristotle
means to say that we can understand something as *hyle* only as
the *hyle* of something; *hyle* is, by definition, that which is
potentially something else, something more organized and actual. So too the movements, the processes of nature, are understood as movements *toward* something, processes *for* something. Aristotle does not deny that there may be characteristics
of matter, or results of movements, which are *not* "for" anything, but to the extent that this is true, these materials
and these movements are not understood at all. For Aristotle,
to apply the word 'necessary' to characteristics of matter

and/or movements without regard to that which the matter can become, is to misunderstand the meaning of the word 'necessity'. At most the individually regrettable concomitants of valuable processes might have some claim to be 'necessary' if one qualifies that necessity as 'accidental'.

In a non-teleological ("mechanistic") understanding of necessity, by contrast, the generation of so-called monsters is not different from the generation of anything else; the generation of monsters would be just as natural as the generation of other things, for it happens, and whatever happens counts as natural. In a non-teleological theory, monsters or mutations might pose the problem of an unexpected irregularity, but they do not at all count as evidence against the explanatory system. Aristotle comes close to saying that monsters are natural, because they happen, but the appearance of dysteleological results tends to cause a more difficult problem for him because such events cast doubt on his system of explanation.

Some of the modern commentators, for example CHARLTON, make out a case for an identification of Aristotle's 'simple' necessity with mechanical necessity; their case might seem plausible if one accepts their description of the mechanistic theory as arguing that, since it always happens, it must be necessary. A theory of this kind would describe as 'necessary' that which always happens, and Aristotle's 'simple necessity' is also ascribed to that which always happens. However, the argument proceeds in opposite directions: Aristotle argues that the process is simply necessary, and therefore that it always happens, while CHARLTON's mechanist seems to argue that, since it always happens, it must be necessary. This is the fundamental mistake made by CHARLTON, as by some of the other commentators, when he compares Aristotle's simple necessity with the necessity which appears in 'regularity' theories. David HUME saw that an observed constant conjunction does not demonstrate a necessary connection; Aristotle knew that the necessity had to be known independently of the phenomenon --

he doesn't even try to show the constancy of the phenomena
regarded as simply necessary. In fact, he is not usually concerned with the frequency of phenomena regarded as conditionally necessary either.

If those who believe that Aristotle has a mechanistic side
would make clear what they mean by "mechanistic" the difficulties would be on the way to resolution. Historically, the
concept of a mechanical explanation of nature was developed
during the sixteenth century, and the consequences of mechanical explanation for a theory of necessity were discussed
during the seventeenth and eighteenth centuries.[37] The original idea of a mechanical explanation of nature derived in
part from Aristotle's analogy of art and nature, with the
Platonistic introduction of God as the artisan of nature (see
ROSSI, appendix 1). The Aristotelian-Ptolemaic picture of the
universe suggested (to Robert BOYLE, among others) a mechanical clock; perhaps the Ptolemaic system, or some version of
it was in fact one of the ideas behind the development of
early clocks. The pictures of the universe developed by CO-
PERNICUS, KEPLER, and NEWTON also seemed comparable to great
machines. Mechanistic theory was not opposed to teleology in
the seventeenth and eighteenth centuries, because it was
supposed that just as the clock exists for some purpose, so
too the mechanism of the heavens was designed by God for some
purpose. For most of the people who developed the mechanistic
explanation of the universe, for DESCARTES and his followers,
as for NEWTON and his followers, there was no conflict between a mechanistic explanation and a teleological explanation.

The classical mechanistic theories distinguish some of
the same senses of necessity as Aristotle distinguished. G.
TONELLI has pointed out (see note 37) that one of the positions proposed in the eighteenth century was that mechanical
necessity is identical with conditional (hypothetical) necessity. The mechanists did not, however, mean by conditional
necessity just what Aristotle means; for the mechanists, efficient causal relationships are examples of conditionally

necessary relations, whether or not they are aiming at some
end. For Aristotle, however, the relation between mover and
moved is conditionally necessary if the process has some end.
But I suspect that the major difference between Aristotle and
the classical mechanists on the matter of conditional necessity is the emphasis which each places on this sort of necessity. For Aristotle, the explanation of terrestrial events
can at best appeal to conditional necessity, while for the
mechanists, some things can be found to be simply necessary.
TOLAND, for example, used the analogy of the universe and
the mechanism, and thought that the movement of matter was
absolutely (simply) necessary; this account of simple necessity looks more like Plato's use of the concept of *anagkē* of
the *Timaeus* than it does like Aristotle's notion of simple
necessity. One could, however, use the more truly Aristotelian
notion of simple necessity within a mechanistic system, by
arguing that it is 'mechanically' necessary that any individual event within a system be determined by the structure
of the entire system. Indeed, an Aristotelian mechanist of
this kind might even say that an examination of the structure
of the system could enable one to predict future events. For
Aristotle himself, only the structure of the heavens had that
kind of necessity, however; events on the terrestrial sphere
are, for him, made unpredictable by the fact that the movement of matter is *not* simply necessary. The concept of 'accidental necessity' can also be explicated within a classical
mechanistic theory: eclipses, which can be made to look like
counter-examples to Aristotle's generalization that regularly
occurring events are pointed events, occur in the astronomy
of Aristotle and in the astronomy of the mechanists in the
way in which the hands of a clock 'happen' (as it may chance)
to be in conjunction eleven times in twelve hours. For Aristotle, and for the classical mechanist, these 'necessarily
accidental' events do not have a point, but the heavens and
the clock do, none the less, exist for some purpose. For most
of the mechanists, however, the heavens were created, while

208

for Aristotle the heavens have always existed.

This is not the place to explore further the relationships which may exist between Aristotle's system and the development of classical mechanistic theories. It can be pointed out, however, that classical mechanism resembles more closely the cosmological theory developed by Plato in the *Timaeus* than it does anything in Aristotle. To be sure, both the mechanist and Aristotle (like Plato) point to the regularity of the heavens as a paradigm of the comprehensible, but classical mechanics went on to find regularities on the atomic level, which Plato had expected to exist, but which Aristotle (and HARVEY) denied as a basis for explanation. Also, classical mechanics, like Plato and unlike Aristotle, made a creator God the apparent basis for the existence of teleological relationships in the world. Although classical mechanistic theories are usually not anti-teleological, Aristotle would have used against them some of the criticisms used against Plato's *Timaeus*, as well as some aimed at Democritus.

In philosophical literature of the twentieth century it seems that mechanistic theories are opposed to teleological theories; the mechanism remains but not the Engineer. At least to the extent that a mechanistic theory is anti-teleological (and many who use the word 'mechanistic' assume that it is), Aristotle's theory is not mechanistic and cannot be, for his theory is thoroughly teleological, and cannot admit anti-teleological elements. His system of explanation is consistent in this respect, despite the apparent attempts of some to find this sort of inconsistency lurking in the biollogical books.

5. Formal necessity in nature: structure and species

Commentators have more often found a necessity of matter and movement opposed to finality than a necessity of form opposed to finality. It might, however, be thought plausible that

Aristotle would oppose form to end occasionally; passages
which might be used to support such a suggestion will help
us to understand Aristotle's teleology and his concept of natural necessity.[38]

Aristotle distinguishes, as we have noted, two modes of investigation; the one attempts to discover how a part belongs
to the essence of the species, the other tries to show how
the part contributes to the life and well-being of the species. One might be tempted to identify these methods, or to
reduce the one to the other. The passages which we now discuss may discourage such a reduction, for they show an 'es-
sentialist' side of Aristotle's teleology. We will look at
three different notions in examining this aspect of his
thought: a) the idea of the 'logos of the entity', b) dualizing and the scale of nature, c) the principle of natural
directions.

a) "ὁ λόγος τῆς οὐσίας"

The phrase, 'the logos of the entity', is used several times
in explanations, as if it were explanatory, and not always
with an indication that it refers to something of utility to
the entity. We would expect from Cat. and Met. that the phrase
should mean 'definition of the entity' or something closely
related.[39] As applied to explanation, the logos of the entity
would be its formal cause, as is stated rather clearly in GC
II.9, 335b7. Aristotle even says, at GA I.1, 715a5, that of
the four causes, the final cause (hou heneka, telos) and the
logos of the ousia should be understood as "just about the
same". As we have seen, they usually are just about the same,
for example at PA IV.5, 678a34, the animals which have blood
have it, and the ones which do not do not, because it is in
the logos which defines their ousia, for the ones which have
it, have a purpose for it, and the others do not.

However, sometimes the phrase 'the logos of the entity' or

210

some similar expression is used to summarize a description
of various structural demands. For example, a certain kind
of octopus has only one row of suckers on its tentacles, necessarily, because the tentacles are so long and narrow:
"They are this way not because it is best, but necessarily
through the peculiar *logos* of the entity" (*PA* IV.9, 685b15).
The same sort of necessity seems to be involved at III.3,
664a30, in the case of air-breathing animals, which must have
a neck so that the trachea may have some length, and that
consequently there must be an oesophagus to unite mouth and
stomach (see OGLE's note to the passage). Similarly, birds
and serpents are said not to have the penis and testes externally because their structure would not permit it (*GA* I.5,
717b14ff). Furthermore, cephalopods 'necessarily' copulate
at the mouth because 'nature has bent the end for the residue
alongside the mouth' (I.15, 720b18).

Aristotle seems to think of this reference to the form of the
entity as something a bit different from either a straightforwardly functional account, or from a reference to matter
and movement. At the beginning of *GA* II.1, he says that he
has already explained that male and female are principles of
generation, and has stated the powers and the *logos* of the
ousia of each; now he will go on to explain the existence of
the differentiation between male and female both on the basis
of matter and movement, and on the basis of the 'better'. The
part of his book which, he says, states the *logos* of the
ousia was discussed in Chapter II.A, above; the part which
states the purpose, and the matter and movement, was discussed in II.B. If we are to discern a general difference
between these parts of the *GA*, we would say that the part
which states the *logos* of the *ousia* is more descriptive in
character, and the part which states the 'causes' tends to
range further afield for explanatory principles.

The somewhat separate status of explanations by reference to
the *logos* of the *ousia* is made more precise by a passage in
GA V.1, at 778a32:

> Whenever things are not the product of nature
> working upon the animal kingdom as a whole, nor
> yet characteristic of each separate kind (ἴδια
> τοῦ γένους ἑκάστου), none of these is for a point
> or has been generated for something. For an eye
> is for something, but blue is not for something,
> unless this characteristic is peculiar to a par-
> ticular class. In some cases it doesn't even
> connect with the *logos* of the *ousia*, but happens
> necessarily, leading back the causes to the mat-
> ter and the moving origin.

Aristotle seems to suppose that some characteristics might
belong to the essence of the species, yet not have a specifically discernible function; a species in which all the
animals had the same color of eyes would be understood that
way, I think (cf.III.B.1, above). Or else, the fact that
something belongs to the essence of a species is an *additional*
reason for it to be as it is; at *PA* IV.6, 682b28, Aristotle
explains the various advantages gained by insects from their
segmentation, for example the ability to curl up for protection, and then adds: "It is also necessary for them to be
segmented because it is in their *ousia* to have many *archai*,
and in this they resemble plants." The *logos* of the *ousia*
may also be used to explain the absence of something; the
absence of blood in the bloodless animals is explained that
way (*PA* IV.5, 678a34), and the absence of limbs in fish is
explained on the grounds that "they have the nature of swim-
mers, according to the *logos* of the *ousia*, and nature makes
nothing functionless or in vain" (*PA* IV.3, 695b19).
The case of the fish indicates that the *logos* of the *ousia*
is regarded as a convenient explanation of the absence of
something. He cannot refer the absence of an organ directly
to some function, and he cannot always say that the material
as such will not permit the development of an organ of this
kind; he can sometimes say that the absence of the function
for this species explains the absence of the organ. In the
case of the oesophagus, its length is concomitantly caused
by the necessary length of the trachea; there are other examples of this sort of 'essential' causation. But most pe-

212

culiar and most special to Aristotle is the implied claim
that some features simply are indicative of species membership, like the σημεῖον gall-bladder or tail (discussed in
chapter III), the color of eyes in some species, and the segmentation of insects generally. The presupposition which led
him to write in this way is that species and genera are valuable for their own sake, and the characteristics which belong to their definition are thus preserved for their own
sake, even when there is no specific function for these characteristics or organs. This direction of his thought may be
clarified in the following pages.

b) Dualizing and the Scale of Nature

The idea of a scale of nature is one which Aristotle inherited
from Plato; its roots may be discovered in presocratic philosophy and in Greek religious thought.[40] As it is presented in
Plato, the idea is teleological, but not biological; there
seems to be a formal demand that all possible forms of being
be actualized in the course of time; all possible animals and
plants ought to be actualized, as part of this general onto-
logical demand. Aristotle does *not* believe that there is a
formal demand that all potentialities be actualized, so he is
not committed to a scale of nature on metaphysical grounds.
Nevertheless, he supposes that there is some evidence of a
continuum in nature, as a matter of nature's 'style':

> Nature proceeds continuously from inanimate things
> to the animals through living things which are not
> actually animals, so that there seems to be an
> infinitesimal difference from one class to the
> next (*PA* IV.5, 681a12-15).[41]

The statement that there is a scale of nature occurs in the
context of a discussion of entities which seem to be somewhere
between plants and animals, the ascidians (sea-squirts, τήθυα)
sponges, and sea-anemones. Aristotle believes, more or less
correctly, that they are really animals, for they are somehow

fleshy and seem to have sensation. Nevertheless, they 'dualize' with plants, for they live attached, and the food must
come to them, as it does to plants.[42]

The general idea seems to be that plants or animals dualize
when they share characteristics of two different classes; the
rather Platonic presupposition is that there *ought* to be such
species in order to fill the gaps between genera. PECK has
picked out a number of examples which Aristotle gives of such
species: pigs dualize between solid-hooved and cloven-hooved,
hermit crabs dualize between crustacea and testacea, primates
dualize between man and quadruped, ostriches dualize between
bitd and quadruped, seals, whales, and dolphins dualize between land animals and water animals, bats dualize between
quadrupeds and birds.[43]

Since man is superior to quadruped, and quadruped is in turn
superior to bird and fish, which in turn are superior to bloodless animals, which are superior to plants, a dualizing animal
is inferior in those respects, parts, or functions, which are
those of the lower class. In those respects, these animals are
said to be 'deformed', even when the characteristic is functionally necessary or desirable for the manner of life of the
animal (the normal state of affairs in such species); the so-
called deformity is, in fact, natural.

We should contrast those deformities which Aristotle calls
'unnatural'; he says of them, in general, that they are the
result of force (βίο), which is often said to be contrary to
nature. Some such unnatural deformities may be more or less
inherited, and remain 'unnatural', so long as the characteristic is not one which belongs to an entire species.[44]

In some cases we would be tempted to say of such productions
that they are, in a way, natural, since they are not simply
the product of force. Mules are somehow natural, and somehow
unnatural; they are produced in the normal course of events,
not by force, but the copulation which produces them is unnatural in the sense that it is a copulation of two different
species. The consequence is a 'deformity', namely the inability to procreate. Of course the generation of mules has some

214

advantages, if not for the mules, at least for men; as animals, mules are defective simply in their inability to procreate (*GA* I.20, 728b10; II.8, 748b34).

Aristotle seems not sure what to say about moles: at *HA* I.9, 491b28-34, he says that the blindness of moles is a deformity which 'happens in generation'; at *de An.* III.1, 425a10, he seems unsure whether to call them deformed at all, since blindness is a characteristic of the species as a whole.

He does seem to enjoy asserting that the female is a deformed male, even though the female is conditionally necessary for the continued existence of the species.[45] In this case, and in the case of the blind moles, there is no indication that Aristotle is thinking of a case of dualizing; he thinks that to be female (or to be blind) is simply to be inferior. Yet he recognizes that the female must be inferior in the relevant respects in order to function as she must.

We have already noted the peculiarity of the theory that characteristics which are clearly adaptive for a way of life, like the lack of ears and shape of the limbs in the seal, are nevertheless deformities, because they seem to resemble characteristics belonging to a 'lower' class of animals (see III.B.2, above). The whole genus of testaceans (as the snails) is called deformed, for they "move in the manner of an animal with its feet cut off, like a seal or a bat, which are quadrupeds, but badly".[46] The lobster too is universally deformed:

> They have claws because they are members of a
> genus which has claws, but they have them in an
> irregular way because they are deformed and do
> not use them for their natural purpose, but for
> locomotion (*PA* IV.8, 684a35).

The continuation of a species which is, according to Aristotle, deformed in significant respects, raises serious problems for the teleological analysis of biological phenomena. The deformed characteristics of dualizing animals are said to be 'necessary', and this necessity is like that which appears in connection with the idea of the *logos* of the species (*logos* of the *ousia*). Although in some cases (e.g. the seal) the deformity exists to the advantage of the animal, Aristotle continues to distinguish the value of the part from its 'essential' necessity. In other cases, as with the locomotion of the testacea, the deformity seems to be teleologically determined by the concept of the species, and is thought to be good in this way, despite the relative adaptive disadvantage which it poses for the species.

If the species has an intrinsic value, as a way of being in the world, a value which is independent of the ecological efficiency of the species (which would be an extrinsic value), then it seems at least possible that the intrinsic value of various species could be compared and scaled. This is one way in which the idea of a 'scale of nature' might be taken, and it seems to be one of the more important ways in which Aristotle uses this idea. Since man is the only rational animal, or at least the most rational animal, and since reason is 'better' than the other functions of the soul, man is a superior animal, the other animals are inferior and the whole of nature may be arranged in an evaluative series. In the biological books, this arrangement is stated most clearly in those passages which explain the idea of 'dwarflikeness';

> Compared with man, all the other animals are
> dwarf-like. By 'dwarf-like' I mean to denote
> that which is big at the top... and small where
> the weight is supported and where locomotion is
> effected. In man, the size of the trunk is pro-
> portionate to the lower portions... . All children
> are dwarfs. ... The whole groups of birds and
> fishes are dwarf-like; indeed, so is every animal
> with bood in it, as I have said. This is why all
> animals are less intelligent than man. ... The
> reason ... is that in very many of them the
> principle of the soul is sluggish and corporeal
> (*PA* IV.10, 686b2ff, PECK).[47]

Aristotle does not seem to argue in this and similar passages that there ought to be inferior beings, for the sake of a fully differentiated world; rather, he seems to suppose that the material available cannot always accept the best possible form. In the same chapter, *PA* IV.10, he goes on to say that

216

"nature always does the best possible" (687a16). Animals which
dualize, animals which are deformed according to some standard
or other, animals which are regarded as 'dwarflike', are the
best possible organization of the available matter; anyway,
they are better than no organization of that matter, better
than a lower level of organization, but less good than a
higher organization if that were possible, less good than the
higher sort of species to which a dualizing or deformed animal might be thought to belong. In the same passage in *PA*,
the series is seen in terms of the relative proportions of
'heat' and 'earthy body', which correspond to the two polar
extremes of the material elements, fire and earth, or *aither*
and earth; in the *Cael.* and generally, Aristotle arranges the
structure of the universe in accordance with the natural
places of the elements -- that of fire and *aither* is 'up',
that of earth is 'down'. So here in *PA*, man stands erect because of his great 'soul-heat', the quadrupeds need four feet
because they are earthier and consequently heavier, and the
footless animals are even more cold and heavy, without the
heat to lift them toward the heavens.
Aristotle's ordering of the universe as a whole in *Met.* Lambda
10 is well-known: "All things are ordered together somehow,
but not all alike -- both fishes and fowls and plants; and
the world is not such that one thing has nothing to do with
another, but they are connected." This fine ecological principle is not, however, understood democratically as some modern scientists would take the connection,[48] but aristocra-
tically: there is one ultimate ruler, and each lower level
is subordinate to the next higher level, as in an army (1075
b14). Consequently in the *Politics* Aristotle argues not only
for natural slavery (I.5), but also that plants exist 'for
the sake of' animals, and animals exist 'for the sake of'
man (I.8, 1256b15ff). One of the roots of the metaphysical
scale of nature, and of the politically aristocratic ecology,
is the scalar organization of Aristotle's taxonomic scheme;
although this scale is inherited from Plato, and has its roots

217

much farther back in earlier thought, Aristotle has made it
an intrinsic part of his system. Those of us inclined to mis-
anthropy may well note that man's reason is a δύναμις μετὰ
λόγου, a power with contrary effects (*Met*. Theta 5, 1048a3),
with capacity for both good and evil; the evil seems to can-
cel out the good, making man no better, in sum, than the
other animals.

c) The Principle of Natural Directions

The scale of nature is related, by means of the polar opposition of *aither* and earth in the cosmic order, to the principle of natural directions. Aristotle is conscious of having
inherited from the Pythagoreans, if not others, the assumption that 'up' is intrinsically better than 'down', that
'right' is intrinsically better than 'back';[49] the use of
'natural directions' in explanations introduces a formal principle which is more or less independent of function. For many
of his predecessors, sets of opposites constituted reality,
but Aristotle explicitly rejects this polarized system of the
world (*Met*. Lambda 2). For him, the natural directions provide a convenient, if sometimes misleading, frame of reference for the apprehension of the world; as such, they are
used as a formal principle which has no necessary connection
with a specifically biological world.
The principle of natural directions in Aristotle's usage is
teleological in at least two ways. The first way is primitive:
up, right, and front, are regarded as simply and intrinsically
'better' than their opposites; this is the implication of the
Pythagorean tables (*Met*. Alpha 5, 985a21ff). Systems involving
polarities of many kinds have been developed throughout the
world; contrasts between *yin* and *yang*, good and evil, male
and female, as well as more complicated arrangements like that
in the *I Ching*, are the standard fare of several mythologies
and religions.[50] It is not surprising that Aristotle, like

218

many more modern philosophers, supposed that there should
be something true in this intuition of an essential unity
of opposites. He knew the myth of the origin of the sexes
proposed by Aristophanes in the *Symposium* (he refers to it
at *Pol.* II.3, 1262b11), he knew his Hesiod, and he discusses
the philosophy of Heracleitus at length, particularly in *Met.*
Gamma. However, like Plato, Aristotle finds the Pythagorean
version of the myth of polarity most congenial; the ultimate
equality of value of the opposites, as Heracleitus presents
it, seems to Plato and to Aristotle to make evaluative judge-
ments ultimately baseless. In Heracleitus, as in the religion
of the Persians, "To god all things are beautiful and good
and just; but men suppose some things to be just and others
unjust" (DK 22 b 102); for the Pythagoreans, and then for
Plato and Aristotle, there are some things which are really
just and others which are really unjust.
So, one says that up is better than down, because the eternal
beings live above; or perhaps one says that the eternal beings
live above, because up is better than down (some people, even
some Greeks, had chthonic deities). So too, the difference
between right and left, and between front and back, is supported and exemplified by taboos concerning which hand one
ought to use for certain actions, which way one ought to face
on certain occasions, and that sort of thing. But little of
this comes through in Aristotle's version.
Aristotle regards the directions as having a largely biological significance, rather than a primarily religious significance. This appears most clearly in *Cael.*; at II.2, 284b
7ff, he argues that all three directional polarities which
are present in animals are also to be found in the heavens,
on the ground that the heavens are self-moving, and self-
moving entities have all three sets of polarities.[51] In a
rather obscure formula, Aristotle says, "Up is whence the
movement, right the from which, and front the to which", or
as GUTHRIE translates, "If above is the starting point of the
motion of growth, right the place where locomotion originates,

and front the goal of appetitive motion, this too gives above
the standing of a first principle in relation to the other
forms" (285a23). As we saw above (Chapter II.B.1), Aristotle
says that 'the front is more of an $arch\bar{e}$' in explaining why
the nictitating membrane in birds begins its movement from
the side of the eye toward the nostrils. The erect stature of
man, the praise of right-handedness, and so on, are expressed
in emotional terms, perhaps (*PA* IV.8, 684a28ff), but their
basis is for Aristotle something understood biologically
rather than, or much more than, religiously. There is a kind
of conditional necessity in the natural directions of the animal: for any living being, 'up' is where it takes in its food
and the like; the roots of plants are, for them, 'up' (*PA*
IV.10, 686b34).[52] For animals with senses which perceive at
a distance, 'front' is the direction in which sight and
hearing are most efficacious; one naturally moves in that direction (*IA* 14, 712b18). Quite a lot of empirical evidence is
adduced in support of the distinction between right and left,
especially in *IA* 4, the longest discussion of the principle.
It seems that limbed animals start moving with their right
limbs, and even univalve shellfish have their shells on the
right.[53] Men rest on their right foot (as Greek statues are
seen to do, incidentally), and step out with the left foot
first. In fact, the right in man is the most right-handed, so
to speak, for man has his natural directions 'most in accord
with nature' (706a24).

It would not be appropriate to criticize Aristotle too strongly
on this matter, for the most recent investigations in science
seem to indicate that there really are differences corresponding to those which he has picked out, not only among animals
and man, but also in plants, which tend to grow, some of them,
in a spiral to either right or left, and which are oriented
very largely by reaction to the force of grafity (up and down).
Organic molecules are distinguished by their 'right-handedness' and 'left-handedness', and even electrons have a spin
which determines their orientation to the rest of the world.

220

6. Summary of Part A

In this part we have tried to explain the way that Aristotle
uses the notion of necessity in his biological works. Our
major objective has been to show that the form of necessity
which appears in his explanations is conditional (hypothetical) necessity, in nearly all cases. One sort of necessity
which he does not use at all is a non-teleological or 'mechanical' necessity. Aristotle's philosophical system is so
loaded with teleological implications that he would have had
a difficult time expressing a non-teleological concept of
necessity if he had wanted to. Passages in the biological
books and elsewhere which have been taken to indicate the
presence of a non-teleological necessity may be interpreted
teleologically with more consistency; these passages may be
compared with passages which seem to oppose *form* and end,
yet no one supposes that Aristotle's notion of form is sometimes non-teleological. These latter passages, again, make
us aware that for Aristotle the end for a species is not
simply 'the best', but the best possible in the circumstances,
given the matter and the generator, which provides the *logos*
of the species.

B. "NATURE USES..."[54]

We have examined those of Aristotle's explanatory concepts
which are least clearly teleological, and we have tried to
show how even they are dependent upon some notion of finality; to be sure, some of the concepts discussed toward the
end of the previous part are very clearly teleological, but
they were of interest in that one teleological concept was
pitted against another, as it seemed. In this part, we will
look at a group of expressions which are easily taken as

typical of Aristotle's presentation, of his rhetoric in the
biological books; these expressions emphasize teleological
concepts in a way which seems much too personal, in the light
of the interpretation which we have tried to give of his
notion of a final cause. Many of these expressions speak of
nature's 'using' some object or some feature of an organism,
to achieve some end; we saw a number of instances of expressions of this kind in Chapter III.[55] This way of talking
about nature might be taken to indicate the existence of a
transcendent entity called "Nature" who purposefully implants
organic form into disorganized matter. However, such an interpretation of Aristotle's language would be a misunderstanding
of his biological principles and point of view.

The early Greek poets understood much of the world of nature
in terms of the actions of personal or semi-personal deities;[56]
this tendency continued, in a more subdued way, in some of
Aristotle's philosophical predecessors.[57] Plato, in the *Timaeus*,
uses the famous 'demiourgos' and an assortment of lesser deities as persons whose activity is meant to be, however, mytho-
logically, the source of the phenomenal world, or at least of
that which is rational in the phenomenal world.[58] If one looks
in Aristotle's works for some deity who parallels the demiourgos, one might expect to find him in either the prime mover
or Nature. The prime mover does not have the characteristics
of a person, and should not qualify; Nature, on the other hand,
is sometimes said to 'do' something in the world, and might
be thought to occupy the place in Aristotle's system which
the demiourgos occupies in the system of the *Timaeus*. Indeed,
CORNFORD says as much in *Plato's Cosmology*.[59]

I will argue that Aristotle's Nature is not personal, that the
teleology of Aristotle's system does not depend upon the personal intentions of any deity, even one so ubiquitous as Physis.

1. A Philological Introduction

The group of passages to be examined first are those which
contain the phrases χρῆται ἡ φύσις, καταχρῆται ἡ φύσις, παρα-
χρῆται ἡ φύσις, and παρακαταχρῆται ἡ φύσις. We may understand
these phrases as dependent upon the analogy of art and nature,
indeed as derivative from that analogy; but I believe that
these phrases, especially those with prefixed forms of the
verb, became for Aristotle technical terms for certain typical organic phenomena observed in the biological realm. A careful survey of his varying uses of these phrases will serve to
make this point clearer.

Καταχρῆται ἡ φύσις poses special problems because the verb
καταχρῆσθαι shows opposed tendencies in pre-Aristotelian literature. In all cases the verb involves some notion of use,
but sometimes earlier writers use it for wrong or unfortunate
use, and sometimes the use is understood to be good and ad-
vantageous; sometimes the verb emphasizes that the use was
to be expected, but sometimes it indicates that the use was
not the expected use. Some cases are, of course, ambiguous
or borderline. The most striking example of καταχρῆσθαι as a
'bad' use is the constant usage of Herodotus of this verb as
a synonym for 'kill'.[60] In Isocrates and Lysias, however, the
comparatively rare appearances are either neutral or favorable
in tone. Lysias[61] implies a transfer of use (money) from an
expected purpose to an unexpected but necessary use. Isocrates uses the word with no unfavorable overtones, and also
suggests a transfer of use once or twice.[62]

Demosthenes (and the other writers whose speeches we have under his name) and Plato use καταχρῆσθαι in both favorable and
unfavorable senses, and for transferred and non-transferred
uses. In the Demosthenic speeches the tendency is particularly
toward unfavorable senses. The range is from a clear sense of
'abuse' through rather strong suggestions of misuse[63] or sar-
castic suggestions of misuse[64] to rather neutral expressions
of using or consuming.[65] But some of these appearances do imply

223

a transfer of use from an expected to an unexpected use, even
if that unexpected use is supposed by the speaker to be an
abusive use.

Plato uses καταχρῆσθαι in the sense of 'abuse' on several
occasions;[66] and at *Philebus* 51a there is an implication of
turning to a different and better use.

Aristotle uses καταχρῆσθαι in the sense of 'abuse' just once
(*Cael.* I.3, 270b25). Otherwise, all the appearances of the
word seem to be in the biological and psychological books,
and are cases in which the word has some sort of explanatory
force. The senses in which καταχρῆσθαι appears in Aristotle's
biological explanations are not adequately delineated by LSJ,
and the various translators are not always very clear in their
versions of this word. Two closely related senses have their
predecessors in the usage of the earlier Attic orators: 1) The
use (of an organ or part) for an unexpected function; the organ or part in question would normally have some other function
in another species, or would even be quite useless there.
2) The transfer of material from one part (of the body) in
order to strengthen some other part for a particular purpose.
A third sense is, so far as I can tell, original with Aristotle, and used in a technical way: 3) The same organ or part
has more than one use, the additional use or uses being peculiar to a restricted group of animals among those which have
the part. Aristotle sometimes explains this sense of the word
in the context, which leads one to suspect that the sense is
unfamiliar to his audience.

The unprefixed verb χρῆσθαι sometimes has one or another of
these special senses. παραχρῆσθαι, judging from the LSJ entries and my own investigations, *always* means 'abuse' or something closely related, with just one exception, *PA* IV.10, 688
a23-25. Here alone it has the technical sense (3) which Aristotle gave to καταχρῆσθαι. Aristotle seems to have coined
παρακαταχρῆσθαι, partly perhaps out of his 'love for bipre-
positional prefixes',[68] partly to emphasize his peculiar sense
of καταχρῆσθαι.

Aristotle had reasons for giving certain words technical
senses and for inventing technical terms. The colloquial
language often lacks a word which conveys the desired sense,
particularly when a new and/or refined scientific hypothesis
is advanced, as in the biological books. Furthermore, philosophers generally try to pack their philosophical positions
into their terminology.

Aristotle faced a difficult problem in explaining the differences between species of animals. It was particularly difficult for him because he could not, by his own rules, have
recourse either to 'chance' or to 'evolution'. He could not
have recourse to chance because he did not think that an appeal to chance counts as an explanation (*Phys*. II); he could
not explain such variations by an appeal to evolutionary
developments, because the theory of evolution with which he
was familiar (that of Empedocles) depended upon chance variations, and therefore could not count as an explanation. So
he used his four causes and various analogies -- most importantly for us here, the special cases of the analogy of the
operations of *technē* and *physis*. For the explanation of variations he needed a concept which could, on the one hand,
include teleological (functional), formal, and material factors, and on the other recall the operations of *technē*. 'Use'
in all its ramifications suited this purpose.

2. 'Nature uses...' (χρῆται ἡ φύσις)

The notion of 'use' is intrinsically teleological, as Aristotle points out.[69] He often notes parts which have more than
one use, or which may be 'pressed into service' for some unusual use. Sea urchins, for example, normally use their spines
for feet, but these spines are also an admirable means of
defense.[70] Long narrow fish, eels for example, have only two
paired fins instead of the usual four, but they *use* their
length for movement, like snakes, and can manage to move on

land fairly well as a result (*PA* IV.13, 696a18). The human tongue is 'useful' (χρήσιμος) for both taste and speech,[71] and the human hand is 'well designed by nature' for a large number of uses, in which the flexions of the limbs also participate.[72] Nature, whether the nature of the individual animal, or the nature of the species, is often related to the idea of the use of the parts.

> Since every animal needs food in order to exist, and cooling for its preservation, χρῆται ἡ φύσις the same organ (the mouth) for both of these, just as in some the tongue is used for taste and articulation (*Resp.* 11, 476a16ff, after HETT).

> The use of the external parts is not the same in all animals, but each is equipped for its particular way of life and movements; in the same way various internal organs πέφυκεν in various animals (*PA* III.4, 665b2-5).

The verb πέφυκεν is ambiguous: it might mean simply 'have grown' it might 'are naturally present', or it might mean 'are provided by Nature'. The translation is bound to be interpretative.

The system (*physis*) of the bones is described as all connected "in order that χρῆται ἡ φύσις any two bones or more as one, or as two or more for flexing".[73] PECK translates, "this enables Nature to use", while LOUIS translates, "à fin que la nature se serve".[74] The 'nature' here is surely that of the individual animal, but in some other passages nature seems to transcend the individual. For example, Aristotle describes the activity of the carpenter in *GA* II, then says,

> In the same way the *physis* in the male of semen-emitting animals uses (χρῆται) the semen as a tool which has the movement in *energeia* (12, 720b9-21).

To interpret this 'nature' as the nature of the father, we have to say that the nature of the father 'uses the semen as a tool', which may sound odd, but the immediate alternative might be supposed to be that there is a 'power' which transcends the individual male animal and which 'uses the semen as a tool'. This passage may be interpreted as the rhetorical

226

outcome of the analogy of art and nature, as seems to be the
case in a later passage:

> Nature uses both heat and cold; each has neces-
> sarily a power, the one to do this, the other
> than. In generated things, the heating and cool-
> ing happen for some purpose.[75]

I suppose that 'nature' is used here as a generic term for
all individual natures, as a convenient way of talking about
natural processes in general. The final passage in *GA* con-
forms with this interpretation.

> Democritus omitted to talk about purpose, leading
> back to necessity everything which nature uses
> (χρῆται ἡ φύσις); they are necessary, but also
> purposive, and for the sake of the best for each
> thing... . Just as there are some tools in the
> arts which have many uses (πολύχρηστα), so too
> *pneuma* in natural constructions (V. 8, 789b3-6,
> 10-12).

In both of these passages the necessary character (including
movements) is just that which 'nature uses' to produce *everything* natural. We may expect that the compound forms of the
verb will be special cases of this general understanding of
natural processes.

3. Katachresis[76]

Aristotle uses the forms καταχρῆται ἡ φύσις and κατακέχρηται
ἡ φύσις rather often in his explanations of the parts of various animals. The sense of the prefix 'κατα-' is so general
that it gives little hint of the nuance in meaning which it
provides in this word.[77] The clarification of the phrase in
question can best be achieved by collecting the passages in
Aristotle's biological books which give an indication of the
sense in which he uses it. Sense 1), Katachresis as using the
otherwise useless.[78]

> We must tell how rational nature (ἡ κατὰ τὸν λόγον
> φύσις) has used (κατακέχρηται) that which is present
> necessarily from the possession of a necessary nature
> (τῆς ἀναγκαίας φύσεως).[79]

227

The distinction between *physis* as form and *physis* as matter
is familiar from *Phys.* and *Met.*, and is discussed at length
in *PA*.[80] The necessary nature here seems to be the material
nature as defined elsewhere, and the 'rational nature' the
nature as form.

> The word 'nature' has two senses, and there are
> two kinds of nature: a) matter; b) entity, and
> the latter both as mover and as end (*PA* I.1, 641a26).

So 'nature as entity' or 'rational nature' καταχρῆται matter
which is necessarily present, because an animal has a 'necessary nature', or material character.

> In the larger animals there is a residual surplus
> of earthy material which καταχρῆται ἡ φύσις for
> their defense and advantage; that which flows up-
> wards from necessity she has turned away to teeth
> and tusks in some, to horns in others (*PA* III.2,
> 663b32-36).[81]

Similarly the omentum has a 'generation which happens from
necessity', like all parts of the body, and this necessary
generation "καταχρῆται ἡ φύσις for the good concoction of
the food", for the omentum is fat, and therefore hot; this
is why the omentum is attached to the middle of the stomach
(*PA* IV.3, 677b30).

This idea of katachresis is stated gracefully, without (it
is true) using any form of the word, in this passage:

> Like a good housekeeper, nature is not accustomed
> to throw away anything from which something use-
> ful can be made. In housekeeping the best of the
> food available is served to the free men, the next
> best and the residue of the best to the servants,
> and the worst is given to the domestic animals.
> Just as an external mind does these things for
> growth, so the nature in developing animals con-
> structs flesh and the other sensitive parts from
> the purest food, then bones, sinews, and hair
> from the residues, then nails, hooves, and such
> (*GA* II.6, 744b16-27, after PECK).

However, even the best housekeeper cannot use everything:
bile, which is a necessary residue and not for the sake of
anything, is supposed by Aristotle to be totally useless, in
spite of the attempts of his predecessors to find a function
for it (*PA* IV.2, 677a16).

228

Aristotle several times makes use of the idea of nature using
that which is otherwise useless, without making a point of
signalizing this idea with some form of the word 'use'. In
PA III.2, 663a33, the rhinoceros is said to have just one
horn, since that is how much excess material nature was able
to find for it. At IV.10, 689b12ff, Aristotle says that nature takes away the heavy corporeal material from the top
part of the body, in man, and adds it at the bottom, giving
him the buttocks, useful for resting.

Sense 2), katachresis as taking from one part to help another.[83]
"What nature takes from one place, she adds in another" (*GA*
III.1, 750a4). The context of this remark is a discussion of
the multitude of variations in birds: Aristotle discusses how
nourishment is taken from the size and strength of the legs
to add it to the generative residue in some species (the birds
that lay the most eggs have the puniest legs). Katachresis
does not appear here in so many words, but there is already
an indication of the 'turning away' idea suggested in the
passage on horns, teeth, and hooves (*PA* III.2, 663b32), discussed above. This becomes even more clear in the account of
the camel's mouth. Aristotle describes some general rules
about the relationship between stomach structure and dentition,
and horns and hooves. Animals with front teeth in both jaws
(amphidentate), animals with solid hooves, and cloven-hooved
amphidentate animals, have one stomach. The exception would
be an animal with a large body and the habit of eating food
difficult to digest because thorny and woody; such an animal
would have several stomachs, as do the horned animals (which
are also non-amphidentate), and the camel. So the camel is
non-amphidentate and non-horned,

> because it is more necessary for it to have a
> multiple stomach than to have front teeth...
> because front teeth would not be useful (προἔργου).
> But since its food is thorny, and the tongue is
> necessarily fleshy, κατακέχρηται ἡ φύσις the
> earthy material from the teeth to the hardness
> of the roof of the mouth (*PA* III.14, 674a33-b5).

Senses 1) and 2) are closely related, and seem to be combined in at least one passage:

> The female nature, not being able to concoct,
> necessarily generates residues not only of the
> useless food but also in the blood vessels,
> and when they are full the finest vessels over-
> flow. But for the sake of the better and the
> end ἡ φύσις καταχρῆται to this place (the
> uterus) for the sake of generation, in order
> that there might be g enerated another of the
> same kind (GA II.4, 738a34-b3).

According to Aristotle, the periodic overflow of the bloody
residue is by no menas limited to the uterus,[84] and there is
no special reason apart from the purpose of generation why
this residue should particularly congregate there. It does,
however, and in this case, as in the case of the camel's
mouth, final causation seems to have an efficient character.

This notion, of nature taking sometzing from one place
to give it to another, occurs very frequently without the
word καταχρῆται as well as with. Personalization is tempting
with this concept, for there seems to be much more element of
choice when almost equally attractive uses may be made of
the same material or part, and then one occurs rather than
the other. This is most explicit at GA II.7, 757a25, where
Aristotle says that in the case of fish, "Nature prefers to
expend the milt in helping to enlarge the eggs after the
female has laid them, rather tahn in constituting the eggs
at the outset". PA II.14, 658a11-b13, discusses the relative
distribution of hair on various animals, using both utility
(weak conditional necessity) and this sense of katachresis,
for 'nature takes from one part to add on in another', for
example, to "decorate the tails of long-tailed animals"
(658a32). He supposes that the coughness of skin and flexibility of bone of the shark are related, for "nature has
used up the earthy material on the skin" (PA IV.13, 697a9).
What nature takes away from the body of the octopus, she
adds on the tentacles; what she takes from the tentacles of
the squid, she adds on the body (PA IV.9, 685a25).[85] Most

230

anthropomorphically, "Nature, like a prudent man, always
distributes to each one what he can use" (PA IV.10, 687a11).
Here it is the organs, but sometimes it is material, which
is distributed, as at PA II.9, 655a27; sometimes the moving
cause has its direction changed, as at GA V.1,780b10: when
the nature is not able to complete the process of development of the eyes, sometimes one eye of one color, one of the
other, is produced. In this case, one sees again that the
nature is that of the individual.

The idea of 'compensation', as used in biological explanation,
has some relationship with this concept of katachresis. The
mobility of the hard eyes in insects (PA II.14, 657b38) and
crabs (IA 14, 712b18), the peculiar structure of the mouth
of the crocodile (IV.11, 691b9ff), the structure of the legs
of birds (PA IV.12, 695a11), the gizzard instead of teeth in
birds (III.4, 674b30), are all examples of things which 'nature does' to make up for, or repair, an otherwise unsatis-
factory situation. Nature reduces the number of offspring of
lions, but increases their size (GA III.10, 760b27; in fish,
it is just the reverse, nature makes up for the loss of eggs
by their quantity (GA III.4, 755a32). Nature has given man
hands and arms instead of front legs, and instead of weapons
too (PA IV.10, 687a8); in this case, the front limbs and
built-in weapons of the lower animals are the consolation
prizes, for it is best to have hands.

Sense 3), katachresis as multiple use. This is a sense which
I find to be original with Aristotle, as a technical sense
of the verb καταχρῆσθαι.

> a) καταχρῆται ἡ φύσις breathed air for two
> functions (ἐπὶ δύο ἔργα), as she uses the tongue
> for taste and speech (de An. II.8, 420b18).[86]

> b) κατακέχρηται δ'ἡ φύσις respiration for two
> things, as function for the help of the chest,
> as additional function (παρέργῳ) for the sense
> of smell.[87]

> c) Just as nature made the tongue (of man) dif-
> ferent from that of the others, καταχρησαμένη
> for two sorts of function (πρὸς ἐργασίας δύο),

as we say she does in many cases.[88]

d) As we say, ἡ φύσις αὐτὴ καθ' αὐτήν (nature
'all by herself') often καταχρῆται parts
common to all animals for something special.
For example, in the case of the mouth its use
for food is common to all, but its use for
breathing is by no means common to all animals. But nature has brought all these together into one, making a difference in this
part for different sorts of function.[89]

e) It is better, when possible, that the same
organ not be put to unlike uses... . When it is
possible to use two parts for two functions and
they do not get in each other's way, *physis*
does not usually make, like a coppersmith for
cheapness, a spit-and-lampstand (ὀβελισκολύχνιον).
But when it is not possible ἡ φύσις καταχρῆται
for two functions.[90]

f) καταχρῆται ἡ φύσις the same part for the
excretion of liquid residues and for copulation,
both in male and female, with few exceptions in
the blooded animals, and without exception in
the vivipara. The reason is that semen is a fluid,
and a residue (*PA* IV.10, 689a6, after PECK).

g) All animals with bloody lungs, with few
exceptions, have kidneys,

for καταχρῆται ἡ φύσις simultaneously for the
sake of the blood vessels and toward the excretion of the liquid residues.[91]

In all of these passages it is quite unambiguous that a part
which already has a function is to be used for at least one
additional function, and this adding on of function is the
'katachresis'. In all the passages except f) and g) there is
a qualifying phrase, as though the word καταχρῆται by itself
did not have this sense unambiguously. In all but f) the
functions are distinctively dissimilar; there a rather unexpected similarity (demonstrated only in *GA*) of urine, semen
and menstrual fluid, serves to show how the katachresis is
possible or reasonable. The reader would be expected to think
of the excretion of urine and copulation as considerably dissimilar functions.

We also note, especially in the 'obeliskolychnion' passage

(e), that katachresis, or double-function katachresis at
least, is not the best arrangement theoretically, but the
best possible in the circumstances. There is, however, little
or no hint of an inferiority of katachresis in the passages
which discuss the additional use of man's tongue, mouth,
respiration, teeth and lips for speech. On the contrary,
Aristotle seems to be pleased with the effectiveness of his
teleological analysis in giving an explanation of many facets
of physiological characteristics of man which serve non-phy-
siological ends.

4. Parachresis

Like κατα-, παρα- is ambiguous, although perhaps not to the
same degree.[92] In most Greek authors παραχρῆσθαι has such
senses as 'misuse', 'abuse', 'deal wrongly with', 'treat with
contempt', 'disregard' (LSJ). This sense of the word appears
in a reference to Aristotle's lost dialogue *On Wealth* in
Plutarch's *Pelopidas*.[93] In the biological works the word
occurs uniquely, I believe, at *PA* IV.10, 688a23-25; there is
no connotation of misuse. Only additional use is implied, as
LSJ note.
In man the chest is wide, and needs some insulating covering
around the heart; therefore it is fleshy;

> but in females παρακέχρηται ἡ φύσις for another
> function, as we say she often does, for she stores
> the food for the offspring there.[94]

The passage is remarkable in that a general statement, 'as we
say she often does', is applied to a verb which appears in
this sense uniquely here. Aristotle must be thinking of parachresis as equivalent to katachresis for two functions, which
is, as we have seen, a common locution.

5. Parakatachresis

παρακατα- is obviously the combination of κατα- and παρα-.
In other compounds, e.g. παρακατατίθημι, the doubling of the
prefixes serves to permit a double object for the verb; this
seems less true of παρακαταχρῆται, which mainly emphasizes
the double or multiple utilization. This verb occurs twice in
Aristotle's biological works.

> There are many differences in the tails (of
> quadrupeds), and ἡ φύσις παρακαταχρῆται also
> in these cases, not only for the protection
> and covering of the seat, but also for the
> help and use (χρῆσιν) of those which have it.[95]

This sentence serves as a kind of conclusion for his discussion of tails, although all he has really done is to explain
a) why man has fleshy buttocks and no tail (he needs to sit
down, and the nourishment is used up before it gets far
enough to produce a tail); b) why quadrupeds *et al.* do *not*
have fleshy buttocks, but do have some sort of tail (they
are dwarf-like, and therefore do not have much heavy material
in the lower part of the body, but for protection of the seat
nature has taken away something from the legs and given it to
the tails). One might suppose that the prefix παρα- should
refer to whatever additional uses there might be of the tail,
and the κατα- to the fact that the tails are formed by taking
something away from one part to add it on another. The sense
of κατα- in this case is confirmed elsewhere:

> In animals having tails with some length, nature
> decorates it with hair; long hair for tails with
> short stems, as in horses, short hair on long
> stems, and according to the nature of the rest
> of the body; for (nature) everywhere takes away
> from one part to give to another (*PA* II.4, 658a
> 31-37).

But Aristotle does not tell us what the additional use might
be, not even in *HA*, so far as I can tell, and it is rather
hard to imagine what he might have had in mind, unless it
be chasing flies.
The other example of parakatachresis is in the explanation

234

of the elephant's nose.

ἡ φύσις παρακαταχρῆται habitually the same parts
for several functions, using the trunk instead
of the forefeet (*PA* II.16, 659a22-3).

The explanation may be summarized as follows: the nose is
for breathing, in elephants as in all blooded land animals.
But the elephant is also a swamp animal, and being large and
heavy has to have an efficient mode of breathing once it is
in the water; nature made him a snorkel tube of a nose, a
soft, pliable snorkel. However, the elephant is 'polydactylous'
has its feet divided into toes; animals of this class normally
use their forefeet for getting food and conveying it to their
mouths. The elephant cannot do this, because his feet are
spoiled for this function by the necessity of holding up all
that weight. So, "as we say, ἡ φύσις καταχρῆται" the trunk
for the service which normally comes from the forefeet.
There is little indication that the prefix κατα- refers to the
taking of material from one part to add it on another. The
παρα- clearly refers to the additional functions; perhaps the
κατα- is a kind of reference to the multiple (not simply
double) use of the elephant's nose: he uses it for breathing,
breathing in deep water, smelling, and 'like a hand'.

6. What Nature Does: General Principles

We have seen that verbs formed on the stem 'χρα-' are well-
suited to the specification of certain sorts of purposive
processes. Use involves a) something that is used, materials
and tools, or organs, b) a user (agent), or the process of
usage at least, c) the formal and material aspects of that
which is used which make these things suitable for the use,
and d) the object, value, purpose, end, goal, aim, or point
of the use. We have explored ways in which aspects of these
ideas are developed in passages in which 'nature' is the
subject of some form of the verb χρῆσθαι; we will now broaden
the approach to take in some of the other passages in which

an apparently intelligent Nature appears.

There are several expressions involving a concept of nature
which Aristotle uses so frequently as to make them notorious.
"Nature does nothing in vain (ἡ φύσις οὐδὲν ποιεῖ μάτην)",[97]
"Nature does nothing needless (περίεργον)",[98] are common-
places. Nature does not act from chance (*Cael*. II.8, 290a30),
but for the sake of something (*PA* I.1, 641b11); it allots
what is useful for the individual (*PA* IV.11, 691b9), making
the organ for the function, not the function for the organ.[100]
This sort of slogan sometimes descends to banal: "Nature
does nothing contrary to nature" (*IA* 11, 711a7, cf. 12, 711a
17); but sometimes Aristotle captures the imagination with a
play on words: "Nature flees the limitless, for the limitless
is endless, but nature always seeks an end" (*GA* I.1, 715b15).[101]
Several of these ideas are brought together in a rather powerful manner in the passage at the end of *GA*, V.8, 788b10ff,
where Aristotle attacks Democritus' explanation of the generation of teeth.

> Since we hypothesize, on the basis of observation,
> that nature does not omit anything nor do anything
> in vain (μάταιον) of those things which are pos-
> sible in each case, and since, if the animal is
> going to take food after cessation of suckling it
> must have some organ for dealing with the food,
> if this happened, as Democritus says, at the time
> of maturity, nature would be leaving out something
> which is possible, and the work of nature would
> be generated contrary to nature. For 'force' is
> contrary to nature, but he says that the generation
> of the teeth happens by force (b20-27).

There are several passages in which 'nature' is said to want,
desire, or choose something (the verb is 'βούλεσθαι'). "Nature desires, it seems, that there be a feeling of attention
and care for the young"(*GA* III.1, 753a8); "Nature wants to
number generations and destructions of temporal beings by
the numbers of the movements of the heavenly bodies" (*GA*
IV.10, 778a4); "Nature wants to make a unity of the *archē*,
but where it is not possible, she makes more" (*PA* IV.5, 686
a6).[102] Yet as 'theological' or as 'mythic' as these statements may seem, the same verb 'βούλεσθαι' is used in several

236

cases in which the *physis* is explicitly that of the individual, or even of a part of the individual: in *PA* III.7, the 'nature' of the spleen is generated because the 'nature' of the viscera is double, and each wants to be like as possible to its counterpart, just as the two sides of the body 'seek' (ζητεῖ) to be as like as twins (670a1-7). In the following chapter, III.8, "it seems that nature wants to give a bladder only to those with blood in the lung" (670b33). Animals which do not have blood in the lung tend to have feathers, scales, or scaly plates, and no bladder, but the turtle is an exception, for it has a bladder and scaly plates as well; in this case, the 'nature has only been stunted' (671a16). This passage makes clear what is being expressed in the more general or sweeping statements: Aristotle says that 'nature wants' something when he finds a general, but not completely universal, characteristic, a rule with exceptions. Just as there were natural processes which seem more explicable by an analogy with choice, so too there are natural processes which seem most explicable by a comparison with the fallibility of rule-following in man.

But perhaps there is more to it than that, for in some places nature does seem to be some sort of internal conatus. This is most clear in *GA* I.23, 731a13, when Aristotle explains the copulation of animals: "The nature of the male and female wants to become one". Perhaps one may compare I.18, 724a17: "Semen wants to be that sort of nature from which things constructed naturally are first generated." In spontaneous generation too, 'the nature' "moves itself" (*GA* I.1, 715b27); the nature of the testacea "is constructed spontaneously" (συνίσταται αὐτομάτως, III.11, 761b24). In these passages, it is quite clear that the nature is in, with, and identical to, the individual or part.

7. "Nature" and the personal verb

In Aristotle's biological works, the word 'nature' is the
subject of many verbs which would normally take a person as
a subject. I have made a collection of these instances; in
this section a rather miscellaneous group is presented, in
order to give an idea of the range of this type of expression
in Aristotle's writing.

We have already noted a number of occurrences of the verb
'ποιεῖν' with 'nature' (e.g., ἡ φύσις οὐδὲν ποιεῖ μάτην);
nature makes the diaphragm as a partition and fence, separating functions (PA III.10, 672b19); makes hair as a
covering (GA V.3, 782a21); makes the mammae where they are
(PA IV.10, 688b29); makes milk to provide food for the young
externally (GA IV.8, 776a17); makes the yolk in the egg as
a replacement for the milk which feeds young mammals (III.2,
752b24). It was pointless or impossible for nature to make
a combination of medium and organ except in the case of
touch (PA II.8, 653b28); it is also impossible for nature to
do anything through the weak males of insects (GA I.22, 730
b28); but it does appear that nature succeeded in managing
at least one bit of external teleology, making the mouth of
sharks underneath the snout in order to help out the other
fish (PA IV.13, 696b28).[103]

If ever Physis is the Demiourgos of Plato's *Timaeus*, it is
when she δημιουργεῖ something, for example when nature crafts
(δημιουργεῖ) the division into sexes reasonably,[104] or when
'nature herself' δημιουργεῖ the offspring, as in insects,
because there is no semen (GA I.22, 730b31). And yet, just
as often it is quite clear that that which δημιουργεῖ is not
transcendent, for the male semen is often said to δημιουργεῖν
the offspring (GA I.18, 722b2, 723b30; II.4, 738b12; IV.4,
771b22), although Aristotle says once (III.4, 755a20) that
the *physis* of the psychic heat in animals turns the solid to
fluid and the fluid to *pneuma*.

Nature also μηχάνηται a number of arrangements. The verb

derives from μηχανή, 'machine'; we mey recall what was said
about mechanical necessity above. For example, nature 'μεμηχάνηται' the coolness of the brain to counterbalance the heat
in the heart (PA II.7, 652b20); she has 'contrived' the tongue and epiglottis for the protection of the windpipe against
food (III.3, 664b21, 33, 665a8); the bloodvessels were contrived for the blood (III.4, 665b13), and the digestive tract
for treating food and dealing with residues (14, 675b11).
The shape of the hand was "well put together (συμμεμηχάνηται)
for its various uses (IV.10, 687b16, b23), and nature has
well μεμηχάνηται the wearing away of the teeth to coincide
with old age. He does not say specifically that it was nature who 'has contrived' the testes to temper the speed of
copulation (GA I.4, 717a30).
Nature has 'brought together' (συνήγαγεν) the nostrils in
the front of the head (PA II.10, 657a9), probably because the
most natural (εὐφυέστατος) place is the middle; she also
brought together the mouth and the place of residues in the
cephalopods, bending them around (GA I.15, 720b18). The
semen of the male is that which brings things together, at
GA IV.4, 771b22. We may also note that nature sometimes 'se-
parates' (PA III.10, 672b19).
We have already noted, especially under the second sense of
'katachresis', some of the many instances in which nature
'puts' something somewhere (forms of the verb τίθημι) or
'gives' something to some species (forms of the verb δίδωμι).
We may note in addition that nature 'has given an additional
means of defense" (προστέθεικεν) to certain species (PA III.
2, 663a9),[105] and has, in the case of shellfish, 'surrounded'
(περιέθηκεν) the flesh with something hard (PA IV.9, 685a8).
The limbs of animals have been added (προσέθηκεν) for the
sake of the torso (684b30), for nature has put feet under the
quadrupeds (ὑπέθηκεν, IV.10, 686a35), and under the birds
(12, 695a11). Nature has put food in the egg (GA III.2,752b
19, cf. 755a35, IV.4, 771a30), and in the uterus (II.7,
746a3); she has put sense organs in the head (PA IV.10, 686b19)

for the sake of the symmetry of the blood. In the sea urchin,
there is one of each of several organs in each of the five
sectors, "for this way nature could give one to each" (a form
of the verb ἀποδύδωμι, PA IV.5, 681a1). Generally, nature
gives (ἀποδύδωσι) each of the residues to the part fitted to
receive it (GA IV.1, 766b18), but has not given a place for
'colliquescence' (GA I.18, 725a34). Also, nature has given
the use of voice for speech to man alone (GA IV.7, 786b20;
cf. 771a35). There is a limit to the generosity of nature,
however, for she is not able to 'pour out a lot' for both
an abundance of semen and feathers (GA III.1, 749b9), nor
for both milk and menstrual fluid during the period of lac-
tation (IV.8, 777a16). In this last case especially we may
see that the 'nature' is that of the individual; here Aristotle says that the *physis* of milk and of mense is the same,
and therefore that *physis* is not able to produce both.

8. The arts to which nature is compared

It may be of interest to look at the analogy of art and nature from the point of view of the particular sorts of arts
whose activity is thought to be similar to the activity of
nature, or vice versa.

a) Analogies of the graphic arts

Nature is said to 'paint' or 'draw' aspects of the living
organism during the process of development, in several passages in GA; the idea is that nature sketches in the animal
in outline first, then fills in the color (GA II.6, 743b20ff).
This 'sketch' is composed of the bloodvessels, which are
'drawn' from the heart (II.4, 740a28); the sketch is called
a *'kanabos'* at IV.1, 764b30, rather obscurely (see III.A.3.b,
note 46).

240

In *GA* I.18, 725a26, Aristotle argues that semen is a residue
of blood, against the 'pangenesis' theory (see II.A.2, above);
if this is the case, then semen should resemble blood 'just
as the paint left over on an artist's palette resembles that
which he has actually used.'[106]
There are several looser allusions to an analogy between
painting and the activity of nature: the painted person is a
person only homonymously (*PA* I.1, 641a1), although we do de-
light in the productions of the graphic art (I.5, 645a13).
Painters, with their winged cupids, create something which
nature could not, because it would be unnatural (*IA* 11, 711
a1).[107]

b) Analogies of the plastic arts: working in clay

The most striking, and anthropomorphic, example of the use
of an analogy between nature and a worker in clay occurs at
GA I.22, 730b5-32, where 'nature herself' models the offspring in those species which do not have the power to emit
semen. We have discussed this analogy in II.A.4; see especially note 21. Another rather striking analogy is that between
the bones and the armature which modellers in clay use for
building their figures (*PA* II.9, 654b27; see III.A.3.b, with
note 46). We may note in connection with these passages Aristotle's idea that wax and its shape provide a good example
of the relationship between matter and form (*GA* I.21, 729b
19; *de An.* II.1, 412b7); we may also note that the bones are
regarded as similar to earthenware in that they cannot be
dissolved by fire: "they have been baked as it were in an
oven by the heat present at their formation "(*GA* II.6, 743a9).

c) Analogies of the plastic arts: working in metal

Nature does not usually, as the coppersmith for cheapness,
make a spit-and-lampstand combination (obeliskolychnion),
though she will if she has to (*PA* IV.6, 683a23, cf. III.B.
3.f). Both nature and art know how to make non-human beasts
stand on two legs; natural birds have their weight at the
back, for balance, and that is how they make the bronze
horses with their front legs raised (*IA* 11, 710b18). We may
also note the analogies of the automata here, since they
seem to have been made of metal primarily (II.B.3, with note
32; III.A.2; III.A.3.c.i.).
A more general comparison appears at *GA* II.1, 734b27ff, where
Aristotle says that 'as an axe is not simply made by fire,
so a foot or hand is not simply made by heat; the movement
of the instruments employed contains the *logos* of the art,
"since the art is the principle and form of the thing which
is produced, but elsewhere than in the thing, whereas nature's movement is located in the thing itself which is produced" (after PECK). Similarly, in *GA* V.8, 789b10, *pneuma*
serves many uses in the constructions of nature, just as the
hammer and anvil have many uses for the smith.

d) The *tektōn* and the *oikodomos*

The word '*tektōn*' is usually translated 'carpenter', but its
significance is more general, since it is etymologically
related to the word '*technē*'. In practice, Aristotle's 'carpenter' is a person who makes things out of wood; he is
usually making pieces of furniture. There are several passages in which nature is compared with the carpenter at some
length. In *PA* I, at 640b24, the 'bed' is an example of form
and matter, at b36, the 'carpenter' who confused a carved
hand and a real hand would be making the sort of mistake which
Democritus makes; in fact, the 'carpenter' knows that it is

not just a description of the movements which he makes, and
the matter and form, which accounts for what he makes, but
also the purpose of the product.[108] in *GA* I.18ff, the carpenter again plays an explanatory role; we have discussed
this passage in II.A.4.[109] We noted there that Aristotle has
a good deal of trouble over the analogy of the carpenter, and
that he introduced the analogy of the automata to counteract
the 'personalism' of the carpenter analogy.

In the same passages, with very similar purpose, the housebuilder or *oîkodomos* is also mentioned as an analogue of
nature. The *oîkodomos* is contrasted with the *tektōn* in that
the *oîkodomos* works with stone, not wood, Greek houses normally being built of stone. In *PA* I.1, the housebuilder sets
before himself an end, a house (639b16), and carries out the
process in a set order. The order is determined by what the
house will be (640a17); we are not concerned with the character of the material as much as with the ultimate form
(5,645a33). In II.1, the metaphysical order of the housebuilding is said to be the reverse of the material order; in
the material order, the bricks come first, but in the essential order, the whole comes first. In housebuilding, the
stones are laid out along the foundation; just so nature provides for the building of the body with the blood vessels
(III.5, 668a17).[110]

e) Nature as doctor and teacher

The medical art is end-directed (*PA* I.1, 639b16) and so should
nature be end-directed, even though the method of reasoning
in the practical art of medicine is the reverse of that in
the theoretical knowledge of nature (640a1). Of course the
medical art can become a theoretical science (*Resp.* 21, 480
b23).[111] Nature is described as like the doctor who heals
himself (*Phys.* II.1, 192b23ff), and consequently plays the
doctor (ἰάτρευκεν,*PA* III.3, 665a8) in the case of the wind-

pipe, placing the epiglottis over it. She also 'has pre-
scribed' (ὑπέγραφεν, II.14, 658a23) protection for the front
of the body, which is 'nobler', for nature is always the
cause of the best possible.

The distinction between the activity of the medical art and
the activity of nature is that the medical art is exercised
on another, or on oneself *qua* other, while the activity of
nature is on the entity, the nature, itself. Furthermore,
the doctor does not produce another doctor, as exercising
the medical art, but a healthy person from a sick person;
nature, however, produces another nature of the same kind.
This fine distinction between art and nature is at its limit
in the case of medicine, and tends to break down when applied
to the art of teaching; this may be the reason why Aristotle,
himself a teacher, rarely compares nature to a teacher, although such a comparison became popular enough in later literature. In teaching, one might well suppose that the teacher
also teaches himself, and that his production, exercised on
another, is that of another like himself. But teaching is,
according to Aristotle, very like a natural activity in several ways; some of the animals teach their young, which indicates the naturalness of the process (*HA* I.1, 488b25; IX.1,
608a18). One might point out that some animals also build
houses, and housebuilding is undeniably an 'art'. Furthermore,
in *EN* X.9, 1179b20, Aristotle distinguishes between nature,
habituation, and teaching. It may be that the art of teaching
is one which shares many characteristics with nature, as
somehow essential in the nature of man, and some other animals.

9. Nature: a conclusion

The passages which have been discussed in this part cannot
be dismissed simply as rhetorical flourishes, although there
is something of that in them. Aristotle's talk of nature's
'using' parts and materials, etc., may easily suggest an
image of Nature as an independent organizing agency operating
throughout the cosmos. We might think of the "mother" nature
of our literary tradition, the "blessed" nature of Epicurus,
f. 67, or the "common" nature of the Stoics. But in order to
understand correctly Aristotle's teleological but non-trans-
cendentalizing position concerning nature, his definition of
'nature' must be considered carefully. Aristotle accepts as
one sense of the word the typical Ionian account, but with
a twist of his own. Nature is in one sense, to be sure, the
'matter' of things, but there are two sub-senses, 'prime'
matter, and 'proximate' matter; both are understood as conditionally necessary for entities, that is their being, to
be *for* something; they are not essentially necessary in themselves.

Nature is also "the *eidos* and the *ousia*; this is the end of
the generation". By transference from this sense, in general
every *ousia* may be called a 'nature', because nature too is
a certain *ousia*.

> From what has been said, the primary and strict
> sense of 'nature' is 'the *ousia* of those things
> which have the source of movement in themselves
> *qua* themselves'. Matter is said to be a nature
> because it is receptive of this nature; generations
> and growing are called natures because they are
> movements from this nature. And nature in this
> sense is the source of movement of natural beings
> present in them somehow, either in power or in
> actuality.[112]

According to the primary sense, 'nature' seems identical to
the entities which are elsewhere said to be natural entities,
those which are *per se* sources of change; or one might say
that nature is identical to the *ousia* of such beings, which
comes to much the same thing. If we turn to the definition

of *ousia* (*Met.* Delta 8), we find that the senses which fit
the definition of nature most closely are: "that which, being
a constituent in such things as are not predicated of a subject, is the cause of their being, as the soul in an animal;"
(1017b15, Apostle) "The essence, whose formula is a definition,
is also said to be the entity of each thing" (b22). It appears
that the entity of something alive may be spoken of indiscriminately as the soul of that being or as the nature of that
being. In the case of beings investigated in biology, the
soul and the nature are identical.[113]
This identity of soul and nature is especially emphasized in
GA, which is among the very last books which Aristotle wrote.
He says explicitly that "the nutritive soul is the nature of
the individual" (II.4, 741a1), that it is the 'nature' of
the insects which lay imperfect eggs, or larva (III.9, 758b
20), that the 'nature' of the eggs takes food and grows
(758b34), and that lack of family resemblance is to be explained by the failure of the nature (of the individual) to
gain the mastery (IV.3, 768b31); the formal nature "does not
conquer" the material nature (IV.4, 770b18).[114]
To be sure, Aristotle can speak of the 'nature' of a species,
collectively, just as he can speak of the 'entity' of the
species, or the 'soul' of the species (or even of the organs
which belong to the species). We have noted some passages in
which he does do this. 'Nature too is a certain entity.' Does
this mean that 'nature' is an individual separate from other
individuals? No, it means that a nature is a certain *kind* of
entity, a natural being; thus translators usually render the
passage. Aristotle goes out of his way, in Delta 4, to say
that the nature which is the source of movement for natural
beings is *present in* them, as a power or as an actuality. But
if it is present in them, it is *their* power, their actuality,
their 'entity', their soul. This is true no matter how collectively the word 'nature' is used by Aristotle. An expression
such as 'Nature does nothing in vain' does *not* mean that there
is some deity who, although interfering with things in this

246

world, never makes mistakes; rather, it means that any essential process of any species which has in itself, *qua* itself, a principle of movement, is a purposive process.

The talk of 'nature using...', and the like can be understood only in terms of the nature which is the entity of the species. It is the nature of the male animal, and the nature of the species which is his determining form, which 'uses' the semen as a tool for generation; it is the nature of the individual which uses the mouth for respiration, ingesting food, and speech; it is the nature of the species as the dynamic form of the individual which uses materials for growth according to value and need, like a good housekeeper.

We may see from the explanations examined in Chapter III, and the passages discussed in IV.B., that this is, in fact, the limit of Aristotle's commitment to the existence of a purposive nature. Aristotle does achieve a middle position between materialistic reductionism on the one hand, and pantheism or animism on the other. His explanatory techniques and technical terms are drawn into a rather coherent whole; the quiding principle of this whole might be called 'organismic' or 'functionalistic'. We have seen in Part A of this chapter That Aristotle's concept of necessity can be understood only in terms of its intimate relationship with the functionalistic unterstanding of matter itself, and of the manner of generation of the movements in the matter; and further that the central understanding of *form* of natural beings is in terms of their dynamic structure, their organic wholeness.

It is clear that Aristotle believes that biological phenomena cannot be understood in the absence of an account which includes the purpose or point of those phenomena. Aristotle's biology is the investigation of entities and species of entities; no biological phenomenon is understood unless it is in terms of the dynamic structure of the individual, or in terms of the dynamic structure which determines the nature of the species. The matter which figures in the biological explanations is the matter *for* the generation and maintenance

of the individual and the species, and cannot be understood
as matter in any other way. The movement which appears in
explanations in Aristotle's biology is the movement which is
originated by entities, and continued as a strutured movement in entities or for entities; no other movement could
figure in a biological explanation. The form of individuals
is their species, and the species is an end in itself. It is
in terms of this kind of end, this point, that all biological
phenomena are to be understood. Individual minds act for
themselves; mind in general acts for itself. Individual natures act for themselves; species generally act for themselves. Nature, as species, is its own end. This is the meaning of Aristotle's analogy: "Just as the mind acts for the
sake of something, so does nature, and this is its end" (de
An. II.4, 415b16).

GENERAL CONCLUSION

Almost one quarter of Aristotle's works which remain today
are biological in character. In these works, Aristotle attempted to resolve biological and philosophical questions of
continuing importance; his answers depend upon several basic
principles or assumptions, some of which we have discussed.
A basic biological assumption is that there exist in the
world fairly definite species of animals, approximately those
which are named in Greek; Aristotle assumes that each of
these species has a "nature" which may be discovered by investigation. One problem about species as such arises when
one is faced by borderline cases; we have discussed (III.B,
IV.A.5) the ways in which Aristotle deals with some of them.
But the major problems for him are two: a) What is it to be
a particular sort of animal, what *is* the animal? b) How does
a species continue to exist through reproduction? These are
the major subjects of the *Parts of Animals* and the *Generation
of Animals*.
Aristotle thinks that the ground of understanding of a natural
thing must be within that thing, not external to it, and that
it should be empirically observable. In *Physics* II.1, he proposes as the definition of 'a nature' "that which has in itself the ground of explanation of the thing's staying the
same or changing." Animals are natural entities, species of
animals are natural species; animals and species of animals
are assumed from the start to be comprehensible in themselves,
and not in virtue of anything else. This is an important key
for the understanding of Aristotle's biology; indeed, the
general principle that entities are to be comprehended in
themselves and not in terms of something else is a fundamental
principle for the understanding of Aristotle's metaphysics
too.
The assumption that entities must be comprehensible in themselves blocks several paths that Aristotle might have taken
in dealing with biological phenomena. 1) He avoids the myth

249

of a creator God, a myth used by Plato in the *Timaeus*. In the *Timaeus*, the causes of phenomenal things are external, separate from the things. For Plato, the Forms constitute separate paradigms which may explain the structure of phenomenal things, but they cannot bring about the coming-into-being of those things. The Forms cannot bring things into being because they are themselves eternal and changeless, completely separated from the world in process. Because the Forms cannot be active, Plato uses the fiction of an Initiator of change, the Demiurge. Aristotle, by contrast, does not need a creator God, and it would be superfluous for him to introduce such a being; the entity is as it is because it has such and such a nature, and it is not particularly important to discover how it acquired this nature. In our experience, this species has always had this nature, and this nature carries within it the ground of our comprehension of it. If this were not true, we could not understand it at all, for the external causes, Plato's Forms or Demiurge, are not available for our investigation. Aristotle's 'nature' or 'species' can explain both the structure and the development of individual animals because the nature or species itself is both a structure and a process, as we have attempted to show in Chapter II. In comparing the Platonic philosophy of science, as outlined in the *Timaeus*, and the Aristotelian philosophy of science, as put into practice in the biological works, it is worth remembering that Plato's Academy eventually turned to the most absolute skepticism, while Aristotle's Lyceum was responsible for the development of Alexandrian science and medicine. An Aristotelian biology is possible, but a Platonic biology is Utopian.

2) Aristotle avoids determinism. Democritus had developed a kind of deterministic system: each entity, each atom, is a perfect solid, with no internal relations at all; all relations are external relations, all change is change in the relations between things. Although Democritus applied the word '*anagkē*' (necessity) to these relations, for Aristotle the unobservable

250

percussion of minute particles seemed a chance or accidental relationship, rather than an adequate basis for explanation. Aristotle resists the identification of chance and necessity (*Physics* II), because an explanation is a revealing of some necessity, but to say that something happens by chance is to say that it cannot be explained. In order to be a determinist, one must assert that everything happens according to perfectly regular rules, and in no other way. Aristotle is quite willing to find regular rules within a species or entity, but he does not find principles which regulate absolutely the relationships between entities.

The connection between Aristotle's metaphysics and biology is perhaps clearest in the use of the concept of necessity (see IV.A, above). The necessity which the *physikos* (natural scientist) is asked to find is an internal necessity, a conditional or hypothetical necessity; for the *physikos*, relationships between entities are taken to be accidental, unless those entities are parts of a greater entity, conditionally necessary for it. While Aristotle as metaphysician envisages the possibility that the parts of animals may be entities (*Met*. Zeta 2, 1028b9), as biologist he finds the necessity of those parts in relation to the activities of the whole animal. Although individual animals do not exist necessarily (*GA* II.1, 731b33), the species seems to be thought necessary for the world, for what we might call the ecological system.[1]

In general, Aristotle understands individual units (of whatever kind) in terms of the system in which they partake, rather than understanding systems in terms of the units which go toward their construction. His approach is just the reverse of that of the reductionist, as we can see, for example, from the fact that he does not try to explain "events" in terms of preceding events, nor does he expound governing laws as explicative of classes of events. These paradigms of explanation, so current in philosophical literature today, did not tempt Aristotle because the relations between events would

usually be external, and thus not necessary. To the extent
that he does explain events, these events are understood as
moments in a process taken as a whole; the events which occur later are just as important for understanding as the
events which occur earlier.

Some processes which Aristotle investigates are cyclical; to
the extent that a process is cyclical, it is absolutely
(simply) necessary, it is determined. Not all processes are
cyclical, however, so not every event is determined as a
part of such a process. By way of the theory of the cyclical
process, Aristotle influenced the development of the "mechanistic" system of explanation: for Aristotle, the heavenly
bodies moved as a great system of interlocking circles or
spheres; this system suggested to modern philosophers an analogy wiht a mechanical clock, an analogy which survived the
revolution in astronomy in the days of Kepler, Descartes, and
Newton, and was extended to cover all natural events, including the biological world.[2] But although Aristotle may be said
to have been an ancestor of the mechanical philosophy, and although he uses one or two mechanical analogies, like the 'automata' (see II.B.3, above), he does not assert the critical
principle for a mechanistic philosophy, that all natural phenomena may be explained by the analogy with mechanisms. Indeed,
he distinguishes between the kinds of change which occur in
mechanisms and living things (*MA* 7, see III.A.2): mechanisms
or machines can only change in position or place, but living
things can change in quality, grow, generate new members of
the same species.

Aristotle's avoidance of determinism depends in part on his
observation of the difference between astronomical processes
and biological processes. In astronomical processes, every
entity can be depended upon to continue to complete its cycle;
in biological processes, however, many individuals die before
reproducing, many accidents befall the biological entity. Even
if astronomical entities seem to be internally determined,
biological entities as individuals do not.

3) Aristotle is not very interested in evidence which might

252

have led him to develop some sort of theory of evolution, for at least three reasons: a) Evolutionary change is not directly observable, and thus an evolutionary explanation would not be empirical. This is one of his major objections to Empedocles, incidentally. b) Although individual biological events are not absolutely determined by the cyclical process of which they form a part, nevertheless the great processes of nature are still cyclical in form. But in order to have an evolutionary theory of the Darwinian type one must have the idea that the major processes of the world are *not* cyclical, but directional. c) In any case, an evolutionary theory would not constitute an explanation, from Aristotle's point of view. If the ancestors and the descendants are the same, there is no evolution; if the ancestors and the descendants are different, to the extent that they differ they do not properly belong to the same species, and the relation between them is external rather than internal. In evolutionary change, ancestor and descendant would be accidentally related, not essentially related. Indeed, it has often been remarked that some parts of evolutionary theory depend essentially upon 'chance' factors, cosmic rays, radioactivity, or other accidental agents for effecting change. If some such theory is true, as it may well be, then Aristotle would say that no explanation has been given, but evidence has been discovered that some things which exist cannot be fully explained. This consequence would not surprise him at all, since he is not (as we have noted) a determinist.

We have said that Aristotle tries to explain the existence of particular kinds of animals on the basis of internal, rather than external, relations, but we have not determined the sort of internal relations which he expects to find. His assumption that the ground of understanding must be empirically discoverable prevents him from asserting at least two kinds of theory based on internal relations, proposed at one time or another, although one must admit that he sometimes approaches both sorts of theory occasionally in the biological books. 1) One such theory is that "mind" or intentional action manifests itself not only in human conduct but also in all living things generally. Anaxagoras had proposed a rather crude version of this theory, and was attacked by Plato in the *Phaedo* for stopping at a simple assertion of the theory and not going on to explain how things are *rightly* as they are. It should be remarked that for both Plato and Aristotle the discovery that things are rightly as they are is more important for understanding than discovering just how they achieved that happy state.

One might imagine that Aristotle has a theory of an 'immanent mind' on the evidence of the many passages in which 'Nature' is said to plan, contrive, use, heal, arrange, and so on, and of the constant reliance upon analogies between the operations of art and the operations of nature (nature is said to work like a carpenter, painter, bricklayer, gardener, etc.). However, Aristotle also says carefully that there is a difference between intentional action and natural change: intentional action begins from a desired future result, and argues back to what must be done now, while natural processes proceed from the present process of the entity, without an intentional object or argument (see *Physics* II.9, and IV.B. above). Furthermore, art and nature differ in that art is a cause which is extrinsic to the object produced, while nature is intrinsic in the natural product (*Physics* II.1). Since Aristotle had a teleological theory which does not appeal to any sort of intention or even to 'goal-directed behavior', many of the criticisms of teleological explanations which one sees today do not apply at all to it.

2) Another sort of quasi-teleological theory which Aristotle almost completely avoids is that which asserts that there is some mysterious "entelechy" within the organism, guiding its development. This sort of theory, known to the scholastics and popular with modern vitalists, resembles the theory of Empedocles. According to him, there were something like 'broken sticks' in the seminal fluid of the male and female

254

parents, and that in fitting together, these 'sticks' determined the physical characteristics of the offspring. Although we might be tempted to see this theory as a remarkable anticipation of the discovery of chromosomes, Aristotle rejects it on the ground that these "sticks" are unobservable. His own theory is that the male semen is a foam of water and hot air, and that this hot air induces changes in the egg or menstrual fluid of the female according to the form of the male parent who provides it. One might see this hot air or *pneuma* as a vitalistic entelechy, perhaps, but Aristotle thinks that he sees it at work, that he has an observable functional process (II.B and III.A, above).

Aristotle bases his own explanation of the being and becoming of animals on the metaphysical assumption or proposition that "being is better than non-being, living than non-living, that which has soul better than that which does not, having a mind better than not having a mind" (*Generation of Animals* II.1). From this premise, however established (see I.B-C, above), flows the consequence that whatever parts of organic systems serve to perpetuate and preserve those systems, they are understood primarily in their relation to the whole of which they are a part. This is true not only of parts or functions which are necessary conditions for survival, but also of those which serve to improve the life of the species, although not strictly necessary. For example, he says of the tongue of man that it is conditionally necessary, to enable man to move food about in his mouth to chew it, but the tongue is also "for the better" because it provides the possibility for speech (see III.B and IV.A).

The functional relations thus described, and some others, are regarded as "explanatory" or "causative" of the animal. The animal is what it is because its parts are interrelated in such a way that it can continue to live, perhaps to live well, perhaps to reproduce its kind. A description of the functional interrelationships of the parts constitutes, for Aristotle, an

255

explanation of the animal.

A consequence of this functionalistic teleology is a theory
of matter, at least biological matter, which is usually mis-
understood. Since the Renaissance at least, and until quite
recently, the dominant concept of matter was one originally
developed partly by the pythagoreans and Plato, partly by
the atomists. According to this theory, there is a more or
less uniform 'stuff' which might take on various shapes
temporarily, but which continues to have its own ultimate
characteristics independently of the things of which it is
the matter. Aristotle, by contrast, makes the very existence
of matter dependent upon the existence of organized entities;
in the biological books at least (see *Parts of Animals* II),
the entity is clearly prior, and matter ontologically posterior. For Aristotle, to be matter is to be the matter *for*
something. Matter is not simply (absolutely, independently)
necessary; matter is conditionally necessary for the existence
of organized entities, living things, animals, and man. Only
organized entities make intelligible the existence of matter; we could not posit as comprehensible a world which was
simply matter, a world without organized entities, a world
in which nothing is *per se* valuable.

Aristotle's examples of 'matters' illustrate his theory. Not
only is bronze the matter for the statue, but the egg is the
matter for the chicken, voice is the matter of language, men
are the matter for the state. Aristotle even says that the
genus is the matter for the species ('animal' is the matter
for 'man'). To be sure, if we analyze a man into his parts,
and analyze the parts into their constituents, and so on,
we arrive finally at the four elements (earth, air, fire,
water) or the four elementary powers (hot and cold, fluid and
solid). But this analysis does not bring us to something which
is more truly matter, more basic (as a modern physicist might
suggest); rather, we have proceeded to that which is less
truly matter, less basic, less real, less *defined*. Instead
of arriving at that which everything "really is", as a ma-

256

terialist would think, we only approach the indefinite, or that which is not really anything.

Another consequence of Aristotle's functionalism is an account of movement which also differs from many modern concepts. For Aristotle, the source of any change must ultimately be a living organism, and must be in principle *for* an organism. To the extent that changes are not describable in this way, they are accidental, not comprehensible, not necessary. Because this is his general position, he finds supposed examples of spontaneous generation an embarrassment for his theoretical position, rather than an integral part of the theory; in fact, he accounts for the cases which people ordinarily understood to be spontaneous generations by finding the source of movement to be the sun or other heavenly bodies, which are indeed living entities for him, and which normally are thought to cooperate in bringing about sexual generation as well. Thus he attempts to make generations which seemed both accidental and natural to be a little less accidental, and thus more comprehensible.

Aristotle even has some difficulty with the idea of a source of movement in ordinary sexual generation, because according to his theoretical position, a source of movement must be an entity which has the actuality which it brings about; in sexual generation, however, semen seems the mover, and semen is not actually that which it brings about. As we have seen in Chapter II, Aristotle's resolution of this problem is the major objective of the *Generation of Animals*.

Aristotle's theory of change and of the source of change differs from the modern sort of theory most clearly in its complete dependence upon the existence of living things for the initiation of movements; it also differs from most modern theories in distinguishing approximately ten different kinds of change, one for each of the categories. Life is a process not only of changes in place and position, but also of changes in quality and quantity and relation; life is a coming-into-being and a passing-away; life is that kind of being which

257

is necessarily also a becoming. Aristotle can have a philosophical biology because his concept of change and the source
of change is sufficiently rich to include all the sorts of
changes which make up the functioning of the living being;
by comparison, the atomist seems to reduce life to non-life,
and the Platonist seems to make life a miracle or a mystery.

Historically, perhaps the most important characteristic
of Aristotelian biology is its overwhelming emphasis upon
the notions of 'form' and 'end', defined in biological terms.
For Plato, the forms were indeed 'ends', but they could not
help us to understand the world, because they were separate
from the world. Although Plato makes clear in the *Parmenides*
the serious difficulties which the separation of the forms
from the phenomenal world raises, he does not succeed in re-
solving those difficulties in any of his dialogues. Aristotle saw that the theory of forms had to work for the natural world if it was to work at all, but the natural world
is, most importantly, a living and changing world, a world
in process. Animals and plants are remarkable in that they
continue to show the same form in different individuals; this
fact does not, however, support the Platonic theory of forms
(*Met*. Zeta 7-9), but rather suggests strongly that the *eidos*
exists in, through, and solely in virtue of the individual
entities which have that form. The form does regulate the
possible ways of change, does continue to exist when the individual dies, does relate the individual to an entire systematic structure of the world, but all of these functions
of form are possible only because the form is within the individuals, not anywhere else. Aristotle does not see any objection to accepting Plato's idea that the form is a kind of
standard, to which individuals measure up only imperfectly;
for Aristotle, this standard is within the individual as the
sum of its potentialities for a better, fuller, existence,
as the possible ways of becoming for that entity. The goal
for the entity, its *raison d'être*, is within it; any goal
which would be outside the entity would be an accidental goal,

258

not essential. Any form which is external to the entity is not the form of that entity. The *eidos* within is that which makes change possible and intelligible.

Aristotle's work in biology was crucial for the further development of the life sciences in antiquity. As it happened, Theophrastus and others in the Lyceum continued biological study, and Aristotelians carried the tradition to the Museum in Alexandria. The Alexandrian school remained the leading center of research in biology and medicine for centuries. This historical development should not be surprising, for Aristotle had developed a comprehensive theoretical system which strongly encouraged biological investigation. Certainly the Hippocratic tradition, as well as Empedocles, Democritus, and Plato, had contributed much to the development of the life sciences, but as Aristotle had assimilated their thought in his terms, so later scientists like Erasistratus, Galen, Ibn Sina, and even HARVEY, could work most easily with Aristotelian problems and terminology. Although the ancient world would probably have developed biological investigation in any case, without Aristotle the forms and aims of that investigation would have been quite different.

Aristotle was the first philosopher we know to make biological individuals metaphysically primary. Just as Pythagoreanism and Platonism encouraged the development of mathematics by giving metaphysical priority to the objects of that science, and just as ancient atomism was to provide an impetus for modern physics by making inanimate entities primary, so Aristotle developed a philosophical foundation for biological research. He also posed many of the problems which later scientists tried to solve. His concept of the living entity as a continuing process of interaction between the organic parts, and his demand for observational evidence, led him to do many dissections, and eventually led to the Alexandrian practice of vivisection; his use of the notion of *pneuma* as an escape hatch in the *GA* and *MA* strongly encouraged the development of *pneuma* theories not only among the Peripatetics, but also

259

in the Stoic school and elsewhere; his analysis of the organism in terms of homoiomeries contributed to the medical theory of humors familiar in GALEN.

Historically, many biologists and medical writers have come to develop philosophical positions on the basis of their scientific investigations, but Aristotle is one of the few people who investigated biological phenomena as an essential and central part of his philosophical investigations. The close relationship between metaphysical theory and scientific curiosity is largely responsible, I believe, for the many unique characteristics of Aristotle's biological works, and for much of their influence and charm.

NOTES TO CHAPTER I

1. For comment on the chronological relationships between
Aristotle's works, see section E below.

2. There are some exceptions, for example the passage describing the "scale of nature", *HA* VIII.1, 588a12ff, but theory is rare in *HA*.

3. The present form of the *GA* is later than the present form
of the *PA*, and it is reasonably placed after *PA* in the standard editions. We have reversed the order in our study for
the following reasons: a) the conflict between philosophy and
observation is more dramatic in the *GA*; b) the central problem of the *GA* is more obviously crucial for Aristotle's philosophical position; c) our Chapter III discusses not only
the *PA* but also some of the later chapters of *GA* which depend
upon the chapters discussed in our Chapter II.

4. *Phys.* VII.3, 246b4-10, HARDIE and GAYE's Oxford translation (Oxford, 1930), which is prolix but clear. The last,
and operative, phrase is, in Aristotle's telegraphic style:
"Proper: that by which naturally generated and destroyed".

5. Ludwig von BERTALANFFY, *Modern Theories of Development*
(Oxford, 1933) p. 12. The major difference between this position and that of Aristotle is the substitution of the word
'significance' for the word 'good'. In fact, many biologists
concern themselves with functional questions, depending upon
their field of investigation. A technical example is *Function
and Taxonomic Importance*, edited by A.J. CAIN (London, 1959).
Several of the articles point out in detail the importance of
functional concepts for the taxonomist; see especially those
by A.J. CAIN, Julian HUXLEY, S.M. MANTON, W.D.L. RIDE, and
D. NICHOLS.

6. Morton BECKNER, *The Biological Way of Thought* (New York,
N.Y., 1959) chapters VI and VII, does this, and he refers to
several similar works. Ernest NAGEL, *The Structure of Science*

(New York, N.Y., 1961) Chapter XII, and "Teleological Explanation and Teleological Systems", in *Vision and Action*, ed. S. RATNER (Rutgers, N.J., 1953), reprinted in H. FEIGL and M. BRODBECK, eds., *Readings in the Philosophy of Science* (New York, N.Y., 1953), includes extensive references to those who use this approach. The major source of the analysis of teleological explanation by comparison with intention, in the recent literature, seems to be the article, "Behavior, Purpose, and Teleology", by A. ROSENBLUETH, N. WEINER, and J. BIGELOW, in *Philosophy of Science* 10 (1943) 18-24, reprinted in J.V. CANFIELD, ed., *Purpose in Nature* (Englewood Cliffs, N.J., 1966). CANFIELD's volume collects half a dozen articles all stuck in this same problem.

7. In this brief suggestion, I have benefitted from discussions with Leon J. GOLDSTEIN, Jerrold ARONSON, and Donald D. WEISS. I find that the account which Maurice MANDELBAUM gives of functional explanation in anthropology does apply to biology, done in the Aristotelian manner, and does involve teleology, of the Aristotelian sort; see "Functionalism in Social Anthropology", *Philosophy, Science, and Method*: Essays in Honor of Ernest NAGEL, ed. MORGANBESSER, SUPPES and WHITE (New York, N.Y., 1969) 306-332. See also L.J. GOLDSTEIN, "The Logic of Explanation in Malinowskian Anthropology", *Philosophy of Science* 24 (1957) 156-177 (an extensive bibliography is included); "Recurrent Structures and Teleology", *Inquiry* 5 (1962) 1-11. The claim in moral philosophy that evaluative properties are 'non-natural' was partly motivated by a desire to avoid reduction of value to non-value; if one assumes that 'nature' is evaluatively neutral, the problem of relating the 'realms' of fact and value becomes very real. In the recent literature, this problem centers on the question of deriving ought from is (as they put it); see the bibliography in W.D. HUDSON, ed., *The Is/Ought Question* (London, 1969), and G.C. KERNER, *The Revolution in Ethical Theory* (Oxford, 1966). The connection between this issue and biological teleology was

262

clarified for me by Emilio ROMA III.

8. *Phys.* II.4-6; *GA* IV.4, 770b9ff; *Met.* Eta 4, 1044b12. Cf.
A. MANSION, *Introduction à la physique aristotélicienne*[2]
(Louvain, 1945) 292-314; F. SOLMSEN, *Aristotle's System of
the Physical World* (Ithaca, N.Y., 1960) 102ff; M. EVANS, *The
Physical Philosophy of Aristotle* (New Mexico, 1964) 21-23.

9. "Nothing occurs at random, but everything for a reason
and by necessity", Leucippos, fragment 2 (DK). W.K.C. GUTHRIE,
A History of Greek Philosophy (Cambridge, 1965) vol. II, pp.
414-419, discusses the concept of necessity in Leucippos and
Democritus. He says that Democritus has the following theory:

> 1. Every event is determined. There is no such
> thing as chance if the term is used in an absolute
> or objective sense.
> 2. The notion of chance may be retained and used
> in a qualified sense to mean a cause which is, and
> must remain, obscure to us.
> 3. The incomprehensibility of such a cause lies in
> the fact that it is always, so far as we are con-
> cerned, one of an indefinitely large number of pos-
> sibilities (p. 419).

10. *Phys.* VIII.1, 252a31ff, my translation. Cf. Plato, *Phaedo*
97c-99d; S. TOULMIN, *Foresight and Understanding* (Evanston,
Ind., 1961) chapter 2.

11. In *Div. Somn.* 1, 462b27ff, he says that there are three
sorts of relationships possible between dreams and actual
events: causes (*aitia*), signs (*sēmeia*), or coincidences
(*symptōmata*).

12. *GA* IV.4, 770b20: the 'smoky' grape is a natural product,
to be sure. The color of grapes is not an essential attribute; this lessens the difficulty. Cf. *APo.* II.2, 90a3ff, *et
al.*, on eclipses; these matters are discussed again in Chapter
IV.A.

13. *The Causes of Evolution* (London, 1932) p. 168. See also
the "Conclusion" of DARWIN's *Origin of the Species,* and Marjorie
GRENE, *A Portrait of Aristotle* (Chicago, Ill., 1963).

14. Some puzzles arise from the application of this distinction to particular cases. a) Is the doctor who doctors himself
acting naturally or according to the art of medicine? The
activity of medicine is in other cases clearly that of an
art, but here the source of movement is internal. The solution
of the puzzle is not essential for Aristotle, since the doctor is understood to be acting purposively, whether medicine
is an art or 'natural' in this case. b) The art of teaching
seems to be somehow natural too, according to the version of
the distinction which appears in *GA* II.1, 735a2ff: "Art is
the source and form of that which is generated, but in something else; but the movement of nature is in the thing itself from another nature which has the form in actuality."
The flute-player, by teaching, produces another flute-player.

15. *PA* I.1, 640b24; 641a30; 5, 645a33; II.1, 646a25; III.5,
668a14; *GA* I.18, 723b30; 724a18; 725a25; 21, 729b14; 22,
730b5; II.6, 743a19; III.11, 762a15.

16. *PA* I.1, 642a10; 5,645b15; II.7, 652b13; IV.10, 687a; *GA*
I.2, 716a25; II.1, 734b27; 4, 740b25; 6, 742a19; V.8, 789b6.

17. *PA* I.1, 642a19; IV.10, 686b25ff.

18. *PA* I.1, 639b29; 640a17; *GA* V.8, 789b3ff.

19. H. RASMUSSEN and M.M. PECHET, "Calcitonin", *Scientific
American* 233.4 (October, 1970) 42-50. The quotation comes
from pp. 45-46.

20. A.L.PECK has re-examined the taxonomy of Aristotle in the
LOEB editions of the biological works, most recently and
thoroughly in *Aristotle: Historia Animalium*, vol. I (London,
1965) v-xxxii, lxii-lxxxix. See also his *Aristotle: Parts of
Animals* (London, 1961) 22, and *Aristotle: Generation of Animals* (London, 1953) lxix. H.A.T. REICHE, *Empedocles' Mixture,
Eudoxan Astronomy, and Aristotle's Connate Pneuma* (Amsterdam,
1960) 105, makes clear that Aristotle's notion of a species
or class of living beings is 'immanently teleological' "in
the manner of a norm".

21. BECKNER, *Biological Way of Thought*, 11; NAGEL, *Structure of Science*, 523-6, senses 3-6 of 'function'.

22. This account is adapted from BECKNER, p. 82, with reference to SOLMSEN, *Aristotle's System*, 74-91. Cf. NAGEL, *Structure of Science*, 567-8.

23. Cf. H.B. TORREY and F. FELIN, "Was Aristotle an Evolutionist?" *Quarterly Review of Biology* XII (1937) 1-18; L. EDELSTEIN, "Aristotle and the Concept of Evolution", *Classical Weekly* 37 (1943/4) 148-50.

24. One should also note that Aristotle's notion of explanation has something of the character of 'gaining satisfaction'; see J.-M. LE BLOND, *Eulogōs et l'argument de convenance chez Aristote* (Paris, 1939); *Aristote philosophe de la vie* (Paris, 1945) 71.

25. NAGEL, *Structure of Science*, 21; C. HEMPEL and P. OPPENHEIM, "The Logic of Explanation", *Philosophy of Science* 15 (1948); reprinted in FEIGL and BRODBECK, pp. 319-352.

26. C. HEMPEL, "The Logic of Functional Analysis", in *Symposium on Sociological Theory*, ed. L. GROSS (New York, N.Y., 1959); reprinted in CANFIELD, *Purpose in Nature*. See CANFIELD's bibliography for other articles in the same vein.

27. "Functionalism in Social Anthropology", p. 323. See also articles by L.J. GOLDSTEIN, n. 7 above, and Jerrold ARONSON, "Explanations without Laws", *Journal of Philosophy* (1969) 541-557. Mr. ARONSON showed me the relationship between my description of Aristotle's position and current accounts of explanation in the social sciences.

28. *PA* II.1; *GA* I.1, 715a9ff; PECK *GA* xlvii-lvii. When one analyses matter in this way there is a temptation to finish in 'prime matter' or 'ultimate substratum'; this concept does not, however, figure in the biological books. According to the traditional interpretation, based other works of Aristotle (see especially *GC* II.1, 329a32; *Cael.* III.6-7;

IV.4) 'prime matter underlies and is inseparable from' the qualities or powers. H.R. KING, "Aristotle without *Prima Materia*", *Journal of the History of Ideas* 17 (1956) 370-389, attempted to debunk the notion that Aristotle uses this concept, but see F. SOLMSEN's reply to KING in the same journal, 19 (1958) 243-252. I discuss this concept in Chapter II, note 15, below, and in Chapter IV; see also "The Continuous Analogy", *Agora* I (1970) 20-42, where I argue that Aristotle has the concept of prime matter but ought not. Most recently, W. CHARLTON, *Aristotle's Physics Books I & II* (Oxford, 1970), has argued that Aristotle does not have the concept of prime matter in the sense in which it has been traditionally ascribed to him (see appendix, pp. 129-145). His analysis of *GC* II.1 and the passages in *Cael.* is attractive. On the "powers" see A.D.P. MOURELATOS, "Aristotle's Powers and Modern Empiricism", *Ratio* (1967).

29. '*Logos*', when used in this sort of context, means both definition and form. Cf. *GC* II.9, 335b7: ὡς δὲ τὸ οὗ ἕνεκεν ἡ μορφὴ καὶ τὸ εἶδος. τοῦτο δ'ἐστὶν ὁ λόγος ὁ τῆς ἑκάστου οὐσίας.

30. 1019a22-26, after TREDENNICK. Cf. Theta, especially 1.1046a22ff. On the relation of *energeia* to *entelecheia* see *Met*. Theta 8, 1050a21-23, and H. BONITZ, *Index Aristotelicus* (Berlin, 1870) 253b39. For the definition of *entelecheia* see Charles KAHN's note to F.J.E. WOODBRIDGE, *Aristotle's Vision of Nature* (New York, N.Y., 1965) 36.

31. This section owes something to P. LOUIS, *Aristote: Histoire des Animaux* (Paris, 1964) t. 1, pp. xxxiv-xliv, and to the sources which he used, P. MORAUX, *Les listes anciennes des ouvrages d'Aristote* (LOUVAIN, 1951) and M. MANQUAT, *Aristote naturaliste* (Paris, 1932); however, these accounts have been limited almost entirely to the *HA*, while I attempt to correlate some passages from the *PA* and *GA*, and from other works of biological interest. LE BLOND, *Aristotle philosophe*

266

de la vie, 24-27, has a cursory and partially mistaken attempt at something similar. G.H. LEWES, *Aristotle: A Chapter from the History of Science* (London, 1864), is still one of the best guides to Aristotle's biology, partly because he is well acquainted with the tradition and with the biology of his day, and yet rather antagonistic to some of Aristotle's typical positions. See also T.E. LONES, *Aristotle's Researches in Natural Science* (London, 1912); Louis BOURGEY, *Observation et experience chez Aristote* (Paris, 1955), especially 85-94; H. CHERNISS, *Aristotle's Criticism of Presocratic Philosophy* (Baltimore, Md., 1935) Chapter 5, pp. 327ff; I. DÜRING's essay in *Aristote et les problèmes de méthode* (Symposium Aristotelicum, ed. S. MANSION, Louvain, 1961) 218ff.

32. LEWES is conscious that much of his book seems rather a polemic, and expresses appreciation of the *GA*, and of Aristotle's biology generally, pp. 380-1.

33. A judicious appreciation of Aristotle's science is presented by H.D.P. LEE, *Aristotle: Meteorologica* (LOEB, London 1952) Introduction pp. xxv-xxviii. As I cannot write without my own prejudices, let the reader be warned that I am aware of having been influenced by the British school of the philosophy of science, Karl POPPER, Stephen TOULMIN, and Rom HARRÉ, in addition to those people already mentioned in the previous sections. For a considerable contrast, philosophically speaking, see BOURGEY, *Observation et experience*; although he is aware of other traditions, he is solidly within that of BERGSON and BACHELARD.

34. Cf. LE BLOND, *Aristote philosophe de la vie*, p. 15; W.D. ROSS, *Aristotle*[3] (London, 1937) 11-12; for an account of some of the more obvious suspected passages. A more technical account may be found in I. DÜRING, *Aristoteles, Darstellung und Interpretation seines Denkens* (Heidelberg, 1966), at the beginning of his analysis of each book.

35. LOUIS, *HA* p. xl, note 10, gives a long list of such ci-

tations, to which we may add: *HA* II.14, 505b21; III.1, 510
a6; III.11, 50812; IV.1, 523b24; 525a21; VI.4, 562b27; 12,
566b12; 14, 568a32; 16, 570a13; 18, 572b9, 13; VII.4, 584a
18; VIII.28, 607a3; there are surely more. MANQUAT, LOUIS'
source, devotes a chapter to a general discussion of such
references. These impersonal references are rather less frequent in the *PA* and *GA*, I think.

36. *HA* V.5, 541a3 (here fishermen are said to believe the
story, see below on fishermen as an oral source); *GA* III.5,
756b7; Herodotus II.93.

37. Cf. also *HA* IV.1, 524a, with THOMPSON's note in the Oxford *Aristotle: Historia Animalium* (Oxford, 1910); *PA* IV.9,
685a1; *GA* I.15, 720b15-36; III.8, 757b31; LEWES pp. 197-201.

38. *HA* VIII.2, 590a18; the same account appears at *Meteor*
II.3, 358b35. In the same chapter of *Mete.*, at 358b19ff,
Aristotle says that wine, like salt water, becomes pure water
upon being evaporated and condensed. Of course this does work
rather well with salt water, but if he had done the experiment with wine, he might have made a brandy.

39. *Hist. An.* IX.64; Aelian has been edited by HERCHER, in
the TEUBNER series.

40. *HA* VI.5, 563a5; IX.12, 615a10, for a rather ignorant
story about the abode of the vulture, and *GA* III.6, 757a1,
for an even more ignorant story about the sexual characteristics of the hyena and the badger. See CHERNISS, *Presoc*,.
327, 337.

41. Cf. MANQUAT, *Aristote naturaliste*, ch. V, 37-47; he prints
parallel passages.

42. III.22, 523a17; Herodotus III.101; the same story is discussed again at *GA* II.2, 736a10. See CHERNISS, *Presoc.*, 337.

43. Herodotus II.68-70. Aristotle seems to insist upon this
story: *HA* I.11, 492b24; III.7, 516a23-25; *PA* II.17, 660b27;
IV.11, 691b5; the same chapters of Herodotus are used or even

paraphrased in *HA* V.33, 558a18; I.1, 487a23; II.1, 498a14;
10, 502b28-503a14; 15, 506a17-20; 17, 508a5; III.1, 509b5-8;
VIII.2, 589a22; 15, 599a30; IX.6, 612a20.

44. II.1, 500a3; Herodotus II.74.

45. VIII.28, 606a22; Herodotus II.67.

46. IX.17, 617b30; Herodotus II.75.

47. Herodotus II.71; *HA* II.1, 499b10; 7,502a9 (stigmatized
by THOMPSON); VIII.2, 589a24.

48. I.5, 490a12; Herodotus II.75, 76.

49. III.11, 508a35; Herodotus I.175; VIII.104.

50. IX.13, 606a7; Herodotus III.111.

51. Herodotus III.108; *HA* V.31, 579b2; cf. Herodotus VII.126;
HA VIII.28, 606b14.

52. *PA* II.16, 659a19; Herodotus IV.183.

53. *HA* III.22, 523a27; *GA* II.2, 736a1. See CHERNISS, *Presoc.*,
337.

54. IX.36, 620a33; cf. Ktesias *apud* Aelian IV.26, as noted by
THOMPSON.

55. See P. MORAUX, *Les Listes anciennes*, 108-9.

56. *HA* VI.30, 579b2; cf. Herodotus III.108.

57. At VIII.12, 597a6, he says that the stories about birds
which fight pygmies are *not* fabulous; at IX.34, 620a, he tells
an Egyptian myth without noting it as such, which may mean a
somewhat uncritical acceptance of a written source; for the
story of the oriole born from a funeral pyre (*HA* IX.1, 609
b10) and the story of fire animals (V.19, 552b10ff) see W.
LAMEERE, "Au temps où Franz Cumont s'interrogeait sur Aristote", *L'antiquité classique* 18 (1949) 279-324. In *de An.*
I.3, 407b22, the Pythagorean theory of the transmigration of
the soul is called a "*mythos*".

58. A book entitled "Homeric Problems" is ascribed to him by Diogenes Laertius V.26; he is supposed to have made an edition of the *Iliad* for Alexander, which that prince was supposed to have kept in a box under his pillow, even on campaign.

59. *HA* VI.20, 574b32; *Od*. XVII, 326.

60. *HA* VI.21, 575b5; *Il*. II.403; VII.315; *Od*. XIX.420; X.19. It is not clear what Homer has in mind, since in the first three verses cited there is a *bous* of five years, and in the fourth, a *bous* of nine seasons.

61. *HA* VIII.28, 606a19; *Od*. IV.85; Herodotus IV.29.

62. VI.28, 578b1, called by Thompson a "travesty" of *Il*. IX. 539 and *Od*. IX.190, but see LOUIS, *ad loc*.

63. IX.12, 615b8; *Il*. XIV.291.

64. IX.44, 629b20; *Il*. XI.553; XVII.663.

65. *GA* V.5, 785a15; *Il*. VIII.83-84.

66. *HA* IX.32, 618b26; *Il*. XXIV.316.

67. *HA* III.3, 513b27; *Il*. XIII.546ff.

68. *PA* III.10, 673a15; *Il*. X.457; *Od*. XXII.329. Together with this story we may note *de An*. III.3, 427a26, where *Od*. XVIII. 136 is quoted as sustaining an identification of thought and perception. Cf. also *de An*. I.2, 404a30, which refers to *Il*. XXIII.698 in the context of a comment on it, apparently by Democritus, although at *Met*. Gamma 5, 1009b26, it appears that the comment was made by Anaxagoras. There is a somewhat jumbled version of *Il*. VIII.20-22, used to illustrate the theory of the First Mover, at *MA* 4, 699b37. The short *MA* has several passing references to mythological themes: Atlas, at 3, 699a27; Tityos and Boreas, at 2, 698b25, are examples.

69. *GA* II.1, 734a15. They are also cited in *de An*. I.5, 410b28 for the theory that the soul enters the body from the universe, carried by the wind.

270

70. *GA* I.18, 724a18. See Athenaeus, *Deipnosophistae* II.36, in vol. I of C. GULICK's Loeb edition (Cambridge, Mass., 1927). Other poets are cited in the psychological books for illustrations of philosophical points. At *de An.* I.3, 406b17, Philippus the comic poet is noted for his idea that Daedelus made his wooden Aphrodite move by pouring in mercury; this is used in an argument against Democritus, whose theory is taken to be tantamount to that of Philippus. In *Div. Somn.* 2, 464b3, it appears that the poems of Philaegides, such as the *Aphrodite*, are beloved by the insane, because all the ideas are associated. In *Sens.* 5, 443b1, there is a reference to STRATTIS, the poet of New Comedy, who parodied Euripedes (see PAULY-WISSOWA, *Real-Encyclopädie*, IV.1.1, 336-338, 1931).

71. *GA* III.2-4, 511b11-515a26; see below, on dissection, and CHERNISS, *Presoc.*, pp 334-5.

72. *HA* I.16, 494b25ff; cf. Hippocrates *Morb.* II.8, The vocabulary of *HA* I.16 agrees with that of several Hippocratic works, see THOMPSON *ad loc. Morb.* is *peri nouson*, "On Illnesses"; *Morb.* II is in E. LITTRE, ed., *Hippocrate, Oeuvres complètes* (Paris, 1839-61) vol. VII.
In using the name 'Hippocrates' I do not mean to assert that any book which we now have was actually written by the great doctor; rather, I refer to the books known under that name, although manifestly by several hands. See L. EDELSTEIN, "The Genuine Works of Hippocrates", *Bulletin of the History of Medicine* 7 (1939) 236-248, reprinted in *Ancient Medicine* (Baltimore, 1967) 133-144. EDELSTEIN argues that one cannot know whether any of the books are genuine, but one can know that some of them are spurious.

73. *HA* VII.2-3, 482ff; Hippocrates *Septim.* I (*peri heptamenou*, "The seven-month fetus", Littré vol. 7); *Oct.* I (*peri octamenou*, "The eight-month fetus", Littré vol. 7); *Morb. Mul.* (*gynaikeia*, "Illnesses of women", Littré vol. 8); *Sterilit.* III (*peri aphoron*, "Sterility in women", Littré vol. 8); *et.al.*

271

74. *PA* I.1, 640b5. In the psychological books, Thales is
noted at *de An.* I.2, 405a20; 5, 411a8. Two other writers,
rarely cited, are mentioned in the same chapter of *de An.*:
Hippo, at 405b3, and Critias, at 405b7.

75. *GA* II.6, 742a16; V.1, 778b7. Cf. *de An.* III.2, 426a21;
Sens. 4, 441b2.

76. *GA* III.6, 756b17; IV.1, 763b32.

77. Cf. *Sens.* 1, 436a17ff; *Resp.* 21, 480b21; *GA* II.6, 742a1.

78. *Vict.* (*peri diaitēs*, "On Diet", Littré vol. 6): I.9, at
PA I.1, 640b15; I.25ff, at *GA* IV.1, 766a20ff; I.35, at *PA*
II.2, 648a5; II.3, 650b20; IV.10, 686b25; *GA* II.6, 744a30.
The theory of blend, or '*krasis*', which Aristotle may have
derived in part from this or a related work, appears most
clearly in these passages. Cf. *GA* IV.2, 767a20. See also
EDELSTEIN, *Ancient Medicine*, 84 and 303ff. The writer of
Vict. shares Aristotle's habit of beginning by criticizing
his predecessors, and also shares his aristocratic bias.
VM (*peri arch. iatrikēs*, "On Ancient Medicine"),W.H.S. JONES,
Hippocrates (London, 1929-31, LOEB): *GA* II.4, 737b30, on
cupping glasses. Littré (I, 294ff) believed that Plato refers
to this treatise at *Phaedrus* 270c, thus ensuring the authenticity of the treatise; this judgement is challenged by L.
EDELSTEIN, "The Genuine Works of Hippocrates", *Ancient Medicine*, 136. In "The Role of Eryximachus in Plato's *Symposium*", *Transactions of the American Philological Association*
76 (1945) 85-103, reprinted in *Ancient Medicine* 153-171,
EDELSTEIN finds that the opinions of Eryximachus are similar
to those of *VM*. The *VM* is notable for its rejection of *a
priori* reasonings and its praise of empirical investigation;
Aristotle sometimes follows its good advice.
Genit. (*peri gonēs*, "On Seed", Littré vol. 7): the theory
of pangenesis, *GA* I.17, 721b20, cf. 725b5, see Chapter II.
A.1, below. The theory that semen is a foam is used at *GA*
II.2, 736a10; Aristotle agrees that semen is a foam, but

272

not that it comes from the entire body. This book seems rather clearly to be one of Aristotle's sources in the *GA*.
Carn. (*peri sarkōn*, "On Flesh", Littré vol. 8): one of the
treatises relating *pneuma*, *aither*, and soul, as Aristotle
does at *GA* II.3, 736b35, cf. II.4, 739a1, and Chapter II,
below. Aristotle may have depended upon this treatise in his
account of the development of various tissues, *GA* II.6, for
in II.7, 746a19, he attacks the theory that children suckle
a piece of flesh in the womb, a theory expounded in *Carn.*
6. See PECK's note *ad. loc.*; PECK says that Aristotle was
attacking Diocles of Carystus for this theory.
Nat. Puer. (*peri physeōs paidiou*, "On the Nature of the
Child", Littré vol. 7) is closely related to *Genit.* (*peri
gonēs*). Like the *Carn.*, it contains a theory of the development of the various parts, emphasizing the theory of 'like
to like' which Aristotle often mentions, e.g. at *GA* II.4,
740b15. This treatise also has a *pneuma* theory which Aristotle opposes at II.6, 742a1, i.e. that the child receives
'breath' through the umbilicus; cf. IV.8, 776b30.
Aër. (*aerōn hydatōn topōn*, "Airs Waters Places", Littré vol.
2): Aristotle refers to the theory that climate influences
the character of animals and poeple, *GA* IV.2, 767a20, a
theory argued at length in *Aër*. For more subtle relationships, see L. EDELSTEIN, *"Peri aerōn* und die Sammlung der
Hippokratischen Schriften", *Problemata* IV (1931) 129-137;
"The Genuine Works of Hippocrates", and "Ancient Philosophy
and Medicine", in *Ancient Medicine*.
Many more parallels and related passages between Aristotle's
biological works and the Hippocratic texts could surely be
found by someone willing to look for them.

79. *PA* IV.9, 685b5. Cf. *Div. Somn.* 1, 463a5, 'the more refined doctors', and the extensive discussions of health and
related topics in the last three essays in the *Parva Naturalia*. For the influence of the medical tradition in Aristotle's work more generally, see W. JAEGER, "Aristotle's

Use of Medicine as a Model of Method in his Ethics", *Journal of Hellenic Studies* 78 (1957) 54-61, reprinted in his *Scripta Minora* (Rome, 1960) II.491-509.

80. *HA* VIII.4, 594a24; IX.6, 612a3ff.

81. VI.22, 577a13. Most of the medical writings which we have are both empirical and rational in their approach; this is especially true of *Morb. Sacr.*, *VM*, and *Epid*. But these writers were working in the face of many kinds of superstition. L. EDELSTEIN, "Greek Medicine in its Relation to Religion and Magic", *Bulletin of the Institute of the History of Medicine* 5 (1937) 201-246, reprinted in *Ancient Medicine* 205-246, shows that the main tradition combatted superstitious competitors, while remaining religious. EDELSTEIN also argues that nearly all writers on pharmacology rejected magical aspects of their art, but this often stated rejection is evidence for the continued existence of incantations and amulets in the popular pharmacy. The purpose of the spiders and snakes in the shops of the sellers of *pharmaka* may be obscure, but we should recall the great numbers of ineffective remedies for diseases which do not yet have a cure sold today in the most modern and scientific countries. The pharmacy around the corner from me in Paris still displayed the furs of cats in its window until two or three years ago, although it also carried the modern remedies.

82. Heracleitus figures much more prominently in the psychological books: *de An*. I.2, 405a25 (the *archē* is soul, and in flux); *Sens*. 5, 443a23 (if everything were to become smoke, we would distinguish by smell); and, not by name, *Juv*. 5, 470a4, the fire and river images as applied to human life.

83. *PA* I.5, 656a19. *PA* II most explicitly compares the soul with fire, especially at II.2, 649a22; 7, 652b8ff. Cf. also *Long.*, *Juv.*, and *Resp*. Probably Aristotle's position is

closer to that of Heracleitus than he thought, although one
cannot be sure, because Heracleitus' remaining writings are
fragmentary and obscure or ambiguous.

84. *PA* II.7, 670b20. In the psychological books, the Pythagoreans are frequently noted: *de An*. I.2, 404a17, the soul
identified with particles of air; 3, 407b22, the Pythagorean
soul could find its way into any body at all; *Sens*. 3, 439
a31, the surface of the body is called its 'color'; 5, 445
a16, some of the Pythagoreans say that animals are nourished
by odors.

85. *GA* III.2, 752b25. Both parts are food; this was shown by
W. HARVEY, "On the Germ in the Egge", see PECK at *GA* III.1,
751b7, and W. PAGEL, "William Harvey Revisited", *History of
Science* 8, 9 (1969, 1970). There seems to be an indirect
reference to Alcmaeon at *GA* IV.3, 769a20, cf. DK 24a14,
Aetius V.30. Alcmaeon's theory of the soul is cited at *de An*.
I.2, 405a30.

86. *PA* I.1, 642a25, see GUTHRIE, *History* , vol. III 417-
425, for the meaning of this passage.

87. *GA* IV.1, 765a15; see PECK *ad loc*. for further information
concerning this person.

88. *de An*. I.2, 405a22: the soul is air, etc.; *Resp*. 2, 470
b31: attacked with Anaxagoras for holding that fish and
shellfish breathe; cf. 3, 471b15.

89. *GA* II.2-3; cf. DK 65b6, a24. See also GUTHRIE's discussion of Diogenes in *History* vol. II.

90. Similarly, at *de An*. I.4, 408b32, he attacks Xenocrates
(without naming him) for the theory that the soul is a 'self-
moving number'. Democritus is tarred with the same brush at
409a12, and 5, 409b1, much as he gets part of the criticism
aimed at Plato's *Timaeus* in *Cael*. III, on the basis of a
similar comparison between the atoms of Democritus and the
units of Plato. See Leo ELDERS, *Aristotle's Cosmology* (Assen

1966) 284, 300, 320.

91. Plato is mentioned in *de An.*, e.g. I.2, 404b16; I.3, 406b26. The *Timaeus* and the lectures 'On Philosophy' are cited in *Sens.* 2, 437b12; *Resp.* 5, 472b6. In *Mem.*, the theory of recollection once held by Plato is criticized by implication.

92. *PA* II.6, 652b20; cf. *Tim.* 73c.

93. *PA* III.6, 669a18; cf. *Tim.* 70c.

94. *PA* IV.2, 676b22; cf. *Tim.* 71d.

95. *GA* V.1, 781a5; *Sens. passim*; and "*On Dreams* 2, 459b24-460a33, and Aristotle's *opsis*", *Phronesis* 13 (1968) 175-182.

96. *PA* I.1, 642a15, PECK's translation. See also *de An.* I.5, 410a3. Aristotle is grudging again at *de An.* I.4, 408a19, about his debt to Empedocles for the *logos* theory of the soul.

97. *GA* I.23, 731a5. At *de An.* II.4, 405b28, Empedocles is criticized for his application of the principle of natural directions of movement of earth and fire to the explanation of the growth of plants. Aristotle says that the explanation might have been all right, but plants are upside down.

98. *PA* I.1, 640a20. Issues of this sort are discussed again below.

99. *GA* I.18, 722b8ff; IV.1, 764a1-765a10; IV.3, 769a15.

100. V.1, 779b15; see my note in *Phronesis* 13 (1968). Aspects of Empedocles' theory of perception are discussed frequently in the psychological books; *de An.* I.2, 404b12; 5, 410a27; III.3, 427a23; 6, 430a28; *Sens.* 2, 437b12, b27; 4,441a7; 6, 446a27.

101. *GA* I.10, 718b35; *Resp.* 14, 477b1ff. In *Resp.* 7, 473a15ff, there is a long quotation about respiration, not altogether lucid, and Aristotle's discussion is not as helpful as one might have wished. For possible interpretations, see GUTHRIE, *History*, vol. II, 220ff.

276

102. *PA* I.1, 640b30, PECK. Sextus Empiricus quotes Democritus as saying, "Man is that which we all know" (*Adv. Math.* VII 265; see DK 68b165, and CHERNISS, *Presoc.*, 259).

103. *PA* I.1, 642a25, PECK. Cf. CHERNISS, *Presoc.* 227, n. 44, comparing Aristotle's claim in *Met.* Alpha that the Platonists were the first to recognize essence.

104. *De An.* I.2, 404a28; 405a8; 3, 406b16; 4, 409a12; 5, 409 b1; *Sens.* 2, 438a5; 4, 442a30; *Div. Somn.* 2, 464a5; *Resp.* 2, 470b28; 4, 471b30ff.

105. For more on Aristotle's criticisms of Democritus on necessity, see Chapter IV.A, and "Aristotle's Natural Necessity", *Studi Internazionali di Filosofia* I (1969) 91-100.

106. IV.1, 764b14; 3, 769a17; cf. I.17, 721b10; DK A 141, B32; Chapter II, below.

107. *Resp.* 2, 470b31. Aristotle discusses Anaxagoras on mind and soul at *de An.* I.2, 404a25; 405a13; III.4, 429a19; b25.

108. I. DÜRING, *Aristoteles*, 10-12; *Aristotle in the Ancient Biographical Tradition* (Göteborg, 1957).

109. J. ZÜRCHER, *Aristoteles' Werk und Geist* (Paderborn 1952).

110. In *Diokles von Karystos* (see also second edition, Berlin, 1963); JAEGER supported a later date in *Abh. d. Pr. Ak. d. Wiss.* 1938, *Phil.-Hist. Klasse* 3, but L. EDELSTEIN supports the earlier date cogently, in his review of *Diokles von Karystos*, *American Journal of Philology* 61 (1940) 483-89 (reprinted in *Ancient Medicine*); see also JAEGER, "Diocles of Carystos: a New Pupil of Aristotle", *Philosophical Review* 49 (1940) 393-414. There is also a remote possibility that Aristotle may have known and learned from Praxagoras of Cos; by some accounts Praxagoras could have been a pupil in the Lyceum during the lifetime of Aristotle, before the completion of the *GA*. See Fritz STECKERL, *The Fragments of Praxagoras of Cos and his School* (Leiden, 1958) 1-4.

111. The evidence is more indirect than THOMPSON's Oxford
translation of the *HA* might suggest. He sometimes translates
the phrase that literally means "some say" as "some writers
say" (in one stretch of a few pages, *HA* VI.13, 567b30; 14,
568a32; 15, 569a22; 16, 570a13). THOMPSON may be right, but
he is guessing that the source is written rather than oral.

112. *HA* VIII. 21-26, 603a29ff, deals in turn with the mala-
dies of pigs, dogs, cattle, horses, donkeys, and elephants,
with special richness of detail on horses. A number of remedies accompany description of symptoms. Cf.*PA* III.9, 672a
26ff, where some diseases of sheep are noted.

113. *HA* IX.1, 608b19-610a35. At 608b28 he explains that
manteis find significance in peace between animals normally
at war, and war between animals normally at peace. In fact,
the passage is an early contribution to animal ecology.

114. *HA* IX.5, 611b17-20. Of course it did not grow there,
the stag had been rubbing his horns against an ivy-covered
tree. But the ivy-crowned stag was widely considered to have
magical significance, something which Aristotle quite dis-
regards in the passage.

115. *HA* I.17, 496b16ff (at b25 he mentions with some humor
the use of animals for sacrifice and forecast); II.17, 507
a20; *PA* III.4, 667b1ff (again, sacrificial victims are
mentioned); IV.2, 676b16ff.

116. *Timaeus* 71-72: "The nature of the liver is devised to
give prophetic intimations", and so on. Cf. *Phaedrus* 244c,
where the mantic art comes off better than poetry, but not
as well as philosophy.

117. See *HA* I.17, 496b27. In any case, divination by entrails would not fit very well with Aristotle's biology,
which is built on the assumption that natural facts have
natural explanations, nor with his theology, which has a
most remote and non-interfering sort of deity.

118. *HA* IV.7, 532b20, τινες τῶν ἐμπειρικῶν ἀλιέων.

119. IV.8, 533b29, *et al.*; 535a20 has an argument that mol-
luscs have some of these senses as well, on the basis of
experience with them. Fishermen claim that they net more
fish in the evening because the fish, being short-sighted,
cannot see the net as well, VIII.19, 602b9.

120. Cf. *GA* I.15, 720b35; *HA* V.12, 544a12, and the notes of
PECK and THOMPSON *ad loc.*

121. *HA* VIII.2, 591a2; Aristotle argues that this is not
true, that it is the conger that chews off the arms of octopi. Actually the fishermen were right, cannibalism does
occur in some octopi.

122. Here are some other places: V.17, 549b17; VI.14, 568a
25; 15, 569b7; 570a1; 17, 570b28; 571a8; VIII.13, 598b13ff;
19, 602b8ff; 20, 603a5ff; IX.30, 621a27.

123. *GA* III.5, 756a32; cf. *HA* V.5, 540b13ff, and the story
from Herodotus, noted above.

124. *HA* VIII.12, 597b23; cf. IX.8, 614a10. The same verb is
used of their activity, θηρεύειν.

125. E.C. MARCHANT, *Xenophon: Scripta Minora* (Cambridge,
Mass., 1925, LOEB). The typical word for hunter is *kynēgos*,
or dog-driver. There is doubt about the authenticity of the
book; see A. LESKY, *History of Greek Literature*[2] (London,
1966) 621ff.

126. Cf. *HA* VI.25, 578a6, in close proximity with discussions of camels, elephants, horses, pigs, dogs, cattle,
sheep, goats, mules, asses.

127. VIII.6, 595a22ff; there is a reference to Thracian
practice here. Pella, the Macedonian capital, is not far west
of Thrace.

128. See DÜRING, *Aristotle in the Ancient Biographical Tradition.*

129. *HA* V.21, 553b1; cf. V.22, 553b17, where the source is plainly oral.

130. Two extensive accounts of Aristotle's errors, many of which can be ascribed to gullibility; LEWES, *Aristotle*; LONES, *Aristotle's Researches*.

131. *HA* V.19, 552b10ff, THOMPSON. Cf. IX.1, 609b10, the birth of the oriole from the funeral pyre. On fire-animals in Aristotle, see LAMEERE, *L'antiquité classique* 18 (1949) 279-324. He argues against JAEGER's interpretation (*Aristotle*, pp. 143-146) of these passages, pp. 300ff.

132. IV.4, 382a7. The pieces of evidence which might help to date the *Mete.* are mutually contradictory, but Lee's dating of the *Mete.* as a whole, and of the *HA*, seem reasonable (see his LOEB edition of *Mete.*, xxiii-xxv). DÜRING, *Aristoteles*, p. 51, concurs.

133. PECK, in the introduction to his *HA*, discusses Aristotle's theory of the proportion of the elements in animals in relation to their classification, but he avoids the problem raised by the juxtaposition of these passages.

134. T.E. LONES, *Aristotle's Researches*, 102-106.

135. References to the *Anatomy* include: *HA* I.17, 497a32; III.1, 509b23; 511a13; IV.4, 529b19; 530a31; VI.10, 565a12; 11, 566a14; VII.3, 583b13 (dissection of aborted human embryos, cf. *PA* III.9, 671b7, and IV.2, 676b32, with PECK's notes); *PA* II.3, 650a31; III.4, 666a9; 5, 668b29; 14, 674b16; IV.5, 680a1 ("some things are clearer to vision than in words"); 8, 684b4; 10, 689a18; 13, 697b14; *GA* I.11, 719a10; II.4, 740a24. Diagrams and drawings are mentioned at *HA* I.17, 497 a32; IV.1, 525a8; VI.11, 566a15; *GA* II.7, 746a14; *Somn.* 3, 456b2; *Resp.* 16, 478a25; they are often implied elsewhere. Michael of Ephesus seems to have had a version of the *Anatomy* purporting to show that the source of perception and movement is the heart: *In Parva Naturalia* 106, 9; 107, 4; 135, 2; *In De Partibus Animalium* 34, 23; 44, 33; *In De Animalium Motu*

et Incessu 121, 5; 123,12. See also BOURGEY, *Observation et expérience*, II and III; DÜRING, in MANSION, ed., *Aristote et les problèmes de méthode*, 218-220; CHERNISS, *Presoc.*, 327.

136. *PA* IV.2, 677a9; *GA* II.7, 746a22; IV.1, 764a35; 4, 771 b32; *HA* IV.4, 529a7; V.17, 549a20.

137. *HA* II.3, 513a13, THOMPSON. See also T.H. HUXLEY, "On Certain Errors respecting the Structure of the Heart attributed to Aristotle", *Nature* 21 (1879) 1-5, on the manner of dissecting the heart and aorta; L. EDELSTEIN, "The History of Anatomy in Antiquity", *Ancient Medicine* 247-301. EDELSTEIN is concerned primarily with the dissection of corpses and with vivisection, practices which developed only after Aristotle's death, but see pp. 256, 261, 278, 287-294.

138. *GA* IV.1, 764a35: "Empedocles is wrong about the side of the womb in which male and female fetuses are carried, as we have seen by the dissection of all the vivipara, both land animals and fish." *PA* IV.2, 699a9: 'Anaxagoras is wrong about the gall-bladder, as dissection (of human corpses) would show.' This sort of comment led to dissection of corpses and human vivisection, as EDELSTEIN shows. *GA* II.7, 746a22: unnamed persons (Hippocratic writers or Diocles of Carystos) are mistaken about how infants are nourished in the womb, 'as dissections of other vivipara will show'.

139. T. CASE, "Aristotle", *Encyclopedia Britannica* 11th edition (1911) vol. 2, 502-522. H.D.P. LEE, "Place-names and the Date of Aristotle's Biological Works", *Classical Quarterly* 42 (1948) 61-67; *Mete.* (LOEB) xxv. LE BLOND, *Aristote philosophe de la vie*, 17ff. Auguste MANSION, "La genèse de l'oeuvre d'Aristote", *Revue néoscolastique de philosophie* 29 (1927) 307-341, 423-466, especially 463.

140. DÜRING *Aristoteles*, 49-51, lists a surprising number of such works. Omitting the dialogues and other fragmentary or lost works, with which we are not concerned here, he lists as written in the early 350's, *Cat.*, *Int.*, *Top.* II-VII. VIII,

I, IX; *Anal.*, *Met.* Lambda; *Rhet.* I-II (except II.23-24);
first drafts of *Poet.* and *Magna Moralia.* From 355 to Plato's
death DÜRING lists *Phys.* I, II, VII, III-VI; *Cael.*; *GC*; *Mete*
IV; *Met.* Mu 9, 1086b21-.Nu; Alpha, Iota, Mu 1-9; Beta. *Rhet.*
III; *EE.* This seems more than Aristotle is likely to have
written during Plato's lifetime, but I will not attack the
list in detail at this time.

141. DÜRING lists *HA* I-VI, VIII; *PA* II-IV; IA; the lost books
on biology, e.g. *Anatomy*; *Mete.* I-III; a first draft of *Parva
Nat.* and a first draft of *de An.*, possibly a second as well.
Pol. I, VII-VIII.

142. DÜRING lists the remaining parts of *Rhet.* and *Pol.*; *Met.*
Gamma, Epsilon, Zeta-Eta-Theta; *Phys.* VIII; *PA* I; *GA*; *MA*;
the present version of *Parva Nat.* and *de An.*; *NE.*

143. THOMPSON, Oxford translation of *HA*, p. vii; CASE, *op.
cit.*

144. *Aristotle*, 329ff.

145. H. HANTZ, *The Biological Motivation in Aristotle* (New
York, N.Y., 1939). H.D.P. LEE, "Place-names..." *Classical
Quarterly*, 1948. J.H. RANDALL, *Aristotle* (New York, N.Y.,
1960) 220-4. M. GRENE, *Portrait of Aristotle*. G. RYLE, *Plato's
Progress* (Cambridge, 1966) 91-94, claims to have found evidence that Aristotle was interested in biology from at least
age 23. See also P. LOUIS, Introduction to *HA*; LAMEERE, *L'an-
tiquitè classique* 18 (1949).

146. F. NUYENS, *Ontwikkelingsmomenten in de Zielkunde van
Aristoteles* (Nijmegen-Utrecht, 1939); *L'évolution de la psy-
chologie d'Aristote* (Paris, 1948). He has been followed by
quite a few scholars, especially on the continent: LE BLOND,
Aristote philosophe de la vie, 17ff; R.A. GAUTHIER et J.Y.
JOLIF, *L'éthique à Nicomaque*, vol. 1 (LOUVAIN, 1958 1-36;
GAUTHIER, *La morale d'Aristote* (Paris, 1963); H.J. DROSSAART
LULOFS, *Aristotelis de Insomniis* etc. (Leiden, 1947); W.D.
ROSS, commentaries on the *de Anima* (Oxford, 1961) and *Parva*

282

Naturalia (Oxford, 1955); BOURGEY, *Observation et expérience*, introduction.

147. I. BLOCK, "The Order of Aristotle's Psychological Writings", *American Journal of Philology* 81 (1961) 50-77; W.F.R. HARDIE, "Aristotle's Treatment of the Relation between Soul and Body", *Philosophical Quarterly* 14 (1964) 53-72. See also my articles in *Classical Quarterly* 18 (1968) and *Phronesis* 13 (1968).

148. *GA* II.3, 736b1, to *de An.* II.4; *GA* V.1, 779b23, to *de An.* II.1, 425a and *Sens.* 2, 438ff (see *Phronesis* 13); *GA* V. 7, 786b25, to *Sens.* 6, 446b, and *de An.* II.8, 419b3ff, see also *GA* V.7, 788b1.

149. Cf. I. DÜRING and G.E.L. OWEN, eds., *Aristotle and Plato in the Mid-Fourth Century* (Symposium Aristotelicum, Göteborg, 1960); P. MORAUX, *Aristote, le dialogue sur la justice* (Louvain, 1957); I. DÜRING, *Aristotle's Protrepticus* (Göteborg, 1961); and items listed in DÜRING, *Aristoteles* 639.

* This chapter was published in *Journal of the History of Biology* 3.1 (Spring, 1970) 1-52; minor revisions have been made. I thank the editors and Harvard University Press for the permission to use it here.

1. *Met.* Eta 4, 1044a33-37, translation by W.D. ROSS (Oxford, 1928). Cf. Alpha 6, 988a5-8; Delta 1, 1013a30; Zeta 8, 1033 b23ff; Theta 7, 1049a1ff; Lambda 3, 1070a28; 4, 1070b30; 6, 1071b30; 7, 1072b30ff. For the place of the *GA* in the order of Aristotle's writings, see I.E., above, with JAEGER, *Aristotle* (Oxford, 1934) 329-341; I. BLOCK, *American Journal of Philology* 82 (1961) 50-77; Pierre LOUIS, introduction to his edition of the *GA* in the Budé series (Paris, 1961).

2. I.2, 716a2-b13, applies the distinction to male and female, and Aristotle seems committed to this rigorous distinction and application still at IV.1, 765b9-15; it is all-important in the key passage at II.4, 738b13-27, which summarizes his explanation of sexual generation.

3. Compare the Hippocratic *Airs, Waters and Places* XIV, 19 (W.H.S. JONES, *Hippocrates*, vol. II, pp. 120-123) and *Peri Gonēs* I, III, VIII (E. Littré, vol. VII, pp: 407ff). The arguments in these places closely parallel those refuted by Aristotle in the present passage. For an analysis of all these theories, and others, of animal generation and development, proposed by ancient Greek authors including Aristotle, see Erna LESKY, *Die Zeugungs- und Vererbungslehren der Antike und ihr Nachwirken* (Mainz, 1950). There is a great deal in the present chapter which overlaps material in Dr. LESKY's account; since it is done from a different direction, and from a different point of view, I hope that my treatment of these issues will complement hers.

4. I.18, 722a29-b4. Cf. *Met.* Zeta 17, 1041b11-33.

5. The term "organizer" seems to have been introduced by

H. SPEMANN. L. von BERTALANFFY, *Modern Theories of Development* (Oxford, 1933), explains the concept pp. 121-128, and give a bibliography of works relevant to this topic.

6. 722b5. For a discussion of modern preformationism, see J. NEEDHAM, *History of Embryology*[2], (New York, N.Y., 1959) pp. 34, 43ff. In modern preformationism, the germs of individuals or 'homunculi' were supposed to have existed since the creation of the world; this part of the theory does not appear in the ancient versions. I use the word 'preformationism' of the ancient theory that held that individuals exist, in the form of a 'seed' perhaps, in one of the parents before intercourse (usually the male parent was thought to implant the seed in the female parent, which only nourishes the seed). I use the word 'epigenesis' to name the contrasting theory that individuals do not pre-exist the moment of conception; both parents, according to this theory, contribute something necessary for the existence of this particular individual. Both Aeschylus (*Eumenides* 657ff) and Euripedes (*Orestes* 552) use the 'preformationist' theory as a part of the defense of Orestes' matricide, arguing that the male parent plants the seed or homunculus in the female parent. According to J.S. MORRISON ("Four Notes on Plato's *Symposium*" *Classical Quarterly* 14 [1964] 42-55), Plato in the *Symposium* seems to subscribe to this preformationist position. LESKY, *Die Zeugungs- und Vererbungslehre...*, pp. 18-20, argues that Plato is *not* a preformationist in the *Timaeus*, at least, since he says at 91d that the seed is "still unformed" when put into the womb.

7. Cf. Empedocles fragments 63-70 DK; H. CHERNISS, *Aristotle's Criticism of Presocratic Philosophy* (Baltimore, Md., 1935) 250ff; G.E.R. LLOYD, "Right and Left in Greek Philosophy", *Journal of Hellenic Studies* 82 (1962) 56ff.

8. 724a17. πρώτου (first) poses problems of translation. A.L. PECK, in his Loeb edition of the *GA* (London, 1953), takes it with γίνεται, translating "originally formed"; A. PLATT, in

the Oxford translation, vol. V (Oxford, 1912) and LOUIS, in
the Budé edition of the *GA* (Paris, 1961) correctly bring
πρώτου closer to ἐξ οὗ:"from it as their origin", "le principe d'où sortent", but these translations lead us to expect the word *archē* in the text. The translation which I give
was suggested by L. EDELSTEIN in conversation. "First" here,
as often elsewhere, has something of the sense of "proximate".
On the words which follow, see H.J. DROSSAART LULOFS, *Aristotelis de Generatione Animalium* (Oxford, 1965) at 724a17.

9. The senses distinguished at 724a may be compared with
those distinguished at *Met*. Delta 24, 1023a26ff (the longest
list) and *Met*. 'little alpha' 2, 994a20. The discussion of
the senses of "from" at *Phys*. I.7, 190a22, is closely related to the notion of *genesis*.

10. See PECK's discussion of nourishment and residues in the
introduction to his Loeb edition of *GA*, pp. lxiii ff. HETT,
in the Loeb edition of *de Anima* and *Parva Naturalia* (London
1935), at *Long*. 5, 466b5-28, unwarily translates the word
'*perittōma*' as "waste product" when applied to the spermatic
secretions; at *GA* I.18, Aristotle explicitly contrasts
perittōma with *syntēgma*, which is the word for 'waste product' in that passage.

11. This is one of the more famous of Aristotle's wrong
guesses; it is also one of the more pardonable, given the
difficulty of finding a mammalian egg. Cf. PECK, Introduction
to *GA*, p. xii, noting the discovery of the mammalian egg by
K.E. BAER in 1827; George SARTON, "The discovery of the mammalian egg and the foundation of modern embryology", *Isis*,
16 (1931), 315ff, notes that the discovery was by no means
easy even with a microscope.
"The menstrual fluid", or "mense", is the standard translation
of "the καταμήνια". A problem arises in the interpretation of
Aristotle's theory in that menstruation, properly so-called,
occurs only in primates, but Aristotle ascribes a spermatic

function to the *katamenia* in all mammals. The beginning of
a solution is simple: Aristotle supposes that the menstrual
discharge in primates is the same in character as the
estrous discharge in some other mammals. In *Historia Animalium* (HA) VI.18, 571b3-37, 581a5, Aristotle treats of the
phenomena which appear in connection with heat in the mammals; in this passage he identifies the estrous discharge
with the *katamenia* of human females at 572b28 and *passim*.
S.A. ASDELL, *Patterns of Mammalian Reproduction* (Ithaca, N.Y.,
1946), p. 23, mentions estrous discharges in several mammals,
notably the dog and cow. In the dog, the bleeding is proestrous, while in the cow it is metestrous. Aristotle mentions
the proestrous discharge in dogs as a *katamenia* at *HA* VI.20,
573b30ff, and he supposes that the time of estrous discharge
in the cow is the best time for impregnation VI.18, 573a3ff.

12. "After the flow is over" may seem a peculiar way of describing the period of peak fertility for human females, in
whom ovulation occurs halfway between menses. But Aristotle
might be thinking of some other mammals, particularly dogs,
with proestrous discharges. The fact that he is thinking of
mammals generally in this passage is borne out by the fact
that he finds it necessary to explain fertilization during
the flow, which is highly infrequent if not unknown in human
females, but rather common in mammals which exhibit estrous
bleeding, such as cows. PECK inserts the word "women" in his
translation at 727b; it is not in the text at this point.

13. *HA* III.6, 516a1; *GA* I.20, 729a10; II.4, 739b20; 2, 735b1;
IV.8, 776a15ff; 4, 772a22, cf. 771b23.

14. I.20, 729a24-32. PECK translates, at x, "if the male is
the active partner ..." as though Aristotle were talking about
individual males and females and the manner in which they
have sexual intercourse; PLATT's translation, "if the male
stands for the effective and active ...", is much better. My
translation stresses the account of the meaning of *words*.

PECK and LOUIS have a quite different interpretation at y, where the text reads "κατὰ τὴν πρώτην ὕλην". PECK translates "the natural substance of the menstrual fluid is to be classed as 'prime matter'". LOUIS translates, "la nature des menstrues appartient au domaine de la matière primordiale". Actually, PECK gives a quite good account of "πρώτη ὕλη" as this term is used in the biological books in his introduction pp. xi-xv. Aristotle is *not* referring to the "prime matter" of the *Metaphysics*, e.g. θ 7, 1049a24, for mense is "bloody", which qualifies as some sort of "thaten" in the sense of "thaten" explained in *Metaphysics* θ. *Metaphysics* Δ 6, 1015a8 -12, gives two senses of the phrase πρώτη ὕλη, primary in relation to the thing, and in general first. Menstrual fluid is primary in relation to the thing to be generated, or proximate. Cf. *Metaphysics* Eta 4, 1044a15-b2, where this proximate matter is called 'οἰκεῖον', and BONITZ, *Index Aristotelicus*, 653b25ff.

15. 729b9-22, partly following LOUIS rather than PECK.

16. I.e., that there is an internal entelechy which causes or guides the development of the individual living thing. I am thinking of H. DRIESCH, *Philosophie des Organischen*[4], (Leipzig, 1928) and E. RIGNANO, *Biological Memory* (London, 1926).

17. Aristotle recognizes cases of parthenogenesis. Apart from plants, in which sex differentiation is only analogically present, there are cases of animals which generate another animal like themselves without benefit of males; the fishes which he calls *erythrinoi* and *channai* are examples (II.5, 741a35; III.5, 755b21; III.10, 760a8; *HA* IV.11, 538a19, 567 a27). The *channa* is rather clearly identified with Serranus cabrilla or Serranus scriba, D'Arcy THOMPSON, *A Glossary of Greek Fishes* (London, 1947) 283; the *erythrinos* is somewhat more difficult, but the consensus seems to be that CUVIER was right in identifying it with serranus anthias, a brilliantly red fish (*erythrinos* means red). It might also be any

of several members of the Serranidae or Sparidae, like the "rouget", as this word is used in French (see THOMPSON, 65-67). Some insects, particularly bees (III.10, 759a8ff), generate parthenogenetically, thinks Aristotle, but sometimes they generate something which is different and "lower" in kind than themselves. Aristotle never really resolves the problem that results from observations of parthenogenesis for his general theory; in the case of the generation of bees, he says simply that "like plants, they have within themselves both the female and the male" (759b30). In plants, one may isolate male and female elements in many species (e.g. the pistil and stamen, in many flowering plants), but he does not attempt to isolate the male and female parts in parthenogenetic (and perhaps hermaphroditic) animals; this was done in the case of the hermaphroditic species of Serranidae beginning in the eighteenth century (see THOMPSON, 283-284).

18. The carpenter analogy was first used in the *GA* at I.18, 723b28; it is further developed at I.22, 730b6ff; II.4, 740 b25; and II.6, 743a25. In *PA* I.1, 641a, and II.7, 652b15, there are related uses of this analogy. See also Chapter IV. B, below.

19. E.G. *Metaphysics* Λ (XII) 3, 1070a30; 4, 1070b30; Z (VII) 7, 1032b1ff;Δ (v) 12, 1019a15ff; *Physics* II.1, 192b24; *PA* I.1 639b15ff. Some of the many examples of φύσις ἰάτρευκε and the like are cited by BONITZ, *Index Aristotelicus*, 837a5ff.

20. Wind-eggs are discussed at length at II.5, 741a; III.1, 749a5ff; and briefly elsewhere. Aristotle *might* have concluded that the viviparous animals also produce eggs, by analogy from the oviparous and especially ovoviviparous animals, but the near impossibility of finding a mammalian egg without a microscope effectively prevented this hypothesis; Aristotle is sufficiently empirical in his approach that he must account for the facts as observed. His theory is developed in such a way as to account for the absence of eggs in mammals.

21. He claims that the female inserts a part of herself into the male, and that the material is thus worked up by direct contact with the internal organs of the male insect. This claim may be supported by correct observation of copulation in the odonata (dragonflies etc); the generalization to the entire class of insects may depend upon mistaking the ovipositor, as seen during oviposition, for the phallus, as seen during copulation, and confusing the male and female between the two events. See K.G. DAVEY, *Reproduction in Insects*, (San Francisco, 1965).

22. 730b27-32, after PECK. Incidentally, the passage counts against, rather than for, the notion that Aristotle's *physis* is a transcendent individual, for the *physis* which works here is that of the male animal.

23. PLATT's note to 730a18 tells the source of this notion.

24. "*hexis* ": see his definition at *Metaphysics* Δ (v) 20, 1022b3ff.

25. 732a2-10. PECK's note to the passage is useful.

26. See *Metaphysics* Λ (XII) 10, 1075a12-24, for the ordering of the universe; *GA* IV.10 discusses the cycles of animal generation in relation to the astronomical cycles; PECK's notes to the passage are valuable. One may treat *GA* II-IV as an explication of *Generation and Corruption* II.10.

27. See Chapter IV.A., below, for a complete discussion of this issue.

28. 733b25. This principle is familiar from *Physics, Generation and Corruption, Metaphysics* Ζ (VII) 7-9, θ (IX) 8.

29. Cf. πρός at 730b27; *Physics* VII.2 notes that air is often the medium of movement. We shall see how Aristotle uses *pneuma* as an analogous medium of movement in the solution of this problem.

30. Note that Aristotle does not entertain the notion that there might be such a thing, unobserved by him.

31. 734a28. Aristotle does not seem to notice one possibility: the part in the semen might be the embryonic heart itself. Although his examination of fertilized chicken eggs might have led him to suggest this possibility, it does not seem supportable by observation of semens.

32. *GA* II.1, 734b11-13, after the texts of PECK and LULOFS. Aristotle uses this analogy again at II.5, 741b8-15 (see III. A.2, below), and at *MA* 7, 701b1-32 (see III.A.3.c.i, below). FARQUHARSON and FORSTER in their editions of *MA*, and TORRACA in the edition of *MA* in *Collana di Studi Greci* 30 (1958) suggest, on the basis of the passage in *MA* and on what is known of ancient mechanisms, some system like this: a piece of iron on the end of a string wound around a cylinder, which serves as the axle of one of two pairs of wheels, provides the motive force, by unwinding by the force of gravity (one lets it drop through a slot in a table or some such thing). The axles also have spokes which, rotating, hit some parts of the members of the puppet, agitating them to a somewhat life-like motion. I have seen a mechanism, dating from the fourth century B.C., which might work in this manner; it is a bronze doll about five inches tall, mounted on a four-wheel wagon or chariot. I have not, however, found any very helpful accounts of such mechanisms. The best ancient source is Hero of Alexandria, who is somewhat later; his automata did almost everything but useful work. See Bertrand GILLE, "Machines" in *A History of Technology*, ed. by Charles SINGER *et al.* (Oxford, 1956) pp. 630-636.

One may also recall the legendary statues of Daedelus, which were supposed likely to run away, so that one had to tie them down (Plato, *Euthryphro* 11, 15; *Meno* 97-98).

In sum, the mechanisms which existed in antiquity were not so complex that one could use them extensively in analogies explaining biological phenomena. The idea of an anthropomorphic machine is such an analogy, taken in reverse; the Daedelus statues, and the life-like painted statues of the fifth

and fourth centuries, as well as the moving dolls mentioned
by Aristotle, suggest the attempt to mimic life; to the extent that these attempts are successful, they suggest analogies from the artifact to the original.

33. II.1, 734b18-19. For the idea of an individual in Aristotle, see Joseph OWENS, *The Doctrine of Being in the Aristotelian Metaphysics* (Toronto, 1957) pp. 334-5; *Metaphysics*
Theta 7, 1049a22-36; A.C. LLOYD, "Aristotle's principle of
individuation", *Mind* LXXIX (1970) 519-529.

34. II.1, 735a6-14, after PECK. At *ii* a problem is posed by
the word αὐτοῦ; LOUIS gives an interpretive translation which
gives the correct force to this word: "une même chose peut
être, en puissance, plus ou moin loin de se réaliser". F.
NUYENS, *L'Evolution de la psychologie d'Aristote* (Paris and
Louvain, 1948), pp. 258-259, emphasizes the two negations,
marked a) and b) above. "Les deux négations se complètent
l'une l'autre. L'âme ne se trouve que dans l'être vivant,
mais non dans un organe particulier de celui-ci. Bien plus,
on ne peut même pas parler d'organe à moins que celui-ci
participe à l'âme. L'âme est la force vitale qui, au sein
de l'être vivant, exerce son influence dans tous les organes."
If he had said "puissance vitale" his interpretation would
be more clearly correct. His interest in this passage is its
hylomorphism, easy enough to demonstrate; he does not deal
with the problem which hylomorphism causes here for Aristotle's
account.

35. 735a18-23, after LOUIS in text and translation; LULOFS
supports this text. Cf.*de Anima* II.4; NUYENS, *Psychologie
d'Aristote*, p. 259.

36. A problem remains: semen does not grow, so does it really
have even the nutritive and generative soul? There are at
least two examples of *female* spermata growing, noted by Aristotle (III.2, 752a24ff, III.4, 755a11ff), but none of the
male sperma, semen, which is at issue here.

37. Cf. NUYENS, *Psychologie d'Aristote*, p. 259.

38. "Homonyous" and "synonymous" are, of course, technical terms developed in the context of Aristotle's logic. It may be noted that these adjectives are as applicable to *things* as they are to *words*. Two things are synonymous if they bear the same name and belong to the same class; they are homonymous if they bear the same name but do *not* belong to the same class, i.e. do not have the same *eidos*.

39. Paul MORAUX "A propos du νοῦς θύραθεν chez Aristote", in *Autour d'Aristote, Mélanges Mansion* (Louvain, 1955).

40. *GA* II.4, 739b22; cf. III.4, 755a15ff; IV.4, 771b23,772a22.

41. 736b8. On living the life of a plant, see *GA* II.7, 745b 26; IV.6, 774b26; *Progression of Animals* 4, 705a28; *PA* IV.10, 686b36; II.3, 650a21; IV.4, 678a10.

42. H.A.T. REICHE, *Empedocles' Mixture, Eudoxan Astronomy, and Aristotle's connate Pneuma* (Amsterdam, 1960), pp. 32-36.

43. 736b16ff.

44. This *aporia pleiste* gives problems to modern commentators; one such problem is whether Aristotle thinks that he solves the puzzle in this chapter. NUYENS, having analyzed the kinds of statement of *aporia*, finds that the present instance is the only one called *pleiste* ("biggest"); he concludes that Aristotle would not introduce a definitive solution in such terms (*Psychology d'Aristote*, p. 316). E. BARBOTIN, in *La Théorie Aristotélicienne de l'intellect d'après Théophraste* (Louvain, 1954), pp. 175ff, agrees while REICHE thinks that a solution is offered; although he feels that Aristotle does not find that there is adequate empirical confirmation, nevertheless REICHE believes that Aristotle is satisfied with the conlusion (*Empedocles' Mixture*, p. 98).

45. III.4, 429a24, suggested at II.1, 413a4-7, and II.2, 413b26.

46. See my "On Dreams 2, 459b24-460a33, and Aristotle's

ὄψις", *Phronesis*, 13 (1968), 175-182.

47. For example, "wrapped up in" (ἐμπεριλαμβάνεται), 736a10.

48. *Metaphysics* Eta (VIII) 6, 1045a34-b9 (OWENS, *Doctrine of Being*, chap. 14, pp. 379-399). OWENS does not suggest that the discussion of separate forms is applicable to minds, in this chapter, and even suggests that the question is not raised (440, n. 11). On the other hand, he asserts (p. 444) that Aristotle "supposes without question that a form which is not the form of any matter is a mind". Assuming that the supposed separate forms of *Metaphysics* Eta 6 are minds, are they minds of individual men, or is one of them the mind of the species man, or are they simply disembodied intelligences, while the minds of men are embodied intelligences? I do not think that this question can be answered within the context of Aristotle's own writings, becuse it was not posed in this way until a later time.

49. Fragment 1 a, in Themistius; translated from the quotation given by BARBOTIN, p. 188.

50. 737a8-11; I have followed PECK, LOUIS, *et al.*, in omitting το σπέρμα in line 8, which results in the rendering, "some of the psychic principle" (PECK and LOUIS: "portion"). The preposition and prefixes in ἐν ᾧ συναπέρχεται are difficult to pack into the English.

51. SOLMSEN, "The Vital Heat, the Inborn Pneuma, and the Aither", *Journal of Hellenic Studies*, 77 (1957), 119-123.

52. 736b27. PLATT inserted the word "only" into the translation, SOLMSEN (*J. Hellenic Studies*, 77), and MORAUX (*Autour d'Aristote*) approve, although no one has it in the text. It is not strictly necessary, although it does emphasize the opposition to preformationism, refuted in I.17-18.

53. MORAUX, "Quinta Essentia", PAULY-WISSOWA, Half-volume 47, vol. XXIV, (Stuttgart 1963), 1171-1263, especially 1196ff. Sections A.3 and B are the most important. He provides an

extensive bibliography of discussions of the problem.

54. Note to 737a1 and appendices.

55. LOUIS remarks the reference to Thales (all things are full of soul) which occurs similarly in *de Anima* II.1, 411a 7-11. The difficulties of Thales' thesis, which Aristotle now seems to adopt, are alleviated by the doctrine that the activity of the physical powers needs the physical organ, which cannot be present in fire, or air, alone.

56. PECK's translation favors this interpretation where the Greek is ambiguous: τὸ σῶμα τὸ περιλαμβανόμενον may mean either "the enclosed body" (i.e. the *pneuma*), or "the enclosing body" (i.e. the mixture of earth and so on around the *pneuma*). The latter interpretation would be supported by the words which follow: "in the sea there is plenty of earthly stuff; therefore the nature of the testacea is generated from such a construction".

57. See note 5, above.

58. *Metaphysics* Λ (XII) 5, 1071a15; *Nicomachean Ethics* VI.7, 1141b1; JAEGER, *Aristotle*, p. 143; PECK *GA* appendix B 18ff.

59. Omitted here is a reference to the theory of "like to like", cursorily refuted in this place. Cf. *de Anima* I.2, 404b15; 5, 409b19ff.

60. Secl. τῷ ἐξ αρχῆς μείζων δὲ αὕτη ἐστίν with PECK, LULOFS retains.

61. Cf. *Movement of Animals* 8, 702a12-21, where animal movement is explained in a similar way, including the "immediacy" of action by active and passive powers. See I. DÜRING, *Aristoteles* (Heidelberg, 1966), pp. 337-345.

62. Only roughly, since much of Aristotle's account of the heat of various parts of the body is fantasy, or *a priori* reasoning at best. Cf. G.E.R. LLOYD, "Right and Left in Greek Philosophy", *Journal of Hellenic Studies*, 82 (1962), 56ff; also *On the Heavens (de Caelo)* IV.

63. Aristotle's homoiomeries must not be confused with those attributed to Anaxagoras. Cf. A.L. PECK, "Anaxagoras, Predication as a Problem in Physics", *Classical Quarterly*, 25 (1931), 27-37, 112-120, esp. p. 34.

64. *PA* II.3, 650a5. Concoction and *metabole* occur through the power of the hot.

65. II.2, 736b37, cf. 736a6-8.

66. IV.10, 777b17ff, cf. *Phys*. II.2, 194b13; *Met*. Lambda 5, 1071a15.

67. The word occurs rarely; cf. II.1, 734a30, 734b35, and section II.B.4, above.

68. *Energeia ontos*, 734b22; *entelecheia* is used comparably at a5, b35, and *Met*. Theta 8.

69. As in II.4, 740b21; II.5, 741b15; II.6, 742a13, 744a8.

70. IV.3, 768a13, b4; cf. 769b2.

71. He mentions by name Anaxagoras, Empedocles, Democritus, and Leophanes, and refers to "other physiologers" (763b32). PECK adds references to Aeschylus, and to Hippocrates, "On Diet", "On the Sacred Disease", "Airs Waters Places"; LOUIS adds references to Euripedes and Parmenides.

72. 766a19: μὴ κρατῇ.

73. PECK's translation of γεννᾷ at 767b33.

74. The passages in question are these: IV.3, 768a12-14: ἔνεισι δ'αἱ μὲν ἐνεργείᾳ τῶν κινήσεων, αἱ δὲ δυνάμει, ἐνεργείᾳ μὲν αἱ τοῦ γεννῶντος καὶ τῶν καθόλου, οἷον ἀνθρώπου καὶ ζῴου, δυνάμει δὲ αἱ τοῦ θήλεος καὶ τῶν προγόνων.
768b4: ἔνεισι γὰρ καὶ τῶν μορίων αἱ μὲν ἐνεργείᾳ κινήσεις αἱ δὲ δυνάμει.
768b7: ἔνεισι τῶν κινήσεων αἱ μὲν δυνάμει αἱ δ'ἐνεργείᾳ.

75. 768a25. It does not seem necessary to omit καὶ ἐπὶ τῶν ἀρρένων καὶ ἐπὶ τῶν θηλεῶν with AUBERT and WIMMER, *Aristotelis*

de Generatione Animalium (Leipzig, 1860), and with PECK, or καὶ ἐπὶ τῶν ἀρρένων with LULOFS, but it does not matter for our argument.

76. 768b16-18; cf. *GC* 324a33ff.

77. *GA* II.1; *de An.* I.4, 415a28ff.

78. *Aristotle's Criticism of Presocratic Philosophy*, p. 252.

79. These characterizations more closely resemble those provided by critics of teleology than those given by its defenders, but they do seem common notions.

NOTES TO CHAPTER III

1. *PA* II may have been the first book of *PA* originally; I.2
- 5,645b, seems the sort of section which could have existed
independently or as part or parts of other compositions, and
placed rather loosely here. This is argued by LE BLOND, *Aristote philosophe de la vie* (Paris, 1945) 51ff; see also Chapter
I.E, above.

2. G.E.R. LLOYD, *Polarity and Analogy* (Cambridge, 1966), describes the character and development of these principles in
early Greek philosophy. He tries to show that 'polar' arguments are relatively independent of 'four cause' arguments
in Aristotle.
A.S.L. FARQUHARSON, *Aristotle: De Motu Animalium, de Incessu
Animalium* (Oxford, 1912), lists in a note to *IA* 2 the explanatory principles which he finds used in this very short
treatise.

     1) Purpose, selection of the best possible.

     2) Economy or organic equivalents; compensation.

     3) Bilateral symmetry.

     4) Specialized differentiation.

     5) Secondary adaptation.

     6) Utility: a) for preservation in the environment;
        b) of mechanical structure.

     7) Homology of organs and members.

     8) Serial homology.

     9) Analogy between the parts and works of nature.

    10) Sovereignty, the principle of subordination
        running through creation:
        a) Man's superiority to the rest of the animal
        kingdom;
        b) Of right to left, upper to lower;
        c) The 'gradual scale' from lifeless things
        to the highest animate beings.

FARQUHARSON has constructed this list from the point of view of modern biology; Aristotle would reduce some of these principles to the formal or final cause.

3. E.g., *GA* II.6, 743a29; *PA* IV.12, 694a.

4. *GA* II.4, 740a24-b11. Cf. 745b21ff, and *HA* VII.7, 8.
Aristotle's discussion of the umbilicus was an original contribution, showing considerable care in dissection.

5. The notion of 'blend' (*krasis*) is discussed by A.L. PECK,
Aristotle: Historia Animalium (London, 1965) lxx ff. See *GC*
II.8, 334b32ff; II.3, 330a30ff; *PA* II.9, 647b29ff; III.2,
663b32; 12, 673b28; IV.1, 676a29; Hippocrates, *peri diaitēs*,
peri trophēs; Chapter I. D. 1, above, especially note 78.

6. *HA* III.19, 621a6; *PA* III.4, 666a10; *GA* II.1, 735a20; II.
5, 741b15; II.4, 740a3; *Juv.* 3, 468b31. Cf. Walter PAGEL,
"An Harveyan Prelude to Harvey", *History of Science* 2 (1962)
114-125; "William Harvey Revisited", *History of Science* 8
(1969) and 9 (1970). PAGEL shows how the development of Harvey's theory of the movement of the blood and other theories
were partly effected by his contact with Aristotle's biological ideas.
On the senses of '*archē*' see *Met.* Delta 1. These senses parallel the senses of 'prior' at *GA* II.6, 742a20.
On the relationship between Aristotle's theory of the mean
and his account of the heart, see T. TRACY, *Physiological
Theory and the Doctrine of the Mean in Plato and Aristotle*
(Chicago, Ill., 1969), and my review in *Studi Internazionali
di Filosofia* II (1970) 181-184.

7. *HA* III.2, 511b10ff; *PA* III.4, 665b16ff; *Somn. Vig.* 3,
456b1; *Juv.* 3, 468b31; *Resp.* 8, 474b7. The heart may also
be the source of the 'sinews': *HA* III.5, 515a26.

8. *PA* II.3, 650a3ff; *GA* II.6, 743a1ff; *Somn. Vig.* 3, 456b1
-458a15; *Juv.* 3, 468b31ff; *Resp.* 8, 474b7ff; 20, 479b17ff.

9. No single word in English quite fits this sense of *archē*.
See LSJ s.v. *archē* II, and words beginning in 'arch-' derived

from this sense. At *Met.* Delta 1, 1013a14, the 'architectonic' arts are mentioned as *archai* in this sense.

10. *PA* III.4, 666a11ff; *GA* II.6, 743b25; *MA* 11, 703b23; *Sens.* 2, 439a3; *Somn. Vig.* 2, 456a1ff.

11. *GA* II.6, 742b35; *MA passim*, cf. *IA*; *de An.* I.1, 403a31; 4, 408b8; *Somn. Vig.* 2, 456a1ff; *Resp.* 8, 474b7ff. PECK *GA* appendix B.IV.

12. In addition to the references in notes 10 and 11, see *PA* II.1, 647a25; II.10, 656b10; III.3, 665a10; 6, 670a20ff; 11, 673b10; IV.5, 678b1; *GA* IV.4, 773a10; V.2, 781a20ff.

13. II.4, 740a4ff, PECK's Loeb translation with minor revisions. Note the play on the ambiguity of the word '*archē*'; cf. *PA* III.4, 666a34, where it is argued that the *archē* must be either the heart or the liver, because of the number of blood vessels coming to these two organs, but it cannot be the liver, because the heart is formed before the liver; therefore the *archē* is the heart. Here too the argument uses two senses of *archē* in one argument.

14. G. VERBEKE, *L'évolution de la doctrine de pneuma* (Paris, 1945), traces the traducianism of the stoics to this interpretation of Aristotle's theory of *pneuma* (p. 30). The development may well have been in this direction, but Aristotle's theory is not traducian; rather, his theory is unclear, and lends itself to adaptation by those motivated by theological considerations. See Chapter II.B.7.c, above, and E. BARBOTIN, *La théorie aristotélicienne de l'intellect d'après Théophraste* (Louvain, 1954) p. 181. "Traducianism" is the theory which holds that the soul is inherited from the parents; the opposed theological theory is that the soul is created in individuals, or "creationism". Both of these theories suppose that the soul can be distinguished from the body, but Aristotle's *de Anima* develops a theory which does not permit a distinction between soul and body such that this question could arise. The theory of *pneuma*, as it appears

in *GA* and *MA*, clouds the issue and might be said to have encouraged the development of the traducian theory. It is worth
remembering that for Aristotle, the opposed theological theory
was not creationism, but transmigrationism, favorite of the
Pythagoreans and the early Academy.

15. See also A.L. PECK, "The Connate Pneuma: An Essential
Factor in Aristotle's Solution to the Problems of Reproduction
and Sensation", *Science, Medicine, and History, Essays in
Honour of Charles Singer*, ed. E.A. UNDERWOOD (Oxford, 1953)
111-121; "Aristotle on *Kinesis*", *Essays in Greek Philosophy*,
ed. J. ANTON and G. KUSTAS (Albany, N.Y., 1971) 478-490.

16. "Aristotle on *Kinesis*", 482.

17. This theory is refuted by Aristotle at *GA* I.17-20. For
a description of the position, see F.S. BODENHEIMER, *The
History of Biology* (London, 1958) 115. LEIBNIZ, *Monadology*
65-75, has a classic expression of the theory; LEIBNIZ accepts infinities and infinitesimals easily in his philosophy
but Aristotle is committed to rejecting them. Theological
traducianism does not cause quite the same problem as a
physical preformationism; since the soul is supposed to be
immaterial, there is not a quantity of it. Aristotle's theory
of the active intellect is thus nearer to the spirit of theological traducianism, except that he says that it comes 'from
outside' (*thyrathen*), as the creationists (e.g. Thomists)
do not fail to remind us.

18. II.6, 742a15. The hot is active, the fluid acted upon.

19. *GA* III.11, 762a20. Cf. PECK, "Aristotle on *Kinesis*",
485ff.

20. *Mete.* I.3, 339b1. Cf. II.9, 370a7, which suggests that
the heat of lightning which makes thunder also generates
pneuma by boiling the clouds.

21. *GA* II.6, 741b37ff, quoted above. The ambivalence seems
to stem in part from a disagreement between the Hippocratic

and Sicilian medical traditions about the character of *pneuma*;
thus VERBEKE, *L'évolution*, 1-15, suggests. Aristotle has some
aspects of both theories, as described by VERBEKE. However,
the history of the concept of *pneuma* before Aristotle has
yet to be written; Anaximenes and Diogenes of Apollonia are
outstanding representatives of 'pneumatic' philosophers in
the presocratic period, and there have been suggestions of
some distant connection with Hindu philosophy, in which many
sorts of 'breaths' are distinguished. See W.K.C. GUTHRIE, *In
the Beginning* (Ithaca, N.Y., 1957) 49, 128; Walter WILI,
"The History of Spirit in Antiquity", *Spirit and Nature*, ed.
J. CAMPBELL (New York, N.Y., 1954) 75-106. Whatever may come
of an investigation of the theory of *pneuma* before Aristotle,
it will be an additional problem to clarify the considerations
leading him to adopt *pneuma* as part of his explanation of the
soul, in addition to his quite reasonable hylomorphism.

22. In fact, Aristotle never calls the *pneuma* involved in
generation '*symphyton*'. In *PA* III.6, 669a1, and *Somn. Vig.* 2,
456a12, *symphyton pneuma* seems limited to non-breathing animals, and is contrasted with the external breath, although
it is given the same functions as the external breath. The
textual basis for reading '*symphyton*' before '*pneuma*' whatever it is a question of something inside animals, is *MA* 10,
703a10ff. See "Aristotle's *Parts of Animals* 2.16. 659b13-19:
Is it Authentic?" *Classical Quarterly* 18 (1968) 270-278. On
the meaning of the word '*symphyton*' see BARBOTIN, *La théorie*
177ff.

23. Mechanistic teleology is not uncommon in modern philosophy. Giorgio TONELLI has suggested in conversation that
BOYLE, NEWTON, LEIBNIZ, and the Cartesian school, all held
some version of the theory that the universe was created by
God as a kind of automaton which would carry out his purposes.
This teleological mechanism of the seventeenth and eighteenth
centuries may be said to be a stage intermediate between Aristotle's functionalistic and non-mechanistic teleology, and

302

the anti-teleological mechanism of the nineteenth century materialists. See also Chapter IV.A, below, and "Aristotle's Natural Necessity", *Studi Internazionali di Filosofia* I (1969).

24. *PA* II.10. 656a29, PECK. Besides this functional account, there is a genetic account of the fact that the head has little flesh on it: *PA* II.7, 652a26; 14, 658b3; III.5, 668a 14ff; *GA* II.6, 743a8; 7, 746a18.

25. *PA* II.7, 652b17, after PECK. In fact, it is the skin which performs this function, for the most part. See Edwin CLARKE, "Aristotelian Concepts of the Form and Function of the Brain", *Bulletin of the History of Medicine*, 1963, 1-14.

26. *PA* II.7, 652b15. LLOYD, *Polarity*, Part I, Chapter 1, explores aspects of this problem, particularly in Aristotle's predecessors.

27. See Jan van der MEULEN, *Aristoteles: Die Mitte in seinem Denken* (Meisenheim/Glan, 1951); LLOYD, *Polarity*; TRACY, *Physiological Theory*.

28. *PA* II.14, 658b1; *GA* V.3, 782b10, 783b25.

29. *PA* IV.10, 686a5; CLARKE, *op. cit.*

30. *PA* II.10, 656a37-b7; cf. *GA* V.1, 779b20; *de An.* II.1, 412b20; *Sens.* 2, 437b14ff.

31. *GA* II.6, 744a9ff, PECK. Cf. *Sens.* 2, 438b28. One might suppose that the observation of the close connection between eyes and the brain would lead to a theory of the brain as the organ of sensation; other considerations led Aristotle to reject this theory, although it was well known to him from Plato, *Tim.* 75, see *PA* II.10, 656b14ff, and probably from the Hippocratic writers as well.

32. *PA* II.10, 656b14ff; cf. *GA* V.2, 781a20ff (the authenticity of this passage has been questioned); *de An.* II.8, 419b32; III.1, 425a4.

33. *Sens.* 2, 438b25ff. The argument is clouded by the contra-

diction between an important premiss in 438b1: "Smell is a
certain smoky vapor", and its denial at 443a22.

34. There is an analogy between taste and smell (*de An*. II.
9, 421a17), and the medium of taste is liquid (II.10, 422a
8ff), but taste is a form of touch, and thus closely related
to the heart (*Sens*. 2, 439a1ff, *et al*.).

35. *PA* II.7, 652b34ff, after PECK; cf. *Phys*. II.8, 198b18.

36. *PA* II.7, 653a11ff, PECK; cf. *Somn. Vig*. 3, 457b20ff.

37. *PA* III.10, 673a33-b3. Aristotle does not give a genetic
account of the viscera, other than the heart, in the *GA*.
There is a description, based upon dissection and observation
of the development of these organs in chick and shark embryos, in *HA* VI.3, 516ff; 10, 565a.

38. T.H. HUXLEY, "On Certain Errors Respecting the Structure
of the Heart attributed to Aristotle", *Nature* 21 (1879) 1-5;
see also my review of TRACY, *Physiological Theory*, in *Studi
Internazionali di Filosofia* II (1970). See *HA* I.17, 496a4ff;
III.3, 513a27ff; *Somn. Vig*. 3, 458a10ff.

39. *Mete*. I.12, 348a34; *HA* VI.15, 569b4; *Met*. Alpha 1, 980
a21; *Pol*. IV.11, 1296a18; *Resp*. 12, 476b27; *GA* III.10, 760
b33; and many other places.

40. 'Vestigium' in Latin is approximately synonymous with
'sēmeion' in Greek.

41. There is another sense of the word 'sēmeion', which does
not operate in this passage at all: 'mathematical point'. This
sense appears in *MA* 8, 702a25, *et al*., in the extended application to the 'point' in the joints of animals, the ends
of their bones. At 10, 703a13, this sense is used in an obscure analogy, according to which the *symphyton pneuma* is to
the *archē* of the soul as the *sēmeion* of the joints, which
moves and is moved, is to the 'unmoved'.

42. In *PA* IV.9, 685a34, Aristotle compares the probosces of
the squid with the anchor lines of ships. He often uses nautical

analogies: the nautilus is described as sailing along the surface with a sail made of webbing and tentacles as rudder oars
(*HA* IX.37, 6225b); it is also described as filling its shell
with water in order to sink when faced by danger, which tempts
us to provide an analogy with the submarine. See also *PA* IV.6,
683b1; 8, 684a12; 12, 694b8; *IA* 10, 710a1, 8; *MA* 2, 698b8;
7, 701b25; *PA* IV.10, 687b18.

43. *PA* II.3, 650a13ff, after PECK. Cf. IV.4, 678a4ff (very
similar); *GA* II.4, 739b33ff (a similar analogy used in embryology); 7, 745b26; IV.6, 774b26.

44. *HA* I.16, 495b24; II.17, 507a29; IV.4, 529a25; *PA* III.13,
674a5ff; IV.5, 680b25ff. Diagrams appeared in the lost *Anatomy*.
Digestion is discussed in *PA* II.3, 650a3ff; *Somn. Vig.* 3,
457b11; *Juv.* 3, 469a2 (explicitly referring to the passage in
PA); 5, 460a24.

45. *PA* II.8, 653b22ff. Cf. *PA* III.5, 668a25; *GA* II.6, 743a8.

46. For a general discussion of Aristotle's use of analogies
drawn from the arts, see Chapter IV.B, below. The use of the
potter's art in an analogy has been noted, cf. *GA* I.22, 730
b5ff. In *PA* II.9, 654b27, the system of bones is likened to
the solid core with which modellers in clay begin as they
mold the figures of animals. Nature similarly molds the body
out of flesh around the bones; perhaps the artists imitated
nature originally. See also *GA* II.6, 743a1, where the bloodvessels are compared to the '*kanabous*' traced on the walls
of buildings. There is a problem about the meaning of the
word '*kanabos*' here; PECK refers to *PA* II.9, 654b27, the
comparison of the bones with the armature used by modellers;
LSJ cite Hesychius, and PECK adds Photius, as authority for
the sense of '*kanabos*' as 'the framework around which artists
mould wax or clay'. In *HA* II.5, 515a33, the same analogy appears: "the veins, as in the drawn *kanabois*, have the shape
of the whole body." THOMPSON translates, "like the sketch of
a manikin", while PECK translates, "like the lines of the

wooden skeleton used in modelling." THOMPSON and PECK use
the same evidence, but THOMPSON says that the word "had come
to mean the rough outline of the human figure, such as
children draw upon a wall." LSJ believe him, and give this
as a second sense, referring both to this passage and to
743a1. Two historians of art, John CONNALLY and Vincent BRUNO,
tell me that large statues, like the Athene Parthenos, were
made of plates of metal (in this case, gold) hung on a wooden
frame; there is little evidence, however, that Greek artists
in the time of Aristotle used armatures for their clay and
wax statuettes. If they did (as artists surely did in the
days of Hesychius, 4th century AD, and Photius, 9th century
AD), then the passages would make sense; an armature looks
like a 'stick man', and the word could be used in both ways.
Greek mural painters did make a practice of drawing a pre-
liminary outline, and Professor BRUNO points out that they
used red paint for this sketch, strengthening the resemblance
of a sketch of the blood vessels.

47. *GA* II.6, 744b23-28. This passage is often noted because
there is a strong reference to nature as craftsman, and because there is a reference to 'mind'; see P. MORAUX, "A propos du νοῦς θύραθεν chez Aristote", *Autour d'Aristote* (Mélanges Mansion, Louvain, 1955); and BARBOTIN, *La théorie*.

48. *HA* III.5, 515a26-b26; *PA* III.4, 666b14-17; *GA* V.7, 787
b11,15. In the last passage, the *neuroi* are said to set the
pneuma in the heart in motion. See F. SOLMSEN, "Greek Philosophy and the Discovery of the Nerves", *Museum Helveticum*
19 (1961) 150-167, 169-197.

49. *PA* IV.10-13; *HA* I.5; II.1; *IA*; *MA*. The *MA* is genuine,
although condemned by BRANDIS, ROSE, and ZELLER. W. JAEGER,
"Das Pneuma im Lykeion", *Hermes* 48 (1913) 31ff, makes out a
strong case; further arguments in its favor may be found in
FARQUHARSON's introduction in the Oxford translation, and
in L. TORRACA, "Sull'autenticitá del DMA di Aristotele",
Maia 10 (1958) 220-223.

50. G.E.M. ANSCOMBE, "Thought and Action in Aristotle", *New Essays on Plato and Aristotle*, ed. R. BAMBROUGH (New York, N.Y., 1965); D.J. ALLAN, *The Philosophy of Aristotle* (London 1952) 75-78; JAEGER, "Das Pneuma im Lykeion"; PECK, *GA* appendix B; W.F.R. HARDIE, "Aristotle's Treatment of the Relation between Soul and Body", *Philosophical Quarterly* 14 (1964) 53-72; *Aristotle's Ethical Theory* (Oxford, 1968); H. CHERNISS, *Aristotle's Criticism of Plato and the Academy* I (Baltimore, 1944) 465-469; Alan R. WHITE, ed., *The Philosophy of Action* (London, 1968) bibliography and index.

51. *GA* II.1, 734b10; II.5, 741b9; Chapter II.B.3, above; cf. *Met.* Alpha 2, 983a14.

52. 7, 710b2-10. See Chapter II.B.3, note 32, above.

53. 8, 702a12-16. HARDIE, in *Philosophical Quarterly* 1964, 53-72, emphasizes the qualitative character of the physiology. His interpretation of the *MA* damages the hypothesis of F. NUYENS concerning the development of Aristotle's theory of the soul. See also I. BLOCK, "The Order of Aristotle's Psychological Writings", *American Journal of Philology* 82 (1961) 50-77; "Three German Commentators on the Individual Senses and the Common Sense in Aristotle's Psychology", *Phronesis* 9 (1964) 58-63.

54. Lambda 10, 1075a12ff. Aristotle calls the heart the acropolis, or seat of government, of the body, *PA* III.7, 670a26. The notion of *ethos* used here is related to the discussion of *ethismos* and the *ethikai aretai* in *NE* III-IV.

55. *MA* 11, 703b11. Man is obviously the paradigm case of an animal in this account, since the other animals would be thought to act generally in a non-rational, but teleological way.

56. *GA* V.1-2; *MA*. J.T. BEARE, *Greek Theories of Elementary Cognition* (Oxford, 1906), provides a general account of Aristotle's theory of perception, 56ff, 111ff, 144ff; 174ff; 188ff; 215ff; 276ff.

57. *GA* II.6, 743a8-12, after PECK. In *PA* III.5, 668a14-35, the process is compared to the irrigation of a garden, see n. 43, above.

58. *de An.* II.9, 421a18; III.12, 434b18; *Sens.* 4, 441a3; *PA* II.17, 660a22.

59. *GA* II.6, 744a6-12, PECK; cf. 743b32ff. The eyes shrink only in proportion to the size of the rest of the body, not absolutely as Aristotle thought. See SOLMSEN, *Museum Helveticum* 1961.

60. R. SORABJI, "Aristotle on Demarcating the Five Senses", *Philosophical Review* 80 (1971) 55-79, comments on the functional explanation of the organs of perception. See D.W. HAMLYN, "Aristotle's Account of Aisthesis in the *De Anima*", *Classical Quarterly* 9 (1959) 6-16; "*Koine Aisthesis*", *The Monist* 52 (1968) 195-209; *Aristotle's De Anima II and III* (Oxford, 1968).
PECK's reference to *MA* 8 in support of his notion that there is a non-teleological sense of necessity in this passage fails to make his point. The *MA*, including chapter 8, is as completely teleological as any work of Aristotle; the 'active and passive' factors, which work so 'automatically', are understood as conditionally necessary for animal movement.

61. See L. von BERTALANFFY, *Modern Theories of Development* (Oxford, 1933) chapter 10.

62. See my note in *Classical Quarterly* 1968, and Chapter IV. B.5, below, for further discussion of noses.

63. *PA* II.2, 648a14-19. DÜRING has a slightly different reading of the text, *Aristoteles De Partibus Animalium* (Göteborg, 1943); cf. J.B. MEYER, *Aristoteles Thierkunde* (Berlin, 1855) 91ff.

64. *de An.* II.9, 421a13; *PA* II.13, 657b36.

65. *Sens.* 2, 438a24; *PA* II.13, 657b38. Crabs: *HA* IV.2, 527b11;

4, 529b26; 2, 526a8; *IA* 14, 712b18. Crawfish: *HA* IV.2, 526a8.
Lobsters: *HA* IV.2, 526b1.

66. *PA* II.13, 658a1.

67. *Ibid.* and passages cited in note 65. *IA* 14, 712b18ff, discusses the mobility and hardness of the eyes of crabs in relation to their peculiar direction of local movement.

68. *PA* II.13, 657b8; cf. *HA* II.12, 504a24, where it is said
that owls use the upper lid. Aristotle probably means that
the sharp-eyed fliers are generally similar in this respect;
he implies that it is 'better' to use the upper lid, because
'up' is better than 'down'; see LLOYD, *Polarity*, 52ff, and
Chapter IV.A.5.c, below.

69. 658a8; see Chapter IV.B, below.

70. *GA* V.1, 779a27ff, especially b7.

71. *HA* I.9, 491b26ff; *PA* II.8, 653b25; *Sens.* 2, 438a13; *de
An.* II.1, 413a3.

72. *GA* V.1, 781a8ff. Aristotle seems to have assumed the
'issuing forth' theory in *Cael.* and *Mete.*, but he sharply
criticizes this theory in *de An.* and *Sens.* See my discussion
in *Phronesis* 13 (1968).

73. *PA* II.13, 657b25: eagles, hawks, owls, etc. The habits
of these birds are discussed at *HA* IX.32, 618b13ff, but the
variations in their eyes are not noted. Owls, he says, see
best at twilight and dawn, and the sea-eagle is particularly
keen-sighted. Cf. *HA* VIII.3, 592a28; *PA* IV.11, 691a25. Owls,
of course, do *not* have deep-set eyes. In fact, predators
tend to have their eyes forward and well-spaced across the
plane of the face; this favors good distance judgement. Animals sought as prey tend to have their eyes well round to
the sides of the head, favoring good peripheral vision.
Aristotle seems not to have figured this out.

74. *PA* II.13, 658a4, and passages in note 65. The distinction
between vision at a distance and discrimination is not made

at 658a4; the fluidity of the eyes is thought sufficient ground for good vision at a distance.

75. *PA* II.11-12, 657a12-24. *HA* I.11, 492a13-b4, covers much of the same material. There are some other passages which could be noted; I am not trying to be exhaustive at this point.

76. *PA* II.11, 657a12-17. *HA* I.11, 492a13ff, adds some bits of 'information'; a22, "Man alone, of those having an ear (lobe) has this part immovable"; a32, "Ears may be hairy, smooth, or intermediate; the intermediate is best for hearing, but is no sign of disposition; large projecting ears are a sign of chattering and gossiping". For more of this sort of comment, see Theophrastus, *Characters*.

77. *PA* II.12, 657a18-22; cf. IV.11, 691a13ff.

78. *HA* VI.12, 566b27; VIII.2, 589a29; *PA* III.9, 671b5; IV.2, 676b29; 13, 697b1. "Dualize" is PECK's translation of ἐπαμφοτερίζειν explained and defended in his *HA* introduction paragraphs 28-33.

79. Cf. PECK, *HA* introduction paragraphs 28-60.

80. The parts of the limbs are carefully enumerated and described at *HA* II.1, 498a32ff.

81. In addition to the passages already cited, *HA* II.15, 506 a24; VI.12, 566b31; VIII.6, 594b30.

82. *IA* 19, 714b12: the whole genus of testacea is deformed, and move in the manner of an animal with its feet cut off, like the seal or bat, for these are quadrupeds, but 'badly'. See IV.A.5.b, below.

83. *PA* II.16, 659b34ff; *Resp.* 11, 476a18; *de An*. II.8, 420 b18; *HA* IV.9, 535a31, 536a21, and Chapter IV.B, below.

84. *PA* II.17, 660a17ff; cf. the explanation of the elephant's nose, IV.B.5, below.

85. Taste is a form of touch: cf. *Sens*. 2, 439a1; *de An*.

II.11, 423a17, b17; H. BONITZ, *Index Aristotelicus* (Berlin 1870) s.v. *geusis*.

86. *PA* II.17, 660b4-11; seals are not mentioned. 'Gourmandise' is a compromise translation of '*lichneia*', and suits the habits of reptiles, which eat a great deal at one time, but not often.

87. There is a suggestion of gourmandise in selachia, *PA* IV. 13, 696b31.

88. If they had tongues which were both broad and light, could they really speak? No, Aristotle would say that if they had the power of speech, they would have broad light tongues.

89. *HA* II.17, 508a20; *PA* IV.11, 691a6; II.17, 660b7-11.

90. *HA* II.11, 503a15ff, has been challenged by O. REGENBOGEN, "Bemerkungen zur *Historia Animalium* des Aristoteles", *Studi ital. di filos. class.*, 27/28 (1956) 444-9; PECK, *HA* vol. 1, p. 238, disagrees.

91. LOUIS *ad loc.* says that γλύσχρον is used metaphorically here, and means 'little, mean'; he therefore translates the words "τρόπον τινὰ γλύσχρον" as "un organe rudimentaire". This is not necessary; Aristotle means that there is a soft gummy place in the mouth which serves to sense tastes.

92. A. DORIER et G. BELON, "Sur l'organe palatin des Cyprinidés", *Travaux du laboratoire d'hydrobiologie et de pisciculture de l'Université de Grenoble* 44 (1952) 47-60.

93. *HA* IV.4, 530b30, describes the part; IV.7, 532a7, says that they all have it; *PA* IV.5, 678b11, tells the function; cf. b23, and below.

94. "Mosquitoes" translates 'κώνωπες'; PECK, at *GA* I.16, 721 a10, says, "It is not possible to say exactly what insects are meant"; he now has (at 532a14) "vinegar fly" on the strength of V.19, 552b4. But drosophila melanogaster is not a notable stinger, while the κώνωψ is. LOUIS has 'moustiques'

311

and refers to Herodotus II.95 for the sense. He must be right: in the first place, mosquitoes are the only Mediterranean stinging insects not otherwise noted by Aristotle, and in the second place, in modern Greek the mosquito is known as κώνωφ or κουνοῦπι.

95. Bees: *HA* V.22, 554a14; Testacea: *PA* IV.5, 678b11, 679b6.

96. Cf. *HA* V.15, 547b7; IV.4, 528b28.

97. Cf. *PA* IV.12, 692b17: as the elephant's trunk replaces a hand; so the tongue of some insects replaces a mouth. These two cases seem to be taken as paradigms.

98. PECK says, 'grasshoppers' for '*tettigoi*', but he has it right in *HA* vol. II, pp. 373-4. We hope that future editions of the other volumes of the LOEB Aristotle will be corrected accordingly. See also *HA* IV.7, 532b11; A.N. BRANGHAM, *The Naturalist's Riviera* (London, 1962); my note in *Classical Quarterly* 18 (1968).

99. PECK translates the word 'κατά' at the places marked (a) with 'by', 'at', and 'alongside', respectively. LOUIS translates consistently 'à', which is fine in French. 'Alongside' is the worst of PECK's three versions, for that would be 'παρά' in Greek. The sense of the passage demands that the tongue and sting be fused together, since the sting-tongue is said to taste as well as to exercise the other functions of conveying food and defending the animal. 'On' is consistent and accurate, but there is also a suggestion of the 'κατα-' in 'καταχρῆται', conveying the idea of the unity of the functions of sting and tongue (see Chapter IV.B, below).

100. His description of the mating process in insects is accurate enough for the dragonflies and damselflies (Odonata), see John BURTON, *The Oxford Book of Insects* (London, 1968) 194; K.G. DAVEY, *Reproduction of Insects* (San Francisco, Cal., 1965) 45. DAVEY's chapter IV is very helpful in claryfying the details in this part of *HA*.

101. The name for most lepidoptera in Aristotle's Greek is
'psychē', which is also the word for 'soul'. He classifies
the psychē on the basis of 'the antenna in front of the eyes'
(HA IV.7, 532a27). Some species of this class produce a hard
larva (V.19, 550b26), but others, thinks Aristotle, are generated spontaneously. His favorite is one which he supposes
to be generated by the leaves of cabbages (V.19, 551a14); he
has an account of the life cycle from the beginning of the
activity of the larva, through the formation of the chry-
sallis, to the development of the adult butterfly, but he
did not notice the adult depositing eggs on the developing
cabbages. W. CAPELLE, "Zur Entomologie des Aristoteles und
Theophrast", Rheinisches Museum für Philologie 105 (1962)
56-66, discusses the passages. See BRANGHAM, p. 118, for a
discussion of the tongue of butterflies, and see PECK ad loc.
for possible identifications of Aristotle's species.

102. J.B.S. HALDANE, The Causes of Evolution (London, 1932);
W.H. DOWDESWELL, The Mechanism of Evolution[2] (New York, N.Y.
1958); Jean ROSTAND, Evolution (New York, N.Y., 1961).

103. Aristotle does not suppose that every place on earth
always keeps the same climate. In Mete. I.14, 351a19-353a27,
he argues that climatic changes are cyclical; the effect of
this argument is support for a theory of permanence of the
terrestrial climate taken as a whole, in contrast to linear
development, a theory refuted in this passage. See W.K.C.
GUTHRIE, In the Beginning (Ithaca, N.Y., 1957) Chapter IV.

104. W.J. VERDENIUS, "Der Logosbegriff bei Heraclit und Parmenides", Phronesis 11 (1966) 81-98; 12 (1967) 99-117;
GUTHRIE, History vol. 2, 260-1.

NOTES TO CHAPTER IV

1. See Hippocrates, *On the Sacred Disease*, ch. 20; Jane HARRISON, *Themis* (reprinted New York, N.Y., 1962) chapter X; Werner JAEGER, *The Theology of the Early Greek Philosophers* (Oxford, 1947) p.158.

2. Much of this section was published as "Aristotle's Natural Necessity", in *Studi Internazionali di Filosofia* I (1969) 91-100. I thank Professor Augusto GUZZO, editor of that journal, for permission to use this material in this place; I also thank all those who commented on earlier versions of this paper at several colloquia.

3. *PA* II.14, 658b3-10; 15, 658b14-26; III.2, 663b13-20, 21ff; 9, 672a13; 10, 673a33; IV.3, 677b22ff; *GA* II.1, 731b18ff; 4, 738a33ff; 739b29ff; III.4, 755a22; IV.8, 776a15, b32; V.1, 778a33; b19; *Mem.* 2, 451b12, and elsewhere. We raised this topic in chapter I.B.2, and discussed aspects of it in chapter III: in III.A.3.b, the 'necessary but not very' spleen was examined; in III.A.3.c.i, we noted the contrast between purpose and necessity in the account of the locomotive parts and their various forms in birds (*PA* IV.12, 692b3ff), and in the account of the generation of marrow (*PA* II.6, 651b33; II.7, 652a27); in III.A.3.c.ii, we noted the way in which 'necessity' enters in the explanation of the eyes.

4. *PA* III.3, 664a30; IV.6, 682b21ff; 9, 685b15ff; *GA* I.5, 717b14ff; 15, 720b18. See section A.5, below.

5. *Met.* Delta 5, 1015a20-b15; Lambda 7, 1072b11; *PA* I.1, 639b23; *Phys.* II.9. The "absolute" necessity of modern philosophy, which is supposed to be discovered *a priori*, owes most to Aristotle's simple necessity.

6. This position has been argued by D.M. BALME, "Greek Science and Mechanism: I. Aristotle on Nature and Chance", *The Classical Quarterly* 33 (1939) 129-138; and by Helene WEISS, *Kausalität und Zufall in der Philosophie des Aristoteles*

(Basel, 1942; reprinted Darmstadt, 1967). Wolfgang WIELAND,
Die Aristotelische Physik (Göttingen, 1962) has a position
which is similar in several respects; see especially pp. 254
-277. For example, he says on p. 264, "Um von Notwendigkeit
in der Natur sachgerecht sprechen zu können, muss man den
Zweck selbst *voraussetzen* und dann fragen, was *für ihn* not-
wendig ist." Again, in the passage which follows, he writes,
"*Zufall und Notwendigkeit gibt es bei Aristoteles nicht trotz
der Teleologie, sondern wegen ihrer*" (the italics are his).
"Auf keinen Fall darf man der Materie als solcher irgendeine
inhaltlich bestimmbare Kraft zuschreiben, die nun 'teleolo-
gisch' zur Vollendung in der Form streben würde." He correctly
argues (p. 266) that Aristotle did not have one of the modern
concepts of causation; those against whom I argue in this
section seem to assume that he must have had such a concept.
I also agree with WIELAND's conclusion that Aristotle is at-
tempting to found a non-theological teleology, having seen
that the anti-theological presocratics had thought themselves forced to be anti-teleological as well.
We may also note that Harold CHERNISS, in *Aristotle's Criticism of Presocratic Philosophy* (Baltimore, 1935) pp. 246ff,
distinguishes Aristotle's concept of necessity from that of
the presocratics, but thinks that Aristotle is 'embarrassed'
about mechanism (p. 257).

7. S. MANSION, *Le jugement d'existence chez Aristote* (Louvain, 1946) p. 81. ("In a general way, Aristotle assigns to
'necessity', that is to mechanical causes, every result ob-
tained without having been pursued as an end.") On the same
page she says, "le Stagirite n'a certainement pas su faire
la synthèse parfaite des deux points de vue" (he didn't know
how to make a perfect synthesis of mechanism and finalism).

8. J.-M. LE BLOND, S.J., *Aristote philosophe de la vie* (Paris,
1945) p. 136.

9. W.D. ROSS, *Aristotle* (London, 1949), pp. 78-81. F.M. CORN-
FORD, in his note to *Physics* II.9, 200a31 (Philip WICKSTEED

translation, London, 1929, 1957, Loeb), finds evidence in that passage for a 'mechanical necessity' which works 'blindly from cause to effect', contrasted with conditional necessity in which a final cause "fixes the goal to which the mechanical chain shall lead, rather than in other directions." See CORNFORD's *Plato's Cosmology* (London, 1937) pp. 159-177 for a more accurate appraisal.

10. *Introduction à la physique aristotélicienne*[2] (Paris, 1946) p. 288.

11. *La notion de force dans le système d'Aristote* (Paris, 1923) p. 177.

12. A.L. PECK, *Aristotle: Generation of Animals* (London, 1953) pp. xlii-xliv; M. GRENE, *A Portrait of Aristotle* (Chicago, 1963) p. 145 (she has a correct interpretation on pp. 222-3). F. SOLMSEN, *Aristotle's System of the Physical World* (Ithaca, N.Y., 1960) p. 104, strongly opposes purpose and necessity in Aristotle; I. DÜRING, "Aristotle's Method in Biology", *Aristote et les problèmes de methode*, ed. S. MANSION (Symposium Aristotelicum, Louvain, 1961) 213-221, and *Aristotle's De Partibus Animalium* (Göteborg, 1945) p. 84, argues for an identification of the modes of necessity found in natural philosophy, metaphysics and mathematics. DÜRING's position depends partly on his reading of *PA* I.1, 640a1ff, which says that the '*tropos*' of demonstration and of necessity in the natural and theoretical sciences differs from that in the practical sciences. We discuss this passage below.

13. W. CHARLTON, *Aristotle's Physics Books I and II* (Oxford, 1970) pp. 115ff.

14. *PA* I.1, 639b24, cf. 641b16; 5, 644b22ff; *GA* II.1, 731b 18ff.

15. In *GC* the temporary and changeable character of matter is explored at length; cf. *Met.* Lambda 2.

16. *Kausalität*..., p. 76 ("... the fundamental being of Hyle itself as ... Hyle, accordingly, is indeed necessary for that which becomes, the being of hyle is *ex anagkēs*. But this 'from necessity' is not *haplōs*, but purely *ex hypotheseōs*.") Cf. p. 78, and *passim* for the interpretation of *Phys.* II.9.

17. There is a large and growing discussion of this chapter; a bibliography may be found in *William OCKHAM:Predestination, God's Foreknowledge, and Future Contingents* (translated with introductions, notes, and appendices, by M.M. ADAMS and N. KRETZMANN, New York, N.Y., 1969). Discussion in English has been stimulated by G.E.M. ANSCOMBE's "Aristotle and the Sea-Battle", *Mind* 1956, in which she says (rather elaborately) that Aristotle's position is similar to that held by Ludwig WITTGENSTEIN in *Tractatus Logico-Philosophicus* 5.1362: "The freedom of the will consists in the fact that future actions cannot be known now. We could only know them if causality were an *inner* necessity, like that of logical deduction. -- The connexion of knowledge and what is known is that of logical necessity." In the preceding statement, 5.1361, WITTGENSTEIN says, "superstition is the belief in the causal nexus." The point which Miss ANSCOMBE tries to make, and with which Jaako HINTIKKA struggled in several articles, is that Aristotle does not share this superstition. HINTIKKA's articles on this topic include: "Necessity, Universality, and Time in Aristotle", *Ajatus* 20 (1957); "An Aristotelian Dilemma", *Ajatus* 22 (1959) 87-92; "Aristotle's Different Possibilities", *Inquiry* 3 (1960), reprinted in J. MORAVSCIK, ed., *Aristotle* (Garden City, N.Y., 1967); "Aristotle and the 'Master Argument' of Diodorus", *American Philosophical Quarterly* I (1964) 101-114; "The Once and Future Sea Fight", *Philosophical Review* 73 (1964) 461-492. See also J.L. ACKRILL *Aristotle's Categories and de Interpretatione* (Oxford, 1963) and Philip MERLAN in *Phronesis* 15.2 (1970).
Although most of this discussion has been developed in the

317

context of Aristotle's works on logic, rather than in relation to his natural philosophy, the consensus has been to
reaffirm the clear sense of *Int.* 9, that according to Aristotle many future events are indeed contingent; this position
is incompatible with any sort of determinism which would
claim that all events are brought about by, caused by, previous events or initial conditions.

18. Cf. Jacques CHEVALIER, *La notion du nécessaire chez Aristote...* (Paris, 1915) pp. 160ff. CHARLTON, *op. cit.*, finds a
number of passages which ascribe regular, cyclical change
both to astronomical and to sublunar phenomena; these phenomena are indeed explained by reference to simple necessity,
but they are not explained by reference to matter, which he
fails and must fail to show.

19. *Introduction à la physique aristotélicienne*, 326-7, especially note 22.

20. One may add *HA* VII.7, 586a17; *GA* II.4, 739a3ff; IV.8,
777a18; similar distinctions are made in these passages.

21. *Plato's Cosmology*, 159-177.

22. *A History of Greek Philosophy* (Cambridge, 1965) vol. II,
pp. 414-419.

23. *De An.* II.2, 413a31, HETT. *PA* III.4, 666a34; *GA* II.4,
740a4ff; *Juv.* 4, 469a24.

24. '... This is what it is to be for man': τοῦτ'ἦν τὸ
ἀνθρώπῳ εἶναι, which is a particular instance of τὸ τι ἦν
εἶναι, traditionally translated 'essence'. J. OWENS, *The
Doctrine of Being in the Aristotelian Metaphysics* (Toronto,
1963) p. 184, translates the general phrase, 'the what-IS-
being' and says (p. 185) that it "expresses the formal intelligible perfection of a thing." See also LE BLOND, p. 144
n. 38; in his translation of this passage he does not supply
the λεκτέον of 640a33, at a35, but the ταῦτ' ἔχει of line 34,
which does not make as good a translation.

25. One may compare the discussion of essential and accidental predication in *APo.* I.4; Aristotle says there that
something 'belongs *per se*' to something else if one of two
conditions are met: 1) that "it belongs to it as an element
in its essence" (ἐν τῷ τί ἐστιν), or 2), "if it is an attribute the formula of whose essence includes the subject
to which the attribute itself belongs" (73a38, TREDENNICK);
the examples are taken from geometry, although the examples
of the corresponding accidental predications are 'musical'
and 'white' as attributes of an animal or man.
Two other sorts of *per se* existence are noted: 3) "Something
exists *per se* if it is not predicated of a subject..., *ousía*
and whatever denotes an individual is nothing other than itself." 4) "That which happens to something else in virtue
of the latter's own nature is said to happen *per se*; while
that which does not so happen is called an accident." Lightning occurring while one walks is an accident, but the animal dying while its throat is being cut is *per se*, or essential.
This account seems to draw a rather rigid distinction between essential and accidental predication, allowing only for
the 'best' way of *PA* I.1; the *PA* seems to ease the restrict-
ions on knowledge and understanding in comparison with the
APo., trying to find a middle path between the certitude of
knowledge of the essence and the unknowability of that which
is purely accidental. The fourth application of the term
'*per se*' in *APo.* comes closest to the 'second best' mode of
statement in *PA* I.1; it would be difficult to include all
possible manners of death in the definition of the species,
but it would not be very difficult to argue that one gains
an understanding of the species through the examination of
the ways in which death comes to its members. In *APo.* I.4,
there is also a distinction between that which is 'true in
every instance' and 'essential predication', which may well
parallel the distinction between the two modes of statement
in *PA* I.1.

26. See also, at the beginning of this section, the passage in which the diaphragm is described as separating the 'end' and 'that which exists for the sake of the end' (*PA* III.10, 672b21).

27. Cf. the language at 640b16, ἀναρραγῆναι. LE BLOND, oddly enough, takes this passage as support for his interpretation, p. 141, n. 32; it clearly cannot be that.

28. This passage is often noted because it is thought to provide information concerning Aristotle's idea of Socrates. See GUTHRIE, *History*, vol. III, p. 417.

29. Not following PECK, who inserts 'οὕτως' at this point in the text.

30. This phrase is quite obscure, but LOUIS translates it just about the same way. OGLE says, "This passage defies all other than a paraphrastic rendering with some expansion" (*ad loc.*).

31. A more lucid account of respiration may be found in *Resp.* 21, 480a15ff.

32. E.g., *PA* IV.3, 677b22; 5, 679a27; 11, 692a4; 12, 694a22.

33. Cf. *Phys.* II.8, 199a33ff; *Met.* Epsilon 2.

34. There are many other places: see BONITZ *Index* 136b20-137a9.

35. 767b22, 768a28-769a7. Cf. *GC* I.10, 328a18-32, and Chapter II, above.

36. 'The way is prepared': πρωδοποιῆται, a suggestive word. 'Symptom' is a transliteration; the word is used here in the medical sense, which is similar in Greek and English ('Characteristic sign of a particular infirmity'). Aristotle says here that this 'symptom' ἐπαλλάτει, which is translated 'occurs occasionally', but this word also has connotations of dualizing.

37. See E.J. DIJKSTERHUIS, *The Mechanization of the World*

Picture (Oxford, 1961), especially pp. 241-271; E.A. BURTT,
The Metaphysical Foundations of Modern Science (New York,
N.Y., 1932); Paolo ROSSI, *I filosofi e le macchine (1400-
1700)* (Milano, 1962); Giorgio TONELLI, "La nécessité des
lois de la nature au XVIIIe siècle et chez Kant en 1762",
Revue d'histoire des sciences XII (1959) 225-241; I thank
Professor TONELLI for his helpful comments on this topic.

38. Aspects of formal necessity have been discussed in Chapter III; the spleen which is 'necessary but not very' in
PA III.7, 669b27, was noted in III.A.3.b, and the relationship between the *logos* and the entity was discussed in relation to the explanation of the brain, in III.A.3.a. 'Dualizing' and 'dwarflikeness' have been noted several times,
for example in III.A.3.c.i and B.2.

39. See *Cat.* 1a2, with John ANTON, "The Meaning of ὁ λόγος
τῆς οὐσίας in Aristotle's *Categories* 1a", *The Monist* 52.2
(1968) 252-267. Aristotle tends to use this, or a similar
phrase, when he is defining 'same' and 'other': in *Met.*
Delta 6, 1016a33, he says that things are one when the *logos*
of τὸ τί ἦν εἶναι are indistinguishable; at Delta 9, 1018a
10, he says, "Things are called 'other' when either the
form or the matter or the *logos* of the *ousia* is more than
one." In general, the word '*logos*' is used of the formal
cause: see, for example, *Phys.* II.3, 194b27; *Met.* Delta 2,
1013a27; 29, 1024a29; 8, 1017b23: the essence, of which the
logos is the definition, is said to be the *ousia* of each
thing; Zeta 7, 1030a7. Sometimes the concept is applied to
mathematical examples; in Iota 3, 1054a35, identity is said
to have several senses: a) one in number, b) one in both
logos and number (a person is identical with himself both in
form and matter), c) if the *logos* of the πρώτη οὐσία is one,
as equal straight lines are the same. This last case is
clarified at Delta 13, 1020a13: some things are said to be
quantities in their *ousia*, as a line, for example (for quantity belongs to the *logos* of its τί ἐστι). In general, the

natural philosopher is supposed to know how to state the
logos of the *ousia* (Kappa 7, 1064a22).

40. The fundamental recent investigation of this aspect of
ancient thought is A.O. LOVEJOY, *The Great Chain of Being*
(Cambridge, Mass., 1936) chapter II; Plato's *Timaeus* is the
essential ancient source of this notion: see the commentaries
by TAYLOR and CORNFORD. We have discussed aspects of the
great chain of being or the scale of nature in II.B.7.d,
where the 'relative value' of different lots of *pneuma* and
aither are said to determine the character of the animal,
and in III.B.2., where the seal as a dualizing animal is
examined as a gap-filler in the scale of nature. See also
my "The Continuous Analogy", *Agora* I.2 (Spring, 1970) 20-42.

41. *HA* VIII.1, 588b4-17, is verbally very similar; in *PA* II.
9, 655a17, a special case of this continuum is described,
that of the relative rigidity of the skeletal structure from
sharks to large land mammals (he says, "παραλλάτει κατὰ μικρὸν
ἡ φύσις"). One should also note the statements in *GA* II.1,
733a34, that 'nature gives generation' to species in a continuous series, and II.3, 736b32, often used in the later
passages of *GA*, that as the soul differs in value, so the
relative 'nature' (*pneuma*), or the nature in the *pneuma*, differs. When he speaks of 'monsters', he says that they 'go out
of' (παρεκβαίνοντα) their proper nature (*GA* IV.4, 771a12);
in fact, even in the case of those offspring which, although
not monsters, do not resemble their ancestors, their nature
"παρεκβέβηκε" (IV.3, 767b7), and the smoky grape is a "meta-
basis" into another nature. In these cases it is clear that
the nature is intrinsic in the individuals, not a universal
artisan of the world. There is an inevitable similarity in
Aristotle's treatment of lower species and of inferior members of the same species.

42. In fact, the ascidians or sea-squirts have two stages,
one attached and looking like vegetation, the other a larval

322

stage; in this stage there is a notochord and other chordate characteristics. Modern biologists think that ascidians 'dualize' (if we may use Aristotle's word in this context) between chordate and non-chordate. See BERRILL and BERRILL, *1001 Questions Answered about the Seashore* (New York, N.Y., 1965) 240f. Aristotle describes the adult, attached, form adequately at 681a29, but does not seem to know the larval form; this is no surprise, since this stage swims freely for only a few hours before attaching itself, and it is very tiny.

43. See PECK, *HA* Intro. paragraphs 28-33, especially 29; LE BLOND, *Aristote philosophe de la vie*, pp. 41ff, discusses the biological scale of nature at some length. See also III. B.2, above. Actually, man is said to dualize with all classes in respect to number of offspring (*GA* IV.4, 772b1). At IV.6, 774b18, Aristotle uses the word ἐπαλλάτει as equivalent to ἐπαμφοτερίζειν, also in reference to number and type of offspring, but this time in pigs (see BONITZ *Index* 264b37ff). "ἐπαμφοτερίζειν" is used in another sense at *GA* IV.8, 777a 18: Nature cannot do two things with one material.

44. While Aristotle envisages the possibility of the inheritance of acquired characteristics, we refer here to deformities of the offspring which can be traced to characteristics of the parents, not necessarily identical to the deformity which appears. This is the subject matter of *GA* IV. 3-4, and is also discussed in 6, 775a4; II.6, 743a30; 7, 746b 22, 32; 8, 749a2ff; in these passages the result of the process which generates the deformity is an infertile generation -- this would clearly be unnatural, for the species could no longer reproduce were the character to be universal. Cf. *de An.* II.4, 415a27; *Met.* Zeta 9, 1034b4; 16, 1040b16.

45. *GA* I.18, 724a4 and *passim*; II.3, 737a25; IV.6, 775a16. He does have some kind words to say about friendship between husband and wife, *EN* VIII.12, 1162a15, but he never forgets who is to be the ruler of the family, *Pol.* I.12-13, for example.

323

46. *IA* 19, 714b8-19; I paraphrase somewhat. FORSTER's interpretation and interpolations are incorrect; the legs of a seal are, as it were, footless, and the bat's forefeet are not much good for walking in their winged form.

47. Aristotle speaks of 'dwarflikeness' fairly frequently in the later biological books, but not in *HA*; this should mean that it is an idea which is grafted on to that of a scale of nature. See *PA* IV.10, 689b26; 12, 695a5; *GA* II.8, 748b33ff; *Mem.* 2, 453a31; *Somn. Vig.* 3, 457a25. In *GA* V.3, 784a5, he says that women don't become bald because 'their nature is like that of children'; in *Long.* 6, 467a33, he says, on the contrary, that the male is more dwarflike than the female.

48. By a 'democratic' theory of ecology, I mean a theory which supposes that all living things have an intrinsic value which is absolute, that the value, merit, or worth of any living thing is to be regarded as intrinsically equal to that of any other; living things are not arranged in a scale of value. Aristotle's 'aristocratic' theory of ecology supposes that beings of different sorts have qualitatively more or less valuable characteristics, that the intrinsic value of various things can be compared and scaled. He does not say or imply that there is a quantitative measure of intrinsic value. He does seem to imply that man exists 'for the sake of' some higher level of being, and this differentiates his ecology from the ecology of systematic self-interest. An ecology of systematic self-interest supposes that all value is determined by and from the vantage point of the individual entity, on the ground of its necessity or utility for the continued existence of itself. If the reader is confused by these comments, he may forget about them.

49. G.E.R. LLOYD discusses the principle of natural directions rather exhaustively in *Polarity and Analogy* (Cambridge, 1966) Part I, especially 51ff, and in "Right and Left in Greek Philosophy", *Journal of Hellenic Studies* 82 (1962). John ANTON,

324

Aristotle's Theory of Contrariety (London, 1957), explores
the systematic position in which the theory of natural directions plays a part. Aristotle avows his debt to the Pythagoreans in this regard at *Met*. Alpha 5, 986b22-987a8,
and *Cael*. II.2, See also above, III.B.1,

50. See Alan WATTS, *The Two Hands of God* (New York, N.Y.,
1969). Giorgio TONELLI has pointed out to me that the Cab-
balistic movement and the related Christian Mosaic philosophy
(e.g. Fludd) founded their philosophy on a universal sexual
bipolarism, probably of hermetic origin. Among the thousands
of adepts may be counted the Rosicrucians.

51. See GUTHRIE's notes to this passage in the LOEB edition
of *Cael*.; it is worth remarking that this passage refers to
the *IA*. Also, compare I.8, 276a23, where the doctrine of natural places is used to argue for the uniqueness of this
earth, and III *passim*, where the elements are distinguished
in terms of 'up' and 'down', and so on.

52. Cf. Plato, *Tim*. 90a; Aristotle, *de An*. II.4, 416a4ff,
where Empedocles' use of the principle of natural directions
is criticized in this regard.

53. Plants, by contrast, have no distinction between right
and left, front and back; they have only up and down (*Cael*.
II.2, 285a18). See LLOYD, *Polarity* 54-5, for some incon-
sistencies in Aristotle's treatment of right and left.

54. An earlier version of this section was published in
Apeiron III.2 (1969) 20-33; I thank the editors and Monash
University for permission to use it here.

55. The analogy of art and nature in its general significance
was discussed in I.B.3 and II.C.1. The idea of a nature
which 'uses' things, or does things of one sort or another,
arose in chapter II (e.g. at A.4) as well as in III. 'Nature
does nothing in vain' (and so does not give eyelids to fish,
PA II.13, 658a8) was noted in III.B.1; the same principle
applied to the absence of a tongue in the crocodile was noted

in III.B.3.d. 'Katachresis' in the explanation of the tongue
and sting of insects was discussed in III.B.3.f.

56. Cf. KIRK and RAVEN, *The Presocratic Philosophers* (Cambridge, 1957) chapter 1; F.M. CORNFORD, *Principium Sapientiae*
(Cambridge , 1952).

57. Cf. W. JAEGER, *The Theology of the Early Greek Philosophers* (Oxford, 1947).

58. *Tim.*29e-30b, 39e-41d.

59. *Plato's Cosmology* (London, 1937) p. 39, n.1; "It has been
observed that Aristotle's personified Nature, who aims at a
purpose and does nothing in vain, may be regarded as equivalent to Plato's Demiurge." See also SOLMSEN, *Aristotle's
System...*, p. 443.

60. I. 82, 117; IV.146; IX.120, *et al.*

61. Lysias 19.22.

62. *Pros Nikoklea* 48, *Panegyrikos* 174, are examples of transfer of use; *Pg.* 9 is similar. *Helenē* 38, *Pg.* 74, and *Panathēn-
aikos* 127 are other appearances of the word (cf. S. PREUSS,
Index Isocrateus); the sense is 'use up' or 'consume'.

63. 18 (*On the Crown*) 150; 19 (*On the False Legation*) 277.
49 (*Against Timotheus*) 36; 23 (*Against Aristocrates*) 128, e.g.

64. 35 (*Against Lacritus*) 44; 49.45, 39, 57; 47 (*Euergos*)
9,40.

65. 47.30, 50; 49.4, 44.

66. *Lg.* III.700c; *Rep.* VII.539b4; cf. *Mx* 247b (LSJ has the
Lg. reference in the wrong place).

67. *Rep.* VII.520a; *Crat.* 426e. Cf. J. BRUNEL, *L'aspect verbal
et l'emploi des préverbes en Grec* (Paris, 1939) p. 248.

68. Cf. G. RYLE, "The Timaeus Locrus", *Phronesis* 10 (1965)
189.

69. *GA* II.6, 742a24ff. Cf. Plato *Lg.* X.888eff, where the

analogy of art and nature is used at length. See also LE
BLOND, *Aristote philosophe de la vie*, p. 47.

70. *PA* IV.5, 681a9; this could serve as an example of katachresis, if Aristotle had chosen to use some form of the
word.

71. *PA* II.17, 660a19 (this is an example of katachresis at
de An. II.7, 420b18, see below, n. 86).

72. *PA* IV.10, 687a7-b8, an admirable essay on the teleological understanding of natural phenomena.

73. *PA* II.9, 654a31-b2. On the *physis* as the system, cf. *HA*
III.7, 516b30; on the use of the bones as one together and
two separately, and so on, see *MA*, especially 8, 702a24
(χρῆται ἡ φύσις), cf. *IA* 11, 710b32.

74. In the Budé *Aristote*.

75. II.6, 743a30-b2; see also the passage which follows. Cf.
PA II.15, 658b24: hair must be formed on the head, unless
nature has another use for that material. See also IV.9,
685a25.

76. I use the noun here and elsewhere to facilitate the
writing about the concept rather than about the word.

77. LSJ, s.v. κατα- in composition, lists the following senses: I. downwards, down; II. In answer to, in accordance
with; III. against, in hostile sense; IV. back, back again;
V. to strengthen the notion of the simple verb; VI. to give
transitive force to an intransitive verb; VII. implying
waste or consumption. Sense V., more than any of the others,
applies to most of the appearances of κατα- in καταχρῆσθαι
in Aristotle, but the definition is too general to give a
clue to the precise sort of 'strengthening' of the verb which
Aristotle might intend. See also BRUNEL, *op. cit.*, 82-102,
226-252, on verbs with κατα-.

78. Cf. e.g. Plato *Phlb.* 51a.

79. *PA* III.2, 663b23. This translation is nearest that of LOUIS; PECK and OGLE err in supposing that what is to be considered is the 'character of the necessary (or material) nature', for Aristotle clearly says that he is going to tell *how* the material is *used* (at least). LOUIS, on the other hand, slides around the tricky ἐχούσης and misplaces ἐξ ἀνάγκης; PECK and OGLE construe these words correctly. PECK's account of the passage in his *GA* introduction♯ 14, xlvi, is clearer than his translation.

80. *Phys.* II.8, 199a31; *Met.* Delta 4, 1014b15-1015a19, especially the fourth and fifth senses; *PA* I.1, 639b21-642b4. Plato makes a comparable but not identical distinction at *Tim.* 47e3-48a5.

81. *PA* III.2, 663b32-36. Cf. the discharge of ink by squid, *PA* IV.5, 679a27, which συμβαίνει ἐξ ἀνάγκης but also ἡ φύσις καταχρῆται. Cf. IV.11, 692a4, where the ability of the snake to turn its head right round 'happens necessarily' but also 'for the sake of the better'.

82. *GA* II.6, 744b16-27, after PECK. I follow BARBOTIN, *La théorie aristotélicienne de l'intellect d'après Théophraste*, Louvain, 1954, p. 188, and H.J. DROSSAART LULOFS, OCT *GA ad loc.*, in rejecting the emendation at b 20 offered by P. MORAUX in "A propos du νοῦς θύραθεν chez Aristote", *Autour d'Aristote*, (Mélanges MANSION, Louvain, 1955). Compare *PA* III.4, 675b21, where the nature (of the individual) is said to "store up" food in the intestine; see also the use of the word "παρασκευάζειν" at *PA* IV.5, 681a7 and *GA* III.2, 753a8.

83. This sense has a number of predecessors in the speeches of 'Demosthenes', e.g. 47. 50, 49.36.

84. Cf. *Insomn.* 2, 459b27-460a9, and my comments on this passage in *Phronesis* 13 (1968).

85. Some other passages which have a similar explanatory idea are: *PA* IV.10, 689b12, 31; 13, 695b16; *IA* 17, 714a16;

GA III.1, 750a4; 4, 755a35; IV.4, 771a30.

86. *de An.* II.8, 420b18. The preservation of the internal heat is the necessary function, speech (in man?) is 'for the better'. In the same way, the tongue is necessary for taste, and articulated speech is 'for the better'. Cf. *Resp.* 8 and 11.

87. *Sens.* 5, 444a25; W.D. ROSS, *Parva Naturalia*, commentary *ad loc.*

88. *PA* II.16, 659b34ff. The tongue for taste and speech, the lips for guarding the teeth and speech. Cf. III.B.3.a, above.

89. *PA* III.1, 662a16-25. On the double function of the teeth see III.1, 661b13ff; that account is assumed here. αὐτὴ καθ' αὑτήν: "of her own accord" (OGLE); "quite spontaneously" (PECK) "de son propre mouvement" (LOUIS).

90. *PA* IV.6, 683a20 (very close to PECK's version). Here a further principle is introduced, that of the division of labor (cf. OGLE's notes to this passage), or the anti-obelisko olychnion principle. LOUIS gives a useful reference to *Pol.* I.2, 1252b1.

91. *PA* III.9, 671b1. PECK translates, "Nature makes use of them for two purposes." How kidneys help the blood is explained at 672a1ff. Most of the viscera are thought of as similar in this respect.

92. LSJ: παρα- in composition means I. alongside of, beside; II. to the side of, to; III. to one side of, by, past; IV. (metaph.) 1. aside or beyond, i.e. amiss, wrong; 2. of comparison; 3. of a side issue. The sense of additional action is clear in such verbs as παραγράφω (which Aristotle does not seem to use); παρατρέφω (which appears at *Ath. Pol.* 62.2); παραφύω and its relatives which Aristotle uses often, in the sense of 'grow beside' or 'grow in addition'. πάρεργον is used in a comparable way at *Sens.* 444a25, quoted above. BRUNEL, *op. cit.*, does not discuss παρα-.

93. ROSS, *Aristotelis Fragmenta Selecta*, (Oxford, 1955) p. 56 = ROSE[3] 56. Plutarch, *On Love of Wealth*, 527a; DE LACY and EINARSON, in the Loeb edition, list a number of manuscript variations, among which are χρῶνται and καταχρῶνται.

94. 688a23-25. The expression 'as we say she often does' also occurs at II.16, 659b34, see c) under sense 3 of katachresis, above; there the verb is καταχρησαμένη.

95. *PA* IV.10, 690a1-4; LOUIS translates, "la nature s'en sert largement"; PECK: "provide another example of Nature's habit of using an organ for secondary purposes."

96. a35, cf. IV.12, 692b17, the elephant uses his trunk 'like hands'.

97. *PA* II.14, 658a8; *IA* 8, 708a10; *GA* II.5, 741b4; in *Cael.* I.4, 271a33, it is said that "God and nature do nothing *matēn*," and at II.11, 291b13, "nature does nothing irrational (*alogos*) or *matēn*." Compare I. DÜRING, *Aristotle in the Ancient Biographical Tradition* (Göteborg, 1957) 396-7.

98. *PA* IV.11, 691b4; *GA* II.4, 739b19; *PA* IV.12, 694a15; neither *matēn* nor *periergon*: *PA* III.1, 661b24; IV.13, 695b19; since neither *matēn* nor *periergon*, therefore neither too early nor too late: *GA* II.6, 744a36.

99. *Cael.* II.5, 288a2; *PA* IV.10, 687a16; not *matēn* but the best possible: *IA* 2, 704b15; compare *GA* II.1, 731b33: the nature of temporal species is unable to be eternal, so it is everlasting in the way open to it.

100. *PA* IV.12, 694b13; cf. 10, 687a11. *GA* IV.1, 766a5: nature gives to each individual the power and the organ at the same time, for it is better thus. *GA* I.4, 717a15: Nature does everything either because of necessity or because of the better, cf. IV.1, 766a5, where it is the division into species which is 'better'.

101. One may discern a fallacy of four terms in this statement, perhaps, but the idea involved is closely related to

that of 'doing the best possible' and 'nothing in vain'. See
also *GA* III.10, 760a32, "The natural always has order
(*taxis*)," (cf. b1); IV.2, 767a17: "Everything generated by
art or by nature exists in virtue of some *logos*"; *PA* II.10
657b27: "The sense organs have been well arranged by nature";
cf. *GA* V.1, 778b4; *PA* III.4, 665b20.

102. Cf. "φύσις ἔβλεψε" at *PA* IV.10, 686a22.

103. Compare the frequent use of the word '*ergon*', the result of a ποίησις, in nature: *IA* 2, 704b14; *GA* I.8, 718b26;
11, 719a14; 23, 731a24; BONITZ *Index* 258b. See also the use
of the verb 'ἀπείργασθαι': *GA* V.2, 781b23, nature ἀπείργασται
the seal's ears εὐλόγως; *Phys.* II.8, 199a16: art completes
what nature cannot ἀπείργασθαι.

104. *GA* I.23, 731a24; cf. *PA* II.9, 654b31, like clay modellers; *GA* II.6, 743b23, like painters; cf. III.11, 762a17;
the verb derives from δυμιουργός, one who works for the
people, a craftsman.

105. In several places, the giving of weapons by nature is
expressed by the verb ἀποδίδωσιν or something similar: *PA*
II.1, 661b30; 2, 662b33; 663a3; 663a18; IV.8, 684a27; *GA*
III.10, 759b4.

106. Cf. *GA* III.11, 762a15, where art and nature 'take material away', which is the reverse procedure from that in
painting, where material is added on, and some may be left
over. The emphasis at 762a15 is on waste materials, whereas
at 725a26 it is on valuable residues.

107. Compare also *GA* I.21, 730b19ff; II.1, 734b21; 735a3;
IV.6, 775a22; 8, 777a7.

108. This comparison continues at 641a30, 642a10; 5, 645b15;
II.7, 652b13, where the 'carpenter' is compared to the heat
in the soul.

109. *GA* I.18, 723b30: the semen does not become part of the
embryo any more than the carpenter becomes part of the house,

cf. 724a18; 21, 729b14; 22, 730b5ff: "Nature, acting in the male of semen-emitting animals, uses the semen as a tool." Cf. II.6, 743a26.

110. See also: *PA* III.7, 670a23; *GA* I.22, 730b8; II.1, 734b18. We have already noted passages in which nature is compared with the gardener, III.A.3.a, and 3.b., note 43. We may also note those passages in which nature is compared, sometimes rather indirectly, with the weaver of cloth: *GA* II.1, 734a19; *PA* III.5, 668b20; IV.2, 676b20; *GA* I.4, 717a35; V.7, 787b22.

111. Cf. *Juv.* 3, 469a10; *GA* I.18, 724a27; 21, 729b21; *PA* IV. 9, 685b4: the suckers which are like the implements for reducing dislocated fingers; *GA* V.8, 789b13.

112. *Met.* Delta 4, 1015a11ff, a conflation of the translations by ROSS, TREDENNICK, and APOSTLE. R.G. COLLINGWOOD, *The Idea of Nature* (London, 1945) 80-85, gives an account which amounts to a brief commentary on this passage. WOODBRIDGE, *Aristotle's Vision of Nature* (New York, N.Y., 1965) is disappointing; on p. 145 he takes examples like those which we have been discussing as 'literary devices' only.

115. What would be the consequent distinction between 'nature' and 'soul'? The idea of 'nature' is more closely connected with the entity of the species, and the soul is the entity of the individual, but there is a great overlapping between these concepts.

114. Other passages in *GA* include I.11, 718b37; II.4, 738a 14 (the coldness of the female 'nature' is unable to concoct the male semen); II.4, 739b26; 6, 743a23; III.4, 755a20 (we have noted this passage before); IV.8, 777a16; V.1, 780b10.

NOTES TO GENERAL CONCLUSION

1. A dilemma (pointed out to me by Hervé BARREAU) may be developed from this statement of Aristotle's position: if entities can become parts of greater entities, then either their relationships are external (between entities), or they are no longer entities but only parts. This dilemma appears to arise from the emphasis which I have put here on the concepts of internal and external. In fact, Aristotle is able to think of individual entities as parts of larger entities, without giving up their status as entities: "By entities, I mean the simple bodies, fire, earth, etc., and everything made of them, for example the whole heaven and its parts, animals and plants and their parts (*Cael*. III.1, 298a29ff)." If entities are parts and parts are entities, the dilemma does not arise, but the contrast between 'internal' and 'external' might be thought weakened. If so, then one may say that for Aristotle necessary relations are always *organic*, and this does not seem to be true of non-Aristotelian theories of necessary relations.

2. For examples, see A. KÄSTNER, *Geschichte des teleologischen Gottesbeweises*, Leipzig 1907 (Diss.), p. 83ff.

BIBLIOGRAPHY

The bibliography is in two parts, the first a list of the texts and translations of Aristotle used, the second a list of other works consulted. Neither list is meant to be exhaustive; the first conspicuously omits the great pre-twentieth century editions and translations; the second does have a large number of items dealing with Aristotle's biology, but no such list can be complete. It does not include works published after 1970, nor does it include works which I have not used, or with which I am acquainted only through some other source.

A. Texts and translations of Aristotle's works

1. Organon

ACKRILL, J.L., *Aristotle's Categories and De Interpretatione*, Oxford, 1963 (English and notes).

COOKE, H.P., *Aristotle: Categories, de Interpretatione*, and H. TREDENNICK, *Aristotle: Prior Analytics*, London, 1938 (Loeb).

EDGHILL, E.M., *Categoriae and de Interpretatione*, and G.R.G. MURE, *Analytica Posteriora*, Oxford, 1928 (Oxford translation I).

POSTE, E., *The Logic of Science, a Translation of the Posterior Analytics of Aristotle*, Oxford, 1850.

ROSS, W.D., *Aristotle's Prior and Posterior Analytics*, Oxford, 1949 (text and commentary).

2. Physics

CARTERON, H., *Aristote, Physique,* Paris, 1926, 1931 (2 vols.);
    2nd ed., 1956 (Budé).

CHARLTON, W., *Aristotle's Physics Books I and II,* Oxford,
    1970 (English and notes).

HARDIE, R.P., and R.K. GAYE, *Aristotle: Physica,* Oxford, 1930
    (Oxford translation vol. II).

ROSS, W.D., *Aristotelis Physica,* Oxford, 1936 (text and
    commentary).

---, *Aristotelis Physica,* Oxford, 2nd ed., 1950 (text).

WICKSTEED, Philip, and F.M. CORNFORD, *Aristotle: The Physics,*
    London, 1929, 1957 (Loeb).

3. Generation and Corruption

FORSTER, E.M., *Aristotle: On Coming-to-be and Passing-away,*
    London, 1955 (Loeb, with Forster, *Sophistical Refutations*).

JOACHIM, H.H., *Aristotelis de Generatione et Corruptione,*
    Oxford, 1922 (text and commentary).

---, *Aristotle: De Generatione et Corruptione,* Oxford, 1930
    (Oxford translation, vol. 2).

4. De Caelo

ALLAN, D.J., *Aristotelis De Caelo,* Oxford, 1936 (text).

GUTHRIE, W.K.C., *Aristotle: On the Heavens,* London, 1939,
    (Loeb).

MORAUX, Paul, *Aristote, Du Ciel,* Paris, 1965 (Budé).

STOCKS, J.L., *Aristotle: De Caelo,* Oxford, 1930 (Oxford trans-
    lation 2).

5. Meteorologica

DÜRING, Ingemar, *Aristotle's Chemical Treatise, Meteorologica
    IV,* Göteborg, 1944.

LEE, H.D.P., *Aristotle: Meteorologica*, London, 1952 (Loeb).

6. De Anima

HAMLYN, D.W., *Aristotle's De Anima Books II and III*, Oxford 1968 (English and notes).

HETT, W.S., *Aristotle: On the Soul, Parva Naturalia, On Breath* London, 1935, 1957 (Loeb).

JANNONE, A. (ed.) and E. BARBOTIN (trans.),*Aristote, de l'âme*, Paris, 1966 (Budé).

ROSS, W.D., *Aristotle: Psychology*, Oxford, 1942 (Oxford translation 3).

---, *Aristotelis de Anima*, Oxford, 1956 (text).

---, *Aristotle: de Anima*, Oxford, 1961 (text, commentary).

SIWEK, Paulus, *Aristotelis Tractatus De Anima*, Romae, 1965 (text, Latin, notes).

TRICOT, Jules, *Aristote, de l'âme*, Paris, 1934, 1959 (French, notes).

7. Parva Naturalia

BEARE, J.T., and G.R.T. ROSS, *Parva Naturalia*, Oxford, 1930 (Oxford translation 3).

BIEHL, Guilelmus, *Aristotelis Parva Naturalia*, Lipsiae, 1898 (Teubner text).

LULOFS, H.J. DROSSAART, *Aristotelis de Somno et Vigilia*, Leiden, 1943 (text and Latin).

---, *Aristotelis de Insomniis et de Divinatione per Somnum*, Leiden, 1947 (text and introduction).

MUGNIER, René, *Aristote, Petits traités d'histoire naturelle*, Paris, 1965 (Budé).

OGLE, William, *Aristotle: On Youth and Old Age, Life and Death, and Respiration*, London, 1897 (English and notes).

ROSS, G.R.T., *Aristotle: De Sensu et de Memoria*, Cambridge, 1906 (text, English, commentary).

336

ROSS, G.R.T., *Parva Naturalia*, Cambridge, 1906 (text, English).

ROSS, W.D., *Aristotle: Parva Naturalia*, Oxford, 1955 (text, commentary).

SIWEK, Paulus, *Aristotelis Parva Naturalia*, Romae, 1963 (text, Latin, notes).

8. History of Animals

AUBERT, H., and F. WIMMER, *Aristoteles' Thierkunde*, Leipzig, 1860 (text, German, notes).

CRESWELL, R., *Aristotle's History of Animals*, London, 1862 (English).

DITTMEYER, L., *Aristotelis de Animalibus Historia*, Lipsiae, 1907 (text).

LOUIS, Pierre, *Aristote, Histoire des Animaux*, Paris, 1964-69 (3 vols., Budé).

PECK, A.L., *Aristotle: Historia Animalium*, London, 1965 (vol. I), 1970 (vol. II), (Loeb).

THOMPSON, D'Arcy W., *Aristotle: Historia Animalium*, Oxford, 1910 (Oxford translation vol. 4).

TRICOT, Jules, *Aristote, Histoire des Animaux*, Paris, 1957 (2 vols., French, notes).

9. Parts of Animals

LANGKAVEL, B., *Aristotelis de Partibus Animalium*, Lipsiae, 1868 (text).

LE BLOND, J.-M., *Aristote, philosophe de la vie. Le livre premier du traité sur les parties des animaux*, Paris, 1945 (text, French, introduction, notes).

LOUIS, Pierre, *Aristote, Les parties des animaux*, Paris, 1956 (Budé).

OGLE, W., *Aristotle on the Parts of Animals*, London, 1882 (English and notes); revised edition, Oxford, 1912 (Oxford translation vol. 5).

PECK, A.L., *Aristotle: Parts of Animals*, London, 1937, 1961 (Loeb).

10. Generation of Animals

AUBERT, H., and F. WIMMER, *Aristotelis de Generatione Animalium*, Leipzig, 1860 (text, German, notes).

LOUIS, Pierre, *Aristote, de la génération des animaux*, Paris, 1961 (Budé).

LULOFS, H.J. DROSSAART, *Aristotelis de Generatione Animalium*, Oxford, 1965 (text).

PECK, A.L., *Aristotle: Generation of Animals*, London, 1943, 1953 (Loeb).

PLATT, Arthur, *Aristotle: De Generatione Animalium*, Oxford, 1912 (Oxford translation vol. 5).

11. Movement of Animals, Progression of Animals

FARQUHARSON, A.S.L., *De Motu Animalium, de Incessu Animalium*, Oxford, 1912 (Oxford translation vol. 5).

FORSTER, E.S., *Aristotle: Movement of Animals, Progression of Animals*, London, 1937 (Loeb, with Peck *PA*).

JAEGER, W., *Aristotelis de Animalium Motione, de Animalium Incessu, Pseudo-Aristotelis de Spiritus libellus*, Lipsiae, 1913 (text).

TORRACA, Luigi, *Aristotelis de Motu Animalium*, Napoli, 1958 (text, Latin, Italian).

12. Metaphysics

APOSTLE, H.G., *Aristotle's Metaphysics*, Indiana, 1966 (English).

JAEGER, W., *Aristotelis Metaphysica*, Oxford, 1957 (text).

ROSS, W.D., *Aristotle: Metaphysica*, Oxford, 1928 (Oxford translation vol. 8).

---, *Aristotelis Metaphysica*, Oxford, 1924, 2 vols. (text, commentary).

TREDENNICK, H., *Aristotle: Metaphysics*, London, 1933, 2 vols. (Loeb).

13. Opuscula and Fragmenta

LOVEDAY, T., and E.S. FORSTER, L.D. DAWDALL, H.H. JOACHIM, *Opuscula*, Oxford, 1913 (Oxford translation vol. 6).

HETT, W.S., *Aristotle: Minor Works*, London, 1936 (Loeb).

ROSE, Valentin, *Aristotelis Fragmenta*, Lipsiae, 1886 (text).

ROSS, W.D., *Aristotelis Fragmenta Selecta*, Oxford, 1955 (text).

---, *Aristotle: Select Fragments*, Oxford, 1952 (Oxford translation vol. 12).

Not much use has been made of the other works of Aristotle for the present study; references to the *Nicomachean Ethics* or to the *Politics*, for example, can be followed up in any of several editions.

B. Works consulted, other than those by Aristotle

AFRICA, T.W., *Science and the State in Greece and Rome*, New York, N.Y., 1968.

AGAR, W.E., "The Concept of Purpose in Biology", *Quarterly Review of Biology* 13 (1938) 255-273.

---, *A Contribution to the Theory of the Living Organism*, Oxford, 1943.

ALBERTUS MAGNUS, *De Animalibus libri xxvi*, ed. H. Stadler, Münster, 1916, 1921.

ALLAN, D.J., *The Philosophy of Aristotle*, London, 1952.

ANSCOMBE, G.E.M., "The Principle of Individuation", *Berkeley and Modern Problems*, Proceedings of the Aristotelian Society, Supplementary Volume XXVII, 1953, pp. 83-96.

---, "Aristotle and the Sea-Battle", *Mind* 65 (1956) 1-15.

---, *Intention*, Oxford, 1958.

ANSCOMBE, G.E.M., "Thought and Action in Aristotle", *New Essays on Plato and Aristotle*, ed. Bambrough, New York, N.Y., 1965, 143-158.

ANTON, J.P., *Aristotle's Theory of Contrariety*, London, 1957.

---, "The Meaning of ὁ λόγος τῆς οὐσίας in Aristotle's *Categories* 1a", *The Monist* 52.2 (1968) 252-267.

---, and G. KUSTAS, editors, *Essays in Greek Philosophy*, Albany, N.Y., 1971.

ARNOLD, Lloyd L., *Aristotle's Biological Concepts and Methods in the Light of Modern Biology*, Baltimore, Md., 1953 (diss.).

ARNOLD, Uwe, *Die Entelechie*, Wien, 1965.

ARONSON, Jerrold, "Explanations Without Laws", *Journal of Philosophy* 1969, pp. 541-557.

ASDELL, S.A., *Patterns of Mammalian Reproduction*, Ithaca, N.Y., 1946.

ATHENAEUS, *The Deipnosophists*, ed. C.B. Gulick (Loeb), Cambridge Mass., 1927 and foll.

BAEUMKER, Clemens, *Das Problem der Materie in der griechischen Philosophie*, Münster, 1890.

BALME, D.M., "Greek Science and Chance. 1. Aristotle on Nature and Chance", *The Classical Quarterly* 33 (1939) 129-138.

---, "Greek Science and Mechanism. 2. The Atomists", *The Classical Quarterly* 35 (1941) 23-28.

---, "γένος and εἶδος in Aristotle's Biology", *The Classical Quarterly* 12 (1962) 81-98.

---, "The Development of Biology in Aristotle and Theophrastus: the Theory of Spontaneous Generation", *Phronesis* 7 (1962) 91-104.

---, "Aristotle's Use of Teleological Explanation", Inaugural Lecture, London, 1965.

BALSS, H., "Präformation und Epigenese in der griechischen Philosophie", *Archivio di storia della scienza* 4 (1923) 319-325.

---, "Die Zeugungslehre und Embryologie in der Antike", *Quellen und Studien zur Geschichte der Naturwissenschaft und der Medizin,* 5 (1936) 193-274.

BAMBROUGH, Renford, editor, *New Essays on Plato and Aristotle*, New York, N.Y., 1965.

BARBOTIN, Edmond, *La théorie aristotélicienne de l'intellect d'après Théophraste*, Louvain, 1954.

BEARE, J.T., *Greek Theories of Elementary Cognition from Alcman to Aristotle*, Oxford, 1906.

BECKNER, Morton, *The Biological Way of Thought*, New York,N.Y. 1959.

BERRILL, N.J. and Jacqueline, *1001 Questions Answered about the Seashore*, New York, N.Y., 1957.

BERTALANFFY, Ludwig von, *Modern Theories of Development*, Oxford, 1933.

---, *The Problems of Life*, London, 1952.

BITTERAUF, Karl, *Der Schlussteil der aristotelischen Biologie: Beiträge zur Textgeschichte und Textkritik der Schrift 'de Generatione Animalium'*, Wissenschaftliche Beilage zum Jahresbericht des Kgl. humanistischen Gymnasiums Kempten, 1913.

---, *Neue Textstudien zum Schlussteil der aristotelischen Biologie*, same publication, 1914.

BLOCK, Irving, "The Order of Aristotle's Psychological Writings", *The American Journal of Philology* 81 (1961) 50-77.

---, "Truth and Error in Aristotle's Theory of Sense Perception", *Philosophical Quarterly* 11 (1961) 1-9.

---, "Three German Commentators on the Individual Senses and the Common Sense in Aristotle's Psychology", *Phronesis* 9 (1964) 58-63.

BLÜH, O., "Did the Greeks Perform Experiments?" *American Journal of Physics* 17 (1949) 384ff.

BOAS, George, "Presuppositions of Aristotle's Metaphysics", *American Journal of Philology* 55 (1934) 36-48.

---, "Presuppositions of Aristotle's Physics", *American Journal of Philology* 57 (1936) 24-36.

---, "Some Presuppositions of Aristotle's Psychology", *American Journal of Philology* 58 (1937) 275-282.

---, "A Basic Conflict in Aristotle's Philosophy", *American*

Journal of Philology 64 (1943) 173-193.

BOAS, G., "Aristotle's Presuppostions about Change", *American Journal of Philology* 68 (1947) 404-413.

---, "Some Assumptions of Aristotle", *Transactions of the American Philosophical Association*, vol. 49, part 6, 1959.

---, *Rationalism in Greek Philosophy*, Baltimore, Md., 1961.

BODENHEIMER, F.S., "Aristote Biologiste", *Université de Paris, Conférences du Palais de la Découverte*, Series D, no. 15, 1953.

---, "Aristotle, the Father of Animal Ecology", *Homenaje a Millás-Valliciosa*, Barcelona, 1954, pp. 165-181.

---, *The History of Biology*, London, 1958.

BONITZ, Hermann, *Index Aristotelicus*, Berlin, 1870; reprinted Graz, 1955.

BOURGEY, Louis, *Observation et expérience chez Aristote*, Paris, 1955.

BRANGHAM, A.N., *The Naturalist's Riviera*, London, 1962.

BRUCHARD, H., *Der Entelechiebegriff bei Aristoteles und Driesch*, Bochum, 1928 (diss.).

BRUNEL, J., *L'aspect verbal et l'emploi des préverbes en Grec*, Paris, 1939 (Collection Linguistique XLV).

BRUNSCHWICG, Léon, *L'expérience humaine et la causalité physique*, Paris, 1922.

BURTON, John, *The Oxford Book of Insects*, London, 1968.

BURTT, E.A., *The Metaphysical Foundations of Modern Science*[2], New York, N.Y., 1932.

BYL, S., "Note sur la place du coeur et la valorisation de la μεσότης dans la biologie d'Aristote", *L'antiquité classique* 37 (1968) 467-476.

CAIN, A.J., ed., *Function and Taxonomic Importance* (Publication 3 of the Systematics Association), London, 1959.

CANFIELD, J.V., ed., *Purpose in Nature*, Englewood Cliffs, N.J., 1966.

CAPELLE, W., "Das Problem der Urzeugung bei Aristoteles und

Theophrast und in der Folgezeit", *Rheinisches Museum* 98 (1955) 150-180.

CAPELLE, W., "Zur Entomologie des Aristoteles und Theophrast", *Rheinisches Museum* 105 (1962) 56-66.

CARLO, W.E., "Mechanism and Vitalism: a Reappraisal", *Pacific Philosophy Forum* 6 (1968) 57-68.

CARTERON, H., *La notion de force dans le système d'Aristote*, Paris, 1924.

CASE, Thomas, "Aristotle", *Encyclopedia Britannica*, 11th edition, Cambridge, 1911, vol. 2, 501-22.

CENCILLO, Luis, "Tres problemas planteados por el concepto aristotélico de Hyle", *Emérita* 25 (1957) 1-13.

CAIGNET, A.E., *Essai sur la psychologie d'Aristote*, Paris, 1883.

CHARLESWORTH, M.J., *Aristotle on Art and Nature*, Aukland University College, Bulletin 50, Philosophy series 2, 1957.

CHARLTON, W., *Aristotle's Physics Books I and II*, Oxford, 1970.

CHERNISS, Harold, *Aristotle's Criticism of Presocratic Philosophy*, Baltimore, Md., 1935.

---, *Aristotle's Criticism of Plato and the Academy I*, Baltimore, Md., 1944.

---, *The Riddle of the Early Academy*, Berkeley, Cal., 1945.

CHEVALIER, Jacques, *La notion du nécessaire chez Aristote et chez ses prédécesseurs, particulièrement chez Platon*, Paris, 1915.

CHROUST, A.H., "The First Thirty Years of Aristotelian Scholarship", *Classica et Mediaevalia* 24 (1963) 27-57.

Chung-Hwan CHEN, "The Relation between the Terms ἐνέργεια and ἐντελέχεια in the Philosophy of Aristotle", *The Classical Quarterly* 8 (1958) 12ff.

CLAGHORN, G.S., *Aristotle's Criticism of Plato's Timaeus*, The Hague, 1954.

CLARKE, Edwin, "Aristotelian Concepts of the Form and Function of the Brain", *Bulletin of the History of Medicine*, 1963, 1-14.

CLOSE, A.J., "Philosophical Theories of Art and Nature in Classical Antiquity", *Journal of the History of Ideas* 32 (1971) 163-184.

COHN-HAFT, Louis, *The Public Physicians of Ancient Greece*, Northampton, Mass., 1956.

COLE, F.J., *Early Theories of Sexual Generation*, Oxford, 1930.

---, *A History of Comparative Anatomy from Aristotle to the Eighteenth Century*, London, 1944.

COLLINGWOOD, R.G., *The Idea of Nature*, London, 1945.

CORNFORD, F.M., *Plato's Cosmology*, London, 1937.

---, *Principium Sapientiae*, Cambridge, 1952.

DARWIN, Charles, *The Origin of the Species and The Descent of Man*, New York, N.Y., n.d.

DAVEY, K.G., *Reproduction in Insects*, San Francisco, Cal., 1965.

DEMOS, Raphael, "The Structure of Substance according to Aristotle", *Philosophy and Phenomenological Research* 5 (1944/5) 255-68.

Demosthenes:

CROISET, Maurice, *Démosthène, Harangues*, (2 vols.) Paris, 1924; 1925 (Budé).

DE WITT, N.W., and N.V. DE WITT, *Demosthenes: Funeral Speech, Erotic Essay, et al.*, London, 1949 (Loeb).

GERNET, Louis, *Démosthène, Plaidoyers civils* (4 vols.) Paris, 1954-60 (Budé).

HUMBERT, Jean, et Louis GERNET, *Démosthène, Plaidoyers politiques* (vol. 2), Paris, 1959 (Budé).

MATHIEU, Georges, *Démosthène, Plaidoyers Politiques* (vols 3 + 4), Paris, 1945, 1947 (Budé).

MURRAY, A.T., *Demosthenes: Private Orations* (3 vols.), London, 1936-9 (Loeb).

NAVERRE, Octave, et Pierre ORSINI, *Démosthène, Plaidoyers politiques* (vol. 1), Paris, 1954 (Budé).

VINCE, C.A., and J.H. VINCE, *Demosthenes: De Corona and de Falsa Legatione*, London, 1926 (Loeb).

VINCE, J.H., *Demosthenes: Philippics, Olynthics, Minor Public Speeches, Speech against Leptines*, London, 1930 (Loeb).

344

VINCE, J.H., *Demosthenes: Against Meidias, Androtion, Aristocrates, Timocrates, Aristogeiton*, London, 1935 (Loeb).

DIELS, Hermann, and Walther KRANZ, *Die Fragmente der Vorsokratiker*, Dublin/Zürich, 1966 (6th edition), abbreviated 'DK'.

DIJKSTERHUIS, E.J., *The Mechanization of the World Picture*, Oxford, 1961.

DILLER, J., "ὄψις τῶν ἀδήλων τὰ φαινόμενα", *Hermes* 67 (1932) 14ff.

DORIER, A., et G. BELLON, "Sur l'organe palatin des Cyprinidés", *Travaux du laboratoire d'hydrobiologie et de pisciculture de l'Université de Grenoble* 44 (1952) 47-60.

DOWDESWELL, W.H., *The Mechanism of Evolution*[2], New York, N.Y. 1958.

DRABKIN, I.E., "Notes on the Laws of Motion in Aristotle", *American Journal of Philology* 59 (1938) 60-84.

DRIESCH, Hans, *The History and Theory of Vitalism* (trans. Ogden), London, 1914.

---, *The Problem of Individuality*, London, 1914.

---, *Philosophie des Organischen*[4], Leipzig, 1928.

DUBARLE, D., "La causalité dans la philosophie d'Aristote", *Histoire de la philosophie et métaphysique*, Recherches de philosophie I, Paris, 1955, pp. 9-55.

DÜRING, Ingemar, *Aristoteles De Partibus Animalium, Critical and Literary Commentary*, Göteborg 1943 (Göteborgs Vetenskaps Samhälles Handlinger, 7. reihe, ser. A, vol. 2, 1).

---, *Aristotle's Chemical Treatise: Meteorologica IV*, Göteborg, 1944 (Göteborg Högskolas Arsskrift 50 (1944) 2).

---, "Notes on the History of the Transmission of Aristotle's Writings", *Göteborg Högskolas Årsskrift* 56 (1950) 37-70.

---, "Aristotle the Scholar", *Arctos* NS 1 (1954), Commentationes in honorem Edwin Linkomies, 61-77.

---, "Aristotle and Plato in the Mid-Fourth Century", *Eranos* 54 (1956) 109-120.

DÜRING, Ingemar, *Aristotle in the Ancient Biographical Trad-ition*, Göteborg, 1957 (*Acta Univ. Gothob.* 63.2).

---, (review of Luigi Torraca's edition of the *MA*), *Gnomon* 31 (1959) 415-418.

---, and G.E.L. OWEN, editors, *Aristotle and Plato in the Mid-Fourth Century*, Symposium Aristotelicum 1957, Göte-borg, 1960.

---, "... *De Part. An.* I.1, 639b30-640a2", *Aristote et les problèmes de méthode*, Symposium Aristotelicum, ed. S. Mansion, Louvain, 1961, 213-221.

---, *Aristotle's Protrepticus*, Göteborg, 1961.

---, *Aristoteles, Darstellung und Interpretation seines Denkens*, Heidelberg, 1966.

---, "Aristoteles", Pauly and Wissowa, *Realencyclopädie*, Supplement-Band XI, Stuttgart, 1968, col. 159-336.

DUPRAT, "La théorie du pneuma chez Aristote", *Archiv für Ge-schichte der Philosophie* 12 (1899) 305-321.

EAST, S.P., "De la méthode de la biologie selon Aristote", *Laval Théologique-Philosophique* 14 (1958) 213-235.

EDELSTEIN, Ludwig, "Περὶ ἀέρων und die Sammlung der hippo-kratischen Schriften", *Problemata* 4, Berlin, 1931.

---, "Die Geschichte der Sektion in der Antike", *Quellen und Studien zur Geschichte der Naturwissenschaft und der Medizin* 3 (1933) 100ff, 148ff. A translation appears in *Ancient Medicine*.

---, "The Development of Greek Anatomy", *Bulletin of the Institute of the History of Medicine* 3 (1935) 241ff.

---, "Greek Medicine and its Relation to Religion and Magic", *Bulletin of the Institute of the History of Medicine* 5 (1937) 201-246, reprinted in *Ancient Medicine*.

---, "The Genuine Works of Hippocrates", *Bulletin of the History of Medicine* 7 (1939) 236-248, reprinted in *Ancient Medicine*.

---, (review of Werner Jaeger, *Diokles von Karystos*), *American Journal of Philology* 61 (1940) 483-89, reprinted in *Ancient Medicine*.

---, "Aristotle and the Concept of Evolution", *Classical Weekly* 37 (1943/4) 148-50.

EDELSTEIN, L., "The Role of Eryximachus in Plato's *Symposium*", *Transactions of the American Philological Association* 76 (1945) 85-103, reprinted in *Ancient Medicine*.

---, "Recent Trends in the Interpretation of Ancient Science", *Journal of the History of Ideas* 13 (1952) 573-604, reprinted in *Ancient Medicine*.

---, *Ancient Medicine*, Baltimore, 1967.

EINARSON, Benedict, "On Certain Mathematical Terms in Aristotle's Logic", *American Journal of Philology* 57 (1936) 33-54, 151-172.

ELDERS, Leo, *Aristotle's Cosmology*, Assen, 1966.

EUCKEN, Rudolf, *Die Methode der aristotelischen Forschung*, Berlin, 1854, 1872.

EVANS, M.G., "Causality and Explanation in the Logic of Aristotle", *Philosophy and Phenomenological Research* 19 (1958/9) 466-485.

---, *The Physical Philosophy of Aristotle*, New Mexico, 1964.

FEIGL, H., and M. BRODBECK, editors, *Readings in the Philosophy of Science*, New York, N.Y., 1953.

FERNÁNDEZ, Luis Gil, *Nombres de insectos en griego antiquo*, Madrid, 1959.

FRANK, Erich, "Das Problem des Lebens bei Hegel und Aristoteles", *Deutsche Vtljrsschr. f. Litwiss. u. Geistgesch.* 5 (1927) 609-643, reprinted in *Wissen, Wollen, Glauben*, Zürich, 1955.

---, "The Fundamental Opposition of Plato and Aristotle", *American Journal of Philology* 61 (1940) 34ff, 166ff, reprinted in *Wissen ,Wollen, Glauben*, Zürich, 1955.

GALEN, *On the Natural Faculties*, ed. A.J. Brock, London, 1952 (Loeb).

GAUTHIER, R.A., et J.Y. JOLIF, *L'éthique à Nicomaque*, Louvain 1958.

---, *La morale d'Aristote*, Paris, 1963.

GIGON, O., "Die Naturphilosophischen Voraussetzungen der Antiken Biologie", *Gesnerus* 3 (1946).

GILLE, Bertrand, "Machines", *A History of Technology* , ed.

347

Charles Singer, *et al.*, Oxford, 1956, vol. II, pp. 630-636.

GOHLKE, Paul, "Die Entstehungsgeschichte der Naturwissenschaftlichen Schriften des Aristoteles", *Hermes* 59
(1924) 274-306.

---, *Die Entstehung der aristotelischen Lehrschriften*,
Berlin, 1933.

---, *Aristoteles und sein Werk*, Paderborn, 1948.

GOLDSTEIN, Leon J., "The Logic of Explanation in Malinowskian
Anthropology", *Philosophy of Science* 24.3 (April, 1957)
156-177.

---, "Recurrent Structures and Teleology", *Inquiry* 5 (1962)
1-11.

GREENE, Murray, "Aristotle's Circular Movement as a Logos
Doctrine", *The Review of Metaphysics* 19 (1965) 115ff.

GRENE, Marjorie, *A Portrait of Aristotle*, Chicago, Ill., 1963.

GRENET, Paul, *Les origines de l'analogie philosophique dans
les dialogues de Platon*, Paris, 1948.

---, *Aristote*, Paris, 1962.

GUERLAC, Henry, "Copernicus and Aristotle's Cosmos", *Journal
of the History of Ideas* 29 (1968) 109-113.

GUTHRIE, W.K.C., *In the Beginning*, Ithaca, N.Y., 1957.

---, *A History of Greek Philosophy*, 3 vols., Cambridge,
1962-69.

HALDANE, J.B.S., *The Causes of Evolution*, London, 1932.

---, "Aristotle's Account of Bees' Dances", *Journal of Hellenic Studies* 75 (1955) 24ff.

HALDANE, J.S., *The Sciences and Philosophy*, Garden City, N.Y.
1929.

---, *The Philosophy of A Biologist*, Oxford, 1935.

HAMELIN, Octave, *La théorie de l'intellect d'après Aristote
et ses commentateurs*, Paris, 1953.

HAMLYN, D.W., "Behaviour", *Philosophy* 28 (1953) 132-145.

---, "Aristotle's Account of Aisthesis in the *De Anima*",
The Classical Quarterly 9 (1959) 6-16.

348

HAMLYN, D.W., *"Koine Aisthesis"*, *The Monist* 52 (1968) 195-209.

---, "Aristotle and Platonism" (a review of G.E.L. OWEN, *The Platonism of Aristotle*), *Classical Review* 18 (1968) 40-41.

HANSON, N.R., *Patterns of Discovery*, Cambridge, 1958.

HANTZ, H.D., *The Biological Motivation in Aristotle*, New York, N.Y., 1939.

HARDIE, W.F.R., "Aristotle's Treatment of the Relation between Soul and Body", *Philosophical Quarterly* 14 (1964) 53-72.

---, *Aristotle's Ethical Theory*, Oxford, 1968.

HARING, E.S., "Substantial Form in Aristotle's *Metaphysics* Zeta", *Review of Metaphysics* 10 (1956/7) 308ff, 482ff, 698ff.

HARRÉ, R., *Matter and Method*, London, 1964.

---, *An Introduction to the Logic of the Sciences*, London, 1960.

HARRISON, Jane, *Themis*, New York, N.Y., 1962 (reprint).

HARVEY, William, *The Works*, ed. and trans. by R. WILLIS, London, 1847, reprinted 1965.

---, *De Motu Locali Animalium*, ed. and trans by G. WHITTE-RIDGE, Cambridge, 1959.

HEATH, Sir Thomas, *Mathematics in Aristotle*, Oxford, 1949.

HEIDEGGER, Martin, "Von Wesen und Begriff der φύσις, Aristoteles *Physica* B.1", *Il Pensiero* (Milan) 3 (1958) 131-156, 265-289.

HEIDEL, W.A., *The Necessary and the Contingent in the Aristotelian System*, Chicago, 1896.

---, *Hippocratic Medicine, Its Spirit and Method*, New York, N.Y., 1941.

HEIN, Hilde, "Mechanism, Vitalism, and Biopoesis", *Pacific Philosophy Forum* 6 (1968) 4-56.

HEMPEL, Carl G., and Paul OPPENHEIM, "The Logic of Explanation", *Philosophy of Science* 15 (1948), reprinted in FEIGL and BRODBECK, listed above.

HERTLING, G. von, *Materie und Form und die Definition der Seele bei Aristoteles*, Bonn, 1871.

HESSE, Mary, "Aristotle's Logic of Analogy", *Philosophical Quarterly* 15 (1965) 328-340.

---, *Models and Analogies in Science*, Notre Dame, Ind., 1966.

HINTIKKA, Jaako, "Necessity, Universality, and Time in Aristotle", *Ajatus* 20 (1957) 65-91.

---, "An Aristotelian Dilemma", *Ajatus* 22 (1959) 87-92.

---, "Aristotle's Different Possibilities", *Inquiry* 3 (1960), reprinted in J. MORAVSCIK, ed., *Aristotle*, listed below.

---, "Aristotle and the 'Master Argument' of Diodorus", *American Philosophical Quarterly* 1 (1964) 101-114.

---, "The Once and Future Sea-Fight", *Philosophical Review* 73 (1964) 461-492.

HIPPOCRATES, ed. W.H.S. JONES, London, 4 vols.,1923-31 (Loeb).

---, *Oeuvres complètes*, ed. E. LITTRÉ, Paris, 1839-61; reprinted Amsterdam, 1961-62.

HUDSON, W.D., ed., *The Is/Ought Question*, London, 1969.

HULL, David L., "The Conflict between Spontaneous Generation and Aristotle's Metaphysics", *Proceedings of the Seventh International Congress of Philosophy*, 1967, vol. II, 245-250.

HUMMEL, K., "Der Begriff des Lebendigen bei Aristoteles und in der wissenschaftlichen Biologie von heute", *Studium Generale* 14 (1961) 413-420.

HUXLEY, J.S., and G.R. DE BEER, *The Elements of Embryology*, Cambridge, 1934.

HUXLEY, T.H., "On Certain Errors respecting the Structure of the Heart attributed to Aristotle", *Nature* 21 (1879) 1-5.

JAEGER, Werner W., *Studien zur Entstehungsgeschichte der Metaphysik des Aristoteles*, Berlin, 1912.

---, "Das Pneuma im Lykeion", *Hermes* 48 (1913) 29-74.

---, *Aristoteles, Grundlegung einer Geschichte seiner Entwicklung*, Berlin, 1923; translated by R. ROBINSON,

Aristotle: Fundamentals of the History of his Development, Oxford, 1934.

---, *Diokles von Karystos*[2], Berlin, 1963.

---, "Diocles of Carystos: a New Pupil of Aristotle", *Philosophical Review* 49 (1940) 393-414.

---, *The Theology of the Early Greek Philosophers*, Oxford, 1947.

---, "Medizin als methodisches Vorbild in der Ethik des Aristoteles", *Zeitschrift für Philosophische Forschung* 13 (1959) 513-30; "Aristotle's Use of Medicine as a Model of Method in his Ethics", *Journal of Hellenic Studies* 77 (1957) 54-61; reprinted in his *Scripta Minora*, Roma, 1960, II, 491-509.

JOHNSON, H.J., "Three Ancient Meanings of Matter: Democritus, Plato, and Aristotle", *Journal of the History of Ideas* 28 (1967) 3ff.

JOLIVET, R., "Aristote et la notion de création", *Revue des sciences philosophiques et théologiques* 19 (1930) 5-50, 209-235.

JOLY, R., "La biologie d'Aristote", *Revue Philosophique* 158 (1968) 219-253.

KAHN, Charles, "Sensation and Consciousness in Aristotle's Psychology", *Archiv für Geschichte der Philosophie* 48 (1966) 43-81.

KERNER, G.C., *The Revolution in Ethical Theory*, Oxford, 1966.

KING, H.R., "Aristotle without *Prima Materia*", *Journal of the History of Ideas* 17 (1956) 370-389.

KIRK, G.S., and J.E. RAVEN, *The Presocratic Philosophers*, Cambridge, 1957.

KOSMAN, L.A., "Aristotle's Definition of Motion", *Phronesis* 14 (1969) 40ff.

KRÄMER, H.J., *Arete bei Platon und Aristoteles*, Heidelberg, 1959.

KROLL, W., *Zur Geschichte der aristotelischen Zoologie*, Wien, 1940.

LAMEERE, William, "Au temps où Franz Cumont s'interrogeait sur Aristote", *L'antiquité classique* 18 (1949) 279-324.

351

LAUDAN, L., "Theories of Scientific Method from Plato to Mach: A Bibliographic Review", *History of Science* 7 (1968) 1-63.

LE BLOND, Jean-Marie, Εὐλόγως *et l'argument de convenance chez Aristote*, Paris, 1939.

---, *Logique et méthode chez Aristote*, Paris, 1939.

---, *Aristote, philosophe de la vie*, Paris, 1945.

---, "The Biological Bias of Aristotle", *The Modern Schoolman* 12 (1958) 82-84.

LEE, H.D.P., "Geometrical Method and Aristotle's Account of First Principles", *The Classical Quarterly* 29 (1935) 113-124.

---, "Place-names and the Date of Aristotle's Biological Works", *The Classical Quarterly* 42 (1948) 61-67.

LEISEGANG, H., "Physik", PAULY and WISSOWA, *Realencyclopädie*, 20.1, p. 1041.

LESKY, A., *History of Greek Literature*[2], trans. WILLIS and DE HEER, London, 1966.

LESKY, Erna, *Die Zeugungs- und Vererbungslehren der Antike und ihre Nachwirkung*, Mainz, 1950.

LEWES, G.H., *Aristotle: A Chapter from the History of Science*, London, 1864.

LEWIN, Kurt, *A Dynamic Theory of Personality*, New York, N.Y., 1935.

LLOYD, A.C., "Genus, Species, and Ordered Series in Aristotle", *Phronesis* 7 (1962) 67-90.

---, "Aristotle's Principle of Individuation", *Mind* 79 (1970) 519-529.

LLOYD, G.E.R., "The Development of Aristotle's Theory of the Classification of Animals", *Phronesis* 6 (1961) 59-81.

---, "Right and Left in Greek Philsophy", *Journal of Hellenic Studies* 82 (1962) 56ff.

---, *Polarity and Analogy*, Cambridge, 1966.

---, "Ancient Medicine and Modern Controversies", (review of L. EDELSTEIN, *Ancient Medicine*), *History of Science* 7 (1968) 125-128.

LLOYD, G.E.R., *Aristotle: The Growth and Structure of his Thought*, Cambridge, 1969.

LONES, T.E., *Aristotle's Researches in Natural Science*, London, 1912.

LOUIS, Pierre, "Sur la chronologie des oeuvres d'Aristote", *Bulletin de l'association Guillaume Budé* ns 5 (1948) 91-95.

---, "Le traité d'Aristote sur la nutrition", *Revue de Philologie* 26 (1952) 29-35.

---, "Le mot ἱστορία chez Aristote", *Revue de Philologie* 29 (1955) 39-44.

---, "Remarques sur la classification des animaux chez Aristote", *Autour d'Aristote*, Mélanges Mansion, 297-304, Louvain, 1955.

---, "La génération spontanée chez Aristote", 12 Congrès international d'histoire des sciences 1968, pp. 291-305.

---, see also his editions and translations in the Budé series.

LOVEJOY, A.O., *The Great Chain of Being*, Cambridge, Mass., 1936.

MC KEON, Richard, "Aristotle's Conception of the Development and Nature of Scientific Method", *Journal of the History of Ideas*, 8 (1947), 3-44.

---, "Aristotle and the Origins of Science in the West", *Science and Civilization*, ed. R.C. Stauffer, Madison, Wisc., 1949, 1-29.

MC MULLIN, Ernan, ed., *The Concept of Matter in Greek and Medieval Philosophy*, Notre Dame, Ind., 1965.

MANDELBAUM, Maurice, "Functionalism in Social Anthropology", *Philosophy, Science, and Method: Essays in Honor of Ernest Nagel*, ed. Morganbesser, Suppes, and White, New York, N.Y., 1969.

MANICAS, P.T., "Aristotle, Dispositions, and Occult Powers", *Review of Metaphysics* 18 (1965) 678ff.

MANQUAT, M., *Aristote Naturaliste*, Paris, 1932.

MANSION, Auguste, *Introduction à la physique aristotélicienne* Louvain et Paris, 1913, 1945.

MANSION, Auguste, "La genèse de l'oeuvre d'Aristote d'après les travaux récents", *Revue néo-scolastique de philosophie* 29 (1927) 307-341, 423-466.

---, "L'objet de la science philosophique suprême d'après Aristote, Métaphysique E.1", *Mélanges de Philosophie Grecque*, offerts à Mgr. Diès, Paris, 1956.

MANSION, Suzanne, *Le jugement d'existence chez Aristote*, Louvain et Paris, 1946.

---, "Les apories de la Métaphysique aristotélicienne", *Autour d'Aristote*, Mélanges Mansion, Paris, 1955, 141-179.

---, ed., *Aristote et les problèmes de méthode*, Symposium Aristotelicum, Louvain et Paris, 1961.

MARX, Werner, *The Meaning of Aristotle's Ontology*, The Hague, 1954.

MEEHAN, F.X., *Efficient Causality in Aristotle and St. Thomas Aquinas*, Washington, D.C., 1940.

Mélanges Auguste MANSION, *Autour d'Aristote*, Louvain, 1955.

MERLAN, Philip, *From Platonism to Neoplatonism*, The Hague, 1953.

---, *Studies in Epicurus and Aristotle*, Wiesbaden, 1960.

---, "Hintikka and a Strange Aristotelian Doctrine", *Phronesis* 15.2 (1970) 93-100.

MEULEN, Jan van der, *Aristoteles: die Mitte in seinem Denken*, Meisenheim/Glan, 1951.

MEYER, Adolf, "The Tradition of Ancient Biology and Medicine in the Vitalistic Periods of Modern Biology and Medicine", *Bulletin of the Institute of the History of Medicine* 5 (1937).

MEYER, A.W., *The Rise of Embryology*, Stanford, Cal., 1939.

MEYER, Hans, *Der Entwicklungsgedanke bei Aristoteles*, Bonn, 1909.

---, "Das Vererbungsproblem bei Aristoteles", *Philologus* 75 (1919, 1920) 333-363.

MEYER, J.B., *Aristoteles Thierkunde, Ein Beitrag zur Geschichte der Zoologie, Physiologie und alten Philosophie*, Berlin, 1855.

354

MICHAEL Ephesios, *In Parva Naturalia Commentaria*, ed. Paulus WENDLAND, Berlin, 1903 (Commentaria in Aristotelem Graeca 23.1).

---, *In Libros de Partibus Animalium, De Animalium Motione, De Animalibus Incessu Commentaria*, ed. Michael HAYDUCK, Berlin, 1904 (Commentaria in Aristotelem Graeca 22.2).

MONOD, Jacques, *Le hasard et la nécessité*, Paris, 1970.

MORAUX, Paul, *Les listes anciennes des ouvrages d'Aristote*, Louvain, 1951.

---, "A propos du νοῦς θύραθεν chez Aristote", *Autour d'Aristote*, Mélanges Mansion, Louvain, 1955.

---, *Aristote, le dialogue sur la justice (à la recherche de l'Aristote perdu)*, Louvain, 1957.

---, "L'évolution d'Aristote", *Aristote et Saint Thomas d'Aquin*, par P. MORAUX *et al.*, Louvain, 1957, pp. 9-41.

---, "Quinta Essentia", PAULY and WISSOWA, *Realencyclopädie*, Halbband 47 (bd. 24) Stuttgart 1963, 1171-1263.

---, ed., *Aristoteles in der neueren Forschung*, Darmstadt, 1968.

---, *D'Aristote à Bessarion*, Québec, 1970.

MORAVSCIK, J.M.E., ed. *Aristotle, A Collection of Critical Essays*, Garden City, N.Y., 1967.

MOREAU, Joseph, "L'éloge de la biologie chez Aristote", *Revue des études anciennes* 61 (1959) 57-64.

---, *Aristote et son école*, Paris, 1962.

MORRISON, J.S., "Four Notes on Plato's *Symposium*", *The Classical Quarterly* 14 (1964) 42-55.

MOURELATOS, A.D.P., "Aristotle's Powers and Modern Empiricism", *Ratio*, 1967.

MUGLER, Charles, "Démocrite et les postulats cosmologiques du Demiurge", *Revue des études anciennes* 69 (1967) 50-58.

MURE, G.R.G., *Aristotle*, London, 1932, 1964.

MUSKENS, G.L., *De Voce* ἀναλογίας *significatione ac usu apud Aristotelem*, Groningen, 1953.

NAGEL, Ernest, "Teleological Explanation and Teleological Systems", *Vision and Action*, ed. S. RATNER, Rutgers, N.J., 1953; reprinted in FEIGL and BRODBECK (listed above), pp. 537-558.

---, *The Structure of Science*, New York, N.Y., 1961.

NEEDHAM, J., *A History of Embryology*, New York, N.Y., 1934, 1959.

---, *Background to Modern Science*, New York, N.Y., 1938.

NUYENS, François (E.J.C.J.), *Ontwikkelingsmomenten in de Zielkunde van Aristoteles*, Nijmegen-Utrecht, 1939; trans., *L'évolution de la psychologie d'Aristote*, Paris, 1948.

OATES, W.J., *Aristotle and the Problem of Value*, Princeton, N.J., 1963.

OCKHAM, William, *Predestination, God's Foreknowledge, and Future Contingents*, trans. *etc.* by M.M. ADAMS and N. KRETZMANN, New York, N.Y., 1969.

OWEN, G.E.L., "Τιθέναι τὰ φαινόμενα" Symposium Aristotelicum, ed. S. MANSION, Louvain, 1961, 83-103.

---, *The Platonism of Aristotle*, London, 1965.

OWENS, Joseph, "Aristotle on the Categories", *Review of Metaphysics* 14 (1960/1) 73-90.

---, *The Doctrine of Being in the Aristotelian Metaphysics*, Toronto, Ont., 1957 (2nd ed.).

---, "Teleology of Nature in Aristotle", *The Monist* 52 (1968) 159-173.

PAGEL, Walter, "The Reaction to Aristotle in 17th Century Biological Thought", *Science, Medicine and History, Essays in Honour of Charles Singer*, ed. E.A. UNDERWOOD, London, 1953, vol. I. 489-509.

---, "An Harveyan Prelude to Harvey", (review of W. HARVEY, *Lectures on the Whole of Anatomy*, trans. O'MALLEY, PAYNTON, and RUSSELL, Berkeley, Cal., 1961), *History of Science* 2 (1963) 114-125.

---, *William Harvey's Biological Ideas*, New York, N.Y., 1967.

---, "William Harvey Revisited", *History of Science* 8 (1969) 1-31; 9 (1970).

356

PECK, A.L., "Anaxagoras, Predication as a Problem in Physics", *The Classical Quarterly* 25 (1931) 27-37, 112-120.

---, "The Connate Pneuma: an Essential Factor in Aristotle's Solution to the Problems of Reproduction and Sensation", *Science, Medicine and History, Essays in Honour of Charles Singer*, ed. E.A. UNDERWOOD, London, 1953, vol. I, 111-121.

---, "Aristotle on Kinesis", *Essays in Ancient Greek Philosophy*, ed. J. ANTON and G. KUSTAS, Albany, N.Y., 1971, pp. 478-490.

---, see also his editions and translations in the Loeb series.

PEYER, Bernard, "Über die zoologischen Schriften des Aristoteles", *Gesnerus* 3 (1946) 58-71.

PHILIBERT, Henri, *Du principe de la vie suivant Aristote*, Paris, 1865.

PHILOPONUS, Joannis, *In Libros De Generatione Animalium Commentaria*, ed. M. HAYDUCK, Berlin, 1903 (Commentaria in Aristotelem Graeca 14.3).

PLATT, Arthur, "Aristotle on the Heart", *Studies in the History of Science*, ed. Charles SINGER, Oxford, 1921, vol. II, 521-532.

PLOCHMAN, G.K., "Nature and the Living Thing in Aristotle's Biology", *Journal of the History of Ideas* 14 (1953) 167-90.

PLUTARCH, *Moralia* vol. VII, ed. P.H. DE LACY and B. EINARSON, Cambridge, Mass., 1959 (Loeb).

POSCHENREIDER, Franz, *Die naturwissenschaftlichen Schriften des Aristoteles in ihrem Verhältnis zu den Büchern der hippokratischen Sammlung*, Bamberg, 1887.

POUCHET, Charles, *La biologie aristotélicienne*, Paris, 1885.

PRECOPE, John, *Medicine, Magic and Mythology*, London, 1954.

---, *Iatrophilosophers of the Hellenic States*, London, 1961.

PREUS, A., "Aristotle's *Parts of Animals* 2. 16. 659b13-19: Is it Authentic?" *The Classical Quarterly* 18.2 (1968) 170-178.

---, "On Dreams 2, 459b24-460a33, and Aristotle's ὄψις", *Phronesis* 13.2 (1968) 175-182.

PREUS, A., "Aristotle's 'Nature Uses...'", *Apeiron* III.2 (1969) 20-33.

---, "Aristotle's Natural Necessity", *Studi Internazionali di Filosofia* I (1969) 91-100.

---, "Science and Philosophy in Aristotle's *Generation of Animals*", *Journal of the History of Biology* III.1 (1970) 1-52.

---, "The Continuous Analogy: Uses of Continuous Proportions in Plato and Aristotle", *Agora* I.2 (1970) 20-42.

---, (review of T. TRACY, *Physiological Theory...*), *Studi Internazionali di Filosofia* II (1970) 181-184.

PREUSS, S., *Index Demosthenicus*, Leipzig, 1892; reprinted Hildesheim, 1963.

---, *Index Isocrateus*, Fürth, 1904; reprinted Hildesheim, 1963.

RANDALL, J.H., Jr., *Aristotle*, New York, N.Y., 1960.

RASMUSSEN, H., and M.M. PECHET, "Calcitonin", *Scientific American* 233.4 (October, 1970) 42-50.

REES, D.A., "Some Aspects of Aristotle's Development", *Proceedings of the XIth International Congress of Philosophy*, Amsterdam and Louvain, 1953, vol. XII, pp. 83-85.

REGENBOGEN, Otto, "Eine Forschungsmethode antiker Naturwissenschaft", *Quellen und Studien zur Geschichte der Mathematik, Astronomie und Physik* I (1931) 131-182 (reprinted in *Kleine Schriften*, München, 1961).

---, "Eine Polemik Theophrasts gegen Aristoteles", *Hermes* 72 (1937) 469-475 (reprinted in *Kleine Schriften*, München, 1961).

---, "Bemerkungen zur *Historia Animalium* des Aristoteles", *Studi ital. di filos. class.* 27/28 (1956) 444-9 (reprinted in *Kleine Schriften*, München, 1961).

REICHE, H., *Empedocles' Mixture, Eudoxan Astronomy, and Aristotle's Connate Pneuma*, Amsterdam, 1960.

---, "Aristotle on Breathing in the *Timaeus*", *American Journal of Philology* 86 (1965) 404-408.

---, (review of P. SIWEK, *Aristotelis Parva Naturalia*), *American Journal of Philology* 87 (1966) 350-354.

REYMOND, A., *History of the Sciences in Greco-Roman Anti-quity*, London, 1927.

RIGNANO, E., *Biological Memory*, London, 1926.

RIST, J.M., "Some Aspects of Aristotelian Teleology", *Trans-actions and Proceedings of the American Philological Association* 96 (1965) 337-349.

RITTER, W.E., "Why Aristotle Invented the Word Entelecheia", *Quarterly Review of Biology* 7 (1932) 377-404.

ROBIN, Léon, "Sur la conception aristotélicienne de la cau-salité", *Archiv für Philosophie* 23 (1910).

---, *La pensée grecque et les origines de l'esprit scien-tifique*, Paris, 1923; *Greek Thought and the Origins of the Scientific Spirit*, New York, N.Y., 1928.

---, *Aristote*, Paris, 1944.

ROSEN, S.H., "Thought and Touch, a Note on Aristotle's *de Anima*", *Phronesis* 6 (1961) 127-137.

ROSENBLUETH, A., N. WEINER, and J. BIGELOW, "Behavior, Pur-pose, and Teleology", *Philosophy of Science* X.1 (1943) 18-24; reprinted in J. CANFIELD, ed., *Purpose in Nature* Englewood Cliffs, N.J., 1966.

ROSS, W.D., *Aristotle*, London, 1923, 1930, 1937.

---, "The Development of Aristotle's Thought", *British Aca-demy,Proceedings* 43 (1957) 63-78; also in Symposium Aristotelicum 1957 (1960).

---, see also his editions, translations, and commentaries of Aristotle's works.

ROSSI, Paolo, *I filosofi e le macchine (1400-1700)*, Milano, 1962.

ROSTAND, Jean, *Evolution*, (Paris, 1960), New York, N.Y., 1961.

RUDBERG, Gunnar, *Textstudien zur Tiergeschichte des Aristoteles*, Uppsala, 1909.

---, "Kleinere Aristotelesfragen", *Eranos* 9 (1909) 92ff.

---, *Zum so-genannten 10. Buch der Tiergeschichte*, Uppsala, 1911.

RÜSCHE, F., "Blut, Leben und Seele", *Stud. z. Gesch. u. Kult. d. Altert.* 5 Ergbd., Paderborn, 1930.

RUSSELL, E.S., *Form and Function*, London, 1916.

---, *The Directiveness of Organic Activities*, Cambridge, 1945.

RYLE, Gilbert, "The Timaeus Locrus", *Phronesis* 10 (1965) 189ff.

---, "Dialectic in the Academy", *New Essays on Plato and Aristotle*, R. BAMBROUGH, ed., New York, N.Y., 1965.

---, *Plato's Progress*, Cambridge, 1966.

SAMBURSKY, S., *The Physical World of the Greeks*, London, 1956.

SARTON, George, "The Discovery of the Mammalian Egg and the Foundation of Modern Embryology", *Isis* 16 (1931) 315ff.

SCHRAMM, M., "Aristotelianism: Basis and Obstacle to Scientific Progress in the Middle Ages", (review of A.C. CROMBIE, *Augustine to Galileo*), *History of Science* 2 (1963) 91-113.

SCHRECKENBERG, H., *Ananke*, München, 1964.

SCHUMACHER, J., *Antike Medizin*, Berlin, 1963.

SENN, G., "Hat Aristoteles eine selbständige Schrift über Pflanzen verfasst?" *Philologus* 85 (1929/30) 113-40.

---, *Die Entwicklung der biologischen Forschungsmethode in der Antike*, Aarau, 1933.

SHUTE, C.W., *The Psychology of Aristotle*, New York, N.Y., 1941.

SIMARD, E., "Aristote et les charactères généraux d'une théorie scientifique", *Laval théologique-philosophique* 10 (1954) 146-166.

SINGER, Charles, *Studies in the History and Method of Science*, Oxford, 1921.

---, "Biology", "Medicine", in: *The Legacy of Greece*, ed. R.W. LIVINGSTONE, Oxford, 1921, 163ff, 201ff.

---, *Greek Biology and Greek Medicine*, Oxford, 1922.

---, *A Short History of Anatomy from the Greeks to Harvey*, New York, N.Y., 1957.

---, *From Magic to Science*, New York, N.Y., 1958.

---, *A Short History of Scientific Ideas*, Oxford, 1959.

SINGER, Charles, (see: E.A. UNDERWOOD, *Science, Medicine and History, Essays in Honour of Charles Singer*, London, 1953).

SINNOTT, E.W., *Cell and Psyche*, Chapel Hill, N.C., 1951.

SKEMP, J.B., *The Theory of Motion in Plato's Later Dialogues*[2], Amsterdam, 1967.

---, "Plants in Plato's *Timaeus*", *The Classical Quarterly* 41 (1947) 53-60.

---, "ὕλη and ὑποδοχή", Symposium Aristotelicum 1957, Göteborg, 1960, pp. 201ff.

---, (review of A. JANNONE and E. BARBOTIN, *Aristote de l'âme*), in: *Classical Review* 18 (1968) 41-43.

SMITH, H.W., *Kamongo: The Lung Fish and the Padre*, New York, N.Y., 1949.

SMITH, J.A., "τόδε τί", *Classical Review* 35 (1921) 19.

SOLMSEN, Friedrich, "Plato and the Unity of Science", *Philosophical Review* 49 (1940) 506ff.

---, "Tissues and the Soul", *Philosophical Review* 59 (1950) 435-68.

---, "Antecedents of Aristotle's Psychology and Scale of Beings", *American Journal of Philology* 76 (1955) 148-164.

---, "The Vital Heat, the Inborn Pneuma, and the Aither", *Journal of Hellenic Studies* 77 (1957) 119-123.

---, "Aristotle and Prime Matter: A Reply to H.R. King", *Journal of the History of Ideas* 19 (1958) 243-252.

---, *Aristotle's System of the Physical World: A Comparison with his Predecessors*, Ithaca, N.Y., 1960.

---, "Aristotle's Word for 'Matter'", in: *Didascaliae, Studies in Honor of Anselm Malbareda*, New York, N.Y., 1961.

---, "Greek Philosophy and the Discovery of the Nerves", *Museum Helveticum* 19 (1961) 150-167, 169-197.

---, "Nature as Craftsman in Greek Thought", *Journal of the History of Ideas* 24 (1963) 473-496.

SORABJI, R., "Aristotle on Demarcating the Five Senses", *Philosophical Review* 80 (1971) 55-79.

STALLMACH, Josef, *Dynamis und Energeia*, Meisenheim/Glan, 1959.

STAUFFER, R.C., ed., *Science and Civilization*, Madison, Wisc., 1949.

STEBBING, L.S., "Concerning Substance", *Proceedings of the Aristotelian Society* 30 (1930) 285-308.

STECKERL, Fritz, *The Fragments of Praxagoras of Cos and his School*, Leiden, 1958.

STEENBERGHEN, F. von, *Aristotle in the West, The Origins of Latin Aristotelianism*, Louvain, 1955.

STEFANI, E.L. de, "Per l'epitome Aristotelis De Animalibus di Aristofane di Bisanzio", *Studi it. di filol. class.* 12 (1904) 421-445.

STENZEL, Julius, "Zur Theorie des Logos bei Aristoteles", *Quellen und Studien zur Geschichte der Mathematik, Astronomie und Physik* I (1930) 34ff.

---, *Zahl und Gestalt bei Platon und Aristoteles*, Bad Homburg, 1959.

STIEBITZ, F., "Über die Kausalerklärung der Vererbung bei Aristoteles", *Archiv für Geschichte der Medizin* 23 (1930) 332-345.

SUNDEVALL, C.J., *Die Thierarten des Aristoteles von den Klassen der Säugethiere, Vögel, Reptilien und Insekten*, Stockholm, 1863 (also in Swedish, in: K. SVENSKA, *Vetenskapsakademiens handlingar* 4.2, Stockholm, 1962).

Symposium Aristotelicum: see S. MANSION, I. DÜRING.

TAYLOR, A.E., *Aristotle*, London, n.d.

TAYLOR, Richard, "Causation", *The Monist* 47 (1962/3) 287-313.

TEMKIN, Owsei, "On Galen's Pneumatology", *Gesnerus* 8 (1951) 180-189.

THEILER, W., *Zur Geschichte der teleologischen Naturbetrachtung bis auf Aristoteles*, Zürich, 1924.

THEOPHRASTUS, *Characters*, ed. and trans. J.M. EDMONS, London, 1929 (Loeb).

---, *Enquiry into Plants, and Minor Works*, ed. and trans. Arthur Hort, London, 1916 (Loeb).

THEOPHRASTUS, *De Causis Plantarum I*, ed. R.E. DENGLER,
Philadelphia, Pa., 1927.

---, *Theophrastus on Stones* (trans. and notes, *De Lapidibus*)
E.R. CALEY and J.R.C. RICHARDS, Columbus, Ohio, 1956.

---, *Theophrastus and the Greek Physiological Psychology
before Aristotle* (trans. and notes, *De Sensibus*),
G.M. STRATTON, London, 1917.

THOMPSON, D'Arcy Wentworth, *Aristotle as a Biologist*, Oxford
1913.

---, *Growth and Form*, Cambridge, 1917, 2nd ed. 1942.

---, "Natural Science", in: *The Legacy of Greece*, ed. R.W.
LIVINGSTONE, Oxford, 1921, pp. 137ff.

---, "Excess and Defect", *Mind* 38 (1929) 43-55.

---, *A Glossary of Greek Birds*, London, 1936.

---, *Science and the Classics*, London, 1940.

---, "Onos: Anthropos", *The Classical Quarterly* 39 (1945) 54ff.

---, *A Glossary of Greek Fishes*, London, 1947.

TIMPANARO-CARDINI, M., "Physis e Techne in Aristotele", *Studi
di filosofia greca*, ed. R. MONDOLFO, Bari, 1950, pp.
277-305.

TONELLI, Giorgio, "La nécessité des lois de la nature au
XVIIIe siècle et chez Kant en 1762", *Revue d'histoire
des sciences* 12 (1959) 225-241.

TORRACA, Luigi, "Sull' autenticità del 'De Motu Animalium' di
Aristotele", *Maia* 10 (1958) 220-223.

---, "Il I libro del 'De Partibus Animalium' di Aristotele",
Rendiconti dell' Accademia di Archeologia 33 (1958).

---, *Ricerche sull' Aristotele minore*, Padova, 1959.

TORREY, H.B., and F. FELIN, "Was Aristotle an Evolutionist?"
Quarterly Review of Biology 12 (1937) 1-18.

TOULMIN, Stephen, *The Philosophy of Science*, London, 1953.

---, *Foresight and Understanding*, Evanston, Ind., 1961.

---, and June GOODFIELD, *The Architecture of Matter*, New York,
N.Y., 1963.

TOULMIN, Stephen, and June GOODFIELD, *The Discovery of Time*, New York, N.Y., 1965.

TRACY, T., *Physiological Theory and the Doctrine of the Mean in Plato and Aristotle*, Chicago, Ill., 1969.

TUGENDHAT, Ernst, τί κατά τινος *eine Untersuchung zu Struktur und Ursprung aristotelischer Grundbegriffe*, Freiburg, 1958.

ULMER, K., *Wahrheit, Kunst und Natur bei Aristoteles*, Tübingen 1953.

UNDERWOOD, E.A., *Science, Medicine and History, Essays in Honour of Charles Singer* (2 vols.), London, 1953.

VATTIMO, Gianni, "Opera d'arte e organismo in Aristotele", *Rivista di estetica* 1960, 358-82.

VERBEKE, Gerard, *L'évolution de la doctrine du pneuma du Stoicisme à St. Augustine*, Paris, 1945.

VERDENIUS, W.J., "Der Logosbegriff bei Heraklit und Parmenides", *Phronesis* 11 (1966) 81-98; 12 (1967) 99-117.

---, and J.H. WASZINK, *Aristotle on Coming-to-be and Passing -away, Some Comments*, Leiden, 1945.

WADDINGTON, C.H., *The Nature of Life*, London, 1961.

WATTS, A., *The Two Hands of God*, New York, N.Y., 1969.

WEISHEIPL, J.A., "The Concept of Nature", *New Scholasticism* 28 (1954) 377-408.

---, "Aristotle and Modern Science: A Reply", *International Philosophical Quarterly* 1962, 629-32.

WEISS, Helene, *Zufall in der Philosophie des Aristoteles*, London, 1935.

---, *Kausalität und Zufall in der Philosophie des Aristoteles* Basel, 1942.

---, "Aristotle's Teleology and Uexküll's Theory of Living Nature", *The Classical Quarterly* 42 (1948) 44-58.

WEISS, Paul, *Principles of Development*, New York, N.Y., 1939.

WELLMAN, Max, *Die Pneumatische Schule*, Berlin, 1895.

WELLMAN, Max, *Fragmentsammlung der Sikelischen Ärzte*, Berlin, 1901.

WHITE, Alan R., ed., *The Philosophy of Action*, London, 1968.

WIELAND, Wolfgang, *Die aristotelische Physik*, Göttingen, 1962.

WILKIE, J.S., "Harvey's Immediate Debt to Aristotle and to Galen", *History of Science* 4 (1965) 103-123.

WOLFSON, H.A., *Crescas' Critique of Aristotle*, Cambridge, Mass., 1929.

---, "The Plurality of Immovable Movers in Aristotle and Averroes", *Harvard Studies in Classical Philology* 63 (1958) 233-253.

WOODBRIDGE, F.J.E., *Aristotle's Vision of Nature*, New York, N.Y., 1965.

WOOLDRIDGE, D.E., *The Machinery of Life*, New York, N.Y., 1966.

XENOPHON, *Scripta Minora*, ed. E.C. MARCHANT, Cambridge, Mass., 1925 (Loeb).

ZELLER, Eduard, *Die Philosophie der Griechen in ihrer geschichtlichen Entwicklung*, Leipzig, 4th ed., 1903-22; vol. 2.2, *Aristoteles und die alten Peripatetiker*, 1921. An earlier edition, trans., *Aristotle and the Earlier Peripatetics*, London, 1897; reprinted New York, N.Y.,1962.

---, *Outlines of the History of Greek Philosophy*, 13th ed., New York, N.Y., 1957.

ZILSEL, E., "The Genesis of the Concept of Physical Law", *Philosophical Review* 51 (1942) 245-279.

ZÜRCHER, Josef, *Aristoteles Werk und Geist*, Paderborn, 1952.

INDICES

There are three indices: the first is of concepts, key words,
and the like; the second is of proper names; the third is of
passages in Aristotle, by chapter. The indices refer not to
pages in the text, but to chapter-part-section, and to notes
to sections. For example, a reference which reads IIIB2 is
to Chapter III, Part B, Section 2. A reference to IVA2n25 is
to Chapter IV, Part A, Section 2, note 25.

Index I: Concepts

The entries in this index are of several sorts; there are
technical terms in English and Greek, both philosophical and
biological concepts, and names of classes of animal and of
parts of animals. Sections which deal with a subject at length
are noted in italics.

Ancestor: IIC5.

Anchor lines: IIIA3b.

Animism: IB, see also 'myth', 'anthropomorphism', 'teleology
of intention'.

Ant: ID3.

Anthropology: IC2.

Anthropomorphism: IIB3n32, IV intro., B, see also 'teleology
of intention'.

Aphrodite: ID1, n70, IIB6.

Aporia: IIB7n44, see also 'dilemma'.

A priori (arguments, principles, *etc.*): IB1, D1n78, 3, IIA2,
B1, C2n62, IIIB3d, IVA1n5.

Archē: IC1b, *IIIA1*, 3b-c, B1, IVA1, B6, see also 'movement,
source of'.

Aretē: IB1, see also 'value'.

Aristocratic: ID1n78.

Art (and nature): *IB3*, IIA4, B3, n32, C1, III intro., A2,
3n46-47, IVA4, *B*, *8*, Gen. Concl.

Ascidian: see 'sea squirt'.

Astronomy, astronomical entities: IIB1, n26, B7, e, C2-3,
concl., IIIA3a, IVA1-2, 4-5, B6, Gen. Concl.

Athens: IE.

Atoms and atomism: ID, 1, n90, II intro., C2, Gen. Concl.,
see also 'matter', and 'Democritus' in Index II.

Augury: ID1.

Authenticity: ID-E, see also 'text'.

Automata: IIB3, 8, IIIA2, 3ci, IVB8, see also 'mechanism'.

Axe: IVB8c.

Backbone: ID1, IIIA1, 3ci, see also 'bone', 'blooded animal'.

Balance: IB1, IVB8c, see also 'mean', 'proportion', 'symmetry'.

Bat (the animal): IVA5b, n46.

Beard: ID1, see also 'hair'.

Bee: ID1-3, IIA4, n17, C2, IIIB3f, n95.

Behavior: IB1, E, IIIA3cii.

Better and worse: see 'value'.

Biaion: see 'force'.

Biology: ID3, E, II intro., and *passim*.

Bird: ID1-2, IIIA3ci, B1, 3c, IVA5a-c, B3, 7.

Blend (*krasis*): ID1n78, IIIAn5.

Bloodvessels: ID3, IIIA3a-b, IVB3, 7, 8a.

'Blooded' and 'bloodless' animals: IC1a, D1, III intro., A3,
        IVA5a-b, B5.

Boat: IIIA3ci.

Boiling: IIIA1, 3a.

Bone: IIIA3ci, IVB2, n73, 8b.

Brain: ID1, IIIA3a, cii, B1, IVA2.

Breathing: see 'respiration', 'pneuma'.

Buttocks: IVB3, 5.

Camel: ID1-2, IVB3.

Cannibalism: ID2.

Carnivore: IIIB1.

Carp: IIIB3e, see also 'fish'.

Carpenter (*tektōn*): IIA4, IVB8.

Cat: IIIB1.

Cataract: IIIB1.

Cattle and cattlemen: ID1n60, 2, IIA2n11.

Causes: IB, C2, II intro., C2, 4, III intro., A3ci, B1, IVA2,
        5, Gen. Concl.

Cell: IIIA summary.

Cephalopod: IIIB3f, IVA5a, B7, see also 'octopus', 'squid'.

Cetacean: IIIB2, see also 'dolphin'.

Chamaleon: IIIB1, see also 'reptile', 'ovipara'.

Chance: IB2, IVA1, n6, A2, B1, Gen. Concl.

Change: II intro., see also 'movement', 'genesis'.

Chicken: IIB2n31.

Children: ID1, IIIB1, IVA5b.

Chordata: see 'blooded animal'.

Chromosomes: Gen. Concl.

Chronology of Aristotle's life and works: IE.

368

Cicada: ID2, *IIIB3f*, n98, see also 'insect'.

Cinnamon bird: ID1.

Circular argument: II concl., see also 'fallacy', 'contra-
    diction'.

Clay: IIA4, IIIA3b, IVB3b, see also 'matter'.

Classification: III intro., B2, 3f, IVA5b, see also 'species'.

Colliquescence: see '*syntēgma*', 'residue'.

Color, variations in: IIIB1, 3.

Coming-into-being: see 'existential change', '*genesis*'.

Communication: IIIB3c, see also 'speech'.

Compensation: III intro., IVB3.

Conger: see 'eel'.

Connate: see '*symphyton*'.

Contradiction: IIIA3ci.

Copulation: IC3, D, 1-2, IIA4, n21, IVB6-7.

Corpus Aristotelicum: IE.

Crab: IVA5b, B3, see also 'crustacea'.

Crane (bird): ID1.

Craft: see 'art'.

Creationism: IIIA1n14.

Criticism of predecessors: ID1, see also Index II.

Crocodile: ID1, IIIB1, *3d*, IVBn55, 3.

Crustacea: IIIB1-3.

Cupid: IVB8a.

Cyclical process: IIIB3n103, IVA1, 4, Gen. Concl., see also
    'astronomy'.

Deductive model: IB, C2, see also 'syllogism', 'explanation'.

Deer: ID1, IIIA3b.

Defense: see 'weapon'.

Definition: see '*logos*', 'species'.

Deformed (*pepēromenon*): IIIB2, IVA3, 5b, n44.

Demiourgos, demiurge: IVB, 7, n104, Gen. Concl., see also
    'Plato' in Index II.

Description: ID1, 2, IIIB3c, IVA5e, see also 'observation'.
    --- and explanation: IB1.

369

Determinism: IB2n9, IVA, n17, Gen. Concl., see also 'neces-
    sity', 'mechanism'.
Development: see 'genesis', 'generation'.
Diaphragm: IVA2, n26, B7.
Digestion: IIIA3, see also 'food', 'nutrition'.
Dilemma: IIB2, Gen. Concl. n1.
Directions, natural: ID1n97, 2, IIIA3a, *IVA5c*.
Disease: IIIB1, see also 'medicine'.
Disposition: see '*dynamis*', '*ethos*', 'habit'.
Dissection: ID1, 3, III intro., An4, 3, n37, n38.
DNA: IIB8.
Dog: ID1, IIIB1.
Dolphin: IIIB3a-b, IVA5b, see also 'cetacean'.
Dream: ID1.
Dualism: IE, IV intro.
Dualize (*epamphoterizein*): IIIB2, 3d, IVA3, n36, 5n38, *b*,
    n43.
Dwarflike: IIIA3ci, IVA5n38, b, n47, B5, see also 'scale of
    nature'.
Dynamis: ID1a, *3*, II intro., 3, B2-5, 7b, C1, 4-5, IIIA2-3,
    IVB2, 9, Gen. Concl.
Dysteleological: IVA4, see also 'teleology'.

Eagle: ID1, 2.
Ears: ID1, IIIA3a, *B2*, see also 'hearing'.
Earthenware: IIIA3c, see also 'clay'.
Earthy matter: see 'matter'.
Eclipse: IB2, n12, IVA4, see also 'astronomy'.
Ecology: ID1n113, IIIA3ci, IVA5b, n48, Gen. Concl.
Education: see 'teaching'.
Eel: ID2, n112, IVB2, see also 'fish'.
Egg: ID1, 3, II A2n11, B2n31 and *passim*, IVB3, 7, 9, Gen.
    Concl., see also 'ovipara'.
Egypt: ID1.
Eidos: IC3, II intro., A1, 3-4, B1-2, 8, IIIA3b, IVA2, B9,
    Gen. Concl., see also 'species', 'form'.

370

Element: IC3, D1, IIA1, C1, IIIA1, see also 'matter'.

Elephant: ID1-3, IIIB1, 3a, f, n97, IVB5.

Embryo, embryology: ID1, IIA4, B7b, C1, IIIA1-3, IVB8n109.

Emphyton: IIIB3f, see also '*symphyton*'.

Empirical evidence: IIA4, see also 'observation', 'experiment', 'description'.

End: see 'teleology'.

Energeia, entelecheia: ID1a, 3, II intro., B2-4, 7b, d, *C*, IIIA1-3, IVB2.

Entelechy: see '*energeia*', 'vitalism'.

Entity: see '*ousia*'.

Entoma: see 'insect'.

Entrails: see 'viscera'.

Environment: IIIB summary, see also 'ecology'.

Epigenesis: IIA1n6, B2, 8.

Epiglottis: IIIB3a, IVB7, 8e.

Erect position in man: IIIA3ci, see also 'directions', 'dwarflikeness'.

Ergon: IC1a, 3, IIIB1, IVB7n103, see also 'function'.

Essence: IC3, IVA2n24-25, *5*, B8d, see also '*eidos*', '*logos*', 'species'.

Estrous flow: IIA2.

Ethics: IB1, IIIA3ci, n54, see also *EN* in Index III.

Ethiopian: ID1.

Ethos: IIIA3ci.

Evaluation: see 'value'.

'Event': Gen. Concl.

Everlasting entities: see 'astronomy'.

Evolution: IC1n23, IIIA3ci, B, IVB1, Gen. Concl., see also Index II, 'Darwin'.

Excretion: see 'residue'.

Existential change: IA, II, see also 'genesis'.

Experiment: ID, 2, 3, IIIA3a, cii.

Explanation: IA, C, II intro., A5, C1, 5, concl., III intro., B3, IV, A4, B3n85, 8d, Gen. Concl., and *passim*.

Eye: IIB5, C5, IIIA3a, *oii*, *B1*, IVA2, 5a, c, B3, see also
      'vision'.

Fact: IC2, see also 'value'.
Falcon: ID1.
Fallacy: IVB6n101.
Farmer: ID2.
Feathers: IVB6-7.
Feedback: IB1.
Female: ID1-2, IIC5 and *passim*, IIIB1, IVA5b, n47, B3-4, 6,
      9n114, Gen. Concl.
Fertility and fertilization: ID1-2, IVA5n44.
Fetation, fetus: ID3, n138, IIB2, IIIA1, see also 'embryo'.
Fig tree: ID2.
Fig juice: see 'rennet'.
Finality: see 'teleology'.
Fire: ID1, see also 'element', 'heat'.
      --- animal: ID1n57, 2.
'First': IIA2n5.
Fish: ID, I, IIA4n17, IIIB3e, IVA5, Bn55, 7.
Fishermen: ID, 2.
Flesh: IIIA3ci, B3a.
Flies: ID2.
Flute, fluteplayer: IBn14.
Food: IIIA, see also 'nutrition'.
Foot: IIIA3ci.
Force (*bia*): IVA *passim*, B6.
Form: IB3, IIB5, 7, C4-5, IIIA, IVA5, 8d, see also 'species',
      '*eidos*', '*logos*'.
      ---, Platonic: see 'Plato', Index II.
      Formal necessity: IVA1, *5*, see also 'necessity'.
Frog: IIIB3d.
'From': IIA2n9.
Front and back: see 'directions'.
Function: IB1, C1, III intro., A, 3, IVA2-3, B1, 9, see also
      '*ergon*'.

372

Gall bladder: ID1.

Garden and gardener: ID3, IIIA3a-b, n43, IVB8n110.

Generation: II *passim*, III intro., 3, IVB3, Gen. Concl.

Generative soul: see 'nutritive soul'.

Genesis: IC1b, D1, IIA2n9, B3, *C*, IVA3, Gen. Concl.

Genetic account: IB-C.

Geometer: IIB5, 7b.

Goat and goatherds: ID1-2.

God: IB1, IVA4, B, 9, Gen. Concl., see also 'myth', 'astro-
    nomy', 'demiourgos'.

Gourmandise: IIIB3n86-87.

Grape: IB2n12.

"Grasshopper": see 'cicada'.

Habit: IIA4n24, B5.

Hair: ID1, IIIA3a, B2, IVA2, B2n75, 3, 5, 7.

Halcyon bird: ID1.

Hand: ID1, IIIA3ci, B3b, IVB2-3, 5, 7, 8d.

Head: ID1.

Health: IB1.

Hearing: IIIA3a, cii, B2, see also 'ear', 'sensitive soul'.

Heart: ID3n137, C1, 4, IIB2, 5, *IIIA1*, 3, IVA2, B8a.

Heat and cold: ID1, IIB4, 6, IIIA1, 3, IVA5b, B2, 7, 8n108,
    Gen. Concl. see also '*pneuma*', 'elements'.

Heavenly bodies: see 'astronomy'.

Hecatolization: ID, 2, n120.

Hedgehog: ID1.

Hermaphroditic: IIA4n17.

Heron: ID1.

Hexis: see 'habit'.

Hierarchy: see 'scale of nature'.

Hieroscopia: ID1.

Hippomanes: ID1.

Hippopotamus: ID1.

Homoiomeries and anomoiomeries: ID1, IIB7a, C2, n63, *IIIA3*, B1.

Homonymous/synonymous: IIB5, IVB8a.

Homunculus: IIA1n6.

Hoopoe: ID1.

Hooves: see 'horn'.

Horn: ID1, IIIA3b, IVB3.

Horse and horsebreeder: ID1, n112, 2, IIIB1-2.

Hou heneka: IB3, IIIB3, IVA2, see also 'teleology'.

Housebuilder: IB3, IIB3, IVB8.

Housekeeper: IIIA1, IVB3, 9.

Hybris bird: ID2.

Hyena: ID1n40, 2.

Hyle: see 'matter'.

Hylomorphism: IE, IIB5n34, 7d, 8, IIIA3cii.

Ibis: ID1.

Immortality: IIB7c, see also 'astronomy'.

Individual: IIB3n33, see also '*ousia*'.

Induction: IB, see also 'observation'.

Infinity: IVB6; Infinite regress: IIIA1.

Insect: IIA4, n17, n21, IIIB1, 3, *f*, n97, n100-101, IVA5a,
     Bn55, 3, 7, 9.

Instrumentism: IE.

Introspection: IIIA3cii.

Irrigation: IIIA3b, see also 'garden'.

Kanabos: IIIA3n46, IVB8a.

Kata-: IIIB3n99, IVB3, n77.

'Katachresis': IIIB3f, n99, IVBn55, *B1-3*, n76, 7.

Kidney: IIIA3b, IVB3n91.

Kinēsis: IIB3, see also 'movement'.

Konōps: see 'mosquito'.

Korē: IIIB1, see also 'eye'.

Krasis: see 'blend'.

Land animal/water animal: ID1, IIIB3b.

Lantern: IIIB1.

Larva: IIC2, see also 'egg'.

Learning: IIB5, see also 'teaching'.

Lesbos: ID1, E.

Light: IIB7e, IIIB1, see also 'vision'.

Linguistic argument, analysis: IB2, D1, IVA2.

Lion: ID1, IVB3.

Liver: ID1n116, see also 'viscera'.

Lobster: see 'crustacea'.

Local movement: see 'movement'.

Location: IIB7c, C1, IIIA3a.

Logic: IC2, see also 'syllogism', 'deductive model'.

Logos: IC3, D1, IIA3, B1, 4, 7c, C5, IIIA3, B2, summary, IV
    intro., A1-5, B3, 6n101, 8c, see also 'species',
    '*eidos*', 'proportion'.

Lung: ID1, 3, IIIA3b, IVB6.

Lyceum: ID1, E, Gen. Concl.

Macedonia: ID2, E.

Male: see 'female'.

Mammae: IIIB2, IVB7.

Mammalia: IIA2, n11, see also 'vivipara' and the various
    species.

Manger: IIIA3b.

Manteis: ID1.

Marrow: ID1, IIIA3ci.

Martichoras: ID1.

Mathematics: ID1, III intro., IVA2.

Matter: IB3, C3, n28, II intro., A3, n14, 4, B1, 4, 7, C1,
    2, IIIA, 1-3, B1, IVA, *4*, 5, n43, B3, n79, 8, n106, 9,
    Gen. Concl.

    Material necessity: IIB1, IVA1, see also 'necessity'.

Mean, the: IIA2, IIIA3a, B1, see also 'proportion', 'logos'.

Measuring techniques: III intro.

Mechanism and machine: IB1, IIB3, n32, IIIA, 2, IVA, *4*, B7,
    Gen. Concl.

    Mechanical necessity: IVA1, 4, B7, see also 'necessity'.

Medicine: ID1, IIA4, C5, IIIA1n21, IVA2, B8e, n111, see also
    'Hippocrates' in Index II.

Menstrual fluid and menstruation: ID1, *IIA2-3*, C4, and *passim*
    IIIA, 3a, IVB3, 7, Gen. Concl., see also 'residue'.

Mesentery: IVA2.

Metamorphosis: IIIB3f.

Metaphysics: IE, II intro., A4, B3, IVA, see also '*Met.*' in
    Index III.

Meteorology: ID1, IIIA3a-b, n103.

Method: ID3, E, III intro.

Microscope: III intro., summary.

Midwife: ID1.

Milk: ID1, IIA3, IIIA, IVB7.

Mind: IE, IIB7, *e*, C4, IIIA3a, n47, IVA5b, B3, 9, Gen. Concl.

Mole: IVA5b.

Mollusc: see 'testacea'.

Monism: IE.

Monkey: see 'primate'.

Monster: see 'terata'.

Moon: ID2, IIIA3a, see also 'astronomy'.

Mosquito: IIIB3f, n94.

Movement, local: IIIA3ci, B1n67, IVA5b.
    ---, source of: IB, C3, IIA4, B1-3, *C3*, 4, IIIA, 1-2,
    IVA2, 4, B2, Gen. Concl., see also '*archē*'.
    Mover, Prime: ID1n68, IVB, see also 'God'.

Mud: IIIA3b.

Mule: ID1-2, IIIB2, IVA5b.

Murex: ID2, see also 'testacea'.

Muscle: IIIA3ci.

Myth: ID1, IIB8, III intro., IVA3, 5b-c, B, 9.

Nature (*physis*): IB2, C3, IIA4n22, B7e, C1, 4, IIIA3, B1, 3d,
    IV, Gen. Concl., and *passim*.
    "... does nothing in vain" *etc.*: IIIB1, IVB6-8.
    Natural directions: see 'directions'.
    ---, scale of: see 'Scale of Nature'.
    see also 'art', 'analogy'.

Necessity: IIIB1, C5, IIIA1-3, B3, *IVA*, B3, and *passim*, Gen.
     Concl.
Nerve: IIIA1.
Neuroi: IIIA3ci.
Nictitating membrane: IIIB1.
Nobility: see 'value'.
Nose: IVB7, see also 'smell'.
Nutrition, nutritive soul: IIB7b, C1, IIIA1, 3ci, IVA2, B7,
     9, see also 'food', 'digestion'.
Nyktalops: IIIB1.

Obeliskolychnion: IIB3f, IVB3.
Observation: ID, 1, 3, IIA4n20-21, B6, C1, III intro., A3a,
     summary, B, Gen. Concl., see also 'description'.
Obstacle avoidance: II concl.
Octopus: ID, 1-2, IVA5a, B3, see also 'cephalopod'.
Offspring: II, IVB7, see also 'generation', 'children'.
Omentum: IVB3.
Ontogeny: IC1b.
Organ, organic part: IA, C3, IIB5, 7-8, C4, *III passim*, IVB1,
     Gen. Concl.
     --- of perception: III intro., see also 'sensation',
     'eyes', 'ears', 'nose', 'tongue', 'flesh'.
Organicism: IB1, IIIA summary, IV intro., B9.
Organizer: IIA1, B2, 7e.
Ostrich: IVA5b.
Ousia (entity): IC1, II intro., B3, 5, C5, IIIA3b, B1-2,
     IVA2, n25, 5n38, a, B3, 9, Gen. Concl.
Ovipara: IIA4n19, C2, IIIB1-3, see also 'egg'.
Owl: IIIB1n73.
Oxen, backwards-grazing: ID1, see also 'cattle'.

Painting: IVB8a, see also 'art'.
Pangenesis: ID1, n78, n106, IIA1-2, IVB8a.
Pantheism: see 'myth', 'religion', 'God'.
Panther: ID2.

Para-: IVB4, n92.

'Parachresis': IVB4.

Paradigm: II intro., III intro.

'Parakatachresis': IVB5.

Part: IIB3, C1, *III*, Gen. Concl., see also 'organ'.

Parthenogenesis: IIA2, 4, C2.

Partridge: ID2.

Passive: see *'dynamis'*, 'female'.

Pephyke: IIIA3cii, IVA3, B2.

Perception: see 'sensation'.

Perittōma: IIA2n10, see also 'residue'.

Personal verb: IVB7, see also 'nature', 'teleology of in-
      tention'.

Persuasive argument: IB.

Phallus: IIA4n21.

Pharmaka, pharmakides: ID1, n81, see also 'medicine'.

Philology: IVB1, 3n77, see also 'text'.

Philosophy: IE, IIB5, IIIA3ci, and *passim*.

Phylogeny: IC1b, see also 'evolution'.

Physikoi, physiologoi: ID1.

Physis: see 'nature'.

Pig: ID1, IVA5b, n43.

Pinna: ID2, see also 'testacea'.

Plant: IIB7n41, IIIA3b.

Pneuma: ID1, n78, n107, E, II intro., B6, *7*, 8, C2-3, Concl.,
      IIIA1 , 3, B3f, IVA5n40-41, B2, 7-8, Gen. Concl.

Poikila: IIIB3b, see also 'color'.

'Point': See 'teleology'.

Polarity: III intro., A3a, IVA5b, c, see also 'analogy',
      'directions'.

Polydactylous: IVB5.

Positivism: ID.

Potency: see *'dynamis'*.

Potentiality: IVA3, see also *'dynamis'*.

Power: see *'dynamis'*.

378

Predecessor: see 'criticism'.

Prediction: ID1, IVA3.

Preformationism: IIA1, B7n52, IIIA1, n17.

Presocratic: see 'criticism', and Index II.

Primate: IVA5b.

Priority,metaphysical: IVA2, see also 'a priori', 'meta-
     physics'.

Probability: IC2, see also 'inductive argument'.

Process: Gen. Concl., see also 'change', 'movement',
     'genesis'.

Prognostication: see 'predication'.

Proportion: ID2, IIC4, III intro., A2, 3a, B1, see also
     'logos', 'symmetry'.

Psyche: see 'soul', 'insect'.

Psychology: IIIA3cii, see also 'soul'.

Pubes: ID1.

Puppets: see 'automata'.

Purpose: see 'teleology'.

Pygmies: ID1n57.

Quadruped: IIIA3b, ci, IVB5, 7.

Quality/quantity: IIB7e, C2, III intro., A3n53.

Rain: IIIA3a.

Random: see 'chance'.

Ratio: see 'logos', 'proportion'.

Rational: see 'mind'.

Reductionism: IIC2, IVB9.

Regularity: II concl., IVA4, see also 'probability'.

Religion: see 'myth'.

Rennet: IIA3-4, B7-8.

Reproduction: see 'generation'.

Reptile: ID1, IIIB3b, d, n86, IVA5a, B2, 3n81.

Resemblance: IIA1, 4, C5, IVB9.

Residue: ID2, IIA2-3, C1-5, IIIA, IVA3, B3, 7, 8a, n106.

Respiration: ID1n101, IIIA3b, IVA2, n31, 5, B3, 5, see also
     'pneuma'.

Rhetoric: IB2, IIB1, IVB9.

Rheumata: IIIA3a.

Rhinoceras: ID1, IVB3.

Right and left: see 'directions'.

Salamander: ID2.

Scale of nature: IIC2, 5, IIIA3ci, B3f, *IVA5b*, n47.

Science: ID, E, III summary, and *passim*.

Sculptor: IC3, D1, see also 'art'.

Sea-anemone: IVA5b.

Sea-squirt: IVAB , n42.

Sea urchin: ID1, IIIB3f, IVB2.

Sea water: ID, IIIB1.

Seal: IB1, *IIIB2*, 3b, IVA5b, n40, n46, B7n103.

Selachia (sharks, rays): ID1, 3, IIIB3n87, IVB3, 7.

Sēmeion: IB2n11, IIIA3b, IVA5a.

Semen: ID1, n78, IIA3, B2, 5-8, see also *'sperma'*.

Sensation, sensitive soul: ID1, n68, IIB5, 7b, IIIA1, 3a, *c*,
      B, IVA2, B6n101, 7, see also particular senses and
      sense organs.

Separable (*choriston*): IIB7c.

Serpent: see 'reptile'.

Sex: ID1, IIA2, B1, IIIB1, IVB7, see also 'female', 'testes',
      'copulation'.

Shark: see 'selachia'.

Sheep and shepherd: ID1n112, 2, IIIB3b.

Shellfish: see 'testacea'.

'Simple necessity': see 'necessity'.

Sinew: see *'neuroi'*.

Skeleton: IB3, IIIB1, see also 'bone', 'backbone'.

Skepticism: ID1-2, Gen. Concl.

Skin: IIIB1.

Sleep: IIIA3a.

Smell, sense of: ID2, IIIA3a, cii, B3f, IVB3, see also
      'sensation', 'nose'.

Snail: see 'testacea'.

Snake: see 'reptile'.

Soul (*psychē*): ID1, IIA5, B5, *7*, C1, IIIA1n14, IVA5b, B9,
      see also 'nutrition', 'generation', 'sensation', 'lo-
      cal movement', 'mind'.

Species: IC1a, 2, IIB7e, IIIA3c, B *passim*, n101, *IVA5b*,
      B6n99, 9, Gen. Concl., see also '*eidos*', '*logos*',
      '*ousia*'.

Speech, power of: *IIIB3a*, n88, IVB2-3, 7.

Sperma, spermatic secretion: IIA1-2, *B3-8*, C4-5, IVA2, B7,
      Gen. Concl., see also 'semen', 'menstrual fluid'.

Sphere: IIIA1, see also 'astronomy'.

Spider: IB3, D1, IIIB3f.

Spine: see 'backbone'.

Spleen: IIIA3b, see also 'viscera'.

Sponge and spongediver: ID2, IIIA3ci, IVA5b.

Spontaneous generation: ID2, IIB7e, IIIA1, B3f, n101, IVB6,
      Gen. Concl., see also 'generation'.

Squid: IVB3, n81, see also 'cephalopod'.

Stag: see 'deer'.

Stageira: ID2, E.

Starfish: ID2.

Sting: IIIB3, see also 'weapon'.

Stoic: IVB9, Gen. Concl.

Stomach: IIIA3b, IVB3, see also 'nutrition', 'viscera'.

Style: IE.

Sun: see 'astronomy'.

Swallow: IB3.

Syllogism: IB2, C2, IIIA3ci, see also 'fallacy'.

Symmetry, *symmetros*: III intro., B3b, see also 'proportion',
      'polarity'.

Symphyēs: IIIB3d.

Symphyton: IIB7c, IIIA1, n22, 3cii.

Symptomata: IB2, n11, IIIA3a, IVA3, n36.

Syntegma: ID1, IIA2n9, IVB7, see also 'residue'.

Synthesis: IIa1.

Systasis: IIIA, 3cii.

Tail: IIIA3b, IVB3, 5.

Tapeworm: ID1.

Taste, sense of: IIIA3a, cii, B3, n85, IVB2-3, see also
    'tongue'.

Taxis: IVB6n101.

Taxonomy: see 'classification'.

Teaching: IB3n14, D2, IVB8e.

Teeth: IB1, D1, IIIB3e, IVB3, 6-7.

Tektōn: see 'carpenter'.

Teleology: IB, IIA1, B, C2, 4, Concl., III intro., A2-3, B,
    IV *passim*, *Gen. Concl.*
        --- of intention: IB, IIIA3ci, IVB6-9, Gen. Concl.
        ---, external: IVB7.

Temperature: IIIB3f, see also 'heat'.

Terata: ID1, IIC5, concl., *IVA3*, 4, 5n41.

Testacea: ID1, 2n119, IIB7n56, IIIB3f, n95, IVA5b-c, B6-7.

Testes: ID1, IVB7.

Tettix: see 'cicada'.

Text (suggested readings): IIB5, n34-35, B7n50, n52, n56,
    C1n60, 5n74-75, IIIA3c, Bn63, 2, 3d, f, n90, IVA2,
    n24, n29, B1, 3n82, 4n93.

Theory, theoretical: ID, 1, IIIA3cii, IVA1-2.

Thermometer: III intro.

Thrace: ID2n127.

Thyrathen: IIB7c, IIIA1n17.

Tongue: IIIB2, *3*, n88, n97, IVB2-3, 7, Gen. Concl., see also
    'taste', 'speech'.

Tool: IC3, IVB2, 9, see also 'organ'.

Touch, sense of: IIIB3, IVB7, see also 'flesh', 'sensation'.

Traducianism: IIIA1n14,

Transmigration: IIIA1n14, see also 'myth'.

Turtle: IVB6.

Umbilicus: ID1, n78, IIIA.

Uniform part: see 'homoiomeries'.

Up and down: see 'directions'.

382

Uterus: II, IVB3, 7.

Utility: IIIB2, IVA5a, *B*, *6*, see also 'function', 'value', 'katachresis', 'teleology'.

Value: IB1, IIB7e, IIIB1, 3, IVA2, *5*, n48, see also 'utility', 'teleology'.

Variation: IIIB.

Vertebra: see 'backbone'.

Vertebrate: see 'blooded'.

Vestigial: see '*sēmeion*'.

Veterinary medicine: ID1, see also 'medicine'.

'Vinegar fly': see 'mosquito'.

Viscera: IIIA3b, IVB3, 6.

Vision: ID1, 2n119, IIIA3a, cii, *B1*, see also 'eyes'.

Vitalism: IIA4, Gen. Concl.

Vivipara: ID3n138, IIA4n20 and *passim*, IIIA, B2-3, IVB3, see also 'mammalia'.

Vivisection: ID3, Gen. Concl.

Vulture: ID1n40.

Water animal: see 'land animal', 'element'.

Wax: IIA4, IVB8b.

Weapon: IIIA3ci, IVB3, 7, n105, see also 'sting', 'horn'.

Weasel: ID1.

Weaver: ID1, IVB8n110, see also 'art'.

Wine: IDn38.

Wolf: ID1.

Woman: see 'female'.

Yin and yang: see 'polarity', 'myth'.

Index II: Proper Names

This index contains references to authors noted by name, to
ancient writers noted by Aristotle, and to other persons
otherwise mentioned. A few of the names may refer to non-
existent people.

Bourgey, L.: IDn31, n33, 3n135, En146.

Boyle, R.: IVA4.

Brangham, A.N.: IIIB3f, n98, n101.

Brunel, J.: IVB3n77.

Burton, J.: IIIB3n100.

Burtt, E.A.: IVA4, n37.

Cain, A.J.: IB1n5.

Canfield, J.V.: IB1n6.

Capelle, W.: IIIB3n101.

Carteron, H.: IVA1.

Case, T.: IE, n139, n143.

Charlton, W.: IC3n28, IVA1, n13, n18, A3.

Cherniss, H.: IDn31, D1, n40, n42, n53, n71, n103, 3n135,
      IIA1n7, concl., IIIA3n50, IVA1n6.

Chevalier, J.: IVA1n18.

Clarke, E.: IIIA3an25.

Collingwood, R.G.: IVB9n112.

Copernicus: IVA4.

Coriscos: ID1.

Cornford, F.M.: IVA1, n9, 5n40, B, n56, n59.

Critias: ID1n74.

Darwin, C.: IB3n13, IIIBsummary, Gen. Concl.

Davey, K.G.: IIA4n21, IIIB3n100.

Democritus: IB1, 2n9, D, 1, n68, n70, n90, n102, n105,
      IIC5n71, IIIintro., IV intro., A1-3, B2, 6, 8d, Gen.
      Concl.

Demosthenes: IVB1, n63-65, 3n83.

Descartes: IIB7e, IIIA3ci, IVA4, Gen. Concl.

Dijksterhuis, E.J.: IVA4n37.

Diocles of Carystus: ID1, n78, 3n138.

Diogenes of Apollonia: ID1, IIB7b, IIIA1n21, 3b.

Diogenes Laertius: ID1n58.

Dorier, A., and G. Bellon: IIIB3n92.

Dowdeswell, W.H.: IIIB3n102.

Heradorus of Heraclea: ID1.
Hero of Alexandria: IIB3n32.
Herodotus: ID, n36, 1, n42-52, n56, n61, IIIB3d, IVB1, n60.
Hesiod: ID1, IIB6, IVA5e.
Hesychius: IIIA3n46.
Hett, W.S.: IIA2n10.
Hintikka, J.: IVA1n17.
Hippo: ID1n74.
Hippocrates and Hippocratic writers: ID1, n72, n73, *n78*,
      n81, 3n138, IIA1, n3, C5n71, IIIAn5, 3a, B1, IVn1,
      A3, Gen. Concl.
Homer: ID1, n58-68.
Hume, D.: IVA4.
Huxley, T.H.: ID3n137, IIIA3b.

Ibn Sina: Gen. Concl.
Isocrates: IVB1, n62.

Jaeger, W.: ID, 1, n79, n110, 2n131, E, n144, IIn1, B7n58,
      IIIA3n49, n50, IVn1, Bn57.

Käsner, A.: Gen. Concl. n2.
Kahn, C.: IC3n30.
Kepler, J.: IVA4, Gen. Concl.
King, H.R.: IC3n28.
Kirk, G.S., and J.E. Raven: IVBn56.
Ktesias: ID1, n54.

Lameere, W.: ID1n57, 2n131, En145.
LeBlond, J.-M.: IC2, Dn31, n34, E, n139, n146, III intro.n1,
      IVA1, n8, 2, n24, n27, 5n43, B2n69.
Lee, H.D.P.: IDn33, 2n132, E, n139, n145.
Leibniz, G.W.: IIIA1n17, 2n23.
Leophanes: ID1, IIC5n71.
Lesky, A.: ID2n125.
Lesky, E.: IIA1n3, n6.
Leucippos: IB2, n9.

Lewes, G.H.: ID, n31, n32, n37, 2n139, IIIA3b.

Littré, E.: ID1n78.

Lloyd, A.C.: IIB3n33.

Lloyd, G.E.R.: IIA1n7, C2n62, IIIn2, A3n26, B1, IVA5n49,
    n53.

Lones, T.E.: IDn31, 2n130, 3n134.

Louis, P.: IDn31, n35, 1n62, E, n145, IIn1, A2n8, 3n14,
    B5n34, 7n55, IIIB2, 3d, f, n91, n94, n99, IVA2n30, B2,
    3n79.

Lovejoy, A.O.: IVA5n40.

Lulofs, H.J.D.: IEn146, IIA2n8, C5n75, IVB3n82.

Lysias: IVB1, n61.

Mandelbaum, M.: IB1n7, C2, n27.

Manquat, M.: IDn31, 1n41, IIIB3d.

Mansion, A.: IB2n8, En139, IVA1.

Mansion, S.: IVA1, n7.

Mendel, G.: IIC5.

Merlan, P.: IVA1n17.

Meulen, J. van der: IIIA3n27.

Meyer, J.B.: IIIB1n63.

Michael of Ephesus: ID3n135.

Monod, J.: IVA2.

Moraux, P.: IDn31, n55, En149, IIB7, n39, c, n52-53, e.
    IIIA3n47, IVB3n82.

Morrison, J.S.: IIA1n6.

Mourelatos, A.D.P.: ID3n28.

Musaeus: ID1.

Nagel, E.: IB1n6, C1a, n21-22, 2n25.

Needham, J.: IIA1n6.

Newton, I.: IVA4, Gen. Concl.

Nuyens, F.: IE, n146, IIB5n34-35, n37, 7n44, IIIA3n53.

Ogle, W.: IIIB3d, IVA2, n30, 5a, B3n79.

Orpheus: ID1, IIIA3b.

Owens, J.: IIB3n33, 7c, n48, IVA2n24.

388

Rossi, P.: IVA4, n37.
Rostand, J.: IIIB3n102.
Ryle, G.: IEn145, IVB1n68.

Sarton, G.: IIA2n11.
Sextus Empiricus: ID1n102.
Simonides: ID1.
Socrates: ID1, IVA2.
Solmsen, F.: IB2n8, C1n22, 3n28, IIB7d, n51-52, IIIA3n48,
        IVA1n12, Bn59.
Sorabji, R.: IIIA3n60.
Spemann, H.: IIA1n5.
Speusippos: ID1.
Steckerl, F.: ID1n110.
Stesichorus: ID1.
Strattis: ID1n70.
Syennesis: ID1.

Taylor, A.E.: IVA5n40.
Thales: ID1n74, IIB7n55.
Themistius: IIB7n49.
Theophrastus: ID1, IIB7c, IIIB1, Gen. Concl.
Thompson, D.W.: ID, n37, 1n47, n54, n62, n72, n111, E, n143,
        IIA4n17, IIIA3n46, B2.
Toland, J.: IVA4.
Tonelli, G.: IIIA2n23, IVA4, n37, n50.
Torraca, L.: IIB3n32, IIIA3n49.
Torrey, H.B.: IC1n23.
Toulmin, S.: IB2n10.
Tracy, T.: ID, IIIA1n6, 3b.

Verbeke, G.: IIIA1n14, n21.
Verdenius, W.J.: IIIB3n104.

Watts, A.: IVA5n50.
Weiss, H.: IVA1, n6.
Wieland, W.: IVA1n6.

Wili, W.: IIIA1n21.
Wittgenstein, L.: IVA1n17.
Woodbridge, F.J.E.: IVB9n112.

Xenocrates: ID1, n90.
Xenophon: ID2, n125.

Zürcher, J.: ID1, n109.

Index III: Passages in Aristotle

This is an index of references which we make to the text of
Aristotle. The works are listed here in the order in which
they appear in the Berlin edition; titles are abbreviated
according to usual practice, and citations are to chapters
of that edition rather than to the standard page numbers,
for the sake of simplicity and brevity.

(*Phys.* II) 2: IIC3n66.

      3: IVA5n39.

      6: IB2.

      8: IB2, 3, IIIA3n35, ci, IVA3n33, B3n80,7n103.

      9: *IVA1*, n5, Gen. Concl.

  III.1: II intro.

   IV.1-5: IIB7c.

     5: IIIA1.

    V.: II intro.

  VII.2: IIB2n29.

    3: IB1, n4, IIA4.

 VIII.1: IB2, n10.

GC: IE, IVA1n15.

   I.4: *IIC2*

    5: IIB7c.

    7: IIC5n76.

  II.1: IC3n28, II intro.

    3: IIIAn5.

    8: IIIAn5.

    9: IC3n29, IVA5a.

   10: IIB1, IVA3n35.

   11: IVA1-2.

Cael.:   IVA5b.

   I.3: IVB1.

    4: IVB6n97.

    8: IVA5n51.

  II.2: IVA5c, n49, n53.

    5: IVB6n99.

    8: IVB6.

   11: IVB6n97.

  III: ID1n90, IVA5n51.

    1: Gen. Concl.

    2: IB2.

    6: IC3n28.

(Cael.) IV: IIC2n62.

    4: IC3n28.

Meteor. (Mete): ID3n132

   I.3: IIIA1n20.

    9: IIIA3b.

    12: IIIA3n39.

    14: IIIB3n103.

  II.3: IDn38.

    7: ID1.

    9: IIIA1n20.

  IV.3: IIIA1.

    4: ID2n132.

De An.:   IE

   I.1: III. Intro., A1n11.

    2: ID1, n68, n74, n82, n84, n88, n91, n100, n104

      n 107, IIC1n59.

    3: ID1n57, n70, n84-85, n91, n104.

    4: ID1n90, n96, n104, IIIA1n11, 3ci.

    5: ID1n69, n74, n90, n96, n100, n104, IIC1n59, IIIA3ci.

  II.1: IC3, En148, IIA4, B7b, n45, n55, IIIA3n30, IVB8b.

    2: IIB7n45, IVB2n23.

    4: IB, C3, D1n+7, IIB1, 5n35, 7n45, concl., IVA5n44,

      n52, b9.

    5: IIB5.

    7: IIB74, IVB2n71.

    8: IIIA3n32, cii, B1n64, 3n83, IVB3, n86.

    9: IIIA3n34, n58, B.

   10: IIIA3n34.

   11: IIIB3n85.

   12: IIIB1, 3f.

 III.1: IIIA3n32, IVA5b.

    2: ID1n75.

    3: ID1n68, n100.

   4-6: IIA3a, IIB7c.

    4: ID1n107, IIB7c.

(*De An.* III) 6: ID1n100.

  12: IIIA3n58.

  13: IIIB3a.

Parva Naturalia: IE.

Sens.: ID1n95, IIIA3cii.

  1: ID1n77, III intro, B.

  2: ID1n91, n100, n104, En148, IIIA1n10, 3n30-34, cii, B1n65, 3n85.

  3: ID1n84.

  4: ID1n75, n100, n104, IIIA3n58.

  5: ID1n70, n82, n84, IIIA3cii, IVB3n87, 4n92.

  6: ID1n100, En148.

Mem.: ID1n91.

  2: IVA1n3, 5n47.

Somn. 2: IIIA1n10-11, n22.

  3: ID3n135, IIIA1n7, 3n36, n38, n44, 5n47.

Insomn. 2: IIIA3cii, IVB3n84.

Div. Somn.: ID1-2.

  1: IB2n11, D1n79.

  2: ID1n70, n104.

Long. 5: IIA2n10.

  6: IVA5n47.

Juv. 3: IIIA1n6-7, 3n44, IVB8n111.

  4: IVA2n23.

  5: ID1n82, IIIA3n44.

Resp.: IE, IIIA3b.

  2: ID1n88, n104, n107, D2.

  3: ID1n88.

  4: ID1n104.

  5: ID1n91.

  7: ID1n101.

  8: IIIA1n8, n11, IVB3n86.

  9: IIIB3f.

  11: IIIB3n83, IVB2, 3n86.

(*Resp.*): 12: IIIA3n39.

14: ID1n101.

20: IIIA1, n8.

21: ID1n77, IVA2n31, B8e.

HA: IA, D, E, IVA5n47.

I.1: ID1n43, IIIA3ci, IVB8e.

5: ID1n48, IIIA3n49, B3f.

9: IIIA3b, IVA5b.

10: IIIB1.

11: ID1, n43, IIIB1n75, n76, 2.

16: ID1n72, IIIA3a, n44.

17: ID1n115, n117, 3, n135, IIIA3n38.

II.1: ID1, n43, n44, n47, IIIA3n49, B2n80.

3: ID1, 3n137.

5: IIIA3n46.

6: IIIB3a.

7: ID1n47, IIIA3b.

10: ID1n43, IIIB1, 3e.

11: IIIB1, 3d, n90.

12: IIIB1n68, 3c.

13: IIIB3e.

14: IDn35.

15: ID1n43, IIIB2n81.

17: ID1n43, n115, IIIA3n44, B3b, n89.

III.1: IDn35, 1n43, 3n135.

2: ID1, n71, IIIA1n7.

3: ID1, n67, n71, IIIA3b, n38.

4: ID1n71, IIIA3b.

5: IIIA3n48.

6: IIA3n13.

7: ID1n43, IVB2n73.

11: IDn35, n49.

17: IIIB3b.

19: IIIA1n6.

20: ID2, IIIB2.

(*HA* III) 22: ID1n42, n53.

    IV.1: IDn35, n37, 3n135, IIIB3f.

      2: IIIB1n65.

      4: ID3n135, n136, IIIA3n44, B1n65, 3n93, n96.

      5: ID1, IIIB3f.

      7: ID, 2n118, *IIIB3f*, n93, n98, n101.

      8: ID2n119, IIIB3e.

      9: IIIB3a, c, d, n83.

     10: ID1.

     11: IIA4n17.

    V.5: IDn36, 2n123.

      6: ID.

      8: ID1.

     12: ID, 2n120, IIIB2.

     15: ID2, IIIB3n96.

     17: ID2n122, 3n136.

     19: ID1, n57, D2, n131, IIIB3f, n101.

     20: ID1n59.

     21: ID1n60, 2, n129.

     22: ID2n129, IIIB3n95.

     30: ID2, IIIB3f.

     31: ID1n51.

     32: ID2.

     33: ID1n43.

  VI: IIA2n11 (18-37).

      2: ID2.

      3: ID1, IIIA3n37.

      4: IDn35.

      5: ID1n40.

      6: ID1.

      8: ID3.

      9: ID2.

     10: ID3, n135.

     11: ID3, n135.

     12: IDn35, 2, IIIB2n78, n81.

     13: ID1n111.

(*HA* VI) 14: IDn35, 1n111, 2n122.

    15: ID1n111, 2n122, IIIA3n39.

    16: IDn35, 1n111.

    17: ID2n122.

    18: IDn35, 1, 2, IIA2n11.

    19: ID2, IIIB3b.

    20: IIA2n11.

    21: ID1, 2.

    22: ID1, n81.

    23: ID2.

    25: ID2n126.

    28: ID1n62.

    29: ID1, 2.

    30: ID1n56.

    32: ID2.

    25: ID1.

    37: ID2.

VII.1: ID1

    2: ID1n73.

    3: ID1n73, 3n135.

    4: IDn35.

    7: IIIAn4, IVA1n20.

    8: IIIAn4.

    10: ID1.

VIII.1: In2, *IIIA3ci*, IVA5n41.

    2: IDn38, 1n43, n47, 2, n121, IIIB2n78.

    3: IIIB1n73.

    4: ID1n80.

    6: ID2n127, IIIB2n81.

    9: ID2.

    11: IIIB3f.

    12: ID1, n57, 2n124.

    13: ID2n122,3.

    15: ID1n43.

    19: ID1, 2n119, n122.

    20: ID2n122.

(*HA* VIII) 21: ID1n112 (21-26).

       28: IDn35, 1, n44, n51, n61.

   IX.1: ID1n57, n113, 2n131, IVB8e.

      3: ID2.

      4: ID2.

      5: ID1, n114, 2, IIIA3b.

      6: ID1, n43, n80.

      8: ID2n124.

      9: IIIB3c.

    12: ID1n40, n63, 2.

    13: ID1n50.

    15: IIIB3c.

    17: ID1n46.

    18: ID1.

    30: ID2n122.

    32: ID1, n66, IIIB1n73.

    34: ID1n57.

    36: ID1n54.

    37: ID2, IIIA3n42.

    38: ID3.

    39: ID1.

    40: ID2.

    44: ID1n64.

   49b: ID1.

PA: IA, n3, E, Gen. Concl.

   I: IE, III intro., n1.

    1: IB3, n15, n18, D1, n74, n78, n86, n96, n98, n102-
       103, IIA4n18-19, B3, IVA1, n5, n12, n14, *2*, 4, B3,
       n80, e, 6, 8.

    5: IB3, n15-16, D1n83, IVA1n14, B8a, d, n108.

   II: Gen. Concl.

    1: IB3n15, C3n28, IIC2, III intro., A1n12, *3b*,
       IVB7n105, 8d.

    2: ID1, n78, n83, IIIB1n63, IVB7n105.

    3: ID1n78, 3n135, IIB7n41, C2, IIIA3n43-44.

(*PA* II) 5: IIIA3ci, *B3F*.

     6: ID1n92, *IIIA3ci*, IVA1n3.

     7: IB3n16, D1n83, n84, IIA4n18, *IIIA3a*, b, *ci*, IVA1n3, 3, B7, 8n108.

     8: IIIA3n45, IVB7.

     9: IIIAn5, 3n46, IVA5n41, B2, n73, 3, 7n104, 8b.

    10: IIIA1n12, 3n24, n30-34, IVB6n101, 7.

    11: IIIB1n75-76.

    12: IIIB1n75, n77, *2*, 3c.

    13: *IIIB1*, n64-68, n73-74, IVBn55.

    14: IIIA3n24, n28, IVA1n3, 2, B3, 6n97, 8e.

    15: IIIB1, IVA1n3, B2n75.

    16: ID1n52, IIIA1n22, B3a, n83, n88, 4n94, IVB5.

    17: ID1n43, IIIA3n58, *B3*, n84, n86, n89, IVB2, n71.

III.1: IIIB3e, IVB3, n89, 6n98.

    2: ID3, IIIAn5, IVA1n3, B3, n79, n81, 7.

    3: IIIA1n12, 3b, B3a, IVA1n4, 5a, B7, 8e.

    4: ID1, n115, 3n135, IIIA1n6-7, n10, n13, 3b, n48, IVA2n23, B2, 3, n82, 6n101, 7.

    5: IB3n15, D3n135, IIIA3n24, b, n45, n56, IVB8d, n110.

    6: ID1n93, IIIA1n12, n22, 3b, *f*.

    7: *IIIA3b*, n54, IVA3, B6, 8n110.

    8: IVB6.

    9: ID1n112, 3n135, IIIA3b, B2n78, IVA1n3, B3, n91.

    10: ID1n68, IIIA3n37, IVA1n3, 2, n26, B7.

    11: IIIA1n12.

    12: IIIAn5.

    13: IIIA3n44.

    14: ID3n135, IVB3, 7.

IV.1: IIIAn5.

    2: ID1n94, n115, 3n135-136, n138, IIIB2n78, IVA3, B3, 8n110.

    3: IVA1n3, 3n32, 5a, B3.

    4: IIB7n41, IIIA3n43, B3f, IVA2.

    5: IDEn135, IIIA1n5, 3n44, B3f, n93, n95, IVA3n32, 5a-b, B2n70, 3n81-82, 6-7.

(*PA* IV) 6: IIIA3n43, B3f, IVA1n4, 5a, B3, n90, 8c.

8: ID3n135, IIIA3n42, IVA5b-c, B7n105.

9: IDn37, 1n79, IIIA3n42, IVA1n4, 5a, B2n75, 3, 7, 8n111.

10-13: IIIA3n49.

10: IB3n16, n17, ID1, n78, 3n135, IIB7n41, IIIA3n29, b, n42, ci, B3f, IVA5b, n47, c, B1-7, n72, n85, n95, n99-101.

11: ID1n43, IIIB1n73, n77, 3b, *d*, e, n89, IVA3n32, B3, n81, n98.

12: IIIAn3, n43, *3ci*, n97, IVA1n3, 3n32, 5n47, B3, 5n96, 6n98, n100, 7.

13: ID3n135, E, IIIB2n78, 3n87, IVB2-3, n85, 6n98, 7.

MA: IE, IIB7a, IIIA1n11, *3ci*, n49, IVA1.

1: IIIA3ci.

2: ID1n68, IIIA3n42.

3: ID1n68.

4: ID1n68.

7: IIB3n32, IIIA2n, 3n42, *ci*.

8: IIC1n61, IIIA3n41, *ci*, ii, n60, IVB2n73.

9: IIIA3ci.

10: IIIA1n22, 3n41.

11: IIIA1n10, 3n55.

IA: IE, IIIA1n11, 3n49.

2: III intro., n2, IVB6n99, 7n103.

4: IIB7n41, IIIB3f, IVA5c.

5: III intro.

8: IVB6n97.

10: IIIA3n42.

11: IVB2n73, 6, 8a, c.

12: IVB6.

14: IIIB1n65, n67, IVA5c, B3.

17: IVB3n85.

19: IIIB2n82, IVA5b, n44.

400

GA: IA n3, E, *II passim*, Gen. Concl.

  I: II intro.

     1: IC3n28, III intro., IVB6.

     2: IB3n16, C3, IIAn2.

     4: IVB6n100, 7, 8n110.

     5: IVA1n4, 5a.

     8: IVB7n103.

    10: ID1n101.

    11: ID3n135, IVB7n103, 9n114.

    15: IDn37, 2n120, IVA1n4, 5a, B7.

    16: IIIB3n94.

    17: ID1n78, n106, IIA1, IIIA1n17.

    18: IB3n15, D1, n70, n99, IIA1n4, n6, 2n10, 4n18, IVA5n45, B6-8, n109, n111.

    19: Id1, IIA2, C4.

    20: IIA3, n13-14, IVA5b.

    21: IB3n15, D2, IIA4, IVB8b, n107, n109, n111.

    22: IB3n15, IIA4, n18, C4, IIIA3n46, IVB7, 8b, n109-110.

    23: ID1n97, IVb6, 7n103-104.

 II: ID1n89, II intro.

     1: IB, 3n14, n16, C3, D1n69, *IIB1-5*, C4, n67, concl., III intro., A1n6, 2-3, n51, IVA1, n3, n14, 5a, n41, B6, n99, n107, n110, Gen. Concl.

     2: ID1n42, n53, n78, IIA3n13, *B6*, C2, 4n68, IIIA1-2, IVB7.

     3: ID1n78, 2, En148, IIA4, *B7*, n41, n47, n50, C4, IIIA3cii, IVA5n41, n45.

     4: IB3n16, D1, n78, 3n135, II intro., An2, 3n13, 4n18, B7n40, *C1*, 4, n69, IIIA, n4, 1n6, n13, 3a, n43, IVA1n3, n20, 2n23, B3, 6n98, 7-9, n114.

     5: ID1, IIA4n17, n20, B3n32, C4, n69, IIIA, 1n6, *2*, 3n51, IVB6n97.

     6: IB3n15-16, D1, n75, n77-78, IIA4n18, C4, n69, IIIA, n3, 1, n6, n10-11, n18, n21, 3a, n24, n31, n45-47, *cii*, IVA2, B2n69, n75, 3, n82, 6n98, 7n104, 8-9.

(*GA* II) 7: ID1, n78, 3n135, n136, n138, IIB7n41, IIIA, 3n24, b, n43, B3.

    8: ID1, IVA5b, n47.

III. 1: ID1n85, 2, IIA4n20, IVB3, n85, n87.

    2: ID1n85, IIB5n36, IVB3n82.

    4: IIB5n36, 7n40, IVA1n3, 3, B3, n85, 9n114.

    5: IDn36, 1-2, n123, IIA4n17.

    6: ID1, n40, n76.

    8: IDn37.

    9: IVB9.

    10: ID2, IIA4n17, C2, IIIA3n39, IVB3, 6n101, 7n105.

    11: IB3n15, D2, *IIB7e*, C2, IIIA1, n19, IVB7n104, 8n106.

IV: ID1, IVA1.

    1: ID1, n76, n78, n87, n99, n106, 3n136, n138, IIAn2, C5, IVB6n100, 7-8.

    2: ID1n78, 2, C5, IVB6n101.

    3: ID1, n85, n99, n106, IIB7b, C4n70, *5*, B1, IVA3, 5n41, n44, B9.

    4: IB2, n8, n12, D1, n78, 3n136, IIA3n13, B7n40, IIIA1n12, 3, IVA5n41, n43-44, B3, n85, 7, 9.

    6: IIB7n41, IIIA3n43, IVA5n43-45, B8n107.

    7: IVA5n44, B7.

    8: ID1, n78, IIA3n13, IVA1n3, n20, 5n43-44, 8n107, 9n114.

    10: IIC3n66, IIIA3a, IVA1, B6.

V: IVA3.

    1: ID1n75, n95, n100, 3n148, III intro., A3n30, *cii*, *B1*, n72, *2*, IVA1n3, 3, *5a*, B3, 6n101, 9n114.

    2: IIIA1n12, 3n32, n56, B1, IVB7n103.

    3: IIIA3a, n28, IVA5n47, B7.

    5: ID1n65.

    6: IIIB3b.

    7: IEn148, IIIA3n48, IVB8n110.

    8: IB1, 3n16, n18, D1, IVA3, B6, 8c, n111.

Met.:   IA, E.

    Alpha (I).1: IIIA3n39.

      2: IIIA3n51.

      3: IC2.

      4: ID1.

      5: IVA5c, n49.

      6: IIn1.

    'little alpha' (II).2: IIA2n9.

    Gamma (IV).5: ID1n68.

    Delta (V).1: IIn1, IIIA1n6, 9.

      2: IVA5n39.

      4: II concl., IVB3n80, 9, n112.

      5: IVA1, n5, 2.

      6: IIA3n14, IVA5n39.

      8: IVA5n39, B9.

      9: IVA5n39.

     12: IC3, IIA4n19.

     13: IVA5n39.

     20: IIA4n24.

     24: IIA2n9.

     29: IVA5n39.

     30: IVA3.

    Epsilon (VI).1: IVA2.

      2: IVA1, 3, n33.

    Zeta (VII).1: IC1a.

      2: Gen. Concl.

      7: IIA4n19, B2, IVA5n39, Gen. Concl.

      8: IIn1, B2, Gen. Concl.

      9: IIB2, IVA5n44, Gen. Concl.

     13: II intro.

     14: II intro.

     16: IVA5n44.

     17: IIA1n4.

    Eta (VIII).4: IB2n8, IIn1, A3n14.

      6: IIB7n48.

Theta (IX).1: IC3n30.

  2: IIC5.

  7: IIn1, A3n14, B3n33, C2.

  8: IC3n30, IIB2, C4n68, IVA5b.

Iota (X).1: IIB7c.

  3: IVA5n39.

Kappa (XI).7: IVA5n39.

Lambda (XII): III intro.

  2: IVA1n15, 5c.

  3: IIn1, A4n19.

  4: IIn1, A4n19.

  5: IIB7n58, C3n66.

  6-7: IIn1, IVA1, n5.

  10: IIB1n26, IIIA3ci, n54, IVA5b.

EN: IB.

III-IV: IIIA3n54.

III.1: IVA3.

VI.7: IIB7n58.

VIII.12: IVA5n45.

X.9:   IVB8e.

Pol. I.2: IVB3n90.

    5: IVA5b.

    8: IIIA3ci, IVA5b.

  12-13: IVA5n45.

II.3: IVA5c.

IV.11: IIIA3n39.

Rhet. I.1: IIB1.

Ath. Pol. 62: IVB3.

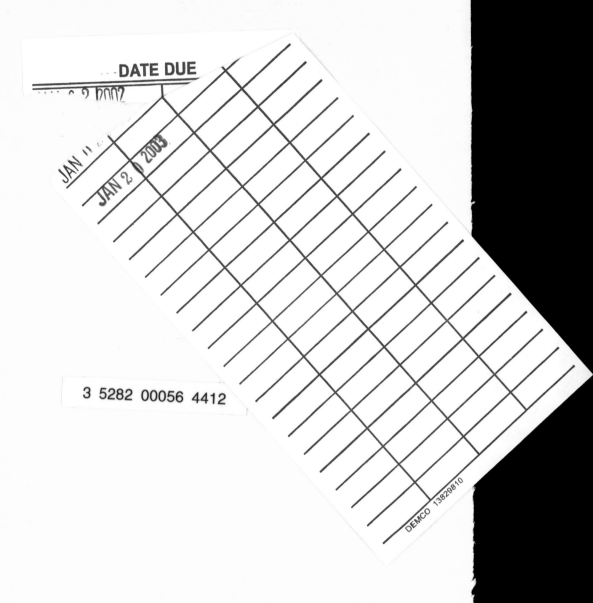